BABY BOOM

Selected titles in ABC-CLIO's Perspectives in American Social History series

African Americans in the Nineteenth Century: People and Perspectives

American Revolution: People and Perspectives

Baby Boom: People and Perspectives

British Colonial America: People and Perspectives

Civil Rights Movement: People and Perspectives

Civil War: People and Perspectives

Cold War and McCarthy Era: People and Perspectives

Early Republic: People and Perspectives

Industrial Revolution: People and Perspectives

Jacksonian and Antebellum Age: People and Perspectives

Jazz Age: People and Perspectives

Making of the American West: People and Perspectives

Reconstruction: People and Perspectives

Vietnam War Era: People and Perspectives

Women's Rights: People and Perspectives

PERSPECTIVES IN
AMERICAN SOCIAL HISTORY

Baby Boom

People and Perspectives

Rusty Monhollon, Editor
Peter C. Mancall, Series Editor

ABC-CLIO

Santa Barbara, California • Denver, Colorado • Oxford, England

Library of Congress Cataloging-in-Publication Data
Baby boom: people and perspectives / Rusty Monhollon, editor.
    p. cm. — (Perspectives in American social history series)
   Includes bibliographical references and index.
   ISBN 978-1-59884-105-3 (hard copy : alk. paper) — ISBN 978-1-59884-106-0 (ebook)
   1. Baby boom generation—United States—History. 2. United States—Social conditions—20th century. I. Monhollon, Rusty L.
  HN59.B233 2010
  305.20973—dc22   2009048618

ISBN: 978-1-59884-105-3
EISBN: 978-1-59884-106-0

14 13 12 11 10   1 2 3 4 5

This book is also available on theWorld Wide Web as an eBook.
Visit www.abc-clio.com for details.

ABC-CLIO, LLC
130 Cremona Drive, P.O. Box 1911
Santa Barbara, California 93116-1911

This book is printed on acid-free paper ∞

Manufactured in the United States of America

To
my mother Anne Monhollon
and
to the memory of my father Ron Monhollon, who together
started their own baby boom.

Contents

Series Introduction, ix
Introduction, xiii
Acknowledgments, xxxiii
About the Editor and Contributors, xxxv
Chronology, xxxvii

1 Baby Boomers and the Family, 1
C. S. O'Brien

2 Women and the Baby Boom, 19
Kimberly Wilmot Voss

3 Students and the Baby Boom, 37
E. Jan Jacobs

4 African Americans, 55
Rusty Monhollon

5 Hispanic Americans, 73
Theodore W. Eversole

6 Poverty and the Baby Boom, 91
Rusty Monhollon

7 Religion and the Baby Boomers, 105
Frank A. Salamone

8 The Counterculture, 117
Scott MacFarlane

9 The Organization Man, 133
Matthew Johnson

10 Suburbanites and Suburbia, 149
Rusty Monhollon

Primary Documents, 165
Reference, 209
Bibliography, 223
Index, 243

Series Introduction

Social history is, simply put, the study of past societies. More specifically, social historians attempt to describe societies in their totality, and hence often eschew analysis of politics and ideas. Though many social historians argue that it is impossible to understand how societies functioned without some consideration of the ways that politics works on a daily basis or what ideas could be found circulating at any given time, they tend to pay little attention to the formal arenas of electoral politics or intellectual currents. In the United States, social historians have been engaged in describing components of the population that had earlier often escaped formal analysis, notably women, members of ethnic or cultural minorities, or those who had fewer economic opportunities than the elite.

Social history became a vibrant discipline in the United States after it had already gained enormous influence in Western Europe. In France, social history in its modern form emerged with the rising prominence of a group of scholars associated with the journal *Annales Economie, Societé, Civilisation* (or *Annales ESC* as it is known). In its pages and in a series of books from historians affiliated with the École des Hautes Études en Sciences Sociale in Paris, brilliant historians such as Marc Bloch, Jacques Le Goff, and Emanuel LeRoy Ladurie described seemingly every aspect of French society. Among the masterpieces of this historical reconstruction was Fernand Braudel's monumental study, *The Mediterranean and the Mediterranean World in the Age of Philip II*, published first in Paris in 1946 and in a revised edition in English in 1972. In this work Braudel argued that the only way to understand a place in its totality was to describe its environment, its social and economic structures, and its political systems. In Britain the emphasis of social historians has been less on questions of environment, per se, than in a description of human communities in all their complexities. For example, social historians there have taken advantage of that nation's remarkable local archives to reconstruct the history of the family and details of its rural past. Works such as Peter Laslett's *The World We Have Lost*, first printed in 1966, and the multiauthored *Agrarian History of England and Wales*, which began to appear in print in 1967, revealed that painstaking work could reveal the lives and habits of individuals who never previously attracted the interest of biographers, demographers, or most historians.

Social history in the United States gained a large following in the second half of the twentieth century, especially during the 1960s and 1970s. Its development sprang from political, technical, and intellectual impulses deeply embedded in the culture of the modern university. The politics of civil rights and social reform fueled the passions of historians who strove to tell the stories of the underclass. They benefited from the adoption by historians of statistical analysis, which allowed scholars to trace where individuals lived, how often they moved, what kinds of jobs they took, and whether their economic status declined, stagnated, or improved over time. As history departments expanded, many who emerged from graduate schools focused their attention on groups previously ignored or marginalized. Women's history became a central concern among American historians, as did the history of African Americans, Native Americans, Latinos and others. These historians pushed historical study in the United States farther away from the study of formal politics and intellectual trends. Though few Americanists could achieve the technical brilliance of some social historians in Europe, collectively they have been engaged in a vast act of description, with the goal of describing seemingly every facet of life from 1492 to the present.

The sixteen volumes in this series together represent the continuing efforts of historians to describe American society. Most of the volumes focus on chronological areas, from the broad sweep of the colonial era to the more narrowly defined collections of essays on the eras of the Cold War, the baby boom, and America in the age of the Vietnam War. The series also includes entire volumes on the epochs that defined the nation, the American Revolution and the Civil War, as well as volumes dedicated to the process of westward expansion, women's rights, and African American history.

This social history series derives its strength from the talented editors of individual volumes. Each editor is an expert in his or her own field who selected and organized the contents of his or her volume. Editors solicited other experienced historians to write individual essays. Every volume contains first-rate analysis complemented by lively anecdotes designed to reveal the complex contours of specific historical moments. The many illustrations to be found in these volumes testify too to the recognition that any society can be understood not only by the texts that its participants produce but also by the images that they craft. Primary source documents in each volume will allow interested readers to pursue some specific topics in greater depth, and each volume contains a chronology to provide guidance to the flow of events over time. These tools—anecdotes, images, texts, and timelines—allow readers to gauge the inner workings of America in particular periods and yet also to glimpse connections between eras.

The articles in these volumes testify to the abundant strengths of historical scholarship in the United States in the early years of the twenty-first century. Despite the occasional academic contest that flares into public notice, or the self-serving cant of politicians who want to manipulate the nation's past for partisan ends—for example, in debates over the Second Amendment to the U.S. Constitution and what it means about potential limits to the rights of gun ownership—the articles here all reveal the vast increase in knowledge of the American past that has taken place over the previous half century. Social historians do not dominate history faculties in American colleges and universities, but no one could deny them a seat at the intellectual table. Without their efforts, intellectual, cultural, and political historians would be hard pressed to understand why certain ideas circulated when they did, why some religious movements prospered or foundered, how developments in fields such as medicine and engineering reflected larger concerns, and what shaped the world we inhabit.

Fernand Braudel and his colleagues envisioned entire laboratories of historians in which scholars working together would be able to produce *histoire totale*: total history. Historians today seek more humble goals for our collective enterprise. But as the richly textured essays in these volumes reveal, scholarly collaboration has in fact brought us much closer to that dream. These volumes do not and cannot include every aspect of American history. However, every page reveals something interesting or valuable about how American society functioned. Together, these books suggest the crucial necessity of stepping back to view the grand complexities of the past rather than pursuing narrower prospects and lesser goals.

Peter C. Mancall

Series Editor

Introduction

No other demographic event in U.S. history—save perhaps for the staggering death toll of the Civil War—has had greater significance than the Baby Boom. Between 1946 and 1964, more than 75 million babies were born in the United States; 4 million were born each year between 1954 and 1964, with a peak of 4.3 million in 1957, or one birth every seven seconds. Between 1950 and 1960, the nation's population increased from 153 million to 170 million, the greatest one-decade increase ever. While the population increase itself was significant, the Baby Boom's greatest impact was on American culture and the economy. At every stage of life—from birth to school to work to retirement—the Baby Boom generation has left, and continues to leave, its mark on American society (Gillon 2004, 1).

The Baby Boom fostered the spread of suburbanization in the United States, contributing directly to significant increases in construction for houses and schools. By virtue of sheer numbers, the Baby Boom fostered the emergence of a unique youth culture and made this generation a cultural and economic force. Teenagers, a new age cohort, were potent consumers, spending billions of dollars annually by 1960; Corporate America took notice, and soon targeted them in advertising, especially through the new medium of television. Rock-and-roll music, movies, and coonskin caps illustrate the consumptive power of the Baby Boom generation and its ubiquitous impact on popular culture.

The emergence of this youth culture created generational tensions never before experienced in the United States. In the 1960s, the Baby Boom generation began straining the resources of the nation's colleges and universities, helping to spur an unprecedented growth in American higher education. It was the Baby Boom generation, too, that abetted the social and cultural movements of the 1960s, which transformed the nation—for better or worse—in numerous ways. In short, the Baby Boom deeply affected the lives of all Americans, in ways sometimes obvious, and others sublime. Americans experienced these changes differently, as they were filtered through the lens of their own race, class, gender, or political leanings.

This collection of essays is about the Baby Boom generation. It examines the lives of the boomers, from birth through their early adulthood, and explores the multiple ways that Americans of every race, class, gender, and political leaning experienced the Baby Boom. The Baby Boom generation was not only the largest in American history, but also the wealthiest and best educated. Given its size, it is not surprising that the boomers were a diverse lot. "If there was a central paradox of baby boomers," writes the historian Glenn Jeansonne, "it was their complexity, leading them in a variety of directions. Theirs was the most idealistic and altruistic—and the most selfish and narcissistic" (Jeansonne 2006, 53).

Indeed, it is difficult to generalize about the baby boomers. These essays, therefore, explore the intersection of the boomers' lives with the historical events that characterize the era: the Cold War, the civil rights movement, Vietnam, the counterculture, Watergate, and September 11, among other events. These essays capture the breadth of the American experience through the lives of the Baby Boom generation.

No one predicted the Baby Boom, and had someone made such a prediction, no one would have believed them anyway. Birth rates in the United States had steadily decreased since the early nineteenth century. People had delayed marriage during the Great Depression and World War II and, with peace and prosperity on the horizon; they now were ready to start families. Americans began marrying younger than previous generations, which meant they started families earlier and had children over a longer period of time. In the 1950s the median age for men getting married was 22.5 years; for women, it was 20.1 years, both historic lows. Nearly 68 percent of all adults were married in 1960 (May 1999, 6).

Yet this alone does not explain why the Baby Boom happened. It was a boom because birthrates had been declining for 150 years or so and all social groups—blacks and whites, rich and poor, college-educated or high school dropouts—contributed to the rise in fertility rates. The birthrate increased no matter the variable factor, whether it was race, ethnicity, education, or class. After World War II, Americans from all socioeconomic categories married younger and had an average of three children.

The Baby Boom, in concert with many other factors, tended to foment a culture of togetherness and domesticity. After World War II, Americans wed young, much younger than their parents. They had babies sooner and more of them. As the historian Elaine Tyler May and others have noted, another factor for the rise in fertility rates was broad acceptance of pronatalism, the idea that having many children was of great value. Additionally, an ideology of domesticity permeated the culture, centered on the nuclear family, and prescribed social roles for men ("the breadwinner") and women ("the homemaker"). Throughout the culture, and especially in popular culture, women were depicted as fulfilled in their lives as wives and mothers. At every level of education, women were discouraged from pursuing careers; those who did were viewed as abnormal and neurotic

(May 1999, 137). Paradoxically, the number of women working in the paid labor force grew steadily after 1945, although employers continued to see women as temporary workers (Chafe 1991, 221–222).

As World War II ended, the United States began preparing for the peace. With more than fifteen years of economic hardship and war behind them, Americans looked confidently to the future, and with good cause. The U.S. industrial might had been crucial to the defeat of Germany and Japan. American technology had developed synthetic substitutes for silk, rubber, and other scarce resources during the war. The United States had also unlocked the secrets of the atom, which had the potential to destroy the world. Unlike Europe and Asia, the United States was unscathed by the war's destruction. The United States in 1945 had its economy and infrastructure intact, had a powerful army and navy, and alone possessed the most powerful weapon the world had ever known. Little wonder many Americans proclaimed it the start of the "American Century."

But demobilization and reconversion would not be easy. Millions of soldiers and sailors would be mustered out of the military. They would need to find jobs and housing. The economy would have to convert back to industrial, rather than military, production. As well, the nation had an inexperienced leader in the White House. Harry S. Truman, who had assumed the presidency upon Franklin Roosevelt's death in April 1945, had been a U.S. senator from Missouri only a short while before Roosevelt tabbed him to be his running mate in 1944.

Demobilization was Truman's first domestic priority. Within months of Japan's surrender, millions of American G.I.s began coming home. Scarred both physically and psychologically from their experiences in combat, many soldiers had difficulty adjusting to civilian life. For many veterans, finding a job was not a problem but holding one was troublesome. The Servicemen's Readjustment Act of 1944, better known as the G.I. Bill, provided veterans with health care and access to medical treatment. The G.I. Bill also was crucial to the nation's economic health. The federal government footed the bill for veterans' college educations, who soon took jobs in key sectors driving the economy, such as the automobile, electronics, and chemical industries.

Many veterans did have difficulty, however, in finding housing immediately after the war. During the war, no new homes had been constructed, and the shortage became acute as the military stood down. After the war, the Federal Housing Administration provided loans, as part of the G.I. Bill, for both the construction and the purchase of new homes, many in suburban developments such as Levittown on Long Island. The impact was significant; homeownership rose to more than 60 percent by 1970 (Marty 1997, 273). It is no wonder, then, that many Americans look back to the 1950s and early 1960s with great nostalgia, as it seemed that the good life, the American Dream, was a possibility for millions.

Truman's foreign policy revolved around the growing distrust between the United States and the Soviet Union, who had been allies during World War II. Truman struck a hard line against what he believed was Soviet aggression in Europe. During the crisis in Greece and Turkey, Truman went before Congress and committed the United States to fighting Communism. The Truman Doctrine, as it was known, promised to "contain" Communism by providing assistance to any country combating "armed minorities." Soon thereafter, the United States launched the Marshall Plan, which provided financial assistance for the rebuilding of Europe. The Cold War had begun.

The Cold War was a contributing factor to the tremendous economic growth in the United States. Although there were brief downturns in the economy, and the national debt rose significantly, the United States during the 1950s had the highest standard of living ever. The greatest economic expansion in the nation's history helped produce, and in turn was fueled by, the Baby Boom. After World War II, the "affluent society," as economist John Kenneth Galbraith called it, permitted millions of Americans, including the white working class, to enjoy a middle-class lifestyle by purchasing homes and sending their children to college. By 1945, the gross national product (GNP) of the United States stood at $200 billion, double what it had been in 1940; it would soar to $500 billion by 1960 (Gillon 2004, 6). The average American earned more than twice the average worker in Great Britain and nearly thirty times greater than those in India. The unemployment rate never exceeded 5 percent during this period and, unlike previous times of economic growth, inflation remained low (3 percent or less) so that rising incomes were not eaten up by rising consumer prices. *U.S. News and World Report* concluded in 1957 that "Never had so many people, anywhere, been so well off" (as quoted in Gillon 2004, 6).

Economic growth after World War II rested on a three-pronged foundation of manufacturing, construction, and defense spending. The aircraft and automobile industries stimulated growth in other industries; their growth was in part the consequence of the availability of inexpensive gasoline to fuel their products. The automobile industry also benefited from massive increases in productivity resulting from automation. After 1950, more than half of the federal budget went to defense spending, on items such as planes, weapons, construction of military bases, and research and development. Much of this money went to the nation's top research institutions and universities. The chemical and electronic industries especially benefited, and grew quickly as a result. Research funds also led to the development of transistors and electronic computers. The computer's impact would be monumental; by 1960, it had become a billion-dollar industry and would only grow larger.

These advances in technology allowed American business to grow larger and stronger. By the 1950s, many of the top U.S. businesses were multinational conglomerates, with business interests ranging from manufacturing to financial services to real estate. Corporate power increased significantly, not only over the economy but politically and in foreign policy, too. As corporations became more bureaucratic, the executives who ran them insisted on loyalty to the company and conformity to the corporate culture.

The working class also shared in the economic bounty. The American Federation of Labor (AFL) and the Congress of Industrial Organizations

(CIO), which had merged in the late 1940s, was content to negotiate labor contracts that provided high wages and good benefits for workers. The price the unions paid was loss of the militancy that had strengthened the labor movement during the Great Depression. In many ways, workers came to see themselves as part of the middle class. Indeed, after World War II, most workers could afford to buy a home, save money, and expect to be financially secure in their retirement. The waning of the unions' strength would be significant as automation and new technology reduced the number of manufacturing jobs.

Consumerism was perhaps the defining characteristic of the Baby Boom era. With the economy focused on war production between 1940 and 1945, Americans had had few consumer goods to purchase. Instead, they banked their savings, which went up 150 percent during the war. They used that money after the war to buy cars, appliances, and other consumer goods in record numbers. New consumer products, such as refrigerators and washing machines, marked the new prosperity of the middle class. Between 1946 and 1970, Americans spent, borrowed, and purchased more goods than at any time in the nation's history. In the 1950s alone, Americans bought 58 million automobiles (Oakley 1986, 239).

The cost of having so many cars on the road was high. As suburban communities grew so too did traffic congestion and the number of car-related deaths. Exhaust fumes polluted the air, and air quality by the 1960s had become a crisis. The greatest cost, however, was that the United States consummated its commitment to oil production. Within two decades, the American dependence on oil, most of which was imported, became the nation's Achilles' heel.

The widespread availability of automobiles combined with government policy that built new roads and encouraged housing developments beyond the city proper, were principal factors for the rapid suburbanization. A trickle before World War II, suburban growth exploded after the war. Nearly nine out of ten new homes built in the 1950s were located in suburban developments.

As the 1960s began, the nation's urban and suburban populations both were about 60 million people. Except for Los Angeles, all major U.S. cities lost population during the 1950s. The greatest growth took place in the so-called Sunbelt stretching from California to Florida, fueled in large measure by Cold War defense and military spending.

But housing and suburban growth were not the only ways that the Baby Boom stimulated the economy. Parents were the first targets for American businesses. The millions of babies born each year needed diapers, formula, clothing, toys, strollers, and cribs, among other goods. Parents spent more than $50 million dollars on diapers alone in 1957, and purchased more than 2 million bicycles (Jones 1980, 42–43).

A distinctive youth culture was cast after World War II, forged in about equal parts by new social identities, affluence, and consumerism. As the historian Steve Gillon has noted, the boomers were "the first generation to have a defined sense of themselves as a single entity." Moreover, he argues, unlike any previous generation, "Boomers were so disproportionately numerous, so affluent, so blessed by the cold peace of the Cold War (Vietnam notwithstanding) that they would have the motive, means, and opportunity to reshape the nation" (Gillon 2004, 1, 4).

This culture was the result of many things. Many parents of the boomers adopted the child-centered ethos of Dr. Benjamin Spock, the author of the best-selling book, *Baby and Child Care*, who emphasized democratic personal relationships and permissive parental discipline. Compulsory school attendance meant that more youths attended high school, contributing to the emergence of the teenager as a distinct age cohort. Between 1930 and 1950 the percentage of children age fourteen to seventeen who were in school grew from 50 to 73 percent. This meant, among other things, a tremendous strain on communities to provide education. New school buildings rapidly cropped up; California in the 1950s opened a new school every week (Gillon 2004, 7).

Freed of economic responsibility to the family by postwar prosperity, teenagers—especially the white middle class—became significant consumers. One industry estimate put the youth market at $10 billion annually, on such products as cosmetics, cars, telephones, televisions, radios, movies, and music. Indeed, rock-and-roll music most powerfully expressed this youth culture. As Landon Jones posits, "Rock was a language that taught the baby boomers about themselves" (Jones 1980, 62).

Advertising targeted teens, especially through the relatively new medium of television. Hollywood churned out movies to appeal to their tastes. Radio stations did the same by playing rock-and-roll music, which provided—in many ways—the first stirrings of rebellion among the baby boom generation. Collectively, these changes contributed to a sense of identity and separateness among youth (Miller and Nowak 1977, 271).

The popular culture—particularly television and advertising—celebrated the Baby Boom. Advertisers increased their spending from $6 billion to $12 billion during the fifties. In 1958, according to Gillon, "64 toy manufacturers spent $3.5 million on television ads. The following year 121 companies spent $6.5 million" (2004). According to advertising experts, American teens each had about $10.00 in disposable income by 1958, which accounted for a $10 billion youth market. Some experts calculated that by the time they were six, most boomers had viewed more than 500 hours of advertising on television, and by the time they turned twenty-one, they watched more than 300,000 commercials (Gillon 2004, 5).

It would be difficult to overstate television's impact on the boomers. Most scholars agree that television more than any other thing gave the boomers their sense of generational identity. Since the beginning of the twentieth century, a national culture had been forged by the spread of mass media, magazines, movies, recorded music, radio, and professional sports. Television molded a mass culture into a common culture as never before. Americans owned 19 million television sets in 1952, up from only 400,000 in 1948. Soon more than 90 percent of all American homes had a set—and many had more than one—which stayed on an average of six hours each day. The political scientist Paul Light calculated that, by age sixteen, the average boomer had watched 12,000 to 16,000 hours of television (Light

1988, 123). In addition to creating a common culture through shared viewing, television profoundly altered American social habits. Americans read fewer books and magazines, went to movies, nightclubs, and restaurants less often, and reconfigured their homes around the television set.

Although on the surface American society appeared calm, clear signs of disquiet were visible on the horizon. The Cold War and the possibility of nuclear annihilation left many Americans anxious. The Korean War and the development of the hydrogen bomb only intensified the anxiety. At the same time, the nascent youth culture exploded into nearly every home in the nation.

That explosion was largely the result of music that Cleveland disc jockey Alan Freed called "rock-and-roll." Rock-and-roll resulted from a confluence of musical influences. Its most direct lineage was rhythm-and-blues, which had been created by African American artists earlier in the twentieth century. White artists such as Bill Haley and the Comets recorded sanitized versions of songs originally written and performed by black artists.

The meteoric success of Elvis Presley provides a glimpse into the rise and spread of the youth culture. Presley exuded rebelliousness and sexuality, not merely through his hip-grinding, gyrating performances, but also through his voice and appearance. Ironically, Presley was not at all a rebel. He was a polite, church-going mama's boy.

Movies also furthered the spread of the youth culture. Marlon Brando, as the leader of a motorcycle gang in *The Wild One*, when asked what he was rebelling against, sneered, "Whatta ya got?" Both Brando and James Dean, in *Rebel without a Cause*, became cult heroes for challenging social mores.

In the 1950s, a perceived increase in the incidence of misdemeanors among teens led many parents and experts to identify juvenile delinquency as an epidemic that threatened the fabric of American society. Blame was hurled at popular culture (film, music, comic books), excessive mothering (Philip Wylie's *A Generation of Vipers*), and the large number of women who worked during World War II.

Allen Ginsburg, Jack Kerouac, and other Beat writers expressed their contempt with middle-class society in their writings. Some educated college-age youth admired Beats, gradually rejected complacency and cautiousness, and heralded the youth movement of the 1960s.

College enrollments grew steadily after the war, from about 1.7 million in 1946 to 3.8 million in 1960 then exploding to 8 million in 1970. Most students were not politically radical but more concerned with seeking educational credentials in their pursuit of the American Dream. While much of the attention was directed at student activism on elite institutions, student activism could be found, to varying degrees, at institutions of every size and kind and in every corner of the nation (Chalmers 1996, 68).

Student activism has often been depicted as a generational struggle, a rejection of the lifestyle and values of the previous generation. Scholars have found, however, that students—activists and nonactivists, from the left and the right—shared to a very large degree the same values as their parents.

Despite claims that the nation's values had deteriorated, religion continued to play a major role in the lives of most Americans. Church attendance rose to 63 percent of the population during the 1960s. The King James Bible was the best-selling book of the decade. Scholars have suggested that the social anxiety created by the Cold War, the nuclear threat, and a rapidly changing popular culture led many Americans to turn to religion for reassurance.

The Cold War cast a long shadow over daily life in the United States. Aside from the anxiety created by the threat of nuclear war, to many Americans, it seemed that the Soviet system was outpacing the United States. The sense that the United States was lagging behind the Soviet Union was amplified when, in October 1957, the Soviet Union launched the first artificial satellite—called *Sputnik*—into Earth's orbit. Americans were stunned. Many blamed the American education system as a main reason for the technological gap between the two superpowers. The federal government poured money into programs that promised to narrow the gap. In 1958, the National Education Defense Act was passed, which funneled billions of dollars into graduate education in mathematics and the sciences.

John F. Kennedy was the youngest man ever elected president. President John F. Kennedy declared in his 1961 inaugural address "that the torch has been passed to a new generation of Americans," and he challenged them to conquer "the common enemies of man: tyranny, poverty, disease, and war itself." He seemed inexperienced and undistinguished to many, especially older Americans, but his youthful appearance and confidence resonated with youth. Kennedy displayed both at his inauguration. Kennedy implored Americans "ask not what your country can do for you, but what can you do for your country." Thus inspired, millions of young people heeded his call. During a campaign trip to Dallas, Kennedy was assassinated. The news stunned the nation, many of whom watched reports on television. Kennedy had captured the American people's imagination, although his record on domestic issues was mediocre at best.

The Baby Boom era coincided with several other significant developments, in particular the civil rights and student activism, and also the peace and antiwar movements. This was not simply a coincidence; the Baby Boom itself was crucial to the evolution of social activism in the 1960s.

The social upheavals and social activism of the 1960s are often associated with the Baby Boom. There is quite a bit of truth in this, but it is also misleading. Many of the leaders of the early civil rights movement, for example, were not baby boomers. Robert Moses, Stokely Carmichael, and the Greensboro Four were all born during World War II or earlier. Mario Savio, who was a prominent figure in the Free Speech Movement, was born in 1942, and Tom Hayden, the principal author of "The Port Huron Statement," was born in 1939. The first baby boomers did not begin college until 1964, just as the Free Speech Movement was beginning, and as Americans were beginning to take note of the U.S. involvement in Vietnam. But the boomers were driving forces in the explosion of the counterculture and the nascent antiwar movement, and contributed to the radicalization of both in the late 1960s.

Black baby boomers, like their white counterparts, were central figures in the social movements of the 1960s. Student activism in the 1960s and 1970s took many forms. As both foot-soldiers and leaders, students played crucial roles in the civil rights, antiwar, feminist, and other reform movements that swept through the United States in this era. Student participation in these movements led to the emergence of a distinct leftist student movement, known as the "New Left" or simply "The Movement," whose goals were to reform not only the university but, in so doing, the whole of American society. Conservative students were also politically active, as critical of American society and politics from the right as others were from the left. Their activism, largely unnoticed at the time, laid the groundwork for the "New Right," whose impact has been equally significant. As well, student activism, and youth more generally, left an enduring cultural legacy, expressed in distinct music, dress, and action, that was transmitted to, and became deeply embedded in, the mainstream culture.

Generally, the course of student activism in the 1960s and 1970s unfolded along these lines. Between 1960 and 1965 both the New Right and the New Left emerged, both of which were critical of Cold War liberalism and sought to wrest power from elites. As American involvement in Vietnam increased between 1965 and 1968, the New Left turned to revolution rather than reform, embodied in the violent confrontations in the streets of Chicago. At about the same time a cultural revolution intensified, exemplified in music, dress, hairstyles, and drug use and experimentation. Between 1969 and the mid-1970s, the youth movement generally faded, the result of state-approved violence but also an inward turn to personal liberation.

Most middle-class Americans were oblivious to the extent of poverty in the United States. Life in suburbia was isolated from the suffering in the inner city and countryside. Popular culture—movies, television programs, prescriptive literature, among others—celebrated the "good life." And most politicians and intellectuals believed that the American economic colossus had the capacity—with a bit of tweaking here and there—to provide material abundance to all Americans and eliminate poverty. Yet, some 35 million Americans lived below the poverty line in 1960, one-third of them in depressed rural regions. The bulk of the poor lived in the crumbling inner city, which millions of whites abandoned for the suburbs. Essential services such as police and fire protection, and trash collection were harder to pay for as the city's tax base eroded. Government programs intended to rehabilitate the cities, such as the urban renewal movement of the 1960s, often displaced the poor and excluded people of color from new housing.

The so-called second wave of feminism in the 1960s owed much of its vitality to women who had been involved in the New Left and the civil rights movement, for several reasons. The experience of fighting racial oppression led women to comprehend fully their own gender oppression, and provided a language through which to express that oppression. Also, the New Left's emphasis on participatory democracy through direct action helped instill the belief that the "personal is political." The patronizing and sexist attitudes of their male colleagues were also factors. Within the New Left, many men expected women to do clerical work and household chores. Men also expected women to reject conventional sexual mores and to confirm their dedication to revolutionary change. Rather than confront such degradation, many women rejected the New Left for a nascent women's liberation movement.

There were several threads within the feminist movement. One focused primarily on workplace economic issues such as equal pay and opportunity. Another emerged primarily from women in the New Left, centered on personal issues that sought to liberate women from second-class citizenship within a male-dominated society. Access to contraceptives, health care, and abortion were major issues.

Students struggled to redefine the paternalistic relationship between them and the university by challenging rules governing personal behavior. For women, this struggle had a larger significance, as many campus regulations had two standards, one for men and one for women. For example, on many campuses, men living in residence halls had a later curfew—or none at all—than women. By the end of the decade, regulations regarding personal behavior had largely been removed from a majority of campuses.

Their fathers had fought World War II and won. The boomers were sent to Vietnam to fight for their country, but with different results. The Vietnam War, perhaps more than any single event, shaped the lives of the Baby Boom. It affected not only the men and women who were stationed there, but the opposition to the war and the divisions it sowed permeated American society and culture.

John Kennedy held fast to the containment policy of his predecessors. Kennedy approved a troop increase from 700 to 16,000 in 1963. He also encouraged the Diem government to enact reforms and end its repressive policies, especially toward Buddhist monks. Diem was overthrown in a coup on November 1, 1963, which Kennedy had tacitly agreed to recognize. Although Kennedy hinted that he would withdraw American troops after the 1964 election, he remained committed to the containment policy.

Lyndon Johnson also held fast to containment. By 1964, Johnson was looking for a way to widen the war and bring American military strength to bear against the Communist insurgents in South Vietnam. He got his chance when an American patrol boat reported being attacked in the Gulf of Tonkin off the coast of North Vietnam. Although it was not clear whether the boat had in fact come under attack, Johnson went to Congress and asked for broad authority as commander in chief to protect American soldiers in Vietnam. Congress delivered the Gulf of Tonkin Resolution, which in effect gave Johnson unfettered license to wage war in Vietnam.

By 1965, Johnson had authorized Operation Rolling Thunder, a sustained bombing of targets in North Vietnam. He also increased the number of American troops in Vietnam to nearly 185,000, a figure that ultimately would exceed 500,000. As Johnson widened the war, he also stirred a nascent peace movement. Pacifists had been protesting American involvement in Vietnam since the early 1960s. But Johnson's escalation of the commitment coalesced the antiwar movement.

Although opposition to the war, by pacifist groups like the Student Peace Union, had been going on for several years, it had not generated much enthusiasm from other students. The first widely known protest was a teach-in held at the University of Michigan in February 1965. Students for Democratic Society (SDS) was a crucial constituency in the antiwar movement, and its leaders encouraged students to protest against the war by marching, burning draft cards, and disrupting the work of draft boards. On many campuses students joined protests against the university's involvement in the war and the military. The Reserve Officers Training Corps (ROTC) was a common target, as it was a visible symbol of the military presence on campus. Activists called into question the legitimacy of awarding college credit for military training, an issue to which students in the 1930s also had objected.

By 1966, more than 250,000 American soldiers were stationed in Vietnam. As the need for more soldiers increased, fewer student deferments were granted, bringing the war home for thousands of male students. Many faculty members refused to fail male students, as grade rank might affect their draft status. More than any other issue in the 1960s, the Vietnam War, and in particular the draft, aroused student awareness and prompted student action.

Vietnam unified the student movement across the nation. Most antiwar protests, and the student movement generally, were peaceful. As the war continued and escalated to more than 500,000 American troops by 1968, demonstrations against the war became more intense and confrontational. As many as 40,000 students from more than 100 campuses joined in antiwar demonstrations in 1968. The peak of the antiwar movement culminated in October 1969, with the March against Death in Washington, D.C.

The Vietnam War radicalized the student movement. Critics of student protests frequently (and correctly) pointed out that "radicals" were only a small minority of students, perhaps 5 percent at most. Yet, as enrollments on college campuses continued to rise throughout the 1960s, a small fraction of a growing student population produced a significant number of "radicals," perhaps something on the order of 400,000 or more. Moreover, while radicals organized and pushed the movement forward, at times "moderate" and "conservative" students could be rallied for specific issues, such as the war or when university administrators were unresponsive to students' needs and demands, or when administrators were pushed by politicians, the public, and governing boards to cede control of the campus to police or other "outsiders." As David Chalmers argues, "It was exciting to be standing up against authority on behalf of moral values, to feel part of a movement that you read about . . . or saw on television" (Chalmers 1996, 74).

The pitch of student protest rose and fell with U.S. involvement in Vietnam. As the nation slowly disentangled itself from Southeast Asia, the frequency and scale of student demonstration withered. Ironically, while the antiwar movement came to include a broad cross-section of American society, few—if any—participants came to accept the radicals' position that the American political and social system needed basic changes.

At the same time that student political activism was spreading, so too was the burgeoning youth culture, often referred to by the broad, nebulous term "counterculture." Many scholars contend that cultural dissent best defines the Baby Boom generation; certainly the legacy of this cultural dissent is great. The counterculture was characterized by many things, and music—rock music, especially—was perhaps the most powerful. Beginning in the 1950s, rock music was a major force in forging a collective youth identity. Then, as it also was in the 1960s and 1970s, rock music was a principal consumption item, whether on records or on the radio. Students could identify with the lyrics of rock music and, to a lesser extent, folk music. Additionally, students could identify with the musicians, who were their age. Their manner of dress reflected a rejection of staid conformity, although the counterculture created its own notions of conformity.

The Beatles almost single-handedly transformed rock music into rock culture. They wore their hair long, wore offbeat clothing, and experimented with drugs and religion. John Lennon was outspoken against the war and promoted peace in his songs and daily life. Moreover, the Beatles' music evolved from simple tunes about young love (*I Want to Hold Your Hand* and *Love Me Do*) to drug experimentation (*Lucy in the Sky with Diamonds* and *I Am the Walrus*) to songs of protest and radicalism (*Revolution* and *Why Don't We Do it in the Road?*). While the music of folk artists such as Phil Ochs, Pete Seeger, Joan Baez, and Bob Dylan seemed to capture the grassroots activism of the early 1960s, folk music's appeal was limited. No one sensed this more clearly than Dylan, who was roundly booed at the Newport Jazz Festival and other venues when he donned a leather jacket and played an electric guitar. Rock music's appeal was vast; it was "where it was at," as Dylan might have said.

Some alienated youth became known as hippies by rejecting middle-class materialism, setting up communes, and experimenting freely with drugs and sex. The hippies were not the only ones experimenting with alternate lifestyles. By 1969, fully one-half of all college students had admitted to smoking marijuana. Others, such as the Harvard psychologist Timothy Leary and countercultural author Ken Kesey promoted the use of a hallucinogenic drug called lysergic acid diethylamide, or LSD. The experimentation with psychedelic drugs, while central to the counterculture, was a major source of contention not only among the counterculture and the mainstream culture but also among the New Left and youth more generally.

A greater openness about sex and sexual issues also characterized the youth culture. Students had won from the university the right to govern their lives, resulting in part in coeducational residence halls and a loosening of sexual taboos. Students explored new living patterns with their girlfriend or boyfriend. Sexual themes and references cropped up frequently in movies and on television. The sexual revolution became a touchstone for the cultural divide of the 1960s. The counterculture touched almost all in one way or another, but it was as much a consumption experience as it was a radical alienation or political potential. The counterculture did not produce a revolution, but it did have a significant impact on values and standards.

Nineteen sixty-eight was a particularly explosive year in the United States, and around the world. Vietnam was the flash point, but the dry tinder had been created by the social and cultural turmoil of the preceding years. The politics of strife by year's end foreshadowed a major realignment of American politics, the first since the New Deal.

On April 2, Martin Luther King, Jr., in Memphis to support striking sanitation workers, was assassinated at his hotel. Violence broke out in more than 100 cities, the result of black anger and frustration. Two months later, Robert Kennedy was gunned down in a Los Angeles hotel, moments after winning the California primary. The assassinations shattered the dreams of activists seeking peace in Vietnam and racial justice at home, students in particular.

The Republican front-runner was Richard Nixon, who eventually claimed the nomination by presenting himself as a leader who would find peace in Vietnam, restore "law and order," and speak on behalf of the "silent majority." Further complicating the presidential campaign was George Wallace, the Alabama governor and defender of segregation. Wallace's rhetoric—sprinkled with thinly veiled attacks on civil rights—struck a chord especially with the white working class and other Americans tired of protests and unrest. Wallace's campaign intensified racial divisions in the United States.

In August, thousands of students and other antiwar activists gathered in Chicago to stage massive protests during the Democratic National Convention. Demonstrators and police in full riot gear squared off in the streets outside the convention hall while the Democrats conducted their business. Television cameras captured the violence, confirming for many Americans that the Democrats were in disarray and incapable of governing.

The beneficiary of the Democratic fratricide was Richard Nixon, who won the election with 43.7 percent of the popular vote. Humphrey polled 42.7 percent, and George Wallace captured nearly 14 percent. Nixon capitalized on turmoil of antiwar protests, racial unrest and violence, campus unrest, school integration, and what seemed, in the minds of many Americans, to be the breakdown of American society. Wallace appealed to the same constituents with coarse tirades against campus radicalism, integrationists, and "welfare mothers." Nixon's election heralded the emergence of a new conservative political coalition, although it would not reach full flower for another two decades. Well more than half of the electorate cast ballots for candidates—Nixon and Wallace—who vowed a return to law and order and opposed further expansion of the Great Society. Student activism, particularly antiwar activism, contributed to the political and social environment in which the election took place.

The breadth of student activism was apparent by the late 1960s. A Red Power movement seeking political and social equality for Native Americans emerged in the late 1960s. Native American students were crucial to the movement, including the planning and execution of the 1969 occupation of Alcatraz, perhaps the best-known episode of Native American activism of the era.

By the late 1960s, student activism in the nation's high schools was becoming commonplace. High school students had long struggled in the civil rights movement. Barbara Johns, for example, led the walkout at Moton High School in Farmville, Virginia, prompting the lawsuit that became one of the five cases in *Brown v. Board of Education*. The first test of *Brown* came in Little Rock, Arkansas, when nine black students integrated Central High School. By placidly enduring racial epithets and white hostility, the students became the public face of integration. High school students, and often junior high and elementary students, participated in civil rights marches in Birmingham, Selma, and throughout the South.

High school students also challenged rules that governed their dress and appearance, another indication of the counterculture's impact. For boys, wearing their hair long became an act of defiance. Wearing "hippie-style" clothing symbolized their challenge to traditional authority. In scores of schools across the country, students and school administrators butted heads over dress codes and acceptable standards of appearance. By the mid-1970s, many school districts had jettisoned their dress codes.

In April 1970, President Richard Nixon ordered an American military invasion of Cambodia. While campaigning for the presidency in 1968, Nixon had promised to reduce U.S. involvement in the war, but the Cambodian invasion widened the war. The response on campus was widespread condemnation of the president and the invasion. Demonstrations erupted on campuses across the nation, including Kent State University in Kent, Ohio. Like countless other campuses, students at Kent State organized protests to "bring the war home" to the United States. In May, the students confronted the local police. The governor sent the Ohio National Guard to campus the following day. Tensions on the campus remained tense. On May 4, several National Guard troops, panicked in apparent retaliation for stones thrown by protestors, fired their rifles into the crowd of students. Four fell, mortally wounded; eleven more were injured. Hundreds of protests ensued, on perhaps 80 percent of all American colleges. Students blame Nixon for the carnage, while Nixon blamed it on "campus bums," an assessment shared by a broad public. More than 100 campuses shut down. On May 14, two more students were killed by law enforcement officials at Jackson State College. Kent State was the turning point in student activism, its "death knell."

The waning of student activism coincided with the end of the Vietnam War. The war was the one issue in the 1960s that could impel widespread student participation along the political spectrum. Radicals had long opposed the war, but they eventually were joined by politically moderate and conservative students. Although some students continued to struggle for such issues as greater minority representation on campus, gender equality, and the environment, their numbers were limited. These issues could not generate broad student interest or participation.

Scholars disagree about the change that student activism brought to higher education, politics, society, and culture. Some argue that while twenty-first-century students participate in many levels of university governance, such as faculty evaluation and university-wide committees, the basic nature of American higher education has not changed much, if at all. While there is disagreement over the impact of student activism, there is little argument that the depth of discontent in the 1960s was unprecedented in the United States.

The move to the Sunbelt represented not only a demographic shift but also a political shift. Indeed, places such as Orange County, California, became the foundation of a conservative majority that has reshaped American politics since 1980. The emergence of the new conservatism resulted, in part, from the changing economic and social changes the nation experienced in the 1960s and 1970s. Middle-class Americans, many of whom held conservative political and fundamental religious beliefs, were enticed to the Sunbelt by employment opportunities with aerospace and defense contractors created during the Cold War.

The silent majority's political clout became evident in the elections of 1968 and 1972. In 1968, George Wallace's strong showing as a third-party candidate appealed to these voters with his promise to return to "law and order"; Nixon was elected and reelected in large measure because of their support. Both Nixon and Wallace made social issues such as busing, crime, and social "permissiveness" campaign issues. Nixon devoted much of his presidency to eliminating the Great Society's policies focusing on racism and poverty. For example, Nixon tried to eliminate the Office of Economic Opportunity, which headed up federal antipoverty programs. The Nixon administration also asked Congress for legislation to counteract school busing decisions handed down by the courts, what he derisively referred to as "judicial activism." This so-called Southern Strategy—characterized by the appointment of conservative judges and Supreme Court justices and opposition to civil rights and cultural permissiveness—transformed the old South from a rock-solid Democratic to a rock-solid Republican stronghold. Not even the Watergate crisis that consumed the Nixon presidency could stem this tide. Jimmy Carter was the only Democrat elected president between 1968 and 1992. Moreover, the Democratic hold on Congress began to wane steadily during the same period, until the Republicans wrested control of both Houses during the 1994 elections.

Carter was elected in the aftermath of Watergate and the turmoil of the 1960s in large part because he presented himself as honest and compassionate. Carter openly declared he was a "born-again Christian," an identity that some 50 million other Americans also claimed. The 1970s saw the marriage of religion and politics. Jerry Falwell, an evangelical minister who broadcast his ministry on television, founded the Moral Majority. At the heart of the evangelical Christians' worldview was an emphasis on the traditional family and moral values. Falwell rejected what he saw as the permissiveness rampant in American society and culture, the result, he believed, of misguided Supreme Court decisions and the 1960s counterculture. The Moral Majority attacked feminism, gay rights, abortion rights, and sexual freedom, claiming they all undermined the traditional family. Unlike previous conservative coalitions, the new conservatism coalesced around social and cultural, rather than economic, interests. The new conservatism transcended class lines, drawing together working-class and middle-class Americans committed to the defense of traditional cultural values.

By the mid-1970s what would become known as the "New Right" had established itself as a force in American politics. The New Right was a coalition of political and economic conservatives and evangelical Christians.

The New Right emerged from the deep social divisions of the 1960s, and the growing mistrust of government that the Vietnam War and Watergate had fostered.

Ronald Reagan was the standard-bearer for the new conservatism. Reagan had once been a liberal New Dealer and hard-line Cold Warrior. By the early 1960s, Reagan had become a well-paid spokesman for General Electric and gave speeches across the country espousing the greatness of American capitalism and American values. He soon entered politics, and in 1966, was elected governor of California. With an eye on the White House, Reagan methodically built his coalition and refined his message. He lost the Republican nomination in both 1972 and 1976, but easily claimed it in 1980.

Reagan was a masterful communicator, no doubt the consequence of his years acting in Hollywood. He believed in limited government and supply-side economics. Soon after taking office, Reagan persuaded Congress to cut spending in social and health programs, to enact a $750 billion tax cut that most benefited the wealthiest Americans, and to increase defense spending significantly. Reagan also began slashing the federal bureaucracy and eliminating regulations that he believed hindered economic growth and development. "Reaganomics," as the president's economic program was known, touted the virtues of a balanced budget, but the United States became the world's largest debtor during the Reagan administration.

Reagan also revived the Cold War. He referred to the Soviet Union as "the evil empire" and promoted the Strategic Defense Initiative, better known as Star Wars, to protect the United States from a Soviet nuclear attack. The Reagan Doctrine, promised American support to any government fighting the Soviets or a Soviet-backed government. The Reagan Doctrine was put to the test in Afghanistan, El Salvador, and Nicaragua. It was the old Cold Warrior Ronald Reagan, however, that ironically negotiated the most significant nuclear arms reduction treaty with the Soviet Union.

The 1980s were noteworthy for what came to be called the "culture wars." The cultural changes that took place in the 1960s did not sit well with all Americans. In the 1980s, a resurgence of fundamentalist Christianity challenged the secular culture that defined American society. These social conservatives decried, for example, the Supreme Court's 1973 decision in *Roe v. Wade*, which permitted a woman to have an abortion in the first two trimesters of pregnancy. The Gay Liberation movement had brought homosexuality into the mainstream culture, which fundamentalists denounced as an abomination. The ill-fated Equal Rights Amendment, they warned, would further erode the "traditional values" on which this nation was founded. Baby boomers were at the center of the culture wars, as they reinforced the frontlines on both sides of these issues.

The 1980s was also a time when corporate mergers and corporate downsizing threatened the stability of the white-collar middle class. As some corporations downsized, they eliminated thousands of jobs for white-collar professionals and managers. Corporate mergers resulted in job losses but also saddled companies with debt and threatened their future.

The boomers' consuming impulses did not fade as they grew older. They accounted for more than 28 percent of the population by the 1980s. "When future historians look back at the contribution made by the Boomer generation," writes historian Steve Gillon, "they will no doubt place the expansion of individual freedom at the top of the list of achievements" (Gillon 2004, 12).

Both a progenitor and the benefactor of this political realignment, Reagan espoused a vision of America that appealed to millions who were disillusioned by the social and economic crises—including Vietnam, urban unrest, the oil embargo, and inflation—of the 1960s and 1970s. The humiliation of the Iranian hostage crisis, which portrayed the United States as weak and powerless, was merely the final straw for many Americans. Reagan promised to make the country great again by refusing to accept any limits on American economic, military, or political power.

Despite his call for limited government, the national debt increased twofold during the Reagan administration. Reagan also sought to roll back government programs that benefited the poor, women, and blacks, although he was not entirely successful. The size of the black middle class grew, the result of greater education and occupational opportunities since the 1960s. The number of African Americans attending college increased fivefold between 1960 and the mid-1970s, from 250,000 to 1.2 million. Women, too, saw similar improvement; the number of women entering professional schools jumped from 5 percent in the mid-1960s to almost 40 percent by 1980 (Chafe 1991, 222).

Despite this progress, the Reagan years specifically and the conservative ascendancy generally did not help the working class. The transformation of the American economy from an industrial to a service economy was nearly complete by 1980. Millions of Americans had access only to low-paying, dead-end jobs. Federal assistance was gutted and did little to help individuals obtain the education and skills required for upward mobility. The new economy disproportionately affected women, blacks, and other minorities.

Some scholars have pointed out that during the Reagan years class divisions within, rather than among, social groups—such as African Americans and women—became more pronounced. While the black middle class grew so, too, did the black working and underclass. The reasons are many. First, the emergence of a service-based economy meant many jobs required little education and were low-paying with few fringe benefits. The economy became increasingly more high-tech, which further widened the gap between those with higher education and those without. In other words, for many Americans with access to education opportunities, racial and gender discrimination became less significant; however, for millions of others, race and gender became even more oppressive.

By the 1980s, the United States was undergoing a wrenching economic transformation, from an industrial-based to a service-based economy. The postindustrial society was characterized by an increasingly automated and technology-driven workplace, which forced workers to struggle to adapt. At the same time, Americans were working more but earning less.

This economic restructuring also resulted in a geographic redistribution of the nation's industry and manufacturing. Until the mid-twentieth century, industry in the United States was concentrated heavily in trapezoid-shaped area, with Boston, Baltimore, St. Louis, and Minneapolis the four end points. Beginning during World War II and accelerating rapidly during the Cold War, American industry migrated to the south and southwest. Several reasons contributed to this, including plenty of land available to construct new plants, plentiful labor, and, because there were few labor unions, inexpensive labor. But the greatest factor was government spending, particularly for defense and space exploration.

When Ronald Reagan assumed the presidency in 1981, the nation was in the throes of another depression and the poverty rate crept upward, cresting at 15 percent before dipping to 13 percent in 1988. Although the proportion of Americans living in poverty declined, millions still lived below the poverty line. The 13 percent rate in 1988 represented some 32 million people, which was 10 million more people living below the poverty line than in the 1970s (Keyssar 1991, 859).

The United States hoped to reap the dividends promised with end of the Cold War. The collapse of the Soviet Union also brought an end to nearly fifty years of a foreign policy that shaped not only international issues but also domestic affairs. The end of the Cold War permitted renewed political discussion of the economy and the plight of working Americans.

William Jefferson Clinton defeated the incumbent George H. W. Bush in the 1992 presidential election by hammering away at the sagging U.S. economy and Bush's inaction to revive it. Clinton, the first baby boomer to hold the office, brought great optimism to the presidency. His first two years in office accomplished little, however, and his national health insurance initiative was a particularly dismal failure. Clinton became a touchstone in the growing culture wars, as he embodied for many the excesses and permissiveness associated with 1960s and Democratic liberalism. In the 1994 midterm elections, Americans elected a conservative Republican majority to both the House of Representatives and the Senate. The Republican "Contract with America" was an ambitious effort to eliminate government programs, even more so than during the Reagan administration. But the public deemed some programs—Aid to Dependent Children and environmental protection, for example—sacrosanct, and it resented Republican efforts to dismantle them.

The U.S. economy fell into recession during George H. W. Bush's term in office, and this no doubt cost him his chance at reelection. During Clinton's presidency, the American economy enjoyed one of its most prosperous periods ever. This had less to do with Clinton and his handling of the economy than with the whirlwind of change in the emerging fields of "information technology," or what some economists called the "new economy." Personal computers, the World Wide Web, cellular telephones, and other forms of digital technology drove the economy into a frenzy. By the late 1990s, the so-called dot-com boom was attracting investors to start up businesses that had not yet shown a profit or paid a dividend. By working to reduce the federal deficit and balance the budget, the Clinton administration did play an important role in the economy.

By the end of the decade, the stock market had soared to new heights. The robust economy and the bullish stock market provided benefits to a wide array of Americans, many of whom had a stake in the market through mutual funds and other financial products. More Americans owned their homes than at any time in the nation's history. Despite this fact, the gap between rich and poor grew even wider in the 1990s.

In 2000, George W. Bush, born July 6, 1946, narrowly defeated Al Gore, born March 31, 1948, in the closest presidential election in history. It perhaps was fitting that, as the Baby Boom generation entered the new millennium and faced the prospect of retirement (the first boomers would turn sixty-five in 2011), they chose between two of their own to be president. The September 11 attacks, the Enron scandal, and the prolonged war in Afghanistan and Iraq have tempered thoughts of retirement for some. The halcyon days of the stock market have passed, and retirement savings have dwindled precipitously. Despite the doom and gloom of the last decade and the graying of the Baby Boom generation, the boomers are not finished leaving their mark on the nation.

Bibliography

Chafe, William H. *The Paradox of Change: American Women in the Twentieth Century.* New York: Oxford University Press, 1991.

Chalmers, David. *And the Crooked Places Made Straight: The Struggle for Social Change in the 1960s.* 2nd ed. Baltimore: Johns Hopkins University Press, 1996.

Gillon, Steven M. *Boomer Nation: The Largest and Richest Generation Ever and How It Changed America.* New York: Free Press, 2004.

Gitlin, Todd. *The Sixties: Years of Hope, Days of Rage.* Toronto: Bantam Books, 1987.

Jackson, Kenneth T. *Crabgrass Frontier: The Suburbanization of the United States.* New York: Oxford University Press, 1985.

Jeansonne, Glen. *A Time of Paradox: America from the Cold War to the Third Millennium, 1945–Present.* Lanham, MD: Rowman and Littlefield, 2006.

Jones, Landon Y. *Great Expectations: America and the Baby Boom Generation.* New York: Coward, McCann & Geoghegan, 1980.

Keyssar, Alexander. "Poverty." In *The Reader's Companion to American History*, edited by Eric Foner and John Arthur Garraty, 858–862. Boston: Houghton Mifflin, 1991.

Light, Paul C. *Baby Boomers.* New York: Norton, 1988.

Marty, Myron A. *Daily Life in the United States, 1960–1990: Decades of Discord.* Westport, CT: Greenwood, 1997.

May, Elaine Tyler. *Homeward Bound: American Families in the Cold War Era.* New York: Basic Books, 1999.

Miller, Douglas T. and Marion Nowak. *The Fifties: The Way We Really Were*. Garden City, NY: Doubleday, 1977.

Oakley, J. Ronald. *God's Country: America in the Fifties*. New York: Dembner Books, 1986.

Patterson, James. *Grand Expectations: The United States, 1945–1974*. New York: Oxford University Press, 1997.

Acknowledgments

I thank all the contributors to this volume for their good work and their patience as it made its way to publication.

I am grateful to James Sherman and Kim Kennedy White at ABC-CLIO for their advice, support, and tolerance. Thanks also go to Jim Ciment and Steve Danver for their help in the early stages of the project, and to Randy Baldini and Jason Kniser for their stellar production work.

My gratitude goes to the support and encouragement my colleagues at Hood College have provided for the past nine years. I extend a special note of appreciation to my colleague and friend, Emilie Amt, whose example of professionalism is one to which I aspire.

I am always grateful for my family, but especially for their support and patience while I finished this volume. Thank you, Sonja, as always, for your unshakable faith and steadfast love. Thank you, Davis and Rachael, for being interested in what I do, for teaching me how to dress Barbies and build with Legos, and for entertaining us with your shows and music.

About the Editor and Contributors

Rusty Monhollon is an associate professor of history and director of the master's program in humanities at Hood College in Frederick, Maryland. He is the author of *This Is America? The Sixties in Lawrence, Kansas,* which received the Edward H. Tihen Publication Award from Kansas State Historical Association.

Theodore W. Eversole studied cultural and intellectual history as well as social history at the University of Cincinnati under the direction of professors Henry D. Shapiro, Zane Miller, and Sheldon Reich. His subsequent career took him into the world of international education, teaching in Jamaica, the Cayman Islands, and for many years in England. He retired in 2001 as assistant principal of Ivybridge Community College, Ivybridge, Devon, one of the few Americans to be promoted to the higher ranks of the British state education system. He is currently an independent scholar pursuing research and writing projects in the United States.

E. Jan Jacobs holds a doctorate in historical studies from Southern Illinois University. Her scholarship focused on civic education programs of the early Cold War period. Since that time, she has been a faculty member of St. Stephens and St. Agnes School in Alexandria, Virginia, where she teaches courses on American and European history at the high school level, advises the student staff of the school's Web-based newspaper, and teaches yoga.

Matthew Johnson is a doctoral candidate at Temple University. He is currently writing his dissertation on "Beyond Affirmative Action: Managing Ethno-Racial Diversity in the Post–Civil Rights Era."

Scott MacFarlane lives in the Skagit Valley of Washington State and is the author of *The Hippie Narrative: A Literary Perspective of the Counterculture* (McFarland, 2007). He is currently working on a book that examines the literature of Kentucky author Ed McClanahan, one of the original Merry Pranksters during the years leading up to the countercultural explosion of the late 1960s.

C. S. O'Brien is assistant professor and Director of the History Department at the University of Maine, Farmington.

Frank A. Salamone is chair of the Sociology-Anthropology Department at Iona College. Salamone is a native of Rochester, New York; is married; and has seven children, ten grandchildren, and one great-grandchild. He has authored many books, including three on the Italians of Rochester, and more than 150 articles.

Kimberly Wilmot Voss is an assistant professor of journalism in the Nicholson School at the University of Central Florida. Previously, she spent five years as an assistant professor at Southern Illinois University Edwardsville and two years at the University of Wisconsin-Stout. Her doctorate in mass communication is from the University of Maryland. She also has a master's degree in mass communication from Towson University and a master's degree in writing from Cardinal Stritch University. Her research specialty is the study of women in journalism and women's clubs from World War II though the women's liberation movement. She has published numerous journal and magazine articles in these areas. Most recently, she appeared as a journalism history expert in the PBS documentary *Texas Trailblazer: Vivian Castleberry.*

Chronology

1944

Congress passes the Servicemen's Readjustment Act, better known as the G.I. Bill.

1945

2,873,000 babies are born this year.

President Franklin D. Roosevelt dies; Vice President Harry S. Truman becomes president.

The first nuclear explosion takes place in Alamogordo, New Mexico.

The United States drops atomic bombs on Hiroshima and Nagasaki, Japan.

World War II ends.

The U.S. population is 139,928,165.

1946

The Baby Boom begins.

Kathleen Casey, who is born in a New Jersey hospital one second after midnight on January 1, 1946, is the first baby boomer. In all, 3,411,000 babies are born this year in the United States.

The U.S. population is 141,388,566.

Dr. Benjamin Spock publishes *The Common Sense Book of Baby and Child Care*.

Truman establishes the U.S. Commission on Civil Rights.

1947

3,817,000 babies are born in the United States.

The U.S. population is 144,126,071.

William Levitt builds his first Levittown home on Long Island, New York.

Jackie Robinson breaks the color line in Major League Baseball.

The Truman Doctrine is proclaimed; Congress enacts the National Security Act, creating the National Security Council and the Central Intelligence Agency.

Truman creates the Federal Employees Loyalty and Security Program amid accusations of Communists in government.

1948

3,637,000 million babies are born in the United States.

The U.S. population is 146,631,302.

The first McDonald's drive-in opens in San Bernardino, California.

Harry S. Truman is elected president.

Congress approves the Marshall Plan.

Truman orders the desegregation of the military.

The Berlin Airlift begins.

1949

3,649,000 million babies are born in the United States.

The U.S. population is 149,188,130.

The Soviet Union successfully tests its first nuclear weapon.

1950

3,632,000 million babies are born in the United States.

The U.S. population is 152,271,417.

David Riesman's *The Lonely Crowd* is published.

Americans own nearly 4.5 million television sets.

Senator Joseph McCarthy launches his anti-Communist crusade, the so-called Red Scare.

The Korean War begins.

National Security Council Report 68 (NSC-68) sets U.S. Cold War policy.

1951

3,820,000 million babies are born in the United States.

The U.S. population is 154,877,889.

Cleveland disc-jockey Alan Freed hosts a rhythm-and-blues radio show, which is popular among white teenagers.

J. D. Salinger publishes *Catcher in the Rye*.

The first color television sets are sold in the United States.

Julius and Ethel Rosenberg are convicted of espionage and sentenced to death.

1952

3,909,000 million babies are born in the United States.

The U.S. population is 157,552,740.

Dwight D. Eisenhower is elected president.

Protestant minister Norman Vincent Peale's *The Power of Positive Thinking* becomes a best seller.

I Love Lucy is the number-one-rated television program.

The U.S. successfully tests the hydrogen bomb.

1953

3,959,000 million babies are born in the United States.

The U.S. population is 160,184,192.

Lawrence Ferlinghetti opens The City Lights Bookstore in San Francisco.

Hugh Hefner begins publishing *Playboy*.

The Korean War ends.

1954

4,071,000 million babies are born.

The U.S. population is 163,025,854.

The Supreme Court rules segregated schools are unconstitutional in *Brown v. Board of Education*.

The U.S. economy is in recession, with a deficit of $12.1 billion and an unemployment rate of 6.4 percent.

The words "under God" are added to the Pledge of Allegiance.

In Pennsylvania, ground is broken for the nation's first commercial nuclear reactor.

The Viet Minh defeat the French at Dien Bien Phu; Geneva Conference partitions Vietnam at the seventeenth parallel.

1955

4,097,000 million babies are born.

The U.S. population is 165,931,202.

According to one survey, 40 percent of middle-class white women believed four to be the ideal number of children.

Allen Ginsburg publicly reads his poem "Howl" for the first time, which he will publish the following year.

The year-long Montgomery Bus Boycott begins.

Disneyland opens in Anaheim, California.

"Rock Around the Clock," recorded by Bill Haley and the Comets hits number one on record charts.

Elvis Presley signs a recording contract with RCA Records.

The first McDonald's hamburger store opens in California.

The Salk polio vaccine is announced.

1956

4,210,000 million babies are born.

The U.S. population is 168,903,031.

Congress passes, and Eisenhower signs into law, the Interstate Highway Act.

Congress passes law adding the words "In God We Trust" to all U.S. coins.

Elvis Presley has his first number one song, "Heartbreak Hotel."

1957

The Baby Boom peaks; 4.3 million babies born.

The U.S. population is 171,984,130.

Americans spend $50 million on diapers.

American Bandstand, hosted by Dick Clark, makes its national television debut.

The Soviet Union successfully launches *Sputnik*, the first manmade satellite to orbit the Earth.

Nine black students integrate Central High School in Little Rock, Arkansas.

Norman Mailer publishes "The White Negro" in *Dissent*; coins the term "hipster."

Jack Kerouac publishes *On the Road*.

1958

4,246,000 million babies are born.

The U.S. population is 174,881,904.

Elvis Presley is inducted into the Army.

Wham-O Toys begins selling the Hula-Hoop.

The U.S. economy experiences another recession; corporate profits are down by 25 percent and the deficit increases.

1959

4,286,000 million babies are born.

The U.S. population is 177,829,628.

Buddy Holly, The Big Bopper, and Richie Valens die in a plane crash in Iowa.

1960

4,257,000 million babies are born.

The U.S. population is 180,671,158.

Twenty-five percent of Americans live in suburbs.

Four students at North Carolina A&T University in Greensboro begin the sit-in movement.

The Student Nonviolent Coordinating Committee is founded.

The first oral contraceptive, Enovid, is licensed by the Food and Drug Administration.

John F. Kennedy is elected president, narrowly defeating Richard Nixon.

Americans own more than 85 million television sets; 90 percent of all American homes have at least one television set.

1961

4,268,000 million babies are born.

The U.S. population is 183,691,481.

Bob Dylan moves to Greenwich Village and visits Woody Guthrie.

In an effort to desegregate interstate transportation, the Congress of Racial Equality launches the Freedom Rides

Alan Shepard becomes the first American in space.

The Peace Corps is founded.

Kennedy establishes the President's Commission on the Status of Women.

1962

4,167,000 million babies are born.

The U.S. population is 186,537,737.

John Glenn becomes the first American to orbit the Earth.

Tom Hayden and others write "The Port Huron Statement."

James Meredith becomes the first African American to enroll at the University of Mississippi.

The first trans-Atlantic television pictures are broadcast by the Telestar satellite.

The Cuban Missile Crisis occurs in October.

Michael Harrington publishes *The Other America*; Rachel Carson publishes *Silent Spring*.

1963

4,098,000 million babies are born.

The U.S. population is 189,241,798.

John F. Kennedy is assassinated in Dallas; Lyndon B. Johnson assumes the presidency.

The number of U.S. troops in Vietnam reaches 16,000.

Quang Duc, a Buddhist monk, immolates self in Saigon, South Vietnam, to protest U.S-backed government of Ngo Dinh Diem.

Alabama Governor George Wallace opposes the admission of black students to the University of Alabama by making a "stand in the schoolhouse door."

In a nationally-televised speech, President John Kennedy promises a civil rights act; civil rights activist Medgar Evers is murdered in Mississippi by a segregationist.

Martin Luther King gives his "I Have a Dream" speech during the March on Washington, the largest civil rights demonstration in the nation's history.

In *Baker v. Carr*, the Supreme Court upholds the principle of "one person, one vote."

The Supreme Court bans mandatory school prayer in *Albington School District v. Schempp*.

Betty Friedan publishes *The Feminine Mystique*.

1964

4,027,000 million babies are born; the Baby Boom ends.

The U.S. population is 191,888,791.

The Beatles perform on *The Ed Sullivan Show*.

SNCC organizes Freedom Summer, and 1,000 white college students participate; three civil rights workers are murdered by the Ku Klux Klan in Mississippi.

Ken Kesey and The Merry Pranksters take their first Magic Bus trip, which Tom Wolfe recounts in *The Electric Kool-Aid Acid Test*.

Congress approves The Tonkin Gulf Resolution, giving President Johnson broad authority to direct the war in Vietnam.

The Warren Commission concludes that Lee Harvey Oswald alone murdered President Kennedy.

The Free Speech Movement begins on the campus of the University of California-Berkeley.

China becomes the fifth nation to successfully test a nuclear weapon.

President Lyndon B. Johnson signs the Civil Rights Act of 1964.

Lyndon B. Johnson is elected president.

1965

The Selma-to-Montgomery march for voting rights is organized in Alabama; federal protection provided for marchers after they are attacked.

The first antiwar teach-in is held at the University of Michigan.

Bob Dylan is booed for "going electric" at the Newport Jazz Festival.

Johnson signs the Voting Rights Act; proclaims his vision of "The Great Society."

Medical Care Act creates Medicare and Medicaid.

Elementary and Secondary Education Act provides direct federal assistance to local school districts.

More than 184,000 American troops are stationed in Vietnam.

Malcolm X is assassinated.

Watts riot in Los Angeles.

1966

The National Organization of Women (NOW) founded.

Stokely Carmichael publicly uses the term "Black Power" for the first time; the Black Panthers are founded.

The Supreme Court upholds the rights of suspects in *Miranda v. Arizona*.

1967

Cesar Chavez, the head of the United Farm Workers, calls for a boycott of grapes.

The first "Be-in" is held in San Francisco.

The Beatles release *Sgt. Pepper's Lonely Hearts Club Band*.

Senator Eugene McCarthy declares himself a candidate for the Democratic nomination for president and runs on a peace platform.

More than 486,000 American troops are stationed in Vietnam.

Race riots occur in Newark and Detroit.

1968

North Vietnam launches the Tet Offensive in February.

Martin Luther King, Jr. is assassinated in Memphis.

Robert F. Kennedy is assassinated in Los Angeles.

The American Indian Movement is founded in Minneapolis.

Jerry Rubin and Abbie Hoffman found the Youth International Party (Yippies).

Lyndon Johnson announces he will not stand for reelection.

Johnson signs the Fair Housing Act.

Police and antiwar protestors clash in the streets outside the Democratic National Convention in Chicago.

Richard Nixon is elected president over Hubert Humphrey and George Wallace.

The number of U.S. troops in Vietnam reaches 586,000.

1969

Woodstock Music Festival is held in upstate New York.

Neil Armstrong and Buzz Aldrin are the first men to walk on the moon.

Six hundred Native Americans occupy Alcatraz Island as a protest against the mistreatment of Indians.

The Tate-LaBianca murders are committed by Charles Manson and his followers.

The prototype of the Internet is launched.

1970

The Beatles break up.

The first Earth Day is held.

President Nixon announces American bombing of Cambodia, prompting campus protests across the country.

National Guardsmen fire on students at Kent State University in Ohio, killing four.

Police fire on students at Jackson State University in Mississippi, killing two.

The Weather Underground forms.

Janis Joplin and Jimi Hendrix die.

The U.S. population reaches 205 million.

Congress enacts the Occupational Safety and Health Act; Nixon establishes the Environmental Protection Agency.

1971

Attica Prison revolt.

The Twenty-fifth Amendment is ratified, giving eighteen-year-olds the right to vote.

Nixon vetoes a comprehensive child care bill.

The *New York Times* publishes the "Pentagon Papers."

1972

"The Plumbers," operatives of the Nixon White House, break into the Democratic National Headquarters in the Watergate complex.

Congress passes Title IX of the Education Amendment Act, which bans sexual discrimination in education.

1973

"Baby Bust"; birth rate falls to lowest point since World War II.

The Supreme Court rules in *Roe v. Wade* that abortion is constitutionally protected.

The United States and Vietnam agree to a ceasefire.

Members of the American Indian Movement occupy the Wounded Knee, South Dakota, courthouse.

Spiro Agnew resigns as vice president of the United States.

Congress passes over Nixon's veto the War Powers Act.

Watergate burglars are convicted; Senate hearings on Watergate reveal the existence of taping system in the Oval Office.

The Organization of the Petroleum Exporting Countries (OPEC) oil embargo is imposed by Arab states.

1974

Heiress Patty Hearst is kidnapped by the Symbionese Liberation Army.

Richard Nixon resigns as president of the United States; Gerald R. Ford sworn in as new president; Ford pardons Nixon for any crimes he may have committed as president.

1975

The U.S. experiences its highest rates of inflation and unemployment since the Great Depression.

The airline industry is deregulated.

The last American soldier leaves Vietnam; Saigon falls to North Vietnamese forces on April 30.

1976

Lowest birthrate of the "Baby Bust."

Steve Jobs founds Apple Computers.

The Dow Jones Industrial Average goes over the 1,000-point mark, a first for the stock market.

Jimmy Carter elected president over Gerald Ford.

1977

President Carter declares that energy conservation is the "moral equivalent of war."

The U.S. dollar plummets in value against the Japanese yen.

Elvis Presley dies of a drug overdose.

Protests against the Seabrook Nuclear Power Plant take place in New Hampshire.

After thirteen consecutive months of deficits, the U.S. trade deficit tops $3 billion; a 26 percent rise in oil imports is largely responsible.

New York City black out; David Berkowitz, the Son of Sam killer, is captured after committing six murders.

George Lucas's *Star Wars* premieres.

1978

Regents of the University of California v. Bakke, the Supreme Court rules against racial quotas and "reverse discrimination."

Jerry Falwell founds the Moral Majority.

President Jimmy Carter helps negotiate the Camp David Accords, a peace treaty between Egypt and Israel.

1979

A disaster is narrowly avoided at the Three Mile Island nuclear plant in Pennsylvania.

Iranian students seize the American embassy in Teheran; they take sixty Americans hostage, whom they will hold for 444 days.

1980

1.2 million divorces granted, the highest total in the nation's history.

The U.S. population reaches 227 million.

Ronald Reagan is elected president.

The United States boycotts the Summer Olympics in Moscow, after the Soviet Union invades Afghanistan.

Cable News Network (CNN) begins broadcasting.

1981

Americans held hostage in Iran are freed moments after Reagan takes office.

Reagan appoints Sandra Day O'Connor to the Supreme Court, the first woman to sit on the court.

President Reagan is wounded in an assassination attempt.

Scientists discover the virus that causes AIDS.

Congress passes Reagan's Economic Recovery Tax Act, the largest tax cut in U.S. history.

1982

The banking industry is deregulated.

Reagan breaks the strike by air traffic controllers.

AIDS recognized as a disease.

The U.S. invades Grenada, a small island in the Caribbean, and overthrows its Communist-backed government.

1983

Reagan announces the Strategic Defense Initiative, commonly known as "Star Wars."

Terrorist bomb a marine barracks in Lebanon, killing 241 Americans; U.S. military forces soon withdraw.

1984

Reagan reelected president in a landslide over Walter Mondale.

The Soviet Union and other Eastern Bloc nations boycott the Summer Olympics in Los Angeles.

1985

Mikhail Gorbachev becomes the leader of the Soviet Union.

The Coca-Cola Company introduces a new Coke formula.

President Reagan and Soviet leader Mikhail Gorbachev continue talks on a nuclear arms limitation treaty.

1986

The Iran-Contra scandal breaks.

The space shuttle *Challenger* explodes minutes after launch, killing all seven crew members.

1987

Congress holds hearings on the Iran-Contra scandal.

President Reagan and Soviet leader Mikhail Gorbachev sign the Intermediate-Range Nuclear Forces (INF) treaty.

1988

George H. W. Bush elected president.

The INF goes into effect.

Columbia space shuttle is launched, the first launch since the *Challenger* explosion.

1989

Communist regimes collapse in Europe; the Berlin Wall comes down.

The Savings and Loan crisis forces government bailout of many institutions.

The United States invades Panama to arrest Manuel Noriega, a one-time U.S. ally, for drug trafficking.

1990

The U.S. population reaches 250 million.

Iraq invades Kuwait, the prelude to the Gulf War.

1991

Congress passes the American with Disabilities Act.

Clarence Thomas becomes the second African American to serve on the Supreme Court.

The Persian Gulf War begins; Iraqis driven from Kuwait.

The World Wide Web is launched.

President Bush and Russian President Boris Yeltsin announce a formal end to the Cold War.

1992

Bill Clinton elected president, the first baby boomer to hold the office.

Four Los Angeles police officers accused of beating Rodney King are acquitted; riots break out in Los Angeles.

1993

Janet Reno becomes the first female attorney general.

Ruth Bader Ginsberg becomes the second woman appointed to the Supreme Court.

The U.S. agrees to the North American Free Trade Act (NAFTA).

Congress passes the Family and Medical Leave Act, which allows both male and female workers leave for childbirth, adoption, and family medical emergencies.

President Clinton proclaims the "don't ask, don't tell" policy regarding homosexuals in the military.

Terrorists explode a bomb in the basement of the World Trade Center, killing six and injuring more than 1,000.

1994

Republicans gain control of both the House and Senate; Newt Gingrich heralds the election as affirmation of conservative Republicans' "Contract with America."

Paula Jones, a former employee of the Arkansas state government, files a sexual harassment suit against President Clinton.

1995

A bomb rips through the Alfred P. Murrah federal building in Oklahoma City; 169 die in the deadliest episode of domestic terrorism in U.S. history. Timothy McVeigh and Terry Nichols, members of a militia group, are soon arrested and charged with the crime.

1996

Bill Clinton elected to a second term over Bob Dole.

Clinton signs into law the Personal Responsibility and Work Opportunity Act, which ends the sixty-year-old U.S. welfare program.

1997

President Clinton signs the largest tax cut in U.S. history.

A U.S. Appeals Court upholds a California law banning affirmative action

1998

President Clinton denies, then later admits, to having a sexual relationship with Monica Lewinksi, a former intern at the White House.

The nation's first balanced budget since 1969 is proposed by the Clinton administration.

The House of Representatives impeaches Bill Clinton on charges of perjury and obstruction of justice.

1999

The Senate acquits Clinton in his impeachment trial.

Two students from Columbine High School in Littleton, Colorado, kill four-teen students and one teacher, and wound twenty-three others before killing themselves.

2000

The U.S. population reaches 281 million.

George W. Bush defeats Al Gore, Jr., in closest presidential election in history.

2001

Terrorists fly planes into World Trade Center and the Pentagon.

The United States launches air strikes against targets in Afghanistan.

Congress passes the U.S. Patriot Act.

President Bush signs the No Child Left Behind Act into law, making schools accountable for their student achievement.

2002

President Bush calls Iran, Iraq, and North Korea "an axis of evil," and commits the United States to waging war against nations that attempt to develop weapons of mass destruction.

Congress creates the Department of Homeland Security.

2003

American and British military forces invade Iraq and topple the government of Saddam Hussein.

The U.S. Supreme Court upholds the limited use of affirmative action in university admissions.

The space shuttle *Columbia* disintegrates on reentry, killing all seven crew members.

Congress passes a $350-billion tax cut.

2004

More than 136,000 American troops remain in Iraq to push back an insurgency against the newly installed Iraqi government.

2005

Hurricane Katrina causes extensive damage in Louisiana and Mississippi. Eighty percent of New Orleans is flooded, displacing hundreds of thousands of residents.

2006

The U.S. Census Bureau estimates that the U.S. population has surpassed 300 million.

2007

Kathleen Casey, the first baby boomer and a retired schoolteacher, files for Social Security benefits.

Baby Boomers and the Family

1

C. S. O'Brien

Tuna fish on white bread, mayonnaise. Pickles or not? Dill or sweet? Salt and pepper? Crusts on or cut them off? Whole, halves, or quarters? Down the middle or diagonal? Soup?

It is somewhat surprising to realize that many Americans believe that families are easier to describe than tuna fish sandwiches. Finding some magical moment in the postwar past, usually in the early years of the Baby Boom, they offer up a picture: mom, dad, son, daughter, Puff, Tip, and a ranch home in Levittown or its local equivalent. Mom stays home to mind the children, who are doing well at their neighborhood school, while Dad takes the Chevrolet to the office. Later, at the family dinner table, they happily share stories of their day.

Happening upon that perfect tuna fish sandwich, however, is considerably simpler than finding that mythical family. If one looked only to the mid-1950s white middle-class family and avoided looking anywhere else, such a family would be easier to identify. Looking at the family of the gardener who comes to tend the lawn complicates matters considerably, as would taking a peek at the family of the woman who cleans dad's office. And, even if we focus only on those white, middle-class "I like Ike" couples, there is a pretty healthy chance that Mom has a job; that debt troubles the family finances; and that divorce looms in the somewhat-distant future. Yet we long to find that family around the dinner table, searching for that momentary ideal as if it were the grail.

A few examples of the folly of even trying to find a "typical" baby boomer family should suffice. George, born in July 1946, was a baby boomer of privilege. His father, a decorated Navy aviator in World War II, parlayed family connections in politics and business into a growing fortune. His mother was an active participant in civic organizations and charities, along with raising her six children. Although he spent most of his childhood in Connecticut, George would come to identify most closely with Texas, where his family moved when he was a young man. He returned to the east coast to continue his education, first at Philips Andover Academy in Massachusetts, then at Yale for a degree in history. As was typical for children of privilege, George did not serve in Vietnam, opting instead for a stint in the National Guard. Rumors that his well-connected father had arranged the appointment haunted George for years to come.

Billy was quite another story. Three months before his birth in August 1946, Billy's biological father was killed in a car accident. His mother, facing an uncertain economic future, signed up for a nursing education program shortly after her son was born. She left Billy in the care of his maternal grandparents, not to return for four years. Shortly after reclaiming Billy, she began dating the co-owner of car dealership in Hot Springs. Nearly eleven years later, Billy adopted his new stepfather's last name. He was the only father Billy had ever known, but it was a problematic relationship. His stepfather, an alcoholic who routinely abused his wife and children, suffered with a gambling problem that often left the family short of cash. Other than a brief stint at a Catholic school, when the family was somewhat flush and able to afford tuition, Billy's education took place in the segregated schools of the South. An exceptional student, he earned a scholarship to the prestigious foreign service program at Georgetown University and then a Rhodes Scholarship at Oxford. Bill, devoid of the political connections or personal wealth that helped George avoid time in Vietnam, instead drug out his student deferment as long as possible, while simultaneously participating in protests against the war. His unwillingness to serve in the conflict that so clearly defined his age-cohort would haunt him for years to come.

Ted was born in November 1946, in the Elizabeth Lund Home for Unwed Mothers in Burlington, Vermont. Raised by his grandparents, he was never certain of his biological father, and believed until adulthood that the woman who was actually his mother was his sister. In fact, he came to believe that his grandfather had molested his mother and was thus also his father. Taken from his home by his "sister," the two moved in with relatives in Washington State. When his sister married, her new husband adopted young Ted. A moderately successful student, Ted earned a scholarship to a local university, but soon withdrew and transferred to another school. He performed well enough to earn admission to an area law school, but once again drifted away from his studies and withdrew to pursue other interests. The ways that he escaped service in the Vietnam war are unclear, but a student deferment and a high lottery number might have done it. Failing to serve, however, was not the most damaging thing to Ted's reputation.

That's two presidents and a serial killer—Bush, Clinton, and Bundy—all born within a few months of each other, and each came from a "family," although none was middle class nor composed of a nuclear set of parents and two children. In fact, when historians confront the idea of "family," they often run headlong into the reality of families as oddly different as the ones above. The one that came closest to mirroring the Ward and June Cleaver image was the one family in which material abundance was ensured. For the other two, the Cleaver ideal was so distant a reality that it might have existed on another planet.

The reason for this seeming disconnect is not complex: the standard image of the early baby boomer family is equal parts Golden Age television and mythologizing nostalgia. In their own lives, boomer families have never been fixed. Simple math dictates that it be so: some 77 million children were born between the years 1946 and 1964. A single model could not fit all. In fact, as children, the oldest baby boomers witnessed a nation that seemed tranquil and static while it underwent tremendous economic and social changes. The youngest boomers, on the other hand, came of age when these changes were evident to all and the chaos of transformation in the economy, family life, and social structures were in full bloom.

For more than thirty years, social and cultural historians have dismantled the notion that the white middle-class family of the Eisenhower era was the typical family structure in American history. Although the dominant trend in the twentieth century has been toward declining family size (because of the increase in the divorce rate and the incidence of single-parent households), from roughly 1949 to 1957, a statistical blip occurred as family sizes briefly grew to 3.7 children, the overall divorce rate declined, and single-occupant households decreased. After this eight-year stretch, the metatrends returned. Historians and sociologists have offered several ideas about why this might be so (ranging from the influence of advanced industrialization, to the liberation of women, to the rise of the welfare state), but no single factor seems to account for the historical divergence of the early Baby Boom from the longer term trends.

Even more difficult for scholars has been the question about how one can most understand the role of families in the past. Historians of families, of children, and of childhood (that is three different sets of scholars), along with anthropologists, psychologists, sociologists, demographers, and others (at least another four or five groups of scholars), have long debated the best ways to define the family, to discuss its workings, to connect individuals to their kin, and to connect those kinship networks to the larger society. While disagreements are rife, two overlapping models seem to dominate the discussion. The first, the "family-strategy" model, understands families by their kinship roles (if the model leans toward the anthropological), or by their attempts to maximize family well-being (if the model leans toward the economic) (Cunningham 1998, 1196). The second model, the "life cycle," takes an individual within the family and traces the major incidents of life (birth, development, marriage, parenting, divorce, death, and the like), through the prism of her experience. As with any model, or any attempt to depict the past, certain limitations are inevitable. In looking at the family-strategy model, the picture is often so large that individual variation is lost. On the other hand, the life-cycle approach can suffer from the opposite problem. In it, individual tales can seem to speak to a much larger reality. In recent years, the two models have begun to fuse, with the broadly sociological and the more decidedly biographical approaches informing each other (Cunningham 1998, 1195–1208). To simplify matters somewhat, we will focus here on the leading edge of the

Jon Provost

In his autobiography, Jon Provost takes on the most famous myth of himself and pronounces it bunk. *Timmy's in the Well: The Jon Provost Story* informs us that Timmy fell off cliffs, was swept into rivers, and tumbled down mineshafts, but he never did fall into a well.

Provost, who joined the cast of the television hit *Lassie* in 1957, was born in 1950, raised in southern California and entered acting before age three. While his mother acted as de facto manager of his acting career, Provost had enormous success. He appeared in more than a dozen films and made frequent appearances on television. But it was in the role of Timmy Martin that Provost achieved fame. In his seven years acting alongside America's most famous collie, he became a child star, a cultural icon, and a troubled young man, a path that several others of his generation also took.

A driver's license made the Sunset Strip accessible and fame opened doors. What he found there was just what might have been expected—sex, drugs, and rock and roll. Within a couple years, he followed a girlfriend north and enrolled in Sonoma State University. The relationship ended but he stayed, finished a degree, and entered a career in real estate.

He married a new girlfriend Sandy Gossens, with whom he had two children. They divorced after several years. The divorce proved devastating. Provost descended into bouts of drinking, depression, and binge eating that left him broken. Returning to the world of the quasi-celebrity, he joined the tour of the once-famous who now make their living by selling their autographs. Oddly, it was at one of these events that he would meet his second wife, Laurie Jacobson. She supported him in his commitment to charitable causes, particularly raising funds for animal shelters and for providing animal companions to people with disabilities. Jacobsen, a screenwriter, also helped Provost write his autobiography. In 1994, Provost was awarded a star on the Hollywood Walk of Fame.

Of course, Provost's life was both typical and atypical for those of his generation. His early fame was something very few achieved—but the temptations he found in later life, and the struggles he underwent when he gave into those demons, were ones that would resonate with many of his age-mates. In important ways, Provost's story is that of the prodigal who returns to the fold by outgrowing his vices. Many of those who ventured into the lifestyles commonly associated with the late 1960s never found their way

---

Baby Boom: those families with children born in the years 1946–1954, or so. Following this cohort through its life cycle as children, newlyweds, parents, and, now, grandparents should prove enough for a single essay.

The image of quiet and harmonious family life in the early postwar years is difficult to dislodge. So let's embrace it for a moment, if only to dismantle it later. In this idealized early boomer family, the parents might be readily pigeonholed as GI Joe and Rosie the Riveter. Themselves children of a decade-long depression, they flooded the World War II workforce, accumulated savings more by a dearth of consumer goods than by habit, then left their wartime lives behind for suburban affluence and an expanding consumer marketplace. Gray flannel for him, an apron and pearls for her, two or three children, a puppy, and a station wagon would

Actor Jon Provost, who played Timmy in the television show *Lassie,* signs copies of his book in Los Angeles in 2008. Provost made his movie debut when he was two and a half years old, playing Jane Wyman's son in *So Big,* and then went on to play the son of Bing Crosby and Grace Kelly in *The Country Girl.* His breakout came at age seven, when his role as Timmy propelled him to international stardom. (AP/Wide World Photos)

back out of the drug-induced haze. Others met their ends in the swamps of Vietnam or the innumerable other conflicts the nation has engaged in since. Thus, the hopeful tale of a troubled life that becomes again respectable is but a small version of a national redemption narrative—the one we hope for, although we do not all achieve.

have earned them a spot on any of the innumerable situation comedies of the 1950s. The stream of their lives goes on beyond this, of course, but this is the spot where the imagination would leave the boomer parents: working, stable, and fixed in place and time.

Their children, in this scenario, start their lives huddled around a television, watching the *Howdy Doody Show* in snowy relief. If boys, they soon join the Boy Scouts and learn how to tie knots and camp out in the snow. If girls, they will disappear until they are ready for a high school dance with a boy that dad does not know but must meet before he approves. Then, perhaps, a stint for son in one of those new-fangled rock-and-roll bands that practices in the basement, but never plays a gig. For both, it is off to college, where daughter will stay for only a year or so before earning her Mrs. degree and beginning the cycle again.

Families are not only economic units but also one place in which cultural values are transferred, and thus are a basic unit of social organization. Yet the family as an object of historical study is of relatively recent vintage. Arising from the trends toward historical demography and social history that emerged during the 1960s and 1970s, the analysis of families has been enormously beneficial in our understanding of life in the past, and has been hamstrung by its own limitations—for example, defining a "family" is a necessarily artificial endeavor. Traditionally, the U.S. Census Bureau has seen families as those related by blood, adoption, or marriage sharing a household. Real families include grandparents, aunts, uncles, cousins, and other relatives, but the standard definition leaves those people out.

Adopting, for a moment, the narrowest definition of a family as a household unit, changes to this definition have been evident over time—but to what extent is the subject of debate. James R. Wetzel, former assistant commissioner for the Bureau of Labor Statistics, who went on to demographic studies at the U.S. Census Bureau, explains the changes as follows:

> The past 75 years brought momentous changes in family life patterns of Americans as we adapted to dynamic economic, social, and demographic developments. Changes in family living arrangements and preferences were particularly pronounced from the early 1960's to the late 1970's, about the time of the transition of the baby-boom generation from adolescence to adulthood. During the 1980's, average family living arrangements and family size exhibited comparative stability, fertility stabilized at a rate just below the replacement level, and the divorce rate leveled off just below the 1979 peak. (Wetzel 1990, 12)

By the early 1990s, Wetzel found, fewer people were living in traditional "nuclear families" for three reasons. First, younger adults were living on their own before marriage for an extended period of nonfamilial living as they entered the workforce. Second, the number of older Americans living alone for longer periods increased as the average life span increased. Third, the incidence of former spouses, stepchildren, and former in-laws expanded the kinship networks (Wetzel 1990, 4–5).

In the midst of those changes, however, it is useful to note that the "average" baby boomer household in 1946 was white, composed of two married parents and their children. A typical family in 2008 is white, composed of two married parents and their children. Thus, in its broadest outlines, families in the United States have been remarkably stable. Nonetheless, Wetzel is correct that, within these broad outlines, great variability took place over time. The likelihood of divorce among those householders in 2008 was roughly twice that of those in 1946 and nearly three times as likely as a similar family in 1956. The rise in the divorce rate has changed the notion of the family for baby boomers. The incidence of stepchildren seems to have grown as nearly 60 percent of those who divorce will remarry. The "family" of 1946 was statistically more likely to be composed of parents and their biological children. But the lure of that early Boom family structure often enters the area of mythic proportions.

To take but one example of how this sepia-toned ideal manifested, the memoirist Susan Allen Toth, who was born slightly before the Baby Boom, but whose memories nicely encapsulate those a few years younger, recalled growing up in the mostly sleepy community of Ames, Iowa. As she explains,

> I have . . . difficulty trying to explain to friends who did not grow up in a small Midwestern college town in the 1950s what life was like then. Those "old days" have disappeared into an irretrievable past that seems only faintly credible to those who did not live it. Does any girl today have the chance to grow up as gradually and quietly as we did? In our particular crucible we were not seared by fierce poverty, racial tensions, drug abuse, street crime; we were cosseted, gently warmed, transmuted by slow degrees. (Toth 1981, 1–2)

It was a life of slow realization, as Toth's girlhood of slumber parties, of self-consciousness about her seeming inability to attract a first boyfriend, and of her own bookishness all melded into her notion of a tranquil life that might be lonely but that she knew would somehow result in a marriage and children of her own. But, even here, the fractures in the idealized narrative emerge: Toth both embraced and rejected the ideals she saw set before her. Longing for the independence that a paycheck would bring, she dreamed of her first job as much as a boyfriend. As the sociologist Wini Breines has argued, white, middle-class girls of the Baby Boom era were torn by the conservative tenor of the times and the liberalizing forces that were changing the country. Indeed, Toth's desire for both a nuclear family and a career was more typical of the young women of her age cohort than one might imagine. As Breines explains,

> [T]he youthful women's liberation movement of the 1960s and 1970s articulated concerns about personal life, sexuality and fulfillment that were generated in the postwar period. Lives changed in ways that were not predictable but close consideration to historical patterns indicates continuity as well as rupture. (1992, xiii)

Further evidence of the "continuity and rupture" thesis can be drawn from what might seem a rather unlikely source: the bible of parenting advice for the parents of boomers, Dr. Benjamin Spock's *The Common Sense Book of Baby and Child Care*, which was first published in 1946. Spock's best-selling book ushered in an era of what has been dismissively called "permissive parenting." In part, this is simply a misunderstanding of his advice; although Spock cautioned against the strict feeding schedules and rejected the expert advice from a previous generation that counseled against regularly touching children, he posited instead that

> good-hearted parents who aren't afraid to be firm when it is necessary can get good results with either moderate strictness or moderate permissiveness. On the other hand, a strictness that comes from harsh feelings or a permissiveness that is timid or vacillating can each lead to poor results. The real issue is what spirit the parent puts into managing the child and what attitude is engendered in the child as a result. (Spock 1968, 7)

Dr. Benjamin Spock

It is quite nearly impossible to discuss baby boomers and not mention one of the most important influences on their generation: Dr. Benjamin Spock. In 1946, as the first boomers entered the world, Dr. Spock's *The Common Sense Book of Baby and Child Care* entered with them. Spock told worried parents: "trust yourself." Within the first year, three-quarters of a million copies of his book had leapt off the shelves. Spock's comforting tone and positive attitude meshed well with the attitudes of the postwar era during which a new sense of national self-confidence struggled against an older mind-set that demanded order over individual freedom. But the transition from one mind-set to the other was never a complete one. Spock's critics eventually would emerge—but they rarely argued with the advice the doctor had given. Instead, they set themselves against the man.

Responding to the behaviorism that dominated professional advice about child care during his own childhood, Spock, who had trained in both pediatrics and psychology, sought to soothe parents' worries about their own inadequacies. In part, these worries grew from the efforts of the professionals themselves who cautioned parents against comforting a crying child, demanded rigid feeding schedules and specified age-appropriate diets, among other things. As Spock understood his task, it was

> just trying to show confidence in parents to reassure them whenever possible. I certainly never advocated a permissive philosophy. I have always believed that parents should respect their children but ask for respect from them, too. It was certainly not my principal aim to give them a whole bookful of "do's" and "don'ts." (Spock and Morgan 1989, 135)

As Spock explained:

> Interviewers often ask me . . . to state my "theories" of childraising. I never set out to impose any such grand design on the parents of the world. In fact, it grew increasingly clear to me as I continued to practice that there were so *many* experts, with the best of intentions, telling parents what to do—that parents' most widespread problem was their own uncertainty, a guilty feeling of "Maybe I don't know enough . . . maybe I need to read another book!" Less secure parents begin to think that only professionals know the answers. They don't dare trust their own judgment or stand firm. It's pathetic, and children can get pesky when they sense their parents' uncertainty. (Spock and Morgan 1989, 133—134)

Yet his advice was controversial in some quarters. He stated that masturbation is normal, for instance, leading several conservative commentators to condemn this portion of his book. He laid most of the burden of childrearing, at least in the early editions, on the mother—earning him critics from an entirely different quarter. The book itself has remained astonishingly successful: seven editions, translated into twenty-six languages and more than 39 million copies sold worldwide. But, oddly, it was the criticism from those who seem never to have read his works that has struck his reputation most.

Spock was an advocate of civil rights, opposed nuclear testing, served on the board of the National Committee for a Sane Nuclear Policy, and came out strongly against continuing American involvement in the Vietnam War. Raised in a Republican household, Spock increasingly became identified with the Democratic Party as it gradually moved closer to the positions he already held. As he became publicly identified with these causes, he became fair game for those who held different views. Yet, it was the nature of their attack—that Spock's "common sense" advice amounted to "permissive parenting" thus condemning the nation to an era of youthful radicalism—that seems to have troubled him most. In part, this was because his political critics warped his advice to

Benjamin Spock, a renowned expert in the field of child development, left his teaching position in 1967 to devote himself to ending U.S. involvement in the Vietnam War. (Library of Congress)

include things he never advocated. This is common play in politics, of course, but the good doctor seemed unprepared for it. That someone might doubt his advice on childrearing simply because he had been indicted for aiding and abetting draft resistance seemed not to have figured into his thinking. Yet, to this day, a significant portion of the American population dismisses his childrearing advice out of hand.

It was ultimately the path of community activism and protest that dominated the remainder of Spock's life. Long after the end of the Vietnam War, he remained active in campaigns to close nuclear power plants, fought to extend civil liberties to ever greater numbers of citizens, and continued to speak out whenever he believed the government had trampled individual liberties. His role as gentle advisor to the parents of the boomers long past, he committed himself to fighting for the well-being of the nation. One might argue that Spock turned more radical, and stayed that way, than many of the young people who were raised on the advice he provided. Thus his critics were wrong: very few rebels emerged from Spock's tutelage, but in confronting problems larger than those of parents and children in the home, Spock himself continued to provide guidance to the generation.

In many ways, Spock was a traditionalist. He assumed that the primary caregiver would be the mother, urged those women with small children to consider nurture as their major responsibility, and yet recognized that some women would have to work and others would choose to do so (Spock 1968, 563–564). Whether the mother stayed home or worked, however, Spock assured them, their children would thrive if they simply trusted their maternal instincts and responded as they believed best. For most baby boomers, it was advice they would embrace when their own children were born.

If, as early as 1946, Spock and others were recognizing the necessity or desirability of work for mothers, how can one explain the persistence of the image of the mother at home in the early years of the Baby Boom? Historians have offered a number of explanations. Elaine Tyler May, for instance, has advanced the now-classic argument that social forces aimed at containing female sexuality tried, albeit mostly unsuccessfully, to hold women within the domestic sphere and limit sexual relations to married couples (May 1999, 109–113). Many mothers embraced the role that was afforded them, but others chafed at the limitations. Other historians, however, have argued that the image of the domesticated mother was more clearly a media construct, pointing to popular magazines, expert prescriptive opinions in women's magazines, or television shows that set this image in the popular mind. In any case, the image of the mother is one that is decidedly stilted by failing to include few who were not white and middle class.

That the Golden Age of television whitewashed the economic and racial diversity of the United States is widely accepted. At the same time, it is also true that the troubled question about the appropriate gender roles within boomer families was the staple of the newest medium of mass communication. Too often in the modern imagination, families of the 1950s were mirrors of Ozzie and Harriet Nelson, the Cleavers, the Reeds, or any of the other television families starring in what critic David Marc describes as "benevolent Aryan melodramas" (as quoted in Englehardt 1995, 146; among the shows that might fit this category, *The Adventures of Ozzie and Harriet* [CBS 1952–1966], *Leave It to Beaver* [CBS 1957–1963], and *The Donna Reed Show* [ABC 1958–1966] are most likely to be recognized by modern audiences due to re-airings on such cable networks as Nickelodeon). But even television, that bastion of illusion, itself proves a bit more complicated. Other than *I Love Lucy*, a show whose very premise was tilting at the domestic ideal, few family comedies cracked the top ten in viewership in the first twenty-five years of the boomer era. Instead, crime dramas, Westerns, medical shows, and, for a brief period, variety shows dominated the airwaves. Thus, those looking to the ideal family of the televised fifties are looking to an image that viewers themselves did not fully accept. Perhaps a more expansive notion of the concept of "family" might be in order, but few have argued that America's domestic ideal was typified by the extended "family" of a salty deputy, a cranky doctor, a reliable bartender, and a spate of dance hall girls that Marshal Dillon built around himself in Dodge City. Nonetheless, the occasional romance of

Matt and Miss Kitty had more viewers than Ozzie and Harriet (MacNeil 1996, 1141–1163).

A simpler explanation might be more compelling: complicating the competing demands on women in the early years of the Baby Boom was the spread of material abundance in the postwar years and its attendant costs. Plainly put, a house in the suburbs was affordable on a single income for only a very brief time in American history. As the wave of industrial and economic expansion—necessitated both by pent-up domestic demand and worldwide need in the shattered years after World War II—crested in the late 1950s, a new reality began to emerge. To afford their acquisitive behavior, families looked even more favorably on the dual-earner model. But this was a slide along a scale, rather than a break with the past. After all, more women worked outside of the home during the 1950s than had during World War II. Indeed, more babies meant a greater need for additional income—and a greater opportunity for women to join the workforce (May 1996, 167–168).

This change in the ordering of the family economic picture emerged over time. In the early years after the war, many women did leave the workforce to dedicate themselves to childrearing. The demographic impact was staggering. Some 79 million children were born during the 1946–1964 Baby Boom. In 1945, approximately 2.8 million children were born. By 1954, the number of births annually topped 4 million, a figure that would be exceeded each year through 1964 (Jones 1980, 396). As demographers have shown, the bulge came from three groups of women: those women who were younger than the historical norm for childbearing, those who were of typical childbearing age, and those who were older than the traditional norm. The declining age of women at marriage explains the first group; the delays in first childbirth due to the absence of men during the war and improvements in health care for mothers explain the latter. Notably, the mothers of the boomers span a nearly two-decade age range. Thus, the mothers of the first wave of boomers had nearly all passed out of their childbearing years by the arrival of the last of the boomers. Women born in the 1920s were the most likely mothers of the original Boomers; the mothers of the children of 1964 would likely have been born in the late 1930s or early 1940s and their experiences differed (Fullerton 1999, 4–5).

In the early years of the Baby Boom, as industrial jobs held by women during the war were taken over by returning soldiers, an ethos of the "career homemaker" took hold among those women who could afford to make this choice. In important ways, the GI Bill made this a possibility. With down payments as low as one dollar, families could acquire a home in the new suburban developments dotting the nation. At the same time, in an embrace of the returning servicemen, universities (the other major beneficiary of Uncle Sam's postwar largess) restricted the number of women they allowed into professional programs. Thus, with jobs filled by their husbands, inexpensive housing at hand, and few opportunities to venture into other roles, the "career homemaker" was a role that was not only expected, but also and often unavoidable. The moment was a brief one—homes, cars, and children cost money and, as those too young to have served began having children, the costs of keeping up with the Joneses increasingly demanded a two-income family. Thus, as their children entered school, more mothers returned to the workforce, either on a part-time basis or, less commonly, as a full-time wage earner. As a woman's work life is not coterminous with her childbearing years, the oldest cohort of mothers of baby boomers likely was still on the job when the youngest cohort moved in, swelling the ranks of women workers overall.

In many ways, it was profoundly important that mothers join the workforce since the economic impact of that massive wave of children was enormous. Both the public and private sector expanded dramatically throughout the 1950s to compensate, in part, for the abundance of new citizens. Throughout the nation, the demand for new schools, hospitals, and roads pushed government expenditures for public works to levels that had not been achieved even during the height of the New Deal. At the same time, pent-up demand for consumer goods like automobiles met new efficiencies in production that had developed during World War II and, after a series of strikes for improved wages in manufacturing, year-over-year income for American families improved steadily throughout most of the 1950s. In a sense, new technology, improved workplace efficiency, and a successful push for higher wages proved the enemy of inflation. Thus, after a brief reconversion period following the war, prices fell in comparison to net incomes. For American families, whether one parent was working or two, it was a good time for the first time in decades.

Within the private sector, the effect of the first wave of baby boomers quite nearly created an entire child-centered sector of the economy. From the massive expansion of toy production, fueled in part by the introduction of television advertisements aimed to sell Mr. Potato Head and other juvenilia, to the expansion of the recording industry as these first boomers entered their adolescence and rock-and-roll swept the nation, the children of the first cohort were an economic gold mine. This massive expansion of demand came at the same time that a push for lengthening the period of compulsory education took root. Thus, with more demand and an absence of children and teens entering the workforce, more positions were available for women workers. The children of the Baby Boom era, whether of the first cohort or the last, grew comfortable with the idea of mothers in the workforce because it was the reality. Nonetheless, this transformation of familial roles for women met with serious opposition from some from quarters of society from the 1940s to the early twenty-first century.

The children of the front edge of the Baby Boom grew into late adolescence and early adulthood in the midst of these demographic changes, but in many ways, the changes were most clearly evident only with historical distance. Those children who grew up in the 1950s tended to see relatively few marriages fail. Throughout the decade, the divorce rate hovered around 25 percent. These children, however, would not have the same experience when they began to wed. As the early boomers entered their own childbearing years, they began to reverse some of the trends established by their parents. The age of first marriage rose for both men and women, divorce resumed its upward slope, and the number of children per family dropped once again.

The first wave of baby boomers began to wed in the early 1960s—and soon challenged the very idea of the "family." Many of those of marriageable age in the late 1960s and throughout the 1970s experimented with more complicated family structures, either in the communal movement that spanned the bridge of years between the decades, or more frequently, by cohabitating before marriage. Of the two, cohabitation has proved to be the more durable trend.

Several other changes in how we understand families have corresponded with the Baby Boom generation. First, family sizes grew (peaking at 3.7 children in 1957), and then fell off by 1972 to below replacement rates. Only recently has replacement again become the norm. Simultaneously, the overall number of families increased, due in part to the demography of the Baby Boom, but also to the increase in immigration since the mid-1960s. Third, families have changed because divorce grew more common (about 25 percent of marriages in 1946 ended in divorce, rising to the 35 percent range in the late 1950s, to nearly 50 percent in 2008). While a declining age at first marriage in the early Baby Boom years (a median of 20.7 years for women in 1950, rising to more than 23.4 now) seemed to cement those marriages, early age at first marriage is now a relatively reliable predictor of divorce.

Taken with the greater incidence of people residing outside of their parents' home before marriage—either for college or work—a new phase of life seems to have emerged in which males and females of marriageable age defer nuptials while they complete their education or begin their careers. For the U.S. Census Bureau, this has increased the number of nonfamily households. Other more complicated arrangements, such as open marriages and multiple-partner marriages, existed in a nearly negligible portion of the population, although they were widely discussed in the press. More telling was the spike in the divorce rate from the 1970s through the 1980s. The increased incidence of blended families complicated the social and demographic picture even more thoroughly. Finally, one of the conventions long associated with marriage in the United States—that is, that the wife takes the last name of the husband and the children share that name—has become common. This simple change in nomenclature speaks to a revised understanding of how and what families are.

Although most forms of nontraditional family structure have faded in recent years, two new forms have gained some level of social acceptance and seeming permanence: (1) same-sex couples and their children are increasingly described as families, and (2) the incidence of unwed motherhood has increased among the late boomers and among the children of the baby boomers. In the former case, the debate over this change in understanding of marriage and family has been fierce. In the latter, a more resigned acceptance reigns.

The struggle over civil and legal rights for gays has laid bare the contest of meaning over the terms "marriage" and "family." In 1996, President Clinton signed into law the Defense of Marriage Act, which stated:

> In determining the meaning of any Act of Congress, or of any ruling, regulation, or interpretation of the various administrative bureaus and agencies of the United States, the word "marriage" means only a legal union between one man and one woman as husband and wife, and the word "spouse" refers only to a person of the opposite sex who is a husband or a wife.

Since then, ballot initiatives in several states have changed either the law or the state constitution to prohibit marriages between partners of the same gender. But, at the same time, several states have adopted "civil union" laws that afford all the protections that accompanied marriage. Massachusetts and California have moved beyond protection to embrace marriage.

The discussion over marriage and parental rights for gay Americans often overlooks an obvious parallel: the rise of single motherhood. Other than a general lament about young women having children out of wedlock, few people have argued that single mothers and their children are not families. In fact, the pressure to put a child up for adoption in such circumstances has all but disappeared. In one case, there is a rush to the altar, in the other an avoidance of it altogether. But those who wish to marry and raise children seem to earn more opprobrium than those who raise the children without "the benefit of clergy."

For early boomers and their own children, families no longer mean simply one father, one mother, and their children all sharing a name and a roof. If one were to look only at the broad outlines provided by the U.S. Census Bureau, remarkably little has changed in the American family in the last sixty years. Astonishingly as it may seem, the family unit composed of two parents and roughly the same number of children remains the societal fundament as it was for those couples of the Eisenhower era. In 1950, when the first baby boomers were four years old, only 66 percent found themselves in married households. In 2006, that number had further declined to 53 percent, a substantial difference, but one whose appearance was deceptively larger since, during the same period, the number of households more than doubled. In the broadest sense, families remain the same. In finer detail, however, families are complicated creatures (U.S. Census Bureau 2006).

So to return to those three boomers who began our tale: George W. Bush married Laura Lane Welch in 1977, and remains married to her to this day. In 1981, they had twin daughters, one of whom married in 2008. William Jefferson Clinton married Hilary Rodham in 1975, and remains married to her to this day. They had a single child, also a daughter, born in 1980. Theodore Bundy, taking advantage of an oddity in Florida law, had his girlfriend called to the stand as a character witness during his trial for murder. In the presence of court officers, Bundy announced that he and Carol Boone were married—sufficient at the time to constitute a valid marriage in the state. They had a daughter, born a short time later. Bundy and Carol divorced in 1989, but he did receive several other marriage proposals while on death row.

Perhaps a more typical boomer is one of the most famous for being born and for leading her generation in each phase of life. In 2006, in one of those recurrent bits of sentimentality, the nation once again trotted out "the first baby boomer" for interviews on *The Today Show*, the *CBS Evening News*, CNN, and innumerable newsmagazines and newspapers. Kathleen Casey-Kirschling, resident of Cherry Hill, New Jersey, born one second after midnight on January 1, 1946, outside of Philadelphia, was hailed as the lucky first of that memorable generation that historian Landon Jones so memorably called "the pig in the python." In fact, it was Jones, in his seminal 1980 book *Great Expectations: America and the Baby Boom Generation* who first nominated Casey-Kirschling, whom he would later call his "ur-boomer" (Welch and Bazar 2005). In many ways, Kathleen Casey-Kirschling was typical of the first wave of her generation. She married, had a career, had a family, divorced, and remarried. On February 12, 2008, she was presented with her first check from the Social Security Administration thereby leading the boomers into retirement as she had into life (Welch and Bazar 2005). As a twice married retiree who is now a grandparent, Casey-Kirschling once again leads the way into a new phase of family life for the boomers.

The families that the first boomers experienced remain the typical families that surround them as they enter retirement. But within that overarching experience, enormous variability is the rule. Suddenly, that tuna fish sandwich seems simple in comparison.

Bibliography

Breines, Wini. *Young, White and Miserable: Growing Up Female in the Fifties.* Chicago: University of Chicago Press, 1992.

Child Study Association of America. *Where We Are: A Hard Look at Family and Society.* New York: Child Study Association of America, 1971.

Chudacoff, Howard. *Children at Play: An American History.* New York: New York University Press, 2007.

Coontz, Stephanie. *The Way We Never Were: American Families and the Nostalgia Trap.* New York: BasicBooks, 2000, 1992.

Cunningham, Hugh. "Histories of Childhood: Review Essay." *American Historical Review* 103, no.4 (October 1998): 1196.

Englehardt, Tom. *The End of Victory Culture: Cold War America and the Disillusioning of a Generation.* New York: Basic Books, 1995.

Friedan, Betty. *The Feminine Mystique.* New York: Norton, 1963.

Fullerton, Howard N., Jr. "Labor Force Participation: 75 Years of Change, 1950–1998 and 1998–2025." *Monthly Labor Review* (December 1999): 4–5.

Hareven, Tamara. "Cycles, Courses and Cohorts: Reflections on Theoretical and Methodological Approaches to the Historical Study of Family Development." *Journal of Social History* 7 (Fall 1978): 97–109.

Hawes Joseph M., and Elizabeth I. Nybakken, eds. *American Families: A Research Guide and Historical Handbook.* New York: Greenwood Press, 1991.

Hawes, Joseph M., and N. Ray Hiner, eds. *American Childhood: A Research Guide and Historical Handbook.* Westport, CT: Greenwood Press, 1985.

Hwang, C. Philip, Michael E. Lam, and Irving E. Sigel, eds. *Images of Childhood.* Mahwa, NJ: Lawrence Earlbaum, 1996.

Jacobson, Lisa, ed. *Children and Consumer Culture in American Society: A Historical Handbook and Guide.* New York: Praeger, 2007.

Jacobson, Lisa. *Raising Consumers: Children and the American Mass Market in the Early Twentieth Century.* New York: Columbia University Press, 2005.

Jones, Landon Y. *Great Expectations: America and the Baby Boom Generation.* New York: Coward, McCann, & Geoghegan, 1980.

MacNeil, Alex. *Total Television: The Comprehensive Guide to Programming from 1948 to the Present.* 4th ed. New York: Penguin, 1996.

May, Elaine Tyler. *Homeward Bound: American Families in the Cold War Era.* New York: Basic Books, 1999.

Meyerowitz, Joanne. "Beyond *The Feminine Mystique*: A Reassessment of Postwar Mass Culture, 1946–1958." In *Not June Cleaver: Women and Gender in Postwar America, 1945–1960,* edited by Joanne Meyerowitz. Philadelphia: Temple University Press, 1994.

"Nation's First Baby Boomer Receives Her First Social Security Retirement Benefit." Press release. Washington, DC: Social Security Administration, February 12, 2008.

Reiss, David, and Howard A. Hoffman, eds. *The American Family, Dying or Developing.* New York: Plenum Press, 1979.

Smith, Judith E. *Visions of Belonging: Family Stories, Popular Culture, and Postwar Democracy.* New York: Columbia University Press, 2004.

South, Scott J., and Stewart E. Tolnay, eds. *The Changing American Family: Sociological and Demographic Perspectives.* Boulder, CO: Westview Press, 1992.

Spock, Benjamin. *Baby and Child Care.* 1946. Reprint, New York: Pocket Books, 1968.

Spock, Benjamin, and Mary Morgan. *Spock on Spock: A Memoir of Growing Up with the Century.* New York: Pantheon Books, 1989.

"The Last Baby Boomer?" BBC News, August 18, 2006. http://news.bbc.co.uk/2/hi/americas/5262500.stm.

Toth, Susan Allen. *Blooming: A Small-town Girlhood.* New York: Ballantine, 1981.

U.S. Bureau of the Census. "America's Families and Living Arrangements, 2006: Living Arrangements of Children Under 18 Years Old: 1960 to Present." http://www.census.gov/population/www/socdemo/hh-fam/cps2006.html.

Welch, William M., and Emily Bazar. "N.J. Woman Enjoys Celebrity of Being 1st Baby Boomer." *USA Today*, December 12, 2005.

West, Elliott. *Growing Up in Twentieth-Century America: A History and Reference Guide*. Westport, CT: Greenwood Press, 1996.

Wetzel, James R. "American Families: 75 Years of Change." *Monthly Labor Review* (March 1990): 12.

Women and the Baby Boom $\Big|\ 2$

Kimberly Wilmot Voss

The 2003 movie *Mona Lisa Smile* depicted the college life of upper-middle-class women in 1953 America. The goal of the college degree for women was to find a man, get married, and fill a home with shiny new appliances. While situation comedies promoted a white, upper-middle-class image of a house in the suburbs that the college students in the movie had dreamed of, the truth is more complicated. That is the heart of social history. Sociologists have shown that the ideal of the nuclear family, typically described as a married working father and a stay-at-home mother, was not as common as once thought. Complicated family structures have long existed. Women, too, were working outside of the home long before the women's liberation movement made the workplace more open to women. (Of course, some women have always worked outside of the home. Many worked as domestic help to upper-class-women, while others worked in traditional female fields such as nursing or teaching.) The groundwork for working women lay in the push for women to fill men's roles during World War II, made famous by the Rosie-the-Riveter propaganda campaigns that tied working to patriotism.

Following World War II, the 1944 G.I. Bill of Rights led to the growth of the suburbs with low-interest mortgages. Couples were marrying young and having more children, thus the term Baby Boom. The government-sponsored daycare centers that existed during the war were closed. Women were encouraged to return to their homes with psychologists warning that motherhood should be women's main occupation. One of the most influential arguments was made in the 1946 book, *Dr. Spock's Baby and Child Care*. The message to women was clear: your place is in the home. Many authoritative studies suggested that women who did not fully embrace their roles as mothers were causing neurosis in their children. A widely cited example is Dr. John Bowlby's 1951 study, *Maternal Care and Mental Health*. The author, who was affiliated with the World Health

Women welders, including the women's welding champion of Ingalls Shipbuilding Corporation, pose for a photo in 1943. (National Archives)

Organization, concluded that, to a child, a mother with full-time employment was trauma equivalent to that of her death.

Experts disagree about the exact years of the postwar Baby Boom, although the most commonly accepted opinion was from 1946 to 1964. In the United States, about 76 million babies were born between those years. In 1946, births grew from 222,721 in January to 339,499 in October. By the end of the 1940s, about 32 million American babies had been born, compared with 24 million in the 1930s. In 1954, yearly births exceeded 4 million for the first time and did not drop below that figure until 1965, which is considered the end of the boom. All those births affected women's lives. Some historians have noted that access to birth control pills in the mid-1960s helped to change the population climb.

World War II

American women took on many of the men's jobs during World War II. In one 1943 *Tampa Tribune* cartoon, a woman is shown sitting on a bed looking at her husband, who was in front of a mirror and wearing a welding-mask. The caption read, "Stop admiring yourself and take it off, Otis; I have to get ready for work" (Weatherford 1991, 145). Across the country, women were taking on new roles, holding positions previously denied to them based on their gender. Women took on a new, public role during World War II. When men went off to war, women were taking their positions in the workplaces. This was most visibly represented by the image of Rosie the Riveter—a woman with muscular arms wearing a bandana over her hair beneath the message "We Can Do It!" She represented the 6 million women who worked in the manufacturing plants that produced munitions and material during the war years. According to the *Encyclopedia of American Economic History*, the number of working American women increased to 20 million by 1944, a 57 percent increase from 1940.

In male-dominated industries, women were taking on new roles. For example, before the war, female reporters typically were restricted to the women's pages, filled with fashion stories and recipes. They were able to cover news and sports after the war began. It is estimated that more than 8,000 male reporters went into the armed forces and were replaced by women during World War II. Many small daily newspapers were often run completely by women, so much so the journalism publication, *Editor & Publisher*, ran the headline: "Man Joins Staff" (as cited in Frank and Sann 1944, 20).

Yet, women who worked during World War II helped create the changes that were obvious more than two decades later. These women knew they could take on new roles in the workplace and women continued to join the workforce in great numbers. According to Elaine Tyler May,

> The number of employed women aged 20 to 34 dropped to one million below the prewar predictions. The retreat of these women made room for more older women to enter the paid labor force in the expanding pink-collar sector. Therefore, the actual number of women in gainful employment continued to rise after the war, even though the range of employment available to them narrowed. (May 1988, 76)

Some high school home economics textbooks included advice for young women to look their best when their husband's came home from work. It is a clear message that a married woman was not part of the workforce.

Women and Consumerism

After World War II, suburban communities across the country grew quickly. The G.I. Bill led to returning men going to school and buying new homes. Many of the women were fired from their jobs after the war when the men returned. Married women returned to the home and homemaking was emphasized. Advertisements featured smiling mothers wearing pearls and an apron marveling over a new appliance. In the five years following the end of the war, not only did consumer spending increase 60 percent, but also the amount spent on household furnishings and appliances rose 240 percent. Prestige was measured by the newest refrigerator or washing machine. In some ways, this consumer growth was a political issue, shopping as a battle against Communism. In the 1950s, the country was in a state of paranoia over Communism and the atomic bomb. Magazines featured photos of bomb shelters and stacks of canned food. According to historian Elaine Tyler May, consumerism was a way of winning the Cold War. She wrote that, in President Richard Nixon's vision,

The suburban ideal of home ownership would defuse two potentially disruptive forces: women and workers. In appliance-laden houses across the country, working-class as well as business-class breadwinners could fulfill the new American work-to-consume ethic. . . . The family home would be the place where a man could display his success through the accumulation of consumer goods. Women, in turn, would reap rewards for domesticity by surrounding themselves with commodities. Presumably, they would remain content as housewives because appliances would ease their burden. (May 1988, 164)

Advertising exploited this approach and appealed to women's patriotism. Shiny appliances and new cars were staples of advertisements in the 1950s. Televisions were advertised as bigger and better. The new technology was in more and more homes. Bright colors were featured and marketing often demonstrated luxury. It was important to impress the neighbors. The tagline for the Ford Edsel was, "They'll know you've arrived when you drive up in an Edsel." Consumers were encouraged to replace the old with the new.

With growing families, women were looking for quick meals. This led to the growth of convenience, or processed, foods. These products were a sign of a growing manufacturing economy and technological advancement. Cookbooks began to reflect semihomemade recipes. These shortcuts allowed busy mothers to continue to fulfill their maternal obligations, as the expectation was that a home-cooked meal was part of being a good mother. Most obvious was the growth of casseroles that typically were made with a base of cream soups. One of the most common kitchen appliances was an electric can opener, an indication that convenience foods were now part of daily recipes. The TV dinner, a packaged, complete meal that only had to be put in the oven for a short time, allowed the family to eat in front of the television.

Giving Advice

Advice columns were a staple of women's pages in newspapers, and an examination of the columns shows some progressive ideas. The columns provide a place to demonstrate a voice of authority. If there was little equality in terms of pay or promotions, women did have the moral authority that allowed them to give advice about relationships and household issues. This was especially important as male experts were reinforcing women's traditional roles, as was explored by Barbara Ehrenreich and Deirdre English in *For Her Own Good: Two Centuries of the Experts' Advice for Women*. As they noted in the introduction, physicians such as stress expert Dr. Hans Selye warned that women working outside the home would run the risk of heart attack: "Some cardiologists even claimed evidence of an 'epidemic' of heart disease among women supposedly liberated by feminism" (Ehrenreich and English 2005, xiii).

While the medical community was talking down to women, a voice of authority was found in these advice columns. Eppie Lederer took over the syndicated Ann Landers column housed at the *Chicago Sun-Times* in August 1955. (Interestingly, Lederer was rejected for a local political position for being too outspoken.) At one point, Lederer, now writing under the pen name of Ann Landers, was getting about 2,000 letters a day, and about a third were from teenagers. A survey in the late 1950s found that 85 percent of all female readers read the column and 45 percent of the male readers read it daily. As an example of how influential her column was, consider her December 1971 column about cancer, a topic that rarely was discussed at the time. She pointed out the statistics—of the 200 million Americans alive, 50 million were likely to develop the disease—and the lack of government dollars spent on cancer research. She urged her readers to contact their senators to support a cancer research bill pending before Congress. An estimated between 300,000 and one million letters came in from Ann Landers readers. She was on hand when President Richard Nixon signed the National Cancer Act (Kogan 2003, 103–104).

Another popular syndicated columnist in the women's pages was Erma Bombeck, whose syndicated column "At Wit's End" began in 1965 running three times a week in hundreds of newspapers across the country. Bombeck's humorous voice was important for her ability to satirize house work. Her jabs at the monotony of cooking, cleaning, and child-raising allowed homemakers to recognize some of the difficulties they faced without disparaging them. Bombeck, for example, told her readers it was fine to keep leftovers in the refrigerator because, "Garbage, if it's made right, takes a full week." On another occasion, Bombeck recounted how she felt being a working mother and "racing around the kitchen in a pair of bedroom slippers, trying to quick-thaw a chop under each armpit." She also poked fun at men and how couples negotiate the responsibilities of parenthood. "Transporting children is my husband's 26th favorite thing," she once wrote, and "it comes somewhere between eating lunch in a tearoom and dropping a bowling ball on his foot" (quoted in Skow 1984, 2). Her columns, and later her books, also highlighted the lack of fatherhood responsibilities while mother's work grew (Weiss 2000, p 93). In her later years, she was a staunch supporter of the Equal Rights Amendment.

Women's Clubs

Women's clubs have a long history in the United States. In the nineteenth century, women were prescribed from participation in the public sphere and, in response, formed clubs directed at self-improvement, social reform, and community service. Women organized around such social issues as temperance, slavery, and voting rights. They provided public service to support Civil War veterans and promote patriotism. And, in the late nineteenth century, they established groups to address such local concerns as health, education, and civic improvement. Mainly, white, middle-class women were attracted to women's clubs, although professional women—such as writers and educators—also joined. African American women were shunned from most clubs, so they formed their own to address the needs

of their communities. Many local clubs were affiliated with national um-
brella associations, such as the Woman's Christian Temperance Union, the
General Federation of Women's Clubs, and the National Association of
Colored Women's Clubs.

Initially criticized for neglecting their responsibilities for their children
and home, by the twentieth century, women's clubs were firmly established and widely respected for their efforts at civic and social reform.

These clubs not only focused on culture, as was common in the earliest days, but also created an element of community development:

> Reform-minded women turned the concept of women's sphere, with its con-
> cern for family well being, into a justification for moving from the home into
> the public arena to confront situations that had an adverse impact on their
> families. (McElhaney 1998, 15)

For example, in 1933, women's clubs were credited with initiating 75 percent of public libraries in the country. James H. Canfield, a librarian at
Columbia University and husband of a club founder, said, "I know of no
one power, no one influence, which has accomplished more for education
in this country than the organization known as women's clubs" (Blair
1980, 101).

Over the years, numerous women's organizations were established
across the country. From modest beginnings, these organizations were
soon tackling social issues. As early as 1922, researchers noted that: "the
one powerful agency through which a woman has been able to express
her individuality is though the woman's club movement" (Roberson 1922,
50). These organizations took on bigger roles supporting the troops on the
home front during World War II. Marie Anderson was one of the women
who volunteered at the Servicemen's Pier in South Florida. In April 1941,
U.S. Army soldiers transformed Miami Beach into a training camp. The
local Junior League asked for women to volunteer at the Filter Center, also
known as the Air Raid Information Center. By October 1942, the Junior
League was a "commanding presence" at the Servicemen's Center, helping
the more than 100,000 Air Force officers being trained in Miami. The
upper-class Anderson said, "It still didn't occur to me to get a job because I
thought you worked only if you needed the money. So I became the
Available Woman. I was available to every cause that came along" (Papers
of Marie Anderson).

It was while Anderson was doing this work that she met Kay Pancoast, who oversaw the volunteers. Anderson and Pancoast would continue to stay in touch over the next few years, and it was Pancoast who
eventually would bring Anderson to the *Miami News* for a brief stay
before her *Miami Herald* tenure began. Many of these women continued
to do important work after the war was over. As Dorothy Roe noted,
"The public began to find out that if a community needs a new school
community center, or somebody to tame its teen-agers, the local wom-
en's clubs could usually get the job done, often succeeding where generations of politicians and aimless 'do-gooders' had failed" (Roe 1961,
124). According to a study of women's clubs, as early as the 1950s, the

clubs' policies supported "a broad set of issues ranging from federally funded day care to education to environmental preservation to equal pay" (Mathews-Gardner 2004, 13).

As Anne Firor Scott has noted, these women "sometimes function as a kind of early warning system, recognizing emergent problems before they were identified by the male-dominated political process" (Scott 1991, p.3). As communities developed, it was clear that women's organizations paved the way for change. In fact, the president of the General Federation of Women's Club said in 1948, "The day of the sewing circle is past. The time has come when we should discard the outmoded idea that we are a non-political organization" (Mathews-Gardner 2004, 3). Little by little, women's clubs were transforming their communities. As recent historians have noted, women's organizations in the 1950s were making a change from civic engagements to political groups: "If the 1950s began as a decade of homemakers and housewives, it opened to a decade for feminists and women's liberation, brining with it new forms and strategies of political action" (Mathews-Gardner 2004, 34). They helped disabled or troubled children, sponsored voting drives, and held family planning workshops in partnership with Planned Parenthood.

Club editor Roberta Applegate was prepared to report on the work of clubwomen. She had noted the activities of these women in their interactions with the governor in Michigan before she was hired by the *Miami Herald*. In 1954, Applegate wrote a two-part series about a home for the disabled. She visited the home and described the setting and the people. Her first story begins,

> The power of women working as a unified group is being recognized more and more. Their material contribution to their communities is recognized in their various projects—school equipment, nurseries, building beautification, etc. More intangible is the influence they exert in civic matters, which sometimes manifests itself in tangible ways. The expanded program at the Florida Farm Colony is one of these. The Florida Federation of Women's Clubs supported the appropriations bill passed by the 1953 legislature. (Applegate October 14, 1954)

The 1953 Florida legislature appropriated much more than was originally requested after being lobbied by the women's organization. The superintendent of the home thanked the women for their help and asked for continued support, saying "because a word from you can mean a great deal" (Applegate October 15, 1954). In the second article, Applegate again pointed out the significant work that the club women did. She wrote about the Junior League women who were working to raise money to buy occupational therapy equipment and about other women's groups who were putting together a survey to identify the needs of children in the state (Applegate October 15, 1954).

Helping marginalized groups was a common cause for women's organization. According to a history of the Federation of Women's Clubs, one of the chief concerns of its members was the welfare of children. The members supported the Proposed Juvenile Court Amendment to the

Florida Constitution, which was intended to establish a statewide uniform of juvenile courts in the 1950s. The organization also passed a resolution urging the legislature to appropriate funds for an industrial school for "delinquent negro girls," which had been built in Ocala but had not been funded for maintenance, operation, and staffing. Other 1950s issues the club examined were crowding in mental hospitals, the dangers of comic books, and fears of nuclear destruction.

Women's Magazines

One of the top women's magazines during the Baby Boom was the *Ladies Home Journal*. Beginning in July 1935, Bruce and Beatrice Gould became the editors of the magazine that was already several decades old. Its circulation that year was 2.5 million and grew to 4.3 million by 1949. The couple remained at the helm until 1962. Under their leadership, the magazine tackled important issues such as crusades for public health, clean politics, and punishment for child-beaters. They attracted significant authors and politicians including Eleanor Roosevelt. Advertising was significant, too. In October, 1948, the magazine sold $2.6 million worth of ads on its 278 pages, more than any magazine had ever run in a single issue. It did more advertising business than the next two women's magazines, *Good Housekeeping* and *McCall's*, combined. At a quarter a copy, circulation was more than 4.5 million, three-quarters of a million over the second-place *Woman's Home Companion*.

Joan Younger was one of the magazine's top writers. A working mother, she traveled the country doing research and wrote at least one article per issue. Most of her articles were about constructive social programs especially those that helped children. She wrote about the low pay of the nation's teachers, quoting one teacher as saying, "For years we appealed to the conscience of the community to pay us living wages; when all else failed, we had a right to strike" (Younger October 1947). In another, she profiled a Louisiana school district that was a role model for a strong education system. This is how she described the district: "The average income of families living in the bayou county is only $500 to $700 yearly—yet they provide their children with schools considered among the best in the country" (Younger September 1947). Other projects she covered were a successful housing project and a productive recreation association. These magazine stories validated the importance of women's work in their communities.

Much of Younger's writing was done at home as daycare was difficult to find. By 1949, she was an associate editor at the magazine. She worked in the Philadelphia office one day a week. The Goulds believed the magazine's mission was to provide mothers and homemakers with information to navigate effectively the modern world. The primary focus was on traditional roles, but it also focused on women taking on public roles, whether in working outside the home or volunteering in the community. Younger wrote a March 1947 story about different volunteer programs across the country. She wrote another of those stories in the April 1947 issue about Red Cross-trained volunteers in Memphis, Tennessee, who helped veterans' hospitals. In the first year of peace time, the 380 women put in more than 124,000 hours of work. Younger wrote, "This is the story of the men whose suffering did not cease with the sound of the victory bells; and this is the story of the women who, because they want to, have learned how to care for these men" (Younger April 1947).

The magazine's editorial agenda was much like a news magazine rather than the traditional women's magazines of the time. Its slogan was "Never Underestimate the Power of a Woman." According to the historian Nancy Walker, the Goulds' magazine was an exception to the fluff found in the other women's magazines. A *Ladies Home Journal* memo from 1950 included the following topics: the Cold War, the United Nations, and union contracts. Much of what Younger covered was political. She noted her reporting plans for a November issue was about election: "Probably our most outstanding fault in making democracy function is the relatively small proportion of people who vote" (Younger memorandum, Joan Younger Dickinson Papers). In January, her attention turned to Congress. She recommended the following story idea: "we might also research those bills most likely to be facing a vote, or those of importance which seem to have been lost in committee in the past" (Younger memorandum, Joan Younger Dickinson Papers).

Younger wrote several of the stories in the acclaimed "How America Lives" series. In researching these stories, she would spend up to three weeks living with the families as she got to know them. The series was intended to run one year, but proved so successful that it ran twenty-one years and featured 250 families. The Goulds noted that the series was meant to allow readers to meet each other. They wrote: "the average proved to be exceptional" (Gould and Gould 1968, 325). The series was primarily about white families in different social classes. The exclusion of minority coverage might have been due to advertisers that paid based on circulation. Editor Bruce Gould noted that when the editor featured the family of an African American physician and referred to his wife by "Mrs." rather than her first name, circulation in the South dropped by 200,000 subscribers. The magazine received thousands of letters from outraged readers. At this point, integration, especially in the American South was rare.

Beginnings of the Civil Rights Movement

Significant demographic changes were occurring in many of America's cities. During the second wave of the Great Migration, many cities grew significantly. Encouraged by stories in black newspapers, many Southern African Americans were relocating in northern cities. One of the most significant of those newspapers was the *Chicago Defender*. It was founded by Robert S. Abbott in 1905 and once heralded itself as "The World's Greatest Weekly." The newspaper was read extensively in the South. According to a history of the newspaper, using editorials and cartoons, the *Defender* addressed the hazards of remaining in the overtly segregated South and lauded a better life in the North. And readers took those words to heart. For example, in Chicago, the African American population grew from 278,000 in 1940 to 813,000 in 1960.

Journalist Charlotta Bass fought for civil rights in California for decades. She took over control of the black newspaper, the *California Eagle,* after the death of its owner John James in 1912. She remained as publisher until 1951. The newspaper investigated discriminatory hiring practices, police brutality, and restrictive housing rules. She was branded a Communist for her crusades and the Federal Bureau of Investigation placed her under surveillance. She retired from the newspaper in 1951 and went into politics. In 1952, she became the first African American woman to run for national office as the vice presidential candidate.

This changing demographic did not mean that segregation was only welcomed. In fact, following two world wars and the Great Depression, a sense of conservative values was spreading. The government stepped in to challenge the status quo. For example, in May 1954, in *Brown v. Board of Education,* the U.S. Supreme Court integrated the country's public schools. (In 1948, President Truman had ordered the integration of the military.) These governmental directives to integrate communities did not happen automatically—social behaviors were more difficult to change.

In the 1950s and continuing throughout the decades, lunch counters were a rather visible sign of a call for change in the South. The discriminatory policies in busses were also addressed. Most famous was Rosa Parks who, in 1955, decided not to give up her seat on a bus in Montgomery, Alabama. But, little more than ten years before Park's arrest, Irene Morgan was arrested in 1944 for refusing to give up her seat on a Greyhound bus to a white couple in violation of a Virginia segregation law. She appealed the Supreme Court. The results was a 1946 landmark decision, the Supreme Court ruled 6-1 that Virginia's state law enforcing segregation on interstate buses was illegal.

Women in Business

Women were making some inroads into the business world by becoming entrepreneurs. For example, in 1950, Marion Donovan patented the disposable diaper and mothers' lives were changed forever. Donovan was a mother unhappy with the era's leaky, cloth diapers that had to be washed. She first invented the "boater," using shower curtain plastic to cover cloth diapers. After creating the new product, she was turned down by manufacturers who responded that the product was not "cost efficient." Instead, she sold them in department stores herself and later sold the business for $1 million.

Another successful female entrepreneur of the Baby Boom was Bette Nesmith Graham who created liquid paper, originally called "mistake out." She was single mother working as a secretary in Dallas when she thought up a way to be more efficient in her typing. She used her kitchen blender to mix up liquid paper to cover up mistakes. Other secretaries began to ask for some and her company was born. In 1956, she started the Mistake Out Company, which was later renamed Liquid Paper, out of her home. Her son Michael Nesmith (who later became part of the band The Monkeys) and his friends helped to sell the product. When she was fired from her secretarial position, she worked on the company full time. It quickly grew, and by 1967, it had grown into a million-dollar business. She died in 1980, a few months after selling her business for $47.5 million.

Cosmetics legend Estee Lauder was another important business entrepreneur of the Baby Boom. A daughter of immigrants, Lauder, who was born Josephine Esther Mentzer, started her company by selling a skin cream that was created by her chemist uncle. She sold her cream to beauty shops and eventually to department stores. She was an ambitious saleswoman

Cosmetics entrepreneur Estee Lauder in 1972. (AP/Wide World Photos)

and, by 1948, she had counter space at Saks Fifth Avenue. She had a personal sales approach, and was one of the first to provide customers with a sample with a purchase. Her company quickly grew and today is worth billions of dollars.

Women and Politics

In the post-World War II years, women were taking on a bigger role in politics. A 1958 women's page article profiled Marion Martin, who was the nation's only woman commissioner of a state department of labor. She had held that position in Maine for eleven years. Martin had gone to Miami to address the Florida Industrial Commission's Workmen's Compensation Conference. In the news story, the reporter included a quote from Martin that spurred some women into action: "Labor-management relations after all are just human relations and the woman in the household is the one who resolved conflicts. The same techniques a woman uses to solve family quarrels are used in labor and management conflicts" (Applegate 1958).

For example, a 1959 women's page story featured the views of a Republican committee woman, Claire B. Williams, and her views on women in politics. Williams, of St. Petersburg, said she was insulted by statements made by male politicians about the woman's vote: "As if we weren't human beings, too." She addressed a stereotype of the female voter: "It's insulting to women to say a candidate must have dimples and wavy hair to appeal to the women. We look for the same thing men do and so often we're better informed." She also said that a woman was not ready to be president. Not for a stereotypical reason, but that the path to the presidency needs to be in place. She believed women would not be ready until more women held office in Congress and more women served as governors (Applegate 1959).

In 1959, the women's sections of many newspapers included a column by Vera Glaser about women and politics. She addressed the increasing role of women in elected positions and their role as voters in the 1960s. She wrote: "There will be a marked increase in the number of women serving in public office from city halls to the United States Congress. This trend can be seen from year to year now." She concluded by pointing out that, by 1970, more than 5 million more women would reach voting age than men (Glaser 1959).

Glaser was the women's press secretary for the Republican Party in the 1950s. In that role, she encouraged women's involvement in politics. She became the Washington Bureau Chief for the North American Newspaper Alliance in the 1960s. In 1963, she wrote a wire story about discrimination against women. In it, she noted a "simmering resentment over the relatively few women in top appointive and career posts" (Papers of Vera Glaser). But Glaser's big moment would occur six years later. During a televised news conference on February 6, 1969, Glaser asked President Nixon the following question: "Mr. President, since you've been inaugurated, you have made approximately 200 presidential appointments, and only three of them have gone to women. Can we expect some more equitable recognition of women's abilities, or are we going to remain the lost sex?" (Papers of Vera Glaser).

The president's initial response was snide: "Would you care to come into the Administration?" He then said, "I really wasn't aware of that. We will do something as soon as possible." The question became a wire story that ran in newspapers across the country. The story began as follows: "President Nixon, chagrined by a charge that women were becoming the 'lost sex' in his administration, promised today to promptly make more high-level female appointments. The complaint was registered by news-woman Vera Glaser" (Papers of Vera Glaser). That question led to a part-nership between Glaser and Catherine East, who had been a member of the Kennedy Commission on the Status of Women. The two gathered sta-tistics and examples of inequities to present to the Nixon administration. The two were aware that some in Washington were implying that women were involved in an unofficial capacity. Glaser wrote to East about how they could build their campaign for more women in high-level positions: "It could alert them to the resentment caused by wives-in-Cabinet-meetings ploy" (Papers of Vera Glaser).

Also in 1969, Glaser wrote a five-part, in-depth series that ran in dozens of newspapers. Called "The Female Revolt," the series addressed "the inequi-ties that women must face in a male-dominated society" (Women's News Service Report memo, March 8, 1969). The final article listed what needed to be done. The requests were as follows: (1) equal protection under the law, (2) daycare centers, (3) legalized abortion, and (4) "a poverty program that does not discriminate against women." Long-time federal employee Cather-ine East wrote in 1970: "Some top Federal officials now expect women's rights to be a major issue of the seventies. It is fair to say Mrs. Glaser's series was a giant step in that direction" (Papers of Vera Glaser). It was Glaser's political training in the 1950s that allowed for her activism years later.

Foundation of the Women's Liberation Movement

The character played by Julia Roberts in *Mona Lisa Smile* was a liberated professor who could have been described as a feminist, although historians have noted that "Fifties 'feminism' was never so labeled" (Kaledin 1984, 218). It was a more subtle force. Yet, at the close of the 1950s and the early 1960s, the rumblings of the women's liberation movement were developing. The Commission on the Status of Women, initially chaired by Eleanor Roosevelt, issued a report in 1963 that documented discrimination against women in virtually every area of American life. States responded by establishing their own commissions for women to investigate discrimi-natory conditions and to recommend changes. In that same year, Betty Friedan published the landmark book, *The Feminine Mystique*, which has been cited as an igniting force for the women's movement. Friedan, a for-mer journalist, explored what she called "the problem with no name" (Friedan 1963), the expectations that women should be fully content with being a wife and mother. She detailed the intellectual oppression that

Hillary Rodham Clinton

Hillary Rodham Clinton is one of the best-known and most powerful women in the world, yet she also elicits great scorn from her detractors. A former first lady (while Bill Clinton was president), Clinton was elected to the U.S. Senate in 2000. In 2008, she mounted the most successful presidential campaign ever by a woman, and in 2009, was named secretary of state by the man who defeated her in the Democratic primaries, Barack Obama.

Born on October 26, 1947, Hillary Diane Rodham grew up in the politically conservative upper-class suburb of Park Ridge, outside of Chicago. Rodham graduated from Wellesley College with a degree in political science before heading to Yale Law School, where she graduated with distinction in 1972. At Yale, Rodham met Marian Wright Edelman, and later interned for the civil rights lawyer at her Washington, D.C., research institution, later known as the Children's Defense Fund. Under Edelman's guidance, Rodham developed a keen expertise in child law, and an affinity for assisting the poor and disadvantaged. Upon graduation from Yale, Rodham took a full-time position with the Children's Defense Fund. She later was assigned as counsel to the House Judiciary Committee as it prepared impeachment charges against Richard Nixon.

When the committee's legal staff was dismissed, Rodham accepted a teaching position at the University of Arkansas Law School. It was in Arkansas that she reunited with Bill Clinton, whom she had met while both were at Yale. In 1975, Hillary Rodham and Bill Clinton were married.

Hillary Clinton became first lady of Arkansas when her husband became governor. She continued to focus her attention on children and children's issues, an effort she continued when Bill Clinton became president in 1992 and she became the nation's first lady.

Bill Clinton was the first baby boomer elected president, and many of his political opponents linked him to the excesses of the 1960s. As first lady, Hillary Clinton was not spared similar attacks. Indeed, her outspokenness on numerous issues only increased the chorus of detractors who criticized her for overstepping boundaries. Clinton was an activist first lady, the likes of which had not been seen since Eleanor Roosevelt. She headed up the administration's effort to overhaul the health care system, which ultimately failed. Her office was located in the West Wing of the White House, near her husband's and symbolic of the role she played within the administration.

Soon after taking her seat in the Senate, rumors arose regarding Clinton's candidacy

middle-class, college-educated women were experiencing because of limited professional opportunities. While the book inspired thousands of women to examine their roles as homemakers, scholars such as Joanne Meyerowitz and others have suggested that postwar culture was more complex than Friedan suggested.

Also at this time, women members of the Student Nonviolent Coordinating Committee (SNCC), the major student organization of the civil rights movement, and Students for Democratic Society (SDS), the student organization for the New Left, began to question their roles in organizations that were not willing to champion gender issues. In media historian Todd Gitlin's book on this period, *The Whole World Is Watching*, Gitlin cites a cartoon of a woman holding a screaming baby, while washing a pile of

Hillary Clinton speaks on the campaign trail in Iowa in October 2007. (Hillary Clinton for President)

for president in 2004. She stayed clear of that race, but threw her hat in the ring for the 2008 nomination. She and Barack Obama staged a historic campaign, with Obama gaining the nomination.

Hillary Rodham Clinton benefited from the many advances gained by women activists during the Baby Boom era, yet her career reflected the difficulties women faced in achieving full equality in American society. Although she has always been an advocate for women and children, she was criticized harshly for stepping outside of her "proper role" as a wife and mother to work on their behalf.

dishes, saying into the telephone, "He's not here, he's out helping the struggle of oppressed people" (Gitlin 1980, 371). The cartoon illustrates the frustration many women activists felt in fighting oppression in one quarter only to experience it in another. This frustration prompted many women to leave the civil rights movement and explore ways to confront their own oppression as women.

According to historian Jo Freeman, the women's movement of the 1960s began with the activities of two different groups. The first was an "older branch" of politically active women who had taken part in the Commission on the Status of Women, and the second a "younger branch" of women who had taken part in the civil rights movement. The older

National Organization for Women president Betty Friedan and other feminists march in New York City on August 26, 1970. The march commemorated the fiftieth anniversary of the passage of the Nineteenth Amendment, which granted American women full suffrage. (Sygma/Corbis)

branch created the National Organization for Women (NOW) in the latter part of the decades. The younger branch developed conscious-raising groups and took on more radical activities on college campuses. Change was on its way. Those young women who grew up during the Baby Boom faced a different future than their mothers.

The experience of women in the Baby Boom era was complex. The changes wrought by the American economic behemoth and the Cold War gave women conflicting messages. On the one hand, they were encouraged to seek fulfillment in the home as wives and mothers, as a refuge against domestic and foreign threats. On the other hand, the needs of the U.S. economy demanded that they enter the paid labor force. This tension prepared the field for the women's movement of the 1960s.

Bibliography

Applegate, Roberta '' 'Children' at Florida Farm Colony Range from 6 to 60.'' *Miami Herald*, October 14, 1954.

Applegate, Roberta. ''Dimples Don't Sway a Woman's Vote.'' *Miami Herald*, August 29, 1959.

Applegate, Roberta. ''Emphasis at Florida Farm Colony Placed on Rehabilitation, Training.'' *Miami Herald*, October 15, 1954.

Applegate, Roberta. ''Women Keep Peace at Home; They Can Do It in Industry.'' *Miami Herald*, October 31, 1958.

Blair, Karen J. *The Clubwoman as Feminist: True Womanhood Redefined, 1868–1914*. New York: Holmes & Meier Publishers, 1980.

Bowlby, John. *Maternal Care and Mental Health*. Geneva: World Health Organization, 1951.

Ehrenreich, Barbara, and Deirdre English. *For Her Own Good: Two Centuries of the Experts' Advice for Women*. New York: Random House, 2005.

Frank, Stanley, and Paul Sann. ''Paper Dolls.'' *Saturday Evening Post*, May 20, 1944, 20.

Freeman, Jo. *The Politics of Women's Liberation*. New York: Longman, 1975.

Friedan, Betty. *The Feminine Mystique*. New York: Bantam Doubleday, 1983.

Gere, Anne Ruggles. *Intimate Practices: Literacy and Cultural Work in U.S. Women's Clubs, 1880–1920*. Urbana: University of Illinois Press, 1997.

Gitlin, Todd. *The Whole World Is Watching*. Berkeley: University of California Press, 1980.

Glaser, Vera. ''What America and Americans Can Expect in National Politics in the Coming Decade, 1960–1970.'' *Miami Herald*, n.d.

Gould, Bruce, and Beatrice Blackmar Gould. *American Story*. New York: Harper & Row, 1968.

Inness, Sherrie A., ed. *Kitchen Culture in America*. Philadelphia: University of Pennsylvania Press, 2001.

Kaledin, Eugenia. *American Women in the 1950s: Mothers and More*. Boston: Twayne Publishers, 1984.

Kogan, Rick. *America's Mom: The Life, Lessons, and Legacy of Ann Landers*. New York: 2003.

''Ladies' Choice.'' *Time*, October 4, 1948.

Mathews-Gardner, A. Lanethea. ''The 1950s, Women, Civic Engagement, and Political Change.'' Presented at American Political Science Association, Chicago, Illinois, September 1, 2004.

May, Elaine Tyler. *Homeward Bound: American Families in the Cold War Era*. New York: HarperCollins Publishers, 1988.

McElhaney, Jaquelyn Masur. *Pauline Periwinkle and Progressive Reform in Dallas*. College Station: Texas A&M University Press, 1998.

Meyer, Jessie Hamm. *Leading the Way: A Century of Service*. Lakeland: Florida Federation of Women's Clubs, 1994.

Meyerowitz, Joanne, ed. *Not June Cleaver: Women and Gender in Postwar America, 1945–1960*. Philadelphia: Temple University Press, 1994.

Morrina, Carmen. "The League Goes to War. The Junior League of Miami." http://www.juniorleagueofmiami.com/warhistory.html. (accessed January 3, 2006).

Morris, Monica. "The Public Definition of a Social Movement: Women's Liberation." *Sociology and Social Research* (1974): 526–543.

Papers of Joan Younger Dickinson. Heritage Center, University of Wyoming, Laramie, Wyoming.

Papers of Marie Anderson. Western Historical Manuscript Collection, University of Missouri, Columbia, Missouri.

Papers of Vera Glaser, Heritage Center, University of Wyoming, Laramie, Wyoming.

Porter, Glenn, ed. *Encyclopedia of American Economic History: Studies of the Principal Movements and Ideas*. New York: Scribner, 1980.

Roberson, Nellie. "The Work of Women's Organizations." *The Journal of Social Forces* (November 1922): 50.

Roe, Dorothy. *The Trouble with Women Is Men*. Englewood Cliffs, NJ: Prentice-Hall, 1961.

Scott, Anne Firor. *Natural Allies: Women's Associations in American History*. Urbana: University of Illinois Press, 1991.

Skow, John. "Erma in Bomburbia." *Time*. July 2, 1984, 2.

Spock, Benjamin. *Baby and Child Care*. 1946. New York: Pocket Books, 1968.

Walker, Nancy, ed. *Women's Magazines 1940–1960*. New York: Bedford, 1998.

Weatherford, Doris. *A History of Women in Tampa*. Tampa, FL: Athena Society, 1991.

Weiss, Jessica. *To Have and to Hold: Marriage, the Baby Boom & Social Change*. Chicago: University of Chicago, 2000.

Younger, Joan. "He's Our Prof." *Ladies Home Journal*, October 1947, 230.

Younger, Joan. "Meriden, Connecticut's Answer on Housing." *Ladies Home Journal*, June 1947, 23.

Younger, Joan. "The Red Cross: Memphis, Tennessee." *Ladies Home Journal*, April 1947, 67.

Younger, Joan. "Schools . . . One Solution." *Ladies Home Journal*, September 1947, 23.

Younger, Joan. "The Smithfield Recreation Association." *Ladies Home Journal*, May 1947, 23.

Younger, Joan. "The Volunteer Worker, 1947 Style." *Ladies Home Journal*, March 1947, 57.

Students and the Baby Boom | 3

E. Jan Jacobs

After World War II, the booming U.S. economy and liberal government policies provided Americans with the highest standard of living in the world. Millions of Americans, including the white working-class, enjoyed a middle-class lifestyle by purchasing homes, taking vacations, and indulging in the purchase of appliances, clothing, and other consumer goods. This affluence contributed to the growth of education, at all levels. Millions of Americans had the means to send their children to college; higher education soon would be available to all, not merely the upper class. More students attended, and completed, high school. The Baby Boom put incredible demands on communities to build new schools and hire more teachers.

By 1960, the United States had produced a consumption-oriented cohort of students, which numbered perhaps 25 million. Compulsory school attendance meant that more young people attended and completed high school. As a result, the teenager emerged as a cohort group for the first time in American history. White, middle-class youths, freed from the economic necessity of contributing to the family income (as their parents had done during the Great Depression and World War II), were expected to go to school and spend their ample spare time wholesomely and appropriately. As they came from affluent families and had significant leisure time, students became significant consumers. Rock-and-roll music was of critical importance, as it tended to reinforce a social identity for high school students, at least those in the suburbs. The lyrics expressed conventional values such as love, marriage, and fidelity, and forged a sense among teenagers that they were a unique social group.

It is tempting to overstate the collective generational identity of the baby boomers. Numerous studies point out that college students in the 1960s shared to a remarkable degree their parents' values. Yet the combined impact of new media, popular culture, a prosperous economy, and sheer numbers cannot be ignored. Students, as a group, were relatively affluent, and certainly higher education was seen as being available to the privileged.

Government Policy and Curricular Changes

To understand the experience of the adolescent student during the latter part of the 1950s, the 1960s through 1975, it is necessary to explore some of the education policy, societal expectations, and cultural expressions that developed over a twenty-five-year period (1950–1975). Government policy focused on the establishment of Cold War policy and politics, which permeated all levels of society. It might be observed that America never quite returned to "normalcy" after World War II because of the perceived threat emanating from the Soviet Union. Response to this threat took up the attention of the whole nation particularly because of the presence, for the first time, of a weapon capable of massive destruction to all life on earth. As so often happened during the twentieth century, the public schools became a focal point for shaping the future of the United States by preparing the rising generation, and helping it understand, its responsibilities to the nation and, by extension, the world.

One of the key curricular programs of the 1950s, which found support from the Office of Education, was Life Adjustment. The Life Adjustment curriculum sought to create a more pragmatic group of adults. The program emphasized preparing students for the workplace and placed less emphasis on the conventional curriculum of math, science, and reading. Schools focused more on the inner life of the child and sought to bring the skills one would need in life, such as those learned in home economic courses for girls and other courses suitable for boys. A great deal of emphasis was placed on citizenship and the knowledge needed to be an active participant in an American democracy. High schools also introduced courses, which gave its student population a way to develop practical vocational skills, such as photography and auto mechanics. By 1956, however, a shift began regarding academic focus. The Council for Basic Education (CBE) encouraged high schools to spend more time developing English, math, science, history, and foreign language skills. Government funding for science and math usually eclipsed that of the humanities and continued to do so with the launch of Sputnik by the Soviets in 1957.

One of the innovations introduced to improve high schools was the concept of tracking. Tracking was a method that allowed educators to identify the skills, talents, and abilities of their students to maximize their potential. This introduced the method of testing as a tool to assess a student's academic talent and ability. If a student could not maintain a particular level of achievement, they would be put on a vocational track over an academic one. This model did not find much popularity because it did not consider the preference of the individual student and it limited a student's right to an education, which had found greater acceptance and popularity throughout the twentieth century.

In 1950, the National Education Association (NEA) organized the Mid-century White House Conference on Children and Youth, which brought together thousands of educators. The participants ended the conference by submitting 67 recommendations. Among them were the following: federal aid that would help equalize education opportunity; financial assistance to qualified youth to attend a college or university; a recognition that church and state needed to be separate but that an individual's understanding of religious and ethical concepts was essential to his or her development; a recommendation that the newly formed Federal Communications Commission (FCC) dedicate some television channels for non-commercial educational programming; children with disabilities must be accommodated; school lunches be provided for those who were unable to pay for them; and, finally, a call for an end to racial segregation in the education system.

The problem of segregated schools, especially in the South, became the focus of the African American community. Spearheaded by the National Association for the Advancement of Colored People (NAACP), *Brown v. Board of Education* charged the public school system in the United States to carry out the policy of integration. This event probably laid the foundation for the activism that became so prominent during the 1960s. High school students in Little Rock, Arkansas, joined the movement in 1957 to resist the federal government's mandate, but much evidence suggests that the African American population born between 1943 and 1957 cleared the path for a wider accomplishment regarding equality of opportunity and the rights of all minority groups.

Students and Popular Culture

The idea of consensus guided much of the cultural development during the 1950s. A sense of conformity and a need to support government policy, especially foreign policy, permeated the era. This common idea found its reflection in the corporate world, but beneath the surface, were those who were ready and willing to break the mold. By 1957, youth culture became a phenomena fueled by a fledgling consumer market, which focused on the high school and college student. Comic books became increasingly popular among the boomer generation. While the evolution of the comic book occurred over a century, it would be publications such as *MAD Magazine*, and its many imitators, that would find a responsive cord. Previously political satire had been aimed at an adult market, but William Gaines targeted *MAD* for a younger audience. By focusing on American culture in general, Gaines was able to create the opportunity for a different perspective that would shape a generation. Certainly his influence could be seen during the antiwar period of the late 1960s through the actions of such groups as the YIPPIES (Youth International Party).

Other comic books that held sway over the boomer generation were Batman, Superman, and other action heroes. There was a tendency during the 1950s to link comic books and juvenile delinquency. In 1954, William

A teacher watches over sixth-grade students reading comic books during class in 1951 as part of an evaluation of leisure activities. (AP/Wide World Photos)

Gaines testified at Senate hearings on behalf of the industry. The comic book industry, aware that the government might impose a code on them, moved to institute their own regulations: that crime could only be displayed as an unsavory activity while pictures of zombies, vampires, and other characters were cut out completely. Where the comic book industry limited its depiction of activities or scenarios, which may have influenced young minds, the movie industry, took over. Films such as *High School Confidential* and the *Blackboard Jungle* depicted life of inner-city teenagers as immoral and the adults who had to cope with their behavior as saviors. But Hollywood increasingly realized the profit potential and began producing films that promoted various musicians and the world of rock and roll. Movie studios also focused on science fiction, producing such classics such as *The Forbidden Planet* and *The Blob*. There were the horror films such as *The Creature from the Black Lagoon, The Attack of the Fifty Foot Woman,* and *I Was a Teenage Werewolf.* These movies brought the teens and preteens of the mid to late 1950s into the single-screen Saturday matinee movie theater.

The adolescent world of the boomer generation contrasted sharply with that of their parents. Those who had grown up in the previous generation were greatly influenced by their experience of the Great Depression of the 1930s, and America's entry into World War II. The youth culture of those born between 1943 and 1957 developed during a time of unprecedented affluence in American society. Many did not experience that affluence, but the images it generated permeated American culture in general. One of the chief vehicles for transmitting the dominant cultural view was through the growing medium of television. Television was a relatively new phenomenon and became available on a mass level during the 1950s. While still in its infancy and experimental, it soon became a tool of advertisers as it opened up the market place to a greater audience. Television served several purposes: it provided entertainment, information, and a way to convey cultural values to a fixed audience. To maximize its potential, those concerned with the development of new markets began to pay more attention to the rising generation's interests. During the 1958 season, television programmers, celebrating ten years of air time, produced twenty-one westerns, introduced Jack Parr to America, put on specials such as *Annie Get Your Gun*, and, for the more intellectually minded, produced shows including *The Twentieth Century*, narrated by Walter Cronkite; Sunday afternoon shows like *Omnibus*; and the *Young People's Concerts* with Leonard Bernstein. Dr. Seuss even had an animated series, "Gerald McBoingBoing."

Beginning in 1957, ABC-TV began to broadcast *American Bandstand*, which would be a staple of American television for the next thirty years. Teens were drawn to the horror film genre and shows such as *Shock Theatre* out of Chicago provided late-night entertainment for the more adventurous viewer. Television became a way of shaping youth culture, although much of the process during the late 1950s through the mid-1960s was more intuitive than calculated. But for the boomers it would be the music that created their cultural paradigm. With shows like *American Bandstand* and the artists that Dick Clark brought to the small screen, the adolescents of the 1950s and 1960s would be keyed into a world and a language that was all their own. One of the major components of rock and roll was the acceptance of musicians and personalities that were more inclusive of minority groups within the United States. One of the cultural focuses of the post-World War II world was recognition of the need to be more inclusive of the diverse cultures that made up the country. It was a time when the leaders of the African American community were able to galvanize their constituency in such a way as to finally break the back of segregation. In doing so, they opened up the possibilities for other disenfranchised groups, and one of the earmarks of the boomer generation thus became its willingness to be shaped by the "other."

Suburbia and Homogenization

Another feature of the boomer generation is where many experienced their adolescence. After World War II, a massive housing shortage came just at the time when those who had to defer marriage to serve their country began to settle down and have families. One of the new features of the American landscape was the rise of the suburban development, which became known as suburbia. Suburbia allowed young families to raise their families in an environment that was more spacious and less frantic then what a city had to offer. Often built on unused farmland, the development of the suburb was a version of small-town America only with an identical floor plan. Much has been made of the tract housing of the 1950s and the conformity that it reflected. Pete Seeger's *Little Boxes* was the critique of his generation's advance toward mediocrity. But the suburbs were also an area of great affluence. In places like Chicago's North Shore, the original migrants from the city had been the McCormicks of the Tribune, the Rosenwalds of Sears, and the Swifts of the meat-packing industry. These families and others like them had built grand summer homes on the lake. It was not unusual for these areas to develop more densely during the 1950s and 1960s as the middle class became more firmly entrenched. This rising middle class was mostly made up of white protestants who were begrudgingly becoming more tolerant of their Jewish and Catholic counterparts, but still it was easy to spot the self-segregation of many religious and ethnic groups. While not every member of the boomer generation experienced the idyllic vision promulgated about the 1950s, their parents attempted to create a world of safety, security, and material success for their children. This relative peace and affluence promoted a youth culture that actually had a hand in dictating trends in American culture. Teenagers toward the end of the 1950s on average had about eleven dollars to spend a week. Still the youth culture of the late 1950s promoted the ideal woman as a wife, mother, and homemaker, while men still formed the economic engine that drove the household toward success. Because of this idealization of gender, young women were more likely not to begin or complete a college education. Young men, on the other hand, were expected to develop some area of expertise, and the opportunities for a college education after World War II expanded enormously.

In hindsight, of course, the first wave of boomers to enter into adolescence in the l950s did so in a world riddled with cracks and fissures. However, the illusion of a society united became a powerful force in maintaining a certain economic and social stability. The stability allowed for some deep reflection and, as the Baby Boom generation came of age, the critical mass of their numbers alone would be a catalyst for change. At the beginning of the 1960s, college-age boomers were part of two nations: white America and black America. One of the consequences of World War II for Americans was the expansion of education opportunity and institutions of higher learning were attempting to be responsive to the issue of integration. While most Americans perceived segregation as a southern issue, colleges and universities in the North also struggled with their traditions of discrimination.

Student Activism

Because of the sheer critical mass of the boomers as they graduated high school, campuses across the country were greatly affected by the influx of students, and a discernable shift occurred in America from one generation to the next. First, the political power of the country came into the steward-ship of younger men when John F. Kennedy became president of the United States. Kennedy urged the rising generation to contribute to the greatness of the nation in tangible ways: "Ask not what your country can do for you, but ask what you can do for your country." In many ways, this phrase defines the students of the 1960s who did not lack for causes, issues, or pragmatic programs to practice the art of citizenship. The move-ment for civil rights within the African American community had gained greater momentum after the success of the Montgomery Bus Boycott. Martin Luther King Jr. emerged as the charismatic leader of the Southern Christian Leadership Conference (SCLC). Inspired by the work of their eld-ers on February 1, 1960, Joseph McNeil, Izell Blair, Franklin McCain, and David Richmond, who all attended North Carolina Agricultural and Tech-nical College in Greensboro, walked into Woolworth's and sat down at the lunch counter in the "Whites Only" section for one hour before the store's closing. The next day they returned with more of their peers, and the press began to notice. The lunch counter seated sixty-six people and, for the re-mainder of the week, an African American student from the college would occupy each seat. Word of the action spread throughout the South and, by the end of April 1960, several more demonstrations of the same type were held, all exemplifying the method of nonviolent confrontation. At their peak, an estimated 50,000 African American students participated in the action. The sit-ins were so powerful that Ella Baker, who had been work-ing for SCLC, organized a conference where students who had taken part in the action could share their insights and experiences. It was at this con-ference at Shaw University in Raleigh, North Carolina, that the Student Nonviolent Coordinating Committee (SNCC) came into being.

As the civil rights movement gained momentum among the African Americans, it spilled over onto college and university campuses that were predominantly white. White involvement peaked in the summer of 1964 with the Mississippi Summer Project. Organized by Bob Moses, the project focused on three goals: voter registration, the organization of Freedom Schools, and the creation of the Mississippi Freedom Democratic Party (MFDP). The voter registration drive attracted hundreds of white students from the North. These students would take the skills that they learned dur-ing their involvement with the civil rights movement and apply them to organizing against the war in Vietnam and the women's movement.

Boomers as a generation did not lack for causes nor were they igno-rant of the workings of their government. This potent combination of ide-alism, injustice, and knowledge drove the engine of protests during the decade. One of the great innovations of the Kennedy administration was the establishment of the Peace Corps in March of 1961. Although an out-growth of the Cold War, the Peace Corps had been designed with youth in mind and provided an opportunity not only to support development in regions such as Africa and Southeast Asia but also sought to create a more personal diplomacy by fostering a greater understanding between Ameri-cans and other people of the world. Along side the Peace Corps and in tribute to the presidency of John F. Kennedy, Lyndon Baines Johnson established Volunteers in Service to America (VISTA). VISTA would be to America what the Peace Corps was to the international community, an opportunity for the youth of the country to give back in tangible ways. VISTA focused on areas of immense poverty in the United States, such as Appalachia. Individuals such as the current senator from West Virginia, John D. Rockefeller, served as volunteers. Although neither the Peace Corps nor VISTA limited the age of service, they both appealed to the boomer generation as a way to put their idealism into practice and repair the world.

In 1962 at Port Huron, Michigan, a group of college students who had been active in more left-leaning liberal politics came together, to explore the possibilities of living in a world free of the Cold War conflict. Most had grown up during the 1950s and were aware of the effects of McCarthyism, the presence of atomic weapons, and the privileges their background gave them. The group had come together because of their involvement in the youth arm of the League for Industrial Democracy (LID), a socialist organization that had denounced Soviet Communism and supported America's stance in the Cold War. The Port Huron Statement laid out the agenda for the organization, but the most striking thing about it was its rejection of Cold War politics. These students, some of whom were the leading edge of the Baby Boom, sought to create a political world that was less violent and more inclusive of differing ideologies. Another movement that gained the attention of the nation and created the political culture of college students during the 1960s happened at the University of California-Berkley. The free speech movement of 1964 was a direct result of the campus administration's attempt to limit the distribution of certain kinds of political material on university property. Mario Salvo became the chief spokesman and symbol of the movement. This kind of rights protest and organization would spread throughout the country. Students on campuses would begin to demand not only their rights as American citizens but would demand changes in housing, hours, and class offerings that would transform college life for future generations. The boomers succeeded in establishing the notion of shared governance between administrators, faculty, and students. Student governments became active participants within the bureaucracy of the campus structure. Students were appointed to various university and college committees, were given some control over the disbursement of student fees, and even gained representation on some school's board of trustees.

As had happened during the abolition movement of the nineteenth century, the civil rights movement early in the decade of the 1960s attracted women young and old into its stream. Coincidental to women's support in the fight for integration and equal rights, Betty Friedan published *The Feminine Mystique*, aimed largely at an audience of women like herself: comfortably middle class, educated, liberal, and of European descent. But her message was heard loudly, clearly, and with energetic acceptance by the young women of the boomer generation. The first inkling of discontent regarding generation came out of the SNCC. In a memo

Charlotte Bunch

Born in West Jefferson, North Carolina, in 1944, Charlotte Bunch grew up in Artesia, New Mexico, and attended Duke University. While at Duke, Bunch involved herself with the Young Women's Christian Association, the Methodist student movement, a poverty program in Oakland, California, and other civil rights work. She graduated magna cum laude in 1966 and shortly thereafter served as a delegate to the World Council of Churches Conference on Church and Society held in Geneva, Switzerland. She also attended a conference in China sponsored by the World Student Christian Federation. She returned to Washington, D.C., serving as the president of the University Christian Movement. In 1967, she became a student intern at the Institute for Policy Studies in Washington, focusing on the interaction between education and politics.

In 1968, Bunch moved to Cleveland, Ohio, where she became active as a leader in the women's liberation movement both locally and internationally. Returning to Washington, D.C., in 1969, Bunch helped to develop a women's studies curriculum, which was taught at the Washington Area Free University, and she also became involved in the antiwar movement. She visited North Vietnam and Laos in 1970. As a feminist and lesbian, Bunch has articulated her point of view as an author and has maintained her activism throughout her life.

Portrait of Charlotte Bunch. (UN Photos)

As a professor at Rutgers University's Bloustein School of Planning and Public Policy, Bunch now serves on the boards of the Ms. Foundation for Women and the Women's Division of Human Rights Watch. She also founded the Center for Women's Global Leadership at Douglass College, Rutgers University. The center focuses on the promotion of women as leaders and addresses issues such as violence against women, sexual and reproductive health, and socioeconomic well-being.

entitled "Women in the Movement," the anonymous authors pointed out that women in SNCC tended to be relegated to subordinate positions not unlike that experienced by African Americans in general. When Stokely Carmichael read the critique, he responded that women had a place in the movement and that it was on their backs. Galvanized by the insensitivity to their position, women throughout the various movements began to unite and organized to remove the obstacles to their progress whether these obstacles were encoded in the law or were part of custom and tradition. Building on the federal government's Presidential Commission on the Status of Women (1961), women demanded equal rights and equal protection under the law as guaranteed by the Fourteenth Amendment. The movement gained great popularity as more and more women attended college during the 1960s. There would be problems because not all women wanted what the founders of the National Organization of Women (NOW) wanted, which was not necessarily to change the structure of hierarchical leadership but to become a player on equal footing within that structure. As often happened in the 1960s, whatever the cause there were radical and conservative offshoots to each movement. But regardless of where the individual stood, the sheer numbers coalescing around the various issues clearly showed that boomers were the deciding demographic of the upheaval of the 1960s.

Vietnam

As the American involvement in Vietnam escalated, students began to turn their attention to the conflict. Beginning with the war effort in the 1940s, universities and colleges had been called on to contribute to the defense of the country. The most famous of these endeavors is the Manhattan Project that brought together an international array of scientists to develop the atomic bomb. There also was the presence of the military on campus through organizations such as the Reserve Officers Training Corps (ROTC), which offered to help young men pay their college expenses and guaranteed the military an influx of willing candidates to serve. The draft had first been used in 1863 during the Civil War. It was reintroduced with U.S. entry into World War I. With the coming of World War II, some were concerned with the military preparedness of the country. In 1940, the Selective Service and Training Act was passed and young men were put into training. After the World War II draft, as it came to be called, Congress passed the Selective Service Act in 1948. The Universal Training and Service Act, which required men between the ages of eighteen and twenty-six to register to serve in the armed forces, would replace this piece of legislation in 1951. It also extended that service from twenty-one to twenty-four months. At the height of the Vietnam War in 1967, the Selective Service Act required all men between the ages of eighteen and twenty-six to register for the draft.

One of the great achievements of the 1960s occurred in the opening up of American higher education to more of the country's youth. The effect of the boomer population coming of age coincided with this great democratization in education. All across the country, young adults between the ages of eighteen and twenty-five were situated in an academic environment, testing out new ideas, learning to be more independent, and shaping their identity as individuals and a generation. Campus life became an incubator for the antiwar movement and student leaders understood the potential power of the collective that existed and took steps to mobilize it. On May 2, 1964, the first demonstrations against the War in Vietnam took place. More than 500 students marched through Times Square in New York City to the United Nations building to protest U.S. involvement in Vietnam. Simultaneously, 700 students marched in San Francisco with other actions taking place in Boston; Madison, Wisconsin; and Seattle. In March 1965, the Students for a Democratic Society (SDS) organized the first Teach-In against the war. The event attracted about 2,500 students who attended lectures, debates, movies, and concerts all designed to foster an antiwar sentiment. Held on the campus of the University of Michigan, the idea spread to thirty-five other campuses. In April 1965, SDS and SNCC organized the first march on Washington against the war. Expecting about 2,000 protestors, 25,000 people showed up lending their voices to a growing dissident voice emerging within the Baby Boom generation. Students were in the forefront of galvanizing the country to search their hearts and minds regarding our involvement in Southeast Asia. Ironically, one of the slogans to emerge during this time "never trust anyone over thirty," originated with Abbie Hoffman who was thirty-one at the time. But the slogan became the label for a generation of students who envisioned a brave new world where the destructive consequences of adult logic would be set aside for a more child-like perception based on peace, love, and understanding.

For every left there is a right, and the students of the Baby Boom generation were no exception. In 1960 about ninety students gathered at the home of William F. Buckley, Jr., the leading intellectual of the conservative movement in the United States. Buckley held the conference to counter the left-leaning organizations being established on campuses. The Young Americans for Freedom (YAF) emerged as the leading political organization for the conservatives of the boomer generation. The Sharon Statement expressed the group's commitment to basic American values as expressed through the Constitution of the United States and an affirmation of the free market economy as an instrument of the democratic order. They gave their support to American foreign policy as it served the interests of the United States. In 1962, Ronald Regan joined the organizations National Advisory Board and, during his lifetime, would remain the honorary chairman of the group. Rather than rejecting the experience and knowledge of their elders, members of the YAF embraced it and mastered it, becoming a movement within the boomer generation that, unlike their counterparts, were able to play and master "the game."

The antiwar sentiment continued to grow throughout the 1960s and spilled into the 1970s. The antiwar movement succeeded in bringing in more than 70,000 people for the March on Washington in October 1967. Students were able to see some of the effects of their work when Lyndon Baines Johnson announced to the nation that he would not seek the nomination of his party for the presidency. The movement, however, was becoming increasingly violent as the radical fringe grew impatient with the slow workings of the American democratic order and the forces of law and order grew impatient with the assault on American policy. There were many clashes and casualties, with the 1968 Chicago Democratic

A Kent State University student lies on the ground after National Guardsmen fired into a crowd of demonstrators on May 4, 1970, in Kent, Ohio. Four students were killed and nine were wounded when the Guard opened fire during a campus protest against the Vietnam War. (AP/Wide World Photos)

Convention being the best example of the conflict between the civil rights and liberties of the individual as interpreted by the forces of the political establishment. Perhaps the most shocking and horror-filled incident of the movement came in May 1970 on the campus of Kent State University in Ohio when National Guardsman gunned down four students in an attempt to control a demonstration against the escalation of the war. That event set off student strikes and protests across the country. Many colleges and universities shut down early that year and cancelled graduation ceremonies. The antiwar movement, like the civil rights movement, gave the students of the Baby Boom generation a sense of mission and identity that they would carry with them into their adult life.

Counterculture

While political culture carried great weight among those born as part of the post-World War II generation, there were more expressions of individualism that affected the social and cultural climate of students. It is hard to discern which came first, the loosening of cultural bonds that allowed for the free experimentation of mind- alternating substances beyond alcohol or the fact that substances such as lysergic acid diethylamide (LSD), peyote, and mescaline were available on a mass level. Regardless, the impact of the introduction of drug use into youth culture was a double-edged sword. On one hand, it created a sense of choice beyond the ordinary. It brought the sense of cosmic order into the common sense of a generation. This perception, the ability to relate to the world in more allegorical and metaphorical terms, had been the domain of artists, poets, and demagogues. During the 1960s, anyone who dared to try psychedelic drugs was opening a pathway to a broader perception, whether real or not. On the other hand, the destructive nature of drugs such as heroin, barbiturates, and amphetamines claimed many casualties. But there is no denying that the drugs combined with the politics of the era created a powerful countercultural movement that affected the flow of American society. It is clear, however, that the use of LSD can be traced to a Harvard professor of psychology named Timothy Leary whose research was being funded as part of a study by the military and Central Intelligence Agency (CIA) regarding the uses of LSD-25. In the early 1960s, research on LSD officially ended, but Timothy Leary and his colleague Richard Alpert refused to comply and were subsequently fired from Harvard University. It was then that Leary came to the attention of mass media, resulting in the popularization of experimenting with LSD. LSD remained legal until 1966, when it became classified as a narcotic by the U.S. government. In the meantime, the uses of other drugs such as marijuana became popular and spread throughout the universities, colleges, and high schools across the country, becoming epidemic. It was apparent that the established institutions of society were at a loss as to how to manage the phenomena. The counterculture became an entity of its own, influencing musicians and civic activists. Students turned away from the traditional and began to establish their own institutions. One of the most notable contributions from the period occurred within the food industry. As students began to branch out, living communally and searching for alternatives popularized organic food and meat, granola, yogurt, and so on. One of the more ironic effects of this movement is the commoditization of these nutritional choices into a mass market. While the majority of the 70 million people who were between the ages of eighteen and twenty-five during the 1960s did not follow the path of countercultural-ism, the dynamics of sheer numbers created the perception that a whole generation had chosen an extreme lifestyle as a way of resisting what had become the Cold War culture of the United States. While there is an argument that the counterculture and the activist culture of the 1960s were separate movements, a more comprehensive consideration of both demonstrates that there was an inflow and outflow between the two spheres.

The counterculture had its clearest expression in San Francisco, as the city became a mecca of sorts for the baby boomers. San Francisco during the 1960s became a center of music, alternative solutions, and literary distinction. Cultural icons, such as Allen Ginsburg, Timothy Leary, and Baba Ram Dass, made it the holy see of the psychedelic movement. The influence of this "city on a hill" could be felt all the way to the east and back again. But the key to the influence of the counterculture lay in its acceptance of the instability of the world. The leaders of the movement stressed the impermanence of experience and encouraged a more flexible approach based on Buddhism and other spiritual philosophies that began to influence the experimentation of the era. The counterculture gave rise to a completely different approach to commercialism particularly as it emphasized the potential of the "youth market" economically. What began as cottage industries such as tie-dye shirts, stringing beads, and so on found its way into the mainstream. Event magazines were not immune. Jann Werner revolutionized the teen magazine market by introducing *Rolling Stone* magazine in 1967. Even the comic strips of the era helped to create a new direction for animation. *MAD Magazine* seemed to be weathering the storm quite nicely under the able steering of William Gaines. Onto the scene came visual storytellers such as R. Crumb whose Mr. Natural became an iconic symbol of the 1960s. "Keep on Truckin" became the slogan and what artists such as Rick Griffin knew as psychedelic poster art adorned the streets advertising concerts. As Marshall McLuhan had pointed out "the medium is the message," and the media helped to popularize and spread a countercultural sensibility throughout the United States.

More so than in the 1950s, it is hard to separate certain aspects of the culture that evolved during the 1960s. For example, the music seemed to become a soundtrack for the surrounding events. Early in the decade, most students were listening to rock music, but it was not as intense as some of the music of the 1950s. Performers like Bobby Rydell, Fabian, and Bobby Vee seemed to be filling in a void that had been created when Elvis Presley was sent off to Germany in 1958 to serve in the U.S. Army. As for female performers, there were not many cutting rock-and-roll records. The greatest activity in popular music seemed to be evolving through folk music. The folk music period coincided with the civil rights and antinuclear movements. Performers such as Pete Seeger, Odetta, and Buffy St. Marie worked alongside more commercial acts like the Kingston Trio and the Chad Mitchell Trio. Younger artists such as Bob Dylan and Joan Baez developed their talent under the auspices of the folk music movement. Folk music seemed to be focused on the east coast, attracting students who were more intellectually attuned. Its counterpart on the west coast could be found in the surf culture of Southern California. Much of the credit for the evolution of the music that expressed that culture can be given to Brian Wilson and the Beach Boys. Although nothing seemed too radical about songs that focused on surf boards, girls, and just having fun, the surf culture brought awareness to the more freewheeling aspect of the baby boomers. When Bob Dylan picked up an electric guitar at the Newport Jazz Festival, he created a bridge between these two worlds that would produce a fusion of lifestyles that would link a generation together. As the bulk of the baby boomers hit adolescence, one other event served as a catalyst that brought the beginning of global awareness. Again music was the medium, and this time it came from Great Britain. With the untimely death of John F. Kennedy in November 1963, a generation lost its center. Kennedy represented all the hope and idealism of the rising generation. He had promoted a sense of confidence regarding the individual's ability to transform the world and had bequeathed to the baby boomers a new frontier. During this time of uncertainty in December 1963, an unknown British group released a record and nothing remained the same afterward. The Beatles success opened the door to an international exchange of music, politics, arts, and letters that reached a generation coming of age. From that point on whatever the social cause, whether it be upholding the American way of life ("The Green Berets" by Barry Sadler), or protesting against the hypocrisy of American ideals in action ("Fixin' to Die Rag" by Country Joe and the Fish), a song would accompanying each point of view.

The Great Society

Overall, the American government, under the leadership of President Johnson, focused on its expanding role in education. His ambitious program began in 1965 with the Elementary and Secondary Education Act, which targeted the children of low-income families. In January 1969, Johnson asked Congress to provide a total of 2 million grants, loans, and

Lady Bird Johnson, wife of President Lyndon B. Johnson, visits with children in a Head Start classroom at Kemper School in Washington, D.C. on March 19, 1968. The goal of the Head Start preschool program is to increase school readiness for young children from low-income families. (Lyndon B. Johnson Library)

interest subsidies to college students, up from 247,000 in 1964. The federal government put resources into assisting in the construction of more college classrooms, libraries, and other facilities. About a half-a-million students received assistance from the G.I. Bill. Johnson's administration also created the Teacher Corps to bring in and perhaps harness the energy of the boomers toward improving education in city slums and poor rural areas. The government also offered graduate fellowships and short-term courses to create a higher standard for teachers that they could then bring into the classrooms.

One experiment that sparked student interest in education was the idea of the Open University. Introduced by sociologist Paul Goodman, the Open University created a student-centered approach to higher education. It was free, and it offered a more hands on learning experience intellectually. Students taught students about topics that may have supplemented but were not offered in the standard curriculum. After 1968, African American students began to apply pressure to colleges and universities to create departments of black studies, something the institutions had a hard time incorporating. Over time, however, the movement spread and black studies became a viable and valid part of the curriculum. Another innovation happened in the discipline of history itself. With the growing focus of society on minority groups, American historians reevaluated their point of view. While the story of the founders and other elites told a story about America, it tended to ignore the everyday life of its people. More and more historians began to uncover "history from the bottom up" rather than the more traditional "top-down" story-telling. In doing so, they created an explosion in the field that created a more complete picture of America's past, warts and all. While not everyone thought this a good approach, the multicultural approach created a more understanding and tolerant society.

The baby boomers who entered the colleges and universities between 1964 and 1972, helped to change the landscape of higher education. Where once *in loco parentis* reigned supreme, by 1968, the colleges and universities were no longer playing that role in the lives of their students. With the civil rights movement came the awareness of rights in general. The feeling was if you were old enough to be drafted into the army, then you ought to be old enough to manage your own life. Many of the smaller protests that occurred on college campuses had to do with restrictions such as dorm hours, who could visit who in their dorm room and student rights in general. As the 1970s approached, students were still agitating about the war and what had begun as the civil rights movement spilled over and fractured into more specific groups. Gay rights became an issue on campus, as did Latino rights and rights of the disabled. As this liberality began to grow more and more popular, the more conservative element of the boomer generation began to react. The YAF was only one such group, and while the conservatives did not show themselves off quite as raucously, they were quietly cultivating their point of view. One such example was the appearance of a new daily newspaper on the University of Wisconsin campus. The paper was called the *Badger Herald* and had been founded as a voice that ran counter to what had become the popular culture of

Norma Norman

Norma Norman was born and raised in Topeka, Kansas, a few years before the landmark 1954 Supreme Court decision *Brown v. Board of Education of Topeka*. Like other African Americans of her generation, Norman had grown up expecting that racial inequality and segregation would soon be a relic of the past. In 1965, while a sophomore at the University of Kansas, Norman participated in a sit-in in the offices of the chancellor. Her parents had always encouraged her to stand up for herself, but to not look for trouble or 'rock the boat.'

While in college, however, Norman found community with other blacks from across the country who had similar life experiences and who were growing increasingly weary with the slow pace of change. It was within this larger group, Norman later recalled, that she was able to articulate what she had long felt and translate those feelings into action.

The protest was prompted by the university's continued acceptance of racial segregation in on-campus and off-campus housing. The chancellor had the protestors arrested; many of them faced the prospect of being expelled or losing scholarships because of their action. Their efforts paid off; within a few weeks the chancellor decreed that the university would not tolerate any form of discrimination in university-approved housing

For Norma Norman, the demonstration was a turning point in her life. While the sit-in was the extent of her direct action as a civil rights activist, she spent her career seeking to address inequality as a teacher and a school administrator.

protest. The *Herald* even attracted the attention of William F. Buckley, the preeminent ideologue of the conservative movement in America.

As the leading edge of the boomer generation graduated college and went on to begin their adult lives, America began to settle down. However, the war continued and so did the protests. When Richard Nixon became president, he had promised that he would end the war. When the press revealed that he and his secretary of state, Henry Kissinger, had actually escalated the air strikes into Laos and Cambodia, students were galvanized to act. When in May 1970 four students were gunned down by the National Guard at Kent State, the event sparked a massive student mobilization on campuses across the country. This event marked the last great antiwar protest of the era. As the 1970s moved forward, the government worked more earnestly toward ending the war. A lasting legacy of the members of the boomer generation is in their actual participation in the democratic process that went beyond the voting booth. The legacy of this activism continued through the first half of the decade of the 1970s on both the right and left.

Bibliography

Avorn, Jerry L. *Up Against the Ivy Wall: A History of the Columbia Crisis*. New York: Antheneum, 1970.

Bedrock, Alan. *The "I was a Teenage Juvenile Delinquent Rock 'n' Roll Horror Beach Party Movie" Book: A Complete Guide to the Teen Exploitation Film, 1954–1969*. New York: St. Martin's, 1986.

Brunsma, David L. *The School Uniform Movement and What It Tells Us about American Education, A Symbolic Crusade*. Oxford: Oxford University Press, 2004.

Burner, David. *Making Peace with the Sixties*. Princeton, NJ: Princeton University Press, 1996.

Cagin, Seth, and Philip Dray. *Hollywood Films of the Seventies: Sex, Drugs, Violence, Rock 'n' Roll and Politics*. New York: Harper & Row, 1984.

Collier, Peter, and Horowitz, David, eds. *Second Thoughts: Former Radicals Look Back at the Sixties*. Lanham, MD: Madison Books, 1989.

Crenshaw, Marshall. *Hollywood Rock*. New York: Agincourt, 1994.

Douglas, Avram. *Born at the Right Time: A History of the Baby-Boom Generation*. Toronto: University of Toronto Press, 1999.

Flesch, Rudolf. *Why Johnny Can't Read and What You Can Do about It*. New York: Harper, 1955.

Freire, Paulo. *Pedagogy of the Oppressed*. New York: Continuum, 1992.

Goodman, Paul. *Growing Up Absurd*. New York: Vintage, 1960.

Heineman, Kenneth J. *Put Your Bodies upon the Wheels: Student Revolt in the 1960s*. Chicago: Ivan R. Dee, 2001.

Hiatt Steil, Janet. *Reflections of a Baby Boomer*. Victoria, BC: Trafford, 2004.

Klatch, Rebecca E. *A Generation Divided: The New Left, the New Right, and the 1960s*. Berkeley: University of California Press, 1999.

Lipset, Seymour Martin, and Sheldon S. Wolin. *The Berkley Student Revolt: Facts and Interpretations*. New York: Anchor Books, 1965.

Michener, James A. *Kent State: What Happened and Why*. New York: Random House, 1971.

Unger, Irwin, and Unger, Debi, eds. *The Times Were a Changin': The Sixties Reader*. New York: Three Rivers Press, 1998.

Weaver, Gary R., and James H. Weaver, eds. *The University and Revolution*. Englewood Cliffs, NJ: Prentice-Hall, 1969.

Wertham, Frederic. *Seduction of the Innocent*. New York: Rinehart & Co., 1954.

Wilson, Laura B., and Sharon P. Simson. *Civic Engagement and the Baby Boomer Generation: Research, Policy, and Practice Perspectives*. London: Hawthorne Press, 2006.

African Americans | 4

Rusty Monhollon

The most common images associated with the Baby Boom—both historical and in popular culture—are of white, middle-class, suburban families. The Baby Boom generation is much more diverse, however, than it is usually depicted. Three of every ten boomers born after 1955—the so-called late boomers—were minorities, nearly double the rate during the Great Depression.

Indeed, the postwar experience of African Americans also was shaped profoundly by the Baby Boom. To a large degree, the formative experiences of all boomers were shaped by significant events, such as the civil rights movement, the Vietnam War, and the growth of a massive consumer culture. The persistence of Jim Crow, however, insured that the experiences of black baby boomers would be quite different from their white counterparts. These differences illustrate the diversity of the Baby Boom generation, and point to one of many sources of potential conflict among the boomers themselves. In ways that have not been fully explored, race has shaped—and continues to shape—the experience and legacy of the Baby Boom generation.

Demographics

Between 1946 and 1964, the birth rate among African Americans increased at a rate greater than the population as a whole. The actual number of black children born annually in the United States nearly doubled during this period, increasing from about 358,000 in 1946 to more than 600,000 births in 1964 (Wellner 2001, 49). The size of this birth cohort might suggest that African American youth were targets of advertisements. One significant difference between black and white baby boomers, however, was the limited participation of African Americans in the consumer culture of postwar America. As consumers, black youths and teenagers were lumped in with the broader youth market. Most advertisements, for example, targeted white, middle-class teenagers exclusively, and rarely, if at all, were African Americans featured in advertisements. The economic marginalization of blacks partially explains why Madison Avenue largely ignored them, but it also was the result of their cultural marginalization within American society.

While there were numerous qualitative differences between the experiences of black and white children born during the Baby Boom, perhaps the greatest difference was not among the boomers themselves, but rather among their parents. The parents of African American boomers were chronically undereducated, primarily because of the lack of equal education opportunities in the Jim Crow South. Only 8 percent of African Americans in 1940 had a high school education, and 42 percent had less than a fifth-grade education; among whites, the numbers were much higher. Fifty years later, this gap had nearly been wiped out, as about eight of ten African Americans had at least a high school education. As many scholars have suggested, this transformation was even more significant than the higher rates of college degrees among white boomers, as it facilitated the entry of many African Americans into the middle class (Wellner 2001, 49).

This transition, however, was not an easy one, nor did it bring about full racial equality. Compulsory school attendance after World War II greatly homogenized popular culture. Most white students spent three or four years in high school, which eroded differences among white ethnics and encouraged a belief in a classless society. Racial distinctions, however, were not so easily removed, and upward mobility still ran hard along class and racial lines. Black high school students, for instance, often were "tracked" by guidance counselors and teachers into vocational, rather than more rigorous academic, courses, which often mirrored class divisions within local communities. For many African Americans, this effectively shut them out of high-paying white-collar managerial and professional occupations.

Equally significant were two additional demographic shifts: the continued migration of African Americans out of the South and the urbanization of the black population. In 1940, 77 percent of African Americans lived in the South, and 48.6 percent lived in cities. By 1960, the percentage of the black population living in the South fell to about 60 percent, but nearly three-fourths of African Americans now lived in cities. These trends would continue; in 1990, 52.8 percent of blacks lived in the South, and 87.2 percent lived in cities. In all, some 5 million African Americans left the South between 1940 and 1950. In the 1950s, Chicago, a popular destination for blacks, often received more than 2,000 new migrants each week (Trotter 2001, A30–31).

African American urbanization was crucial in shaping the experience of blacks during the Baby Boom; indeed, it was crucial to the transformation of American politics and culture after World War II in general. Blacks in the urban North had much greater freedom to exercise their right to vote, thus making them a key political constituency. Moreover, the nation's booming economy produced millions of well-paying jobs open to blacks in factories, mills, and warehouses in Pittsburgh, Detroit, Milwaukee, Baltimore, Cleveland, and other cities outside of the South. Economic gains for African Americans were significant, if uneven and less than whites, between 1940 and 1960.

Urban life was in many ways better than rural life in the South, yet it fell far from fulfilling the American Dream. Since mid-century, the notion of the "American Dream"—living "the good life" through home ownership, financial stability, and job and retirement security—has characterized American culture and society. Popular culture celebrated the ideal, and the federal government provided assistance for citizens seeking that dream, which millions of Americans—the majority of them white—achieved. The dream was much more elusive for African Americans, and for a variety of reasons. One, median income for blacks has remained below that of whites, despite a narrowing in the gap. Two, government policies played a key role, in particular Federal Housing Administration rules that effectively kept African Americans out of the housing market.

The political economy of the city was not open fully to African Americans. Once in northern and western cities, they confronted racial discrimination and exclusion in housing, employment, and education—that severely limited their prospects of upward mobility. During the prosperous 1950s, African Americans had limited opportunities to own their own home and claim their share of the American dream. The Federal Housing Administration and the Veterans Administration would guarantee loans only for homes in white-only neighborhoods, which excluded blacks. New suburban developments also excluded African Americans. In Levittown, developer Levitt declared that if he sold "one house to a Negro family, then 90 to 95 percent of our white customers will not buy into the community" (as quoted in Halberstam 1993, 141). Levitt added that "We can solve a housing problem, or we can try to solve a racial problem. But we cannot combine the two" (as quoted in Jackson 1985, 241).

Discrimination in housing, buttressed by such egregious lending practices as "redlining," relegated blacks to specific neighborhoods, boundaries that whites often defended with violence. With almost no likelihood of finding adequate housing elsewhere in the city, these areas often became poverty-stricken ghettos, which flourished after World War II. As whites fled to the burgeoning suburbs, the cities began to deteriorate and the funding for municipal services such as public transportation and education began to wither.

The federal government contributed to this decline in other ways, too. Urban renewal projects funded by federal money displaced African Americans and other minorities more frequently than they did whites, and they razed neighborhoods inhabited predominately by African Americans. New housing projects built with federal funds generally were located in such a way as to increase the density of African Americans in a specific area. The Civil Rights Act of 1964 and the Fair Housing Act of 1968 slowly made more housing available to blacks by the early 1970s.

Despite these acts, policies contributed significantly to the continued impoverishment of African Americans as a whole. Since the 1950s, blacks entered the middle class in large numbers. Indeed, per capita income among college-educated African Americans has become virtually identical to that of college-educated whites. But the size of the black middle class is small, and does not offset the vast inequality between working-class blacks and whites, and between blacks and whites overall. Nor does it overcome the numerous decades in which African Americans were unable to build any wealth.

Progress was achieved, however, not only on the economic front but also politically and socially. Between 1945 and 1980, the black middle class grew significantly. By the 1980s, one out of five blacks earned more than the median income for whites, a sizable increase from the prewar years. This was the result, in large measure, of increased education opportunities for African Americans, particularly in higher education, which the civil rights movement and federal legislation encouraged.

There was improvement in the quality of daily life in other areas, too. As the standard of living increased for all Americans after World War II, so too did the general health of the population. Life expectancy increased significantly for African Americans, as well. But while some African Americans benefited immensely from the thriving economy, race contin-ued to be a significant predictor of poverty. During the 1950s, a veritable Golden Age for the white middle class, nearly half of all married-couple black families lived below the poverty line (Coontz 1997, 44). Overall, African Americans disproportionately remained mired in poverty, at a rate three times that for whites. Despite the claims of many experts, most prominently Daniel Patrick Moynihan's *The Negro Family: The Case for National Action*, that black families were primarily female-headed and thus "disorganized," African American familial structure remained—as it had been for decades—strong and nurturing. That many black women were the head of household was more the result of being widowed (life expectancy was lower for black men than the national average) than divorce or some so-called pathological legacy of slavery. Until the 1960s, for example, three-fourths of African American households with children under eighteen years of age included a husband and a wife (Franklin and Moss 2000, 518).

The Freedom Struggle

The Baby Boom era coincided with several other significant developments, in particular the civil rights and student activism, but also the peace and antiwar movements. This was not simply a coincidence; the Baby Boom itself was crucial to the evolution of social activism in the 1960s. Perhaps more so than for white boomers, social activism shaped—and continues to shape—the lives of black boomers.

African American boomers, like their white counterparts, were central figures in the social movements of the 1960s. Student activism—and some would say the modern civil rights movement—began properly with the February 1960 Greensboro sit-ins. Four students from North Carolina

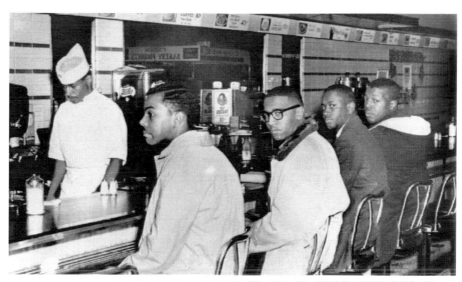

On February 1, 1960, four young African American college students walked into the Woolworth Company, sat down at a whites-only lunch counter, and triggered the civil rights movement that spread across the nation. Shown here on February 2, 1960, are (left to right) Joseph McNeil, Franklin McCain, Billy Smith, and Clarence Henderson. (Library of Congress)

Agricultural and Technical College asked for—but did not receive—service at a segregated Woolworth's lunch counter. They returned the next day with more students, and with more the following day. By challenging Jim Crow head-on, and by enduring threats of violence with quiet dignity, their action sparked a wave of protests across the South and the rest of the nation.

In the 1950s students elsewhere had used the sit-in against segregated public facilities, protests that largely went unnoticed. Not so with Greensboro, as it stirred thousands to action. For some, the simplicity of the students' action, and the moral basis from which it emerged, encapsulated the spirit of the 1960s. The sit-in movement was a watershed, as it ushered in a distinct phase of the struggle for racial equality, nonviolent direct action. As it was both highly visible and psychologically empowering, direct action was an effective means to attack racism. In many ways, the Greensboro sit-in (and the students who initiated it) embodied faith in liberal reform, the belief that the American political system was inherently good and that existing institutions, if the nation was shown the error of its ways, had the capacity to rectify past injustices.

The sit-in movement led directly to the founding of the Student Nonviolent Coordinating Committee (SNCC), the most dynamic civil rights organization of the era. Seeking to build on the momentum of the sit-in movement, SNCC and the Congress of Racial Equality organized the Freedom Rides into the South. The goal was to force Congress to use its power to regulate commerce and desegregate bus travel. Along the way, the Freedom Riders were met with hostility and outright violence from whites;

several riders suffered severe injuries when their bus was attacked and burned. The attention garnered by the attacks compelled President Kennedy to act, although he did so tepidly. It would take another violent confrontation between civil rights activists and southern authorities before Kennedy would act decisively. In 1963, Martin Luther King led the Children's Crusade in Birmingham, Alabama. Again the nation witnessed the depth of racial hatred. Birmingham's police commissioner Eugene "Bull" Connor ordered his men to unleash attack dogs and turn high-pressure water guns on the marchers, many of them children. Kennedy soon proposed legislation to combat racial inequality that eventually would become the Civil Rights Act of 1964.

Not until 1964 or so did black boomers become significant leaders in the freedom struggle, although many had participated in marches when they were younger than eighteen years of age. In 1964, SNCC organized Freedom Summer, an effort to register black voters in the South. SNCC issued a call for volunteers, specifically to white college students from the North, and nearly 1,000—many of them baby boomers—responded. The white students witnessed the grinding poverty and violence that southern blacks encountered daily. The murder of three civil rights workers, two white and one black, vividly illustrated to the rest of the country the extent to which whites would defend the color line in the South. Freedom Summer left a deep mark on the white students. Many continued the struggle in their own communities upon their return, and others used the experience to address other forms of oppression.

In 1964, Congress passed the Civil Rights Act, which prohibited discrimination based on race in employment and education, among other provisions. A year later, Congress enacted the Voting Rights Act. Within a few years of its passage, the number of black voters registered in Mississippi, for example, went from less than 10 percent to nearly 60 percent. The Voting Rights Act transformed southern politics by making African Americans a political force in the region for the first time in nearly 100 years. The two laws culminated a century-old struggle to ensure African Americans equal protection before the law.

The passage of both bills resulted in large measure from activism that forced the nation to look at the ugly side of racism. In Birmingham in 1963, four young girls were killed when Klansmen blew up a church. The murder of James Cheney, Michael Schwerner, and Andrew Goodman during Freedom Summer shocked the nation. And in March 1965, millions of Americans watched footage of Selma, Alabama, police officers brutally beating peaceful civil rights marchers. The Selma campaign, headed by Martin Luther King but manned by hundreds from grassroots efforts, was crucial to the passage of the Voting Rights Act.

Although the Civil Rights Act of 1964 and the Voting Rights Act of 1965 were landmarks in the struggle for racial equality, there were limits to the change legislation could bring to the lives of African Americans. Segregation had been banished, although there had been little integration. Neither act could address poverty, job ceilings, police harassment and brutality, and continued racial exclusion and discrimination. While many pointed to the progress that had been made in civil rights, for most African Americans, and especially the young, equality was still a distant dream.

In 1951, the poet Langston Hughes asked, "What happens to a dream deferred? Does it dry up like a raisin in the sun? . . . Or does it explode?" (Hughes 2001, 145). Between 1964 and 1968, the answer was clear: it explodes. The United States experienced a wave of violence during the "long, hot summers," much of it race related. A race riot erupted in Watts, a black neighborhood in Los Angeles, that left thirty-four people dead and resulted in more than $40 million in property damaged. Rioting in Detroit in 1967 resulted in forty-three deaths and left the downtown in ashes. Twenty-six people were killed in the Newark riots, and some 1,200 more were injured. Smaller conflagrations occurred in cities and towns across the nation.

The Watts riot caught many politicians, black and white, off guard. Three African Americans served on the Los Angeles city council, two

Pictured in front of the Omaha, Nebraska, Central Police Station on June 27, 1969, just after their release from questioning, are (from left to right) Black Panthers Robert Cecil, Robert Griffo, Frank Peate, Gary House, and William Peak. Known for their militancy and Black Power salute, the Black Panthers fought against a society that they claimed unlawfully and unjustly attacked the progress of black people. (AP/Wide World Photos)

John Spearman, Jr.

John Spearman, Jr. was born in Lawrence, Kansas, in 1950. His parents, John Sr. and Vernell Spearman, were long-time residents of Lawrence, and both were members of several civil rights organizations in the community.

Spearman attended Lawrence schools his entire life, and was an outstanding student. At Lawrence High School, he was a member of the student council, the debate team, the Biology Club, and Lawrence High's state champion gymnastics team. He earned several scholarships upon graduation from high school, including a prestigious National Merit Scholarship.

Although he never attended segregated schools, Spearman acknowledged that his education experience was marked by frequent episodes of individual racism. Born just before the *Brown* decision, Spearman and his peers had come of age expecting the promise of *Brown* to be fulfilled. He recalled often being the only black student in class, and never having a black teacher, counselor, or principal. He could not remember being taught anything about black history, literature or culture, or African history. Although the quality of education in Lawrence was generally good, the racist attitudes of some white teachers and students, as well as the physical and cultural isolation and sense of ostracism felt by black students, made their education experience less than ideal.

In 1968, Spearman gave a commencement speech to his fellow graduates. He told his classmates that they "could shape the destiny of man" if they kept "their individuality and convictions." He said that "liberty and justice" were the two ideals most "valued by Americans," and that "one of the most important rights is to determine how you want

represented the city in the state assembly, and another served in the Congress. As well, Watts did not have the same levels of unemployment and economic degradation as other predominantly black urban communities. Yet what seemed to be evidence of progress disguised a simmering discontent. The promise of *Brown v. Board of Education*, the Great Society, and the War on Poverty, while no doubt bringing about positive change, was too little and too slow for many African Americans.

Further contributing to the causes of violence was the chronic tension between the black community and the Los Angeles Police Department, a condition that was replicated in virtually every urban community in the country. The problems were twofold. First, few African Americans served on urban police departments; in some localities there were none at all. Second, white police officers typically shared the same perspectives on race relations as did the greater community from which they came. Communication between the police and African Americans was limited, where it existed at all. Without a doubt, the police mistreated blacks and abused their power, but some of the tension resulted from perceived injustices on the part of African Americans. One white acknowledged that the police in his community too often used "the 'fat end of [their] . . . billy club' to resolve problems" (as quoted in Monhollon 2002, 90). The depth of African Americans grievances against the police became evident as the to live your life." In a tone commensurate with the times, Spearman told his peers that "the path the river is presently following moves in a direction opposing human ideals. Human rights belong to humanity." Therefore, he extolled his classmates not "to be meekly guided. You must be a guiding force, a force which will lead society to a shore of responsibility" (as quoted in Monhollon 1994, 167).

Spearman took his own advice. Before he left Lawrence High School, he led a group of black students into the principal's office and asked that the school add courses on black history, literature, and culture. When he enrolled that fall at the University of Kansas, he quickly became a political force on campus. He was a leader of the Black Student Union (BSU), a student organization modeled on other such groups across the country. Using the Black Panthers' Ten-Point Program as a model, under Spearman's leadership the BSU built black

self-identity and pride, and enacted a measure of African American control over their community.

Unlike his parents, who were activists in the vein of Martin Luther King, Spearman was following a path of activism akin to Malcolm X and Stokely Carmichael; he was committed to the idea of Black Power. In part, his embrace of Black Power stemmed from his frustration over the lack of progress in race relations in Lawrence. The civil rights movement that his parents embraced had, as he put it, "failed to get it done." But it also resulted from the lack of a culture with which he could identify.

Many African Americans who came of age after the *Brown* decision took similar paths as John Spearman. The Black Power movement was dismissed by many white Americans, but African Americans, even those of the older generation, understood that it was part of a larger struggle for freedom and equality.

Black Power movement spread. Stokely Carmichael and Charles Hamilton, in *Black Power*, likened police departments to "occupying forces" in the "black colonies" of America (Carmichael and Hamilton 1974, 52–53). One of the objectives in the Black Panther Party's Ten-Point Platform and Program was "an immediate end to police brutality and murder of black people" (Jones 1998, 274).

The National Advisory Commission on Civil Disorders concluded that the underlying cause of riots were white racism. "What white America had never fully understood—but what the Negro can never forget—is that white society is deeply implicated in the ghetto," the Commission declared in 1968. "White institutions created it, white institutions maintain it, and white society condones it" (National Advisory Commission on Civil Disorders 1968, 2).

The Vietnam War further damaged race relations. Upper- and middle-class whites were able to avoid enlisting by obtaining exemptions, usually college deferments. Others used family connections to join the National Guard, which practically ensured that they would not have to serve in Vietnam. African Americans and other minorities, as well as working-class whites, had limited opportunities to deferments, which resulted in African Americans serving disproportionately overseas.

In 1966, the cry of Black Power altered the nature of the struggle for equality. Carmichael, the chair of the SNCC, and Hamilton, the political

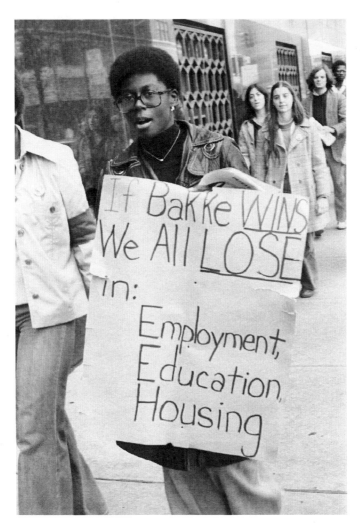

Protesters march around the Detroit federal building during Supreme Court deliberations on the Allan Bakke case, October 3, 1977. Bakke claimed that he was deprived of admission to the University of California Medical School at Davis because of affirmative action. (Bettmann/Corbis)

scientist, defined Black Power "as a call for black people to unite, recognize their heritage, . . . build a sense of community, . . . define their own goals, [and] to lead their own organizations" (Newton and Seale 1970, 2–3).

Black Power emphasized creating black-controlled institutions and self-affirming black consciousness. As an ideology, it was as much a cultural and psychological movement as it was political. Attitude clearly changed among many young African Americans who used the language of Black Power to create institutions that addressed the concerns of people of color and gave them a measure of political power.

In 1966, in Oakland, California, Huey Newton and Bobby Seale founded the Black Panther Party for Self-Defense. Newton and Seale intended the Panthers to protect black neighborhoods from police brutality, but it soon evolved into a revolutionary front seeking the liberation of African Americans. The Panther Party's Ten-Point Platform demanded access to education, land, and employment; the end of the draft; and reparations for past injustices; and it called for blacks to arm themselves in self-defense. Official Panther chapters operated in several major cities, with perhaps several thousand members nationwide.

The Black Power movement reshaped racial dynamics in the United States. It was embraced particularly by high school and college-age African Americans. An example of how the movement seeped into the consciousness of blacks across the nation can be seen in the small college town of Lawrence, Kansas. In September 1968, thirty-seven African American students at Lawrence High School walked out of classes to protest the lack of black teachers, counselors, and administrators; the absence of black history and culture in the curriculum; and the school's limited academic and social opportunities for black students. Their demands were similar to those made by African American students at San Francisco State University in 1967, as well as the University of Kansas, only a few blocks from Lawrence High; in fact, the brother of one of the college students led the high school walkout. Black Power was controversial and divisive, dividing not only blacks and whites but also African Americans.

The Politics of Affirmative Action

The politics of race became entwined with the controversial policy of affirmative action. As President Johnson noted in a speech at Howard University in 1965, the government had a responsibility to help its citizens obtain the training and education necessary to be productive members of society. He also noted that the situation of African Americans, given the nation's long history with slavery, segregation, and exclusion, required efforts not only on behalf of the individual but also on behalf of the group. The resulting effort became known as affirmative action, a policy in which the federal government would make additional efforts to improve the status of African Americans, women, and other economically marginalized groups. These policies sought to overcome decades of racial and gender discrimination in employment and education, among others. Although the intent of affirmative action was to level the playing field for women and minorities, opponents soon derided the policies as giving preferential treatment to blacks and women, claiming they amounted to "reverse discrimination."

Into the twenty-first century, the courts have not resolved the issue. In 1978, the Supreme Court, in *University of California Board of Regents v. Bakke*, ruled that race could be used as an admission criterion in higher education, but it rejected the imposition of strict quotas (specific numbers of admission positions reserved for minorities). In 1989, *City of Richmond v. J. A. Croson Company*, the Court decreed that a government set-aside program, one guaranteed to be given to a minority contractor, was unconstitutional. Later cases in the 1990s, and ballot initiatives in several states, eliminated affirmative action programs. And, in 2003, the Supreme Court ruled in one case that upheld the principle of affirmative action, and in another case struck down provisions of affirmative action admissions plans. In *Grutter v. Bollinger*, the Court rejected the white plaintiff's contention that race had been the deciding factor in her being denied admission to the University of Michigan Law School. In *Gratz v. Bollinger*, the Court struck down Michigan's point-based undergraduate admission process, declaring it amounted to the imposition of racial quotas. In her majority opinion, Justice Sandra Day O'Connor noted that perhaps in twenty or thirty years affirmative action programs would no longer be necessary.

Whether O'Connor's prediction comes true remains to be seen. Affirmative action continues to be a controversial issue. Even some African Americans have decried affirmative action, most notably Supreme Court Justice Clarence Thomas, who, ironically, benefited from education programs that used affirmative action. Affirmative action has helped many African Americans, women, and other minorities reach the middle class. Whether it will continue as public policy is unclear.

The Impact of Deindustrialization

The black middle class has grown significantly since World War II, while at the same time, the rate of poverty among blacks has increased. One factor for these trends has been the erosion of the industrial sector—especially the shift from an industrial-based to a service-based economy—since the late 1960s. While all Americans suffered a loss in purchasing power between the mid-1970s and the mid-1990s, the poorest fifth of Americans suffered the greatest decline. This was due in large measure to the proliferation of service work, which favored well-educated workers but offered low wages to most workers.

Thus, the economic picture for African Americans over the past quarter century is complicated. The black middle class has grown significantly but blacks account for a disproportionate share of the truly disadvantaged. This polarization has led to contention among African Americans regarding the middle class's responsibility to raise others out of poverty. This has been most evident, for example, among professional athletes and entertainers, whose earning potential and visibility provide opportunities to address social issues such as poverty and inequality.

The transition from an industrial-based to a service-based economy had profound consequences for all social groups, but it hit African Americans especially hard. Manufacturing jobs, which provided workers with minimal education high wages, rapidly disappeared from the central city, where many African Americans resided. They were replaced by service-sector employment, in such diverse industries as education, communications, finance, fast food, and retail. Some service industries required high levels of training and education, and offered commensurate wages. Yet other service sectors required little or no training and education and thus were lower paying. This two-tiered occupational structure benefited workers with the resources and access to higher education, especially in the emerging fields of electronic communication and computers. Most of these well-paying jobs in high-tech industries were located outside of the central city, and thus beyond the reach of many African Americans. Not surprisingly then, urban poverty rates climbed during the 1970s and 1980s. Despite some progress, poverty remained a troubling and persistent fact of life for many African Americans. Additionally, African Americans were divided along gender, class, and cultural lines. The number of single black women raising children alone increased during the 1980s and 1990s. The gap between rich and poor blacks widened.

Politics in the 1980s and 1990s

The 1980s and 1990s were politically a mixed bag for African Americans. In 1980, Americans elected Ronald Reagan president by an overwhelming majority, yet Jimmy Carter, the Democratic incumbent, received more than 90 percent of the African American vote. The same pattern would hold true in 1988; George H. W. Bush was elected president but Democratic nominee Michael Dukakis garnered 90 percent of the black vote. In 1992, the Clinton-Gore ticket amassed nearly 85 percent of the African American vote in winning the presidential election. African Americans continue to be a key constituency in national politics.

African Americans have been elected to public office more frequently over the past two decades. Twice, in 1983 and again in 1987, Jesse Jackson announced his candidacy for the Democratic nomination for president. Jackson made a strong showing in the 1988 Democratic primaries, winning seven primary elections and four state caucuses. Douglas Wilder was elected lieutenant governor of Virginia in 1985, and he won the gubernatorial election in 1989, becoming the first African American to serve in both positions. In 1992, Carol Moseley-Braun of Illinois became the first African American woman to serve in the U.S. Senate, and thirty-nine African Americans served in the House of Representatives. Bill Clinton named four African Americans to his cabinet, and Colin Powel became the first African American to chair the Joint Chiefs of Staff, under George H. W. Bush, and the first to serve as secretary of state, under George W. Bush. And, in the historic election of 2008, Americans elected Barack Obama president, the first African American to hold that office.

Neither the Reagan nor Bush administrations promoted policies that benefited African Americans as a group. Reagan especially targeted social programs of which African Americans were the primary beneficiaries. Reagan was slow to respond to the AIDS epidemic, which disproportionately affected African Americans. In many ways, the 1980s and 1990s illustrated a widening gap among African Americans. This gap was in part due to the concomitant growth of the black middle class and the black underclass, but it was also vividly illustrated in the confirmation hearings of Clarence Thomas's nomination to the Supreme Court. One of Thomas's

Spike Lee

Few filmmakers have explored race relations in the United States as deeply as Spike Lee, nor have many matched Lee's penchant for generating controversy. For nearly 25 years, Lee has examined such topics as relations between light-skinned and dark-skinned blacks (*School Daze*, 1988); racial tensions between Italians and blacks in a Brooklyn neighborhood (*Do the Right Thing*, 1989); interracial sex (*Jungle Fever*, 1991); the life of *Malcolm X* (1992); and black-face minstrelsy (*Bamboozled*, 2000).

Shelton Jackson Lee was born in Atlanta on March 20, 1957, the son of a jazz musician and an art teacher. The family soon moved to Brooklyn, which would be the setting for several of his movies. After graduating from Morehouse College, Lee enrolled in New York University's Institute of Film, and received his master's degree in 1982. His final project received critical acclaim and earned Lee several awards.

Lee's career illustrates the difficulties African American baby boomers confronted. While he

loudest critics was Anita Hill, who once worked for Thomas in the Equal Employment Opportunity Commission and accused him of sexual harassment. Although Thomas was confirmed by the Senate despite Hill's allegations, the controversy suggested that gender and class—not only race— would be significant areas of conflict.

But race remained a salient issue in the United States. In March 1991, Los Angeles police officers stopped Rodney King, an African American, for a traffic violation. As the officers arrested King, they beat him with nightsticks, all of which was being videotaped by a nearby observer. Four of the officers were charged with "excessive force" and stood trial. On April 29, 1992, the jury acquitted the officers of any wrongdoing. African Americans were outraged, as the episode conjured up memories of the Jim Crow South. Out of anger and frustration, violence erupted and continued for nearly one week. Buildings were burned and looted, fifty-three people were killed, and some 2,000 more injured. Most of the violence occurred in the South Central section of Los Angeles, inhabited mostly by African Americans and Hispanics. One year later, two of the officers were found guilty of violating King's civil rights; the other two officers were acquitted.

The acquittal of the Los Angeles police officers was not the cause of the riots, but merely the match that touched off the powder keg. The causes were many, and familiar. The grinding poverty of South Central and the lack of employment were major factors. The Los Angeles Police Department, like many urban police forces, used dubious tactics in policing the area, methods that alienated the residents and created distrust. As well, relationships between African Americans and the Korean immigrants that had moved into the area and owned many businesses had worsened; these Korean-owned shops were frequent targets of looters and arsonists during the rioting. While race clearly was an issue in the Los Angeles riots, overtones of class were at the heart of the violence. A lingering image of the did not have a privileged childhood, Lee did have stability and opportunities that many black baby boomers did not. Nonetheless, Lee encountered racism—in both its overt and subtle forms—as he embarked on his film career. In part, many film producers were unwilling to back Lee's films because of their often controversial and sometimes volatile subject matter. His brash self-confidence and unapologetic defense of his film's themes unsettled others. He also has to contend with the notion that he is a spokesman for the African American community, assertions that white filmmakers rarely—if ever—have to refute. Indeed, Lee's films explore the dynamics of intra-racial relationships (*School Daze*, for example) as frequently as they explore interracial relationships. Like other artists and entrepreneurs—both black and white—Lee has used his considerable talents to achieve both critical and financial success. Moreover, his refusal to step back from difficult subjects has, at the very least, opened new dialogue on the dynamics of race relations in the United States.

episode was a tired and forlorn Rodney King, asking the rest of the nation, "Can't we all just get along?"

African American Boomers and the Future

Much had changed for African Americans born during the Baby Boom, and much had remained the same. As black baby boomers approach retirement, they share much in common with their white birth cohorts, but some important distinctions remain.

African Americans made significant gains economically after World War II. Many moved into the middle class, thanks in large measure to the increased education opportunities that prepared them for high-paying careers in medicine, law, education, and other professional fields. For African Americans in the working class, they have had to contend with the vagaries of a fluctuating economy, and the uncertainty and lack of security it engenders. And for those on the bottom rung, their situation has become desperate: there seems to be little, if any, chance that they will be able to climb up the ladder at all. This economic polarization of African Americans mirrors a similar pattern in the larger American economy.

The forecast as the baby boomers move to retirement is somewhat bleak. According to the U.S. Census, only about 200,000 black Americans earn more than $100,000 annually, about 2 percent of all African Americans. Indeed, studies have shown that African American baby boomers have not closed the income gap with whites, just as their parents and grandparents had been unable to do. Black baby boomers are still earning about 66 percent of what their non-Hispanic white age peers earn (Hughes and O'Rand 2005). What this means is that African American boomers likely will have less saved for their retirement and that the struggle for equality will continue.

Bibliography

Branch, Taylor. *Parting the Waters: America in the King Years, 1954–1963*. New York: Simon and Schuster, 1992.

Carmichael, Stokely, and Charles V. Hamilton. *Black Power: The Politics of Liberation in America*. New York: Vintage Books, 1974.

Carson, Clayborne. *In Struggle: SNCC and the Black Awakening of the 1960s*. 2nd ed. Cambridge, MA: Harvard University Press, 1990.

Carter, Dan T. *The Politics of Rage: George Wallace, the Origins of the New Conservatism, and the Transformation of American Politics*. New York: Simon and Schuster, 1995.

Chalmers, David. *And the Crooked Places Made Straight: The Struggle for Social Change in the 1960s*. 2nd ed. Baltimore, MD: Johns Hopkins University Press, 1996.

Coontz, Stephanie. *The Way We Really Are: Coming to Terms with America's Changing Families*. New York: Basic Books, 1997.

Early, Gerald L. *This Is Where I Came In: Black America in the 1960s*. Lincoln: University of Nebraska Press, 2003.

Eskew, Glenn T. *But for Birmingham: The Local and National Movements in the Civil Rights Struggle*. Chapel Hill: University of North Carolina Press, 1997.

Franklin, John Hope, and Alfred A. Moss, Jr. *From Slavery to Freedom: A History of African Americans*. 8th ed. Boston: McGraw-Hill, 2000.

Graham, Hugh Davis. *The Civil Rights Era: Origins and Development of a National Policy, 1960–1965*. New York: Oxford University Press, 1990.

Haines, Herbert H. *Black Radicals and the Civil Rights Mainstream, 1954–1970*. Knoxville: University of Tennessee Press, 1988.

Halberstam, David. *The Fifties*. New York: Villard Books, 1993.

Hughes, Langston. *The Collected Works of Langston Hughes, Volume 3: The Poems, 1951–1967*. Edited with an introduction by Arnold Rampersad. Columbia: University of Missouri Press, 2001.

Hughes, Mary Elizabeth, and Angela M. O'Rand. "The Life and Times of the Baby Boomers." In *The American People: Census 2000*. Edited by Reynolds Farley and John Haaga. New York: Russell Sage Foundation, 2005.

Jackson, Kenneth T. *Crabgrass Frontier: The Suburbanization of the United States*. New York: Oxford University Press, 1985.

Jones, Charles Earl, ed. *The Black Panther Party Reconsidered*. Baltimore: Black Classic Press, 1998.

Kluger, Richard. *Simple Justice: The History of Brown v. Board of Education and Black America's Struggle for Equality*. New York: Alfred A. Knopf, 1976.

Lawson, Steven F. *Running for Freedom: Civil Rights and Black Politics since 1941*. Philadelphia: Temple University Press, 1991.

Malcolm X, with the assistance of Alex Haley. *The Autobiography of Malcolm X*. New York: Grove Press, Inc., 1964.

Marable, Manning. *Race, Reform, and Rebellion: The Second Reconstruction in America, 1945–1982*. London: Macmillan, 1984.

McAdam, Doug. *Freedom Summer*. New York: Oxford University Press, 1988.

Monhollon, Rusty L. "'Away From the Dream': The Origins of Black Power in Lawrence, Kansas." M.A. thesis, University of Kansas, 1994.

Monhollon, Rusty L. *"This Is America?" The Sixties in Lawrence, Kansas*. New York: Palgrave, 2002.

Morris, Aldon D. *The Origins of the Civil Rights Movement: Black Communities Organizing for Change*. New York: Free Press, 1984.

National Advisory Commission on Civil Disorders. *Report of the National Advisory Commission on Civil Disorders.* New York: Bantam Books, 1968.

Newton, Huey P. and Bobby Seale, "October 1966 Black Panther Party Platform and Program: What We Want, What We Believe." In Philip S. Foner, ed., *The Black Panthers Speak.* Philadelphia: J. B. Lippincott Co., 1970, 2–3.

Sitkoff, Harvard. *The Black Struggle for Equality, 1954–1980*. New York: Hill and Wang, 1981.

Stoper, Emily. *The Student Nonviolent Coordinating Committee: The Growth of Radicalism in a Civil Rights Organization*. Brooklyn, NY: Carlson Publishing, 1989.

Sugrue, Thomas J. *The Origins of the Urban Crisis: Race and Inequality in Postwar Detroit*. Princeton, NJ: Princeton University Press, 1996.

Trotter, Joe William. *The African American Experience*. Boston: Houghton Mifflin, 2001.

U.S. Department of Labor, Office of Policy Planning and Research. *The Negro Family: The Case for National Action*. Washington, DC: U.S. Government Printing Office, 1965.

Van Deberg, William L. *New Day in Babylon: The Black Power Movement and American Culture, 1965–1975*. Chicago: University of Chicago Press, 1992.

Weisbrot, Robert. *Freedom Bound: A History of America's Civil Rights Movement*. New York: Norton, 1990.

Wellner, Alison Stein. "The Forgotten Baby Boom." *American Demographics* (February 2001): 46–51.

Whalen, Charles, and Barbara Whalen, *The Long Debate: A Legislative History of the 1964 Civil Rights Act*. New York: New American Library, 1985.

Wilson, William Julius. *When Work Disappears: The World of the New Urban Poor*. New York, Knopf, 1996.

Hispanic Americans | 5

Theodore W. Eversole

The term Hispanic American, and to a lesser extent the phrase Latino American, describes a widely divergent population whose shared commonality is a link to Spanish-speaking countries, primarily Mexico, but also to a range of Caribbean, South American, and Central American nations. As a specific ethnic identity, *Hispanic* emerged as a social appellation in the 1970s and subsequently tied this amorphous group into a coherent whole for largely government statistical purposes. It is a designation that escapes purely racial identities, because Hispanic can include those of any racial background be they black, white, Asian, or of mixed ancestry. This racial dimension is further complicated by the fact that those of Mexican and Central American origins are often of *Mestizo* backgrounds, which involves a Spanish and Amerindian mixture.

What is most significant in the context of the Baby Boom generation is that since 1945 the Hispanic American population has increased enormously, from approximately 4 million nationally in 1950 to an estimated 39 million today, or 14 percent of the total population. This growth has made Hispanics the largest single ethnic minority, surpassing the African American population. This development has increased white America's awareness of a dynamically changing situation in which substantial human impacts are being felt in American politics, business, and society. Furthermore, the Hispanic population growth shows no signs of slowing and has increased by 9.8 percent since the 2000 census. This continued growth appears as an unstoppable upward spiral created by increased immigration and high birth rates. This demographic fact undoubtedly means that additional societal change is inevitable and that greater understanding of this emerging Hispanic reality is needed. The degree of necessary adjustment is seen in projections that suggest that, by 2050, Hispanics will number 25 percent of the nation's total population (U.S. Census 2003, 18).

A Hispanic family walks past a mural in East Los Angeles, California. U.S. Census Bureau figures released in 2000 showed that non-Hispanic whites represent 49.8 percent of the state's population, making them a minority in California for the first time since 1860, when accurate census data were first recorded. (AP/Wide World Photos)

Demographics

Current Hispanic settlement has roots throughout the United States, although the western section of the United States has the largest representation with 44 percent. Within this sector, California is the largest single state on a per capita basis, with 36 percent of the total Hispanic population. States such as Texas, New York, Illinois, and Florida also have large Hispanic populations. In addition, the Hispanic population is following employment opportunities to the south and northeast. For instance, for more than forty years, Miami has been seen as the home of a well-established and large Cuban-American community; however, more recently, many other Hispanic groups have seen the benefits of migration and are moving to new areas in the southeastern United States, including North Carolina and Georgia (U.S. Census 2007).

The Hispanic presence is clearly felt to varying degrees in different regions. The southwest area of the states is the most significant and is closest to the highly accessible Mexican border. New Mexico's relatively small population is currently 43 percent Hispanic, but in the more populous states of California and Texas, with Hispanic populations numbering 35 percent, this Hispanic presence raises general awareness and shapes much of the social fabric of these states. Within California, Los Angeles County's nearly 5 million Hispanics are a considerable political and economic force within the city.

American prosperity, the hope of employment, and political liberties are all facets of the push and pull that draws sizable Hispanic immigration to the states. Mexican immigrants or those Hispanics of Mexican American ancestry make up more than 60 percent of the overall Hispanic grouping, followed by Puerto Ricans at 10 percent, and a variety of other groups such as Cubans, Dominicans, Salvadorans, and others whose origins are in South American and Central American countries.

Roots of Hispanic Americans

The Hispanic dynamic has since the 1980s gained more public attention and become more universally apparent. The Hispanic presence in America was established as early as the sixteenth century, however, making Hispanics far older permanent residents than many of the Anglo populations who trace their roots to the British colonial settlements of Virginia and New England. Spanish claims to Florida were established by Juan Ponce de Leon in 1513. St. Augustine, Florida, became in 1565 the first permanent European settlement in what would become the United States.

Spanish exploration penetrated the heartland of America and ventured as far as the Appalachians, the Mississippi Valley, the Great Plains, the Grand Canyon, and the Pacific coast of Oregon. In 1540, Hernando de Soto and Francisco Vazquez de Coronado made extensive inroads into large areas of the American land mass reaching as far north as Kansas and as far west as California and Arizona. Coronado and de Soto were followed by many other significant explorers who extended Spanish claims in North America, including Sebastian Vizcaino, Pedro Menendez de Aviles, and Juan Rodriguez Cabrillo among many others. Their exploration established Spanish title to vast territories in what was to become the lower portion of the United States. Sectors of the Hispanic population, represented by old family residents of Colorado and New Mexico, claim an ancestry that goes back to these early *conquistadores* and to the earliest Spanish settlements. By the time of American independence in 1783, Spain's rule encompassed half of the present continental United States. In addition, settlement followed these early explorations and Santa Fe, San Antonio, Tucson, San Diego, Los Angeles, and San Francisco remain as permanent reminders of the Spanish colonial legacy and heritage.

American possession of these original Spanish territories was made possible by Spain's declining colonial and military strength as well as by war with Spain's successor on the U.S. southern border, Mexico, whose independence from Spain came in 1821. Beginning with the purchase of Florida from Spain in 1819, and through the Mexican War of 1846–1848 former Spanish territory came under American rule. The subsequent Treaty of Guadeloupe Hidalgo of 1848 ceded to the United States vast tracts of south-western lands totaling more than 525,000 square miles in exchange for $15 million. The later Gadsden Purchase or Melsilla Strip purchase of 1853 added a further 45,000 square miles to American territory, and after payment of $10 million, finally settled the U.S. southern border with Mexico. The United States had by mid-nineteenth century absorbed these former Spanish and Mexican territories and extended America's reach to the Pacific. From these former Spanish territories the economically important and large and politically significant states of Texas, California, and Florida were formed.

The Spanish-American War of 1898 formally ended Spain's long presence in the New World. U.S. victory after only three months of combat resulted in Spain's humiliation and America's emergence as a power on the world stage. The 1898 Treaty of Paris, which formally ended the conflict, brought Puerto Rico, the Philippines, and Guam under American rule. Puerto Rico remains an independently governed American commonwealth territory, and one of the clearest examples of America's continuing Hispanic roots. The war also resulted in an American military occupation of Cuba that established a pattern of involvement in the affairs of Cuba that has been more confrontational since Castro's 1959 Communist takeover of the island and persisting into the twenty-first century.

Immigration

Increasing Hispanic immigration in recent decades from Mexico, Cuba, and Central America has had a dramatic impact on a multitude of levels. Cuban immigration had its roots in the political rejection by many Cubans of Castro's Communist Revolution and its totalitarian aspects. In its earliest days, many of these Cubans fled the political tyranny that undermined their previously held socioeconomic positions and destroyed their property rights. As many as 1 million Cubans fled in this initial postrevolutionary wave and many settled in Miami, bringing with them their language and culture. As time progressed, other Cubans were threatened by Communist rule. As living standards fell, and as Communist pledges failed to deliver the Promised Land, more immigrants willingly faced the risks of escape, and these latter groups represented a broader cross section of the varied strands of the Cuban population.

Mexican immigration, which constitutes the highest proportion of the total Hispanic population, has been largely in the form of poorer economic migrants who have fled poverty, the Partido Revolucionario Institucional (PRI) political monopoly that existed from 1929 until the 1990s, and corruption stemming from the misuse of oil revenues for payments to union and PRI functionaries and have come for the brighter employment, education, and social prospects of the United States. Although settlement has brought greater opportunities, many Hispanic incomes lag behind the American national average. Hispanic entry into professional occupations still produces serious differentials, which through education, acculturation, and assimilation should decline over time. Of these groups, Cuban Americans in both income and professional success are not far off national averages, suggesting that this same upward mobility should translate to other groups.

Hispanic immigration as a whole increased at a time of substantial change in American family patterns with increasing divorce rates, declining birth rates, more single-family living, and later marriages. During an era when baby boomers chose to remain either childless or have but one or two children, Hispanic immigration rose to fill this demographic gap. Without it, an aging American population would have numerically declined, and this decline could create a series of new socioeconomic problems. Hispanic population increases are also occurring at a time when baby boomers are retiring. For further and continued economic progress, the nation requires more workers to remain competitive in a global economy.

The Hispanic demographic edge is seen statistically in these birth rates. As a group, they make up 21 percent of the children under age ten, while accounting for only 14 percent of the total population. While growth among non-Hispanic whites in the important twenty to thirty-five age-group has declined, Hispanic population in this age-group has increased by more than 1.7 million. The Hispanic part of the population is the only segment of the American population that is growing, and this reality clearly raises the visibility and social importance of the Hispanic community (Hamilton, Martin, and Ventura 2007; Pew Hispanic Center 2006).

This weight of numbers is bringing about change to society's overall response to the phenomenon of Hispanic growth. Hispanics are opening many important doors in society as consumers, workers, business, and political forces. For many observers, they hold the key to the future. Their importance has shaped the immigration debate where even among many conservative political factions it is realized that the nation's prosperity depends on Hispanic immigrant labor.

This reality is seen by many to have weakened the introduction of restrictive immigration policies and confused the drive toward a stronger reaction to massive illegal immigration. Demographics have helped overcome some social assimilation barriers and other difficulties facing the Hispanic populations, and this has created a picture that is generally more positive than other previous ethnic groups have experienced.

Culture

This more positive picture has been supported by the growth of a Hispanic cultural community that has preserved traditions through the growth of Spanish-language publications and media outlets throughout the United States, including advertising and marketing of Hispanic-based products. Furthermore, many of these products cater to the different Hispanic groupings within the general population of 38 million. Hispanic purchasing power has now reached $700 billion annually, and this brings increased power and influence. If numbers for wealth and population were combined, the Hispanic American population would be the third largest and the richest Latin American country in existence.

This growth has included sharp rises in the numbers of Hispanic-owned businesses, which now include tens of thousands of firms with more than $1 million in sales. The MasTec Communications firm in Miami is a prominent Hispanic success story with its thousands of employees and billion

Marie Acosta-Colón

Born in 1949, Marie Acosta-Colón was the second of five children born to Frank Acosta, a Native American who served in the Navy, and Beatrice, a Hispanic American. Acosta-Colón has been a tireless advocate for the arts, in addition to being a political activist on behalf of Hispanic Americans.

As a political science major at Los Angeles Valley Junior College, Acosta-Colón became politically active during the 1968 presidential election, where she campaigned for Democratic candidate Eugene McCarthy. While attending the Democratic National Convention in Chicago in August 1968, Acosta-Colón witnessed the street violence between antiwar demonstrators and Chicago police. As with others of her generation, what happened in Chicago, coupled with the prolonged war in Vietnam and the continued racial tensions throughout the nation, led Acosta-Colón to question her faith in the government and the status quo. The experience prompted her to direct her life to working to eliminate economic and political inequality, both in the United States and Mexico.

After transferring to California State University, Acosta-Colón became deeply involved

dollar yearly revenue. Hispanic investment in mainstream businesses has increased dramatically, with an estimated one in twenty American companies now being Hispanic owned or controlled. Spanish-language publications have also expanded, and magazines like Time Warner's *People en Espanol* (which began in 1997) reaching a circulation of more than 400,000, making it the largest Spanish magazine in America and an important advertising outlet.

The evidence of this emerging Hispanic cultural presence is seen everywhere from stores selling exclusively Hispanic products to Spanish-language television and radio programming. Both Spanish language and cross-over programs now feature Hispanic themes and characters, and since 2000, increasing numbers of Hispanic characters are featured in mainstream television shows.

Hispanics are major television viewers, averaging as much as fifty-eight hours of viewing per household per week with widely varied program tastes ranging from dramas and the hugely popular *telenovelas* to variety and reality programs. To cater to such a broad appetite, a number of broadcasting networks have emerged, such as Univision (which is now the fifth-largest network in the country), Telefutura, and Telemundo. As well as popular programming, over the past four decades important films have attempted to capture the Hispanic migration experience in the face of a dominant Anglo culture. Early films in both Spanish and English, such as *El Norte* (1974) and *El Super* (1979) as well as more recent films such as *Mi Familia* (1994) and *Puerto Rican Passage* (1994), have all portrayed the impact of migration and the necessary personal adjustments that are required to meet the demands of a new culture. Given this extensive audience base, organizations such as the National Hispanic Media Coalition, formed in the 1980s, act as pressure groups to promote a greater Hispanic American presence in the general media. The Latino Public Broadcasting in the Chicano student movement. Between 1971 and 1974, she performed with *Grupo Mascarones*, a theater troupe that staged political-themed plays in Mexico and the United States. She also became the troupe's manager, handling publicity and fund-raising activities. She joined the San Francisco Mime Troupe in the mid-1970s, and stayed with the group until 1985.

She married in 1978 and soon had a child, which made touring with the acting company difficult. In 1980, she became the general manager of the troupe, which permitted her to devote time both to the arts and her family. This new role suited her well, and she was asked to join the boards of numerous arts councils and organizations. In 1989, she became the director of the Mexican Museum in San Francisco, which gave her the opportunity to build a cultural site for Hispanics. Under her guidance, the Mexican Museum has thrived; in the late 1990s, it broke ground on a new building to house the institution's impressive collection of Latino art.

group also actively supports and finances cultural programming geared to the Hispanic community.

Popular bilingual programs, such as Nickelodeon's *Dora the Explorer,* have gained a mainstream audience. In addition, Hispanics form 15 percent of cinema box office ticket sales, and many Hispanic stars have emerged such as Jennifer Lopez, Salma Hayek, and Cameron Diaz. Increasingly, Hispanic-themed films produced in both Hollywood and Latin America have drawn large American audiences. Latin radio stations now make up nearly 10 percent of national audiences, and the number of Hispanic performers and musicians are widespread with stars like Shakira, Ricky Martin, Marc Anthony, and Gloria Estefan offering both Spanish and English performances (Hoag 2005; "Hispanic Radio, Asian TV Fuel 16% Increase in Ethnic Media Reach" 2009).

In recent decades, Hispanic inroads in American sports have been equally dynamic. Hispanic athletes can be found in a vast range of sports from ice hockey to speed skating. In particular, in America's national pastime baseball, the growth of Hispanic star players has been phenomenal, making Hispanics the largest minority in the sport. Dominicans, Cubans, Venezuelans, and Nicaraguans all have found representation in the major leagues, and many Hispanic players are now leading performers in the sport, such as baseball's Alex Rodriguez. Spanish-language broadcasting of these sports has followed the growing participation rates. A number of dedicated sports channels, such as ESPN, have Spanish-language broadcasts that include a range of sports coverage, including the National Basketball Association and Major League Soccer among many other sports.

First-generation Hispanic immigrants benefit from such cultural recognition and support. However, the Hispanic community, particularly its second and later generations, accept English as the language of advancement and often are equally bilingual, and use Spanish depending on occasion and circumstance. Present patterns suggest that amalgamation in the larger American community is valued by most Hispanics, and interracial marriage is increasingly common. In language terms, current evidence indicates that 75 percent of the Hispanic population currently speaks English to varying degrees of proficiency.

Upward Mobility

As with other subgroups of the Baby Boom generation, Hispanic boomers have left their mark on the nation's economy, despite historically earning less than the national average. Just as the notion of a cohesive Hispanic community is hard to define so too are average income projections that can vary considerably among groups within the Hispanic community. Cuban Americans have the highest average incomes, and Dominican and Mexican rooted Hispanics the lowest. When grouped together median Hispanic household incomes (2005) were $35,967 as compared with non-Hispanic white median incomes of $50,784. The Asian community maintained the highest median income of all groups at $61,094. Although lagging behind, overall Hispanic median remained higher than that of black Americans (U.S. Census 2005).

In the face of a national poverty average of 12.6 percent, the Hispanic community, many of whom are recent immigrants, face the spectre of poverty to a greater degree than other Americans. With a poverty rate of 21 percent, which is even higher in single-family Hispanic households, the struggle to make ends meet can be quite daunting. Yet the enthusiasm to find a piece of the American dream, as opposed to returning to the even more dire circumstances of their native countries, provides a clear motivation to make the most of the American experience (U.S. Census 2006, 472).

Command of English and other education tools offer the best keys to a more fluid participation in the larger American society, and also offer the best ways for societal and personal progress. Even with some separatist or nonintegrationist tendencies in certain extremist political quarters, Hispanic identities are overwhelmingly being incorporated into the larger American culture, and this can be both confusing and liberating. Greater movement between cultures and communities offers exciting possibilities that often celebrate both the Anglo and the Hispanic cultures to the detriment of none.

Along with the rapid Hispanic growth rate in recent decades the Hispanic student population has naturally risen as well, and with this rise, problems have emerged. Current Hispanic education attainment does not meet that of non-Hispanic students, and the dropout rate in some Hispanic communities remains high. Many students are being underserved, and this can have serious and lasting consequences for those Hispanics entering mainstream public schools. Between 1993 and 2003, the percentage of Hispanic students in the public sector has risen from 12.7 percent to 19 percent of the national student population. In terms of kindergarten through twelfth-grade schools in the western section of the country, between 1972 and 2004, the Hispanic element in the total school population has grown from 15 percent to 39 percent. In the preschool sector, Hispanic children under five now make up 22 percent of this population (Fry and Gonzales 2008).

Concerns exist and improvements are needed because many of these students come from recent immigrant families where income levels are frequently low. In addition, many Hispanic students are held back, and this increases negative attitudes toward school, which later can contribute to increased dropout rates from high school. In comparison with a national white graduation rate at 74 percent, Hispanic graduation rates are significantly lower at 53 percent, although this figure is better than black graduation rates that hover around 50 percent. Nevertheless, this figure remains disappointing and detrimental to many who hope to advance further in a modern economy. In addition, Hispanic participation in higher math and science in high school is underrepresented. These education difficulties are made worse in that many Hispanic students attend schools that serve the poorer and more poverty-affected school districts that have serious issues of per capita underfunding (Tienda and Mitchell 2006; Kohler and Lazarin 2007).

In the postsecondary education sphere, 38 percent of white students go on to further education, whereas the Hispanic rate is only 26 percent. This rate has increased, however, from 16 percent in 1974 to the 26 percent rate recorded in 2003. For many Hispanic students, their progression to higher education is found in two-year colleges that provide further opportunities for 38 percent of those Hispanics enrolled in higher education. This choice is perhaps the result of the cost factors involved in financing a higher education. Such expenses might also pose a factor in college graduation rates. Compared with white graduation rates, Hispanic attainment at bachelor's level lags behind. In 2005, only 12 percent of Hispanics age twenty-five years and older had a college degree (U.S. Census 2006, 179).

Educationally, at a time when Hispanic student numbers have spiralled, their education achievement has been disappointing, and improved outcomes are necessary to correct this degree of underachievement. Hispanic students receive less higher education financial aid than black students. Along with language and other special programs, funding must increase if these gaps are to be filled, and this need affects all levels of the education system from preschool to high school and beyond.

Politics

As the Hispanic population has grown, their political importance has increased correspondingly. Numbers can translate easily into votes, and this has meant that the major political parties throughout the nation have courted the Hispanic vote. In addition, the rising Hispanic presence and, in particular, the tremendous increase in illegal Hispanic migration has created specific political issues that have brought about political divides and tensions as to where this immigration is heading, and how best to accommodate and control it. At the local level, the Hispanic influx can raise political tensions. In North Carolina, the Hispanic numbers have increased so rapidly that local resistance has increased that might threaten ultimate assimilation and acceptance into the majority culture.

Yet fuller participation in the political process, even with such increasing numbers of potential voters, is hampered by a variety of factors, with citizenship status often limiting political influence at the ballot box. Conditions might also be limited by relative poverty, education, and a lack of knowledge of the workings of the U.S. political process. Communities can not be rallied if they lack cohesion and the economic resources to mobilize the vote. Language difficulties can limit participation. A standing issue concerning whether votes cast automatically translate into favourable policies that benefit the Hispanic community both locally and federally. Therefore, the Hispanic political potential exists, but it is not yet a consistent or collective voting block.

Attempts at marshalling the Hispanic vote cross party lines and have confused the nation's response to the illegal immigrant issue. Furthermore, the substantial Hispanic voting potential in areas such as California, Texas, and Florida has meant that Hispanic voices can influence decisions taken at both the state and local levels. In the future, Hispanic concentration in the nine states that control 75 percent of the Electoral College votes might also prove instrumental in presidential elections.

When Hispanic voters became 7 percent of the national electorate in 2000, and with a 45 percent turnout, their electoral potential was starting to be realized. With voter registration rates of 57 percent, the Hispanic vote was clearly becoming important enough that it could influence the outcome of city, state, and federal elections. Both the Democrats and the Republicans have turned to the Hispanic vote, but as yet, Hispanic political affections are not being given overwhelmingly to a particular party. Each party is developing strategies that appeal to Hispanic interests, and this includes Hispanic voter registration drives and Spanish-language Web sites. In addition, Democrats and Republican politicians at state and federal levels are learning Spanish to extend their reach into the Hispanic communities found within their constituencies (Hugo and Taylor 2009; Kaufman 2007; Rosenberg 2006).

Greater participation in national politics is clearly witnessed in Washington, where more and more Hispanics have gained seats in Congress, as well as other senior positions within the federal government and civil service. In 2003, twenty-three Hispanics held seats in the House of Representatives, nineteen Democrats and four Republicans. In addition, the George W. Bush administration promoted a number of Hispanics to key cabinet positions, including Alberto Gonzales, a long-standing political associate from Texas, as attorney general, and Carlos M. Gutierrez as secretary of commerce.

The general operating assumption has been that the Hispanic community has a more natural affinity for Democratic Party platforms, but the actual political situation is more complicated. Evidence suggests that Cubans and Columbians have a more conservative and Republican-orientated agenda than do the Mexicans, Central Americans, and Puerto Ricans. These latter groups seem to fall more consistently into the Democratic camp. In addition, as groups become more established, more economically, educationally, and socially successful, political identities can shift along with interests. The Hispanic community is diverse, and so are its prospective political affiliations.

Given the Hispanic community's shared Catholic faith and generally conservative social values, Republicans have made inroads into the Hispanic vote, particularly in presidential elections. This was revealed in the steady decline from a 72 percent Hispanic vote for Clinton in 1996 to a 60-40 percent split between John Kerry and George W. Bush in the 2004 presidential election. Some of this Republican gain recently has been lost, however, because of the emotive divides stirred up by the illegal immigration debate before Congress. The calls by many Republicans for stronger controls and restrictions have driven many Hispanic voters toward the more liberal Democratic Party policies that offer a greater chance of illegal immigration amnesties. Equally placed Republican and conservative business forces would like to see a more liberal approach to immigration because of the demand for cheap and willing labor that the immigrant community offers. An expanded labor force is needed in many American industries, stretching from agriculture to the manufacturing and service industries.

In addition to the established avenues of elected office in which Hispanic representation is increasing on all levels (city, state, and federal), the lobbying agencies central to the promotion of special interests has been rising substantially. As such, the Hispanic community has a number of important organizations that function to advance Hispanic interests. Founded in 1929, the League of United Latin American Citizens (LULAC) is the oldest and largest of these organizations founded. The Cuban American National Foundation, founded in 1981, is geared to the call for democracy and freedom in Cuba, which gives it great sway in Florida state politics and policy positions. The United Farms Workers Union, founded in 1962 by Cesar Chavez, has established a strong base among Hispanic farm laborers, many of whom are immigrants. The union is an advocate for agricultural worker advancements in pay and conditions, which often has led to boycotts and strikes in defense of these interests. Other Hispanic organizations exist, such as the National Institute of Latino Policy, founded in 1982 in New York City. This group began as an advocacy group for Puerto Rican voting and civil rights but has expanded to represent the broader base of Hispanic affairs. As the Hispanic population grows, organized advocacy and lobbying groups will emerge on all political fronts to push forward Hispanic interests in a variety of areas central to their advancement as a people.

Activism

Hispanic groups also challenge the more corporate and integrationist politics of inclusion, and propose more radical solutions to the Hispanic American situation. These countercultural organizations fall under the broad designation of the *Reconquista* movement and are active in the western areas of the

Cesar Chavez

Cesar Chavez, born on March 31, 1927, near Yuma, Arizona, to a Mexican American family, became in the Baby Boom era one of America's most famous civil rights activists whose reputation rivals that of Martin Luther King in Hispanic circles.

The coming of the Great Depression reversed the meager fortunes of the Chavez family and took them to California where they found work as migrant agricultural workers. This experience introduced Chavez to the hardships and exploitation that went with this way of life. Chavez's education was haphazard as his family moved from job to job, and he finally escaped the fields in 1944 when he joined the navy during World War II.

After his return to California following his military service, his life changed dramatically as he married, had a family, and met and became in involved with Fred Ross' Community Service Organization (CSO), which advocated civil rights and greater civil protections for the Hispanic community. In 1962, Chavez left the CSO and formed the National Farm Workers Association (NFWA) which evolved into the National Farm Workers, now affiliated with the American Federation of Labor and Congress of Industrial Organizations (AFL-CIO).

Chavez came to national prominence in the mid-1960s when he led boycotts and a five-year strike action in support of California grape pickers' demands for higher wages. The union's organizing efforts spread to other areas of the country and involved more crops, such as lettuce, and wider issues and conditions that affected the agricultural labor force. The union opposed the *Bracero* Program of 1942 to 1964 that allowed temporary entry for low-wage Hispanic migrant labor which, in turn, undercut the established workforces and suppressed wages. This concern for the lowering of wages led the union to oppose during the 1970s the rising tide of illegal immigration. Such illegal workers were often exploited by farm owners to lower wages and undercut union strike action. In the current debate over illegal immigration, this stand might appear to be contradictory to Hispanic interests. Chavez and the union wanted tighter immigration regulations to protect wage levels. Nevertheless, immigration amnesties such as that of 1986 were supported along with opposition to sanctions against employer hiring practices.

Chavez protested against excessive pesticide use, as well as the curbing, during the 1980s, of previously gained protections, which directly led in July and August 1988 to Chavez' thirty-six day fast for life.

Chavez gained many accolades during his life, including in 1991, the *Aguila Azteca* (Aztec Eagle), Mexico's highest award to those of Mexican background who make major contributions outside of Mexico. In 1992, he received the *Pacem in Terris* award, papal recognition for promoting peace among mankind.

Chavez died in sleep, of unknown causes, on April 23, 1993; more than 40,000 mourners attended his funeral. Chavez continues to be remembered in many different ways. In California and beyond, residential streets, highways, schools, and parks have been named in his honor. Furthermore, his birthday is now celebrated in four states.

On August 8, 1994, Chavez became the second Mexican American to receive the Presidential Medal of Freedom, the highest civilian

César Chávez organized the first effective migrant worker union in the United States. His political skill and his unswerving dedication to one of society's most unprotected sectors made him a popular hero. (Library of Congress)

honor in the United States. His family traveled to Washington to receive this posthumous award. Also in 1994, the United Farm Workers (UFW) created the Cesar Chavez Foundation to promote the goals and ideals as embodied by Chavez work. In December 6, 2006, Governor Arnold Schwarzenegger of California led the induction of Cesar Chavez into the California Hall of Fame located at the California Museum of History, Women, and the Arts.

The primary Chavez legacy is found in the work of the UFW, which has continued after his death, working for higher wages, benefits, and better conditions for its members as well as preserving its ultimate goal: the establishment of a national farm workers union.

United States. Organizations such as *La Raza Unida,* founded in the 1960s and led by Jose Angel Gutierrez, in addition to the *MECha* (Movimento Estudiantil de Chicanos de Aztlan) have formulated views that contrast considerably with the integrationist melting pot concepts held by the majority of Hispanic Americans. These groups argue that the southwestern United States was seized illegally by the United States in 1848 from its legitimate owners, Mexican Hispanics. Their solution is to return these lands and form an independent *Aztlán* homeland from these recovered territories. They define their struggle in national liberation terms, are active on many western university campuses, and are prominent in marches against stronger immigrant border controls and immigration legislation.

Toward the Future

The growth of the Hispanic American population has been one of the most instrumentally transforming events that has marked the post-World War II Baby Boom generation. The full impact—socially, culturally, economically, and politically—has yet to be fully and comprehensively digested or analysed. The impact of this growth, both through legal and illegal immigration, suggests that more than 100 million people will be added to the American population by 2057, and the overwhelming majority of these people will be Hispanic.

Such a rapid growth has produced concerns from a number of quarters and has raised tensions as part of the ongoing immigration control debate. Some people see such growth as broadening and essential to America's continued industrial and economic development. Higher Hispanic growth rates have been seen as essential to the support of an aging population. American whites have been having fewer children, and these lower birth rates place this section of the population into the same sclerotic birth rate pattern as that of Europeans, where population declines have been reversed only with increased immigration. Much of this immigration has undercut the predominant European Christian identity. The current Hispanic birth rate and its Catholic religion offset a similar long-term decline in American birth rates.

As the House Judiciary hearings in May 2007 indicated, negative consequences stem from such massive immigration and its impact on society as a whole. In one significant area, immigration can undercut American wage rates. This applies especially to those native-born Americans who are unskilled and uneducated. Arguments also express the idea that the immigrant population consumes in civic and other services more than it contributes, therefore increasing the tax burden for many communities. This burden involves such services as health care, housing, and education, where budgets have been squeezed because of the rapid rise in immigrant demands on the system.

These and other demands have resulted in a rise in tensions, and this tension consequently has driven calls for stiffer immigration controls as well as a number of English-only language propositions in several states. This opposition to bilingualism is particularly evident in those states removed from the southwest, where the Hispanic influx has been more recent and more rapid. For instance, in Atkinson County in Georgia, the influx has seen the Hispanic portion of this small community's population rise from 3 percent in 1990 to 21 percent in 2004 (some argue that the actual percentage is much higher at perhaps 33 percent). This type of growth can threaten, or at least challenge, settled communities in a number of ways other than simple economic demands on the public coffers. New cultural and religious orientations as well as perceived rising crime rates can add to public reticence and fears.

Tensions increased, for example, following the Great American Boycott of 2006, which was a protest against tougher immigration laws. Given the possible presence of 12 to 20 million illegal immigrants, some Americans viewed this protest as unnecessary and deeply unappreciative of the opportunities provided in the states. Organized primarily out of Los Angeles, and with more than 1 million protestors on the streets across the nation (many carrying Mexican flags), this protest challenged many Americans and seemed visually unpatriotic.

In addition to issues of primary loyalty to the United States, unease surrounds the potential weight of the Hispanic population as a single voting bloc that could, it is feared in certain conservative circles, spell the emergence of the Democratic Party as a monolithic voice dominating national affairs to the detriment of the democratic system.

Given America's ability in the past to absorb and assimilate huge foreign populations, others dismiss Hispanic growth as not being a serious or long-term problem. The second-generation Hispanic community has become English speaking and seems to be driven along the same lines as other American citizens toward progress and personal improvement. This acceptance of common American work ethic values also includes those patriotic ideals that bind the nation together. By the third generation, this sense of identity becomes even more entrenched, where personal development, marriage, family, and a stake in the future of society undermines any issues involving divided loyalties. This trend is similar to what occurred for the overwhelming majority of immigrant Americans as they became assimilated and settled.

Furthermore, Hispanic growth can be seen as a major economic opportunity for America's national business interests. Companies have the ability to expand their customer base and develop new marketing strategies to envelop a new sector that has tremendous buying potential. As disposable incomes increase along with professional development and education advancement, the Hispanic population can enrich the leadership of America's businesses and develop the potential for new markets at home and abroad.

The Hispanic American experience became during the Baby Boom years a fundamental and transforming aspect of American life. Its significance is still being analysed and tabulated. Projections suggest that the full impact of this immigration phenomenon on American culture, education, society, and politics is far from over. Often difficult to incorporate as a single identified group, Hispanic Americans nevertheless are at the heart of a constantly changing nation and an immigrant force that has not been seen since the late nineteenth and early twentieth century.

Bibliography

Acuña, Rodolfo. *U.S. Latino Issues*. Westport, CT: Greenwood Press, 2003.

Alexander, Sandra C. *Famous Hispanic-Americans in United States History*. Greensboro, NC: Appletex Education Center, 1992.

American Journey: History in Your Hands: Hispanic-American Experience. Woodbridge, CT: Primary Source Media, CD ROM, 1997.

Arreola, Daniel D. *Hispanic Spaces, Latino Places: Community and Cultural Diversity in Contemporary America*. Austin: University of Texas Press, 2004.

Chapman, Charles Edward. *A History of the Cuban Republic: A Study in Hispanic American Politics*. 1927. Whitefish, MT: Kessinger Press, 2005.

Chavez, Linda. *Out of the Barrio: Towards a New Politics of Assimilation*. New York: Basic Books, 1991.

De Varona, Frank, Ron Coleman, and Nick Viorst. *Latino Literacy: A Complete Guide to the Hispanic-American Culture and History*. New York: Owl Books, 1996.

Fry, Richard, and Felisa Gonzales. *One-in-Five and Growing Fast: A Profile of Hispanic Public School Students*. Washington, DC: Pew Hispanic Center, 2008.

Gibson, Campbell and Kay Jung. *The Foreign Born Population of the United States: 1850–2000*. New York: Novinka Books, 2006.

Gibson, Campbell. *Historical Census Statistics on the Foreign Born Population of the United States: 1850–1990*. Washington, DC: U.S. Bureau of the Census, Population Division, 1999.

Hamilton, Brady E., Joyce A. Martin, and Stephanie J. Ventura. "Births: Preliminary Data for 2007." *National Vital Statistics Reports* 55, no. 7 (March 18, 2009). http://www.cdc.gov/nchs/data/nvsr/nvsr57/nvsr57_12.pdf.

Hill, Gene. *Americans All-Americanos Todos: A Bilingual History of the Contributions of Hispanics to the Development of America*. Albuquerque, NM: Añoranza Press, 1997.

"Hispanic Radio, Asian TV Fuel 16% Increase in Ethnic Media Reach." *New American Media*, June 11, 2009. http://www.marketingcharts.com/television/hispanic-radio-asian-tv-fuel-16-increase-in-ethnic-media-reach-9419/.

Hoag, Christina. "Hispanic Television Networks Booming." *Miami Herald*, January 10, 2005.

Iber, Jorge, Arnold DeLeon, and Scott Zeman. *Hispanics in the American West*. Santa Barbara, CA: ABC-CLIO, 2005.

Kanellos, Nicolás, and Cristelia Perez. *Chronology of Hispanic-American History: From Pre-Columbian Times to the Present*. New York: Gale Research, 1995.

Kanellos, Nicolás, and Helvetia Martell. *Hispanic Periodicals in the United States: Origins to 1960: A Brief History and Comprehensive History*. Houston, TX: Arte-Publico, 1999.

Kaufman, Stephen. "Hispanic Americans' Political Clout Expected to Increase," *USINFO*, October 11, 2007. http://www.vamosavotar.org/political%20clout.pdf.

Kohler, Adriana, and Melissa Lazarin. "Hispanic Education in the United States." National Council of La Raza Statistical Brief, January 8, 2007. http://www.nclr.org/content/publications/detail/43582/.

Laezman, Rick. *100 Hispanic-Americans Who Changed American History*. Milwaukee, WI: World Almanac Library, 2005.

Lopez, Mark Hugo, and Paul Taylor. "Dissecting the 2008 Electorate: The Most Diverse in U.S. History." Pew Hispanic Center, April 30, 2009. http://pewhispanic.org/reports/report.php?ReportID=108.

Meyer, Nicholas E. *Biographical Dictionary of Hispanic Americans*. New York: Checkmark Books, 2001.

Navarro, Sharon Ann, and Armando Xavier Mejia, eds. *Latino Americans and Political Participation: A Reference Handbook*. Santa Barbara, CA: ABC-CLIO, 2004.

Nordquist, Joan. *Latinas in the United States; Social, Economic and Political Aspects: A Bibliography*. Santa Cruz, CA: Reference and Research Service, 1994.

Novas, Himilce. *The Hispanic 100: A Ranking of the Latino Men and Women Who Have Most Influenced American Thought and Culture*. New York: Carol Publications, 1995.

Ochoa, George. *Atlas of Hispanic-American History*. New York: Checkmark Books, 2001.

Owsley, Beatrice Rodrquez. *The Hispanic-American Entrepreneur: An Oral History of the American Dream*. New York: Twayne Publishing, 1992.

Pew Hispanic Center. "A Statistical Portrait of Hispanics at Mid-Decade." Table 8: Fertility. Pew Hisplanic Center, August 29, 2006. http://pewhispanic.org/reports/middecade/.

Rosales, Francisco A. *Chicano: The History of the Mexican-American Civil Rights Movement*. Houston, TX: Arte Publico, 1997.

Rosenberg, Simon. "Speak in Spanish." *New Politics Institute*, October 20, 2006. http://www.newpolitics.net/node/180?full_report=1.

Schultz, Jeffrey D., Andrew L. Aoki, Kerry L. Haynie, and Anne M. McCulloch. *Encyclopedia of Minorities in American Politics*. Phoenix, AZ: Oryx Press, 2000.

Stafford, Jim. *Puerto Ricans' History and Promise: Americans Who Cannot Vote.* Philadelphia: Mason Crest Publishers, 2005.

Tienda, Marta, and Faith Mitchell, eds. *Hispanics and the Future of America.* Washington, DC: National Academies Press, 2006.

U.S. Census Bureau. "Facts For Features: Hispanic Heritage Month 2007: Sept. 15 – Oct. 15." CB077-FF.14, July 16, 2007. http://www.census.gov/Press-Release/www/releases/archives/facts_for_features_special_editions/.

U.S. Census Bureau. "Hispanic Heritage Month 2005: September 15-October 15." CB05-FF.14, September 8, 2005. http://www.census.gov/Press-Release/www/releases/archives/facts_for_features_special_editions/.

U.S. Census Bureau. *Statistical Abstract of the United States: 2003.* 124th ed. Washington, DC: U.S. Government Printing Office, 2003, 18: Table 15.

U.S. Census Bureau. *Statistical Abstract of the United States: 2006.* 127th ed. Washington, DC: U.S. Government Printing Office, 2006, 170: Table 270; 472: Table 693.

Vargas, Zaragosa, ed. *Major Problems in Mexican American History: Documents and Essays.* Boston: Houghton-Mifflin Co., 2005.

Whately, William, Jr., ed. *Studies in Hispanic-American History.* Chapel Hill: University of North Carolina Press, 1927.

Poverty and the Baby Boom 6

Rusty Monhollon

An idealized image of the American family emerged after World War II. The typical American family, as depicted in popular culture, was a nuclear unit consisting of a mother and father, and perhaps three or four children. They lived in the suburbs in a relatively new, single-family house. The father wore a suit and commuted to work in the city, where he earned a salary large enough for the family to live comfortably; the family enjoyed all the latest consumer goods, such as televisions, radios, and automobiles. His company would provide him with a pension when he retired, so the family could save now for the children's education. The mother stayed at home tending to the children and the house. She filled her day with cooking, cleaning, and other household chores, as well as chauffeuring the children to school and other activities. Their neighborhood was clean and safe. They knew nothing of want and depravation.

For millions of Americans, however, this was not the case. In the Deep South, countless families earned only a few hundred dollars each year. In Appalachia, whole communities lived without running water or electricity. And in the cities, families lived in appalling housing and, with few job or education opportunities, faced a bleak future with little chance of change.

Although the United States had the highest per capita income in the world, in 1960, about one-fourth (40–50 million) of all Americans lived below the poverty line. Nearly that many lived barely above the poverty line, and more than one-quarter of the nation's housing units were substandard. Michael Harrington referred to these people as the "Other America," in his influential book of the same title. Harrington noted that the poor in the United States were everywhere. Poverty was perhaps most apparent in urban slums, but rural America—Appalachia, southern tenant farms, and California vegetable and fruit farms—experienced it too. What was striking about poverty in the United States during the Baby Boom era, aside from

These wooden homes are typical of the living accommodations in the poverty-stricken, flood-wracked mountains of eastern Kentucky. This scene at Hazard, Kentucky, shows a resident of the area carrying a box uphill past a wooden home in 1963. (AP/Wide World Photos)

the fact that it was a stark contrast to the vast wealth and affluence that often defines the period, was how few Americans took notice of it.

After 1945, daily life in the United States was shaped in part by lingering memories of the Great Depression and World War II. In both domestic and foreign policy, as well as personal choices individuals made, were configured by past experiences. Generally, postwar Americans held similar views on Communism (bad) and economic growth (good), a set of beliefs that scholars often refer to as the "liberal consensus." As a result, a new ideal of the American dream and family life—with attendant assumptions about class, race, and ethnicity—dominated American culture and society for a generation, despite social tensions and conflict simmering just beneath the surface.

At the root of this consensus was an abiding faith that economic progress would provide abundance so great and widespread that poverty and inequality would be eradicated. Indeed, many touted the prospect of a classless society, where all citizens would enjoy material comfort and stability. Accordingly, not only would class distinctions disappear but so too would poverty itself. Wide disparity still existed between rich and poor but even the poorest Americans would enjoy a standard of living unparalleled in human history.

That was not the case, however. While per capita income did increase in the United States between 1945 and 1970, not all Americans shared equally in the bounty. Before Harrington's work, most scholars and policy makers acknowledged that poverty existed in the United States, but it was found in isolated pockets scattered about the country. Harrington argued that poverty in America was systemic, structural, and widespread, and that it demanded attention at the national level. Others argued that a "culture of poverty" existed, a condition in which the poor had been destitute for so long that they were unable or unwilling to alter their economic situation.

A glaring aspect of the American economic structure was the increasing gap between the wealthiest and poorest Americans. In 1960, half of all American families had no savings at all, while the richest 1 percent held one-third of the nation's wealth and the wealthiest 5 percent held more than half. In addition, the wealthy often took advantage of loopholes in the tax code to pay little or no federal taxes (Chafe 2003, 137).

Few Americans, and in particular the suburban, white middle-class, perceived the extent of social injustice in the United States. Suburban life and culture was a self-contained community; it was not necessary for suburbanites to go to the city to shop, which effectively isolated most Americans from the poverty of the city and rural America. Suburban life as depicted in popular culture, especially the new medium of television, emphasized enjoying the good life away from the problems besetting the city; few—if any—characters on television appeared to be poor.

After World War II, the U.S. economy grew at a staggering pace, thanks to massive federal expenditures on defense spending and highway construction, as well as massive consumer spending. Millions of well-paying industrial jobs helped move the working class to a middle-class lifestyle. The middle and upper classes, however, benefited most from the postwar economic growth.

Poverty affected every social group, but some more than others. Women suffered more than men, and African Americans, Latinos, and other minorities suffered more than whites. Both the very young and the very old knew poverty. The elderly—those over sixty-five years of age—were among the nation's poorest citizens. According to one account, perhaps half of the elderly lived in poverty, unable to afford adequate housing, proper nutrition, and access to medical care. Many of these were driven into poverty by mandatory retirement. The monthly pension provided by Social Security was too little to provide adequate housing and nutrition for millions of elderly Americans.

Poverty during the Baby Boom era afflicted both rural and urban dwellers alike, although not to the same extent. Beginning in the nineteenth century and accelerating in the twentieth, rural residents migrated to the cities in waves. This migration was largely the result of the commercialization of agriculture, and especially technological advances in farming such as the mechanical cotton picker in the South and large, diesel-powered tractors in the Midwest and the Great Plains. Although fewer rural Americans were affected by poverty—simply because fewer people lived in rural areas—during the Baby Boom era, rural poverty was as debilitating as was urban poverty. Indeed, Appalachia and many parts of the South were among the poorest regions in the nation.

That poverty had long been true in the South. By any measure of wealth and income, the South lagged far behind other regions of the nation. On the eve of the Great Depression, perhaps a quarter of southerners lived without indoor plumbing, electricity, or running water. During the Baby Boom era, the gap between the South and the rest of the country began to narrow, albeit slowly. A primary factor for this was Cold War defense spending, which diversified the economies of the so-called Sunbelt, a geographic swath stretching from Florida to California.

Migrant farm workers also suffered alarming rates of poverty after World War II. Estimates ran as high as 1.5 million farm workers living in poverty, earning less than $3,000 annually. A large number were tenant farmers—both black and white—residing in the South, often in ramshackle houses that lacked modern plumbing or electricity. Migrant farm workers were common in Florida and especially in California, where Mexican Americans and Mexican immigrants accounted for a large percentage of the region's farm workers. Farm workers faced numerous challenges in scratching out a living. Because they were poor, they had little political power. Their work was seasonal, which meant the demand for workers would be high during planting and harvest seasons, but limited at other times. They also felt the vagaries of the weather. Severe weather could damage crops and reduce, or even eliminate, the need for farm workers. For people living on the fringes of economical survival, such occurrences could be devastating.

Minority populations also suffered high rates of poverty, both in rural and urban America. Puerto Ricans, Native Americans, Mexican Americans, and Asian Americans earned low wages, typically in jobs (such as agriculture or service work) that were exempt from minimum wage laws.

Of these groups, Native Americans suffered the highest incidence of poverty, which often was three times the national average. Lured by jobs in wartime production, Native Americans migrated to the city in large numbers; the urban Native American population doubled during the 1940s. After the war, however, Native Americans faced discrimination in employment, housing, and education. They were denied the ballot in two southwestern states, and federal and state officials routinely denied them veterans' benefits. It was common for unemployment rates on Indian reservations to reach 50 to 70 percent or more (Frantz 1999, 128).

Much as African Americans had been doing for some time, Native Americans and Hispanics during the 1960s began organizing and demanding full equality as American citizens. Their activism, like that of blacks, turned to economic justice. Native Americans were perhaps the most impoverished minority group in the United States. The Kennedy administration had addressed the needs of Native Americans by encouraging tribal economic development. The Area Redevelopment and Manpower-Training Acts established job-training and public works programs on reservations. Johnson's War on Poverty reached out to Native

Americans by establishing an office in the Equal Opportunity Employer (EOE) for Indian affairs. In response, the government provided funding for housing, electrification, health care, and jobs. As the so-called Red Power movement grew and demanded more control over Indian communities, tribal councils began administering federal grants through the Community Action Programs.

Hispanics, and Mexican Americans in particular, also suffered high incidences of poverty during the Baby Boom era. During World War II, amid an acute labor shortage and under the auspices of both the American and Mexican governments, some 4 million Mexican workers were brought to the United States under the *Bracero* (helping hands) Program to help American farmers with their harvest. The program continued after the war, but the workers were temporary, needed seasonally at harvest time. Many, however, did not return to Mexico and remained in the United States illegally, and soon millions more were crossing the border illegally. Nearly 4 million Mexican Americans resided in the United States by 1960, and four out of five lived in a metropolitan area. Some 600,000 million resided in Los Angeles alone (Acuña 1996, 47; Gutiérrez 2004, 53; Schultz et al. 2000, 505).

Mexican migrant workers, employed under the *Bracero* Program to harvest crops on Californian farms, are shown picking chili peppers in this 1964 photograph. The *Bracero* Program, a labor agreement between the United States and Mexico, supplied Californian farms in 1964 with 100,000 Mexican laborers. *Bracero* stems from the Spanish word for arm (brazo) and refers to the hard manual labor. (AP/Wide World Photos)

The most ambitious effort to eradicate poverty was President Lyndon
B. Johnson's War on Poverty, a key part of his Great Society. During a
commencement speech at the University of Michigan in 1964, Johnson
declared that:

> We have the opportunity to move not only toward the rich society and the
> powerful society, but upward to the Great Society. . . . It is a place where
> men are more concerned with the quality of their governments than the
> quality of their goods. The Great Society rests on abundance and liberty for
> all. It demands an end to poverty and racial injustice. (as quoted in Unger
> and Unger 1998, 40)

Before his death, Kennedy had launched an antipoverty program aimed
at Appalachia, one of the most destitute regions of the nation. Johnson took
Kennedy's plan and expanded it to the entire nation. In declaring an
"unconditional war on poverty," Johnson reflected the promise of liberalism and the general optimism of the era. What Johnson envisioned was the
Great Society, a "place where the city of man serves not only the needs of
the body and the demands of commerce by the desire for beauty and the
hunger for community" (as quoted in Unger and Unger 1998, 40).

Both Kennedy and Johnson believed, as did numerous other politicians
and government officials, that poverty resulted from weak economic
growth and the limited education and training that poor people had. An
$11 billion tax cut stimulated the economy between 1964 and 1970 (aided
significantly by military spending on the Vietnam War). This growth led
many in power to conclude that the nation's economy was basically sound
and thus poverty resulted from the inability or reluctance of the poor to
capitalize on the opportunities afforded by the burgeoning economy. Not
surprisingly, then, many politicians and citizens came to see poverty as a
pathology among poor people, an unwillingness to help themselves.

In 1965, Johnson and the Democratic majorities in both houses of
Congress enacted some eighty major pieces of legislation, including Medicare, Medicaid, Head Start, and the Equal Opportunity Employment Act.
In many ways, the Great Society was similar to—and certainly was a kin-
dred spirit to—Franklin D. Roosevelt's New Deal. Johnson affirmed that
access to health care, adequate housing, and equal opportunity in education and employment were basic rights of all Americans, and it was the
government's responsibility to protect and ensure those rights.

While the Great Society encompassed a range of proposals, at its heart
was the elimination of poverty. Johnson believed the best way to do this
was through education. The Equal Opportunity Employment Act was the
primary instrument aimed specifically at eradicating poverty, but others
were equally as important. Head Start provided early childhood education
to disadvantaged children. The Job Corps established training programs for
the poor to learn new job skills. The Model Cities program was directed at
rebuilding urban slums. Aid to Appalachia sought to relieve the suffering
in one of the most impoverished parts of America. The government also
poured money into education and job training through the Office of
Economic Opportunity (OEO), nearly $1 billion in all.

At the heart of Johnson's antipoverty program was the OEO, headed by Kennedy's brother-in-law Sargent Shriver. Although many critics lambasted the OEO for providing "handouts" to the poor, in practice, it sought to help the poor acquire the skills and education necessary to escape their condition rather than simply provide assistance. The OEO offered other programs aimed at assisting the poor. Medicaid was intended to provide health care to the poor and indigent, while Medicare did the same for the elderly. It also provided direct assistance to elementary and secondary schools, especially those that served low-income families. Among the many initiatives designed to address housing was the creation of a cabinet-level office of Housing and Urban Development (HUD).

The War on Poverty also provided direct assistance to poor people through food stamps and housing supplements, and Aid to Families with Dependent Children (AFDC). Most Great Society programs, however, were directed at helping the poor obtain an education and secure a job. Congress also raised the minimum wage from $1.25 to $1.60, and included more workers under its provisions.

Many Great Society programs were popular and free of controversy, primarily because they benefited the middle class as well as the poor. Programs such as Medicare became known as "entitlements," and the middle class came to expect that these programs would continue. When Johnson declared the War on Poverty, however, popular support waned significantly.

The Great Society came with a steep price tag; it more than doubled the nation's spending on social welfare. While many programs proved to have broad support, the cost of funding them, coupled with the rising costs of the Vietnam War, resulted in greater budget deficits and inflation.

Johnson believed that the economy could sustain two wars: one abroad in Vietnam and the War on Poverty, but he was mistaken. Johnson hoped he could pay for American military involvement in Vietnam without raising taxes or cutting his Great Society program. By 1966, the United States was spending $2 billion per month in Vietnam. The consumer price index—which measures inflation—rose steadily after 1966, reaching 170.5 in 1976, up from a base of 100 in 1967. Inflation would dog the U.S. economy for the next two decades. Spending on both the war and the Great Society substantially increased the federal deficit, which doubled between 1966 and 1967, and increased threefold between 1967 and 1968 (Mann 2001, 451; Patterson 1994, 629).

The War on Poverty produced significant results. By 1990, the percentage of Americans living below the poverty line had decreased by some 50 percent (from 21.3 percent to 13.3 percent) between 1959 and 1989. Nonetheless, the depth and breadth of poverty of the United States was great. Millions of Americans remained mired in poverty, giving rise to what some called "the working poor" (Mink and O'Connor 2004, 37).

The plight of the poor became enmeshed with the broader struggle for civil rights. During the 1960s, the National Urban League established a National Skills Bank, supported on-the-job training for African-American workers, and initiated a program to assist blacks seeking employment in television and radio. By 1967, the mainstream civil rights movement headed by Martin Luther King, Jr. and the Southern Christian Leadership Conference (SCLC), had turned its attention to economic issues and helping the impoverished. It launched Operation Breadbasket to provide assistance to the needy. In early 1968, King took up the cause of sanitation workers in Memphis, Tennessee, on strike for better wages and working conditions. After King's assassination in April, Ralph David Abernathy, King's successor as head of SCLC, led the Poor People's Campaign and marched on Washington, D.C. The marchers camped on the National Mall near the Lincoln Memorial, dubbing the site Resurrection City. The marchers wanted an "Economic Bill of Rights," including a federal commitment to full employment, a guaranteed annual income, and the construction of low-income housing. At its peak, some 3,000 people encamped on the mall and lobbied federal officials with protests and information about the campaign's goals. Ultimately, the protestors were evicted by the police without making much progress toward their goals. Later that year, Congress passed the Fair Housing Act, which required housing transactions to be completed without regard to race (McKnight 1998, 112–121).

The 1970s were difficult years economically for all Americans. Economic growth had stagnated by mid-decade, and inflation rose, leading economists to coin the phrase "stagflation." One—if not the—reason for the economic woes was the oil embargo by the Organization of Petroleum Exporting Countries (OPEC). The price of gasoline soared, as crude rose to $34 per barrel in 1979, up dramatically from $3 per barrel in 1973. The cost of living increased by 8 percent annually, the highest ten-year increase ever (Patterson 2005, 65, 127).

The troubles continued into the 1980s. By 1982, the unemployment rate was more than 10 percent, the highest it had been since the Depression; for African Americans, the rate was more than double the national average. Twelve million Americans were out of work as much of the nation's manufacturing sector lay dormant. The Reagan administration had made tax cuts—especially for the middle and upper classes—a priority. When coupled with massive defense spending, the tax cuts stimulated consumer spending, rallied the stock market, and created new jobs. Many of the new jobs, however, were in the service sector, typically paying less and offering fewer (if any) benefits to workers, unlike industrial jobs (Keyssar 1991, "Unemployment").

By the 1980s the United States was undergoing a wrenching economic transformation, from an industrial-based to a service-based economy. The postindustrial society was characterized by an increasingly automated and technology-driven workplace, which forced workers to struggle to adapt. At the same time, Americans were working more but earning less.

This economic restructuring also resulted in a geographic redistribution of the nation's industry and manufacturing. Until the mid-twentieth century, industry in the United States was concentrated heavily in trapezoid-shaped area, with Boston, Baltimore, St. Louis, and Minneapolis marking the four end points. Beginning during World War II and accelerating rapidly during the Cold War, American industry migrated to the south and

Randy Pearl Albelda

One the best-known advocates for women and children is Randy Pearl Albelda, a professor of economics at the University of Massachusetts-Boston and a foremost authority on poverty and gender.

Albelda was born on October 18, 1955, in Wilmington, Delaware. Her parents both were immigrants from Bulgaria. Albelda earned her bachelor's degree at Smith College in 1977 and her doctorate from the University of Massachusetts Amherst in 1983, both in economics.

Albelda is best known for her work on gender, poverty, and public policy, in particular the impact of public policy on working families and single mothers. An avowed feminist, Albelda is highly critical of conservative economic policies, especially those enacted during the Reagan administration, that she claims adversely affect female-headed households. In *Glass Ceilings and Bottomless Pits*, which she co-authored with Chris Tilly, Albelda argues that all working women, regardless of income or social class, confront discrimination and wage inequality. In *Dilemmas of Lone Motherhood: Essays from Feminist Economics* (co-authored with Susan Himmelweit and Jane Humphries), Albelda explores the difficulties that single mothers confront in trying to balance work and family responsibilities. Public policy, she argues, largely ignores single mothers, who—without adequate networks of support—are more likely to live in poverty than women with spouses.

Randy Pearl Albelda's scholarly work has given advocates for women, children, and the poor much needed rhetorical and analytical ammunition to refute traditional explanations of poverty. Perhaps most significant, she has forced policy makers to consider the impact of seemingly neutral economic policies on women and children.

Portrait of Randy Albelda. (Courtesy of Randy Pearl Albelda)

southwest. Several reasons accounted for this migration: plenty of land was available to construct new plants; labor was plentiful and, because few labor unions existed, inexpensive. But the greatest factor was government spending, particularly for defense and space exploration.

The nation as a whole suffered from this transformation. The United States lost its position as the leading industrial nation to Germany and Japan. American manufacturers responded to the economic downturn by cutting costs, often by closing plants or moving production to other countries, where the cost of labor, both in terms of wages and benefits, were much lower.

The shift to a service-based economy had life-altering consequences for millions of baby boomers, both blue- and white-collar workers, who were in the prime of their earning years. Many had to seek new training, especially in the highly technical fields, such as the emerging fields of computers and data systems. Many workers had to adjust to a lower standard of living, as their new jobs typically paid less than their previous ones and offered fewer benefits, such as pensions and health insurance. Both access to and the cost of health insurance left many families in a precarious condition, a significant health crisis away from bankruptcy and destitution. To maintain their middle-class lifestyle, or to stave off a possible financial crisis, many families needed the income from two full-time earners (some of whom worked more than one job), or took on heavy mortgage and credit card debt at high rates of interest.

This all occurred simultaneously with other developments that shaped poverty in America. White Americans abandoned the cities after World War II, resulting in suburban growth that was 95 percent white. Racial boundaries were distinct: white suburbs surrounding cities populated with racial and ethnic minorities. Poverty rates in central cities rose between 1970 and 1997, a time during which the overall poverty rate declined.

Over the course of the twentieth century, the poverty rate in the United States did decline. During the 1920s, industrial growth raised the per capita income, but those gains were wiped out during the Great Depression. Indeed, during the 1930s, the poverty rate was perhaps 40 percent or more. After World War II the poverty rate dropped, falling to about 30 percent in 1950, 20 percent in 1960, and to 11 percent in 1973. This decline was largely the result of unprecedented economic expansion, fueled by defense spending and mass consumerism. By the early 1970s, the economy stagnated and inflation rose, in large measure by escalating crude oil prices. When Ronald Reagan assumed the presidency in 1981, the nation was in the throes of another depression and the poverty rate crept upward, cresting at 15 percent before dipping to 13 percent in 1988. Although the proportion of Americans living in poverty declined, millions still lived below the poverty line. The 13 percent rate in 1988 represented some 32 million people, which was 10 million more people living below the poverty line than in the 1970s (Keyssar 1991, "Poverty").

Historically, poverty has affected blacks and other racial and ethnic minorities more than whites, and immigrants typically more than the native born. In general, these trends have continued into the twenty-first century. The rates of poverty for blacks and Hispanics were about three times that for whites in the late twentieth century.

As Harrington (1962) noted in *The Other America*, poverty after World War II increased significantly among women and children. In 1960, about 25 percent of poor families were headed by women; forty years later, that rate had soared to more than 50 percent, and children constituted around 40 percent of the nation's poor.

Also during this period, poverty among the elderly declined. Before 1945, older Americans accounted for a significant part of the nation's poor. Social Security and corporate pensions were primarily responsible for reducing the incidence of poverty among the elderly (Rodgers 1996, 35).

One reason for the persistence of poverty in the United States is that there is little agreement on the causes of poverty. For Harrington, the answer was simple: the poor were where they were because "they made the mistake of being born to the wrong parents, in the wrong section of the country, in the wrong industry, or in the wrong racial or ethnic group" (Harrington 1962, 14–15). There are two distinct views on the causes of poverty, and the inability of policy makers to bridge the gap between these perspectives has contributed to the continuation of poverty in the United States. The first view views poverty as a moral failing of the impoverished. Indeed, in the late nineteenth and early twentieth centuries the prevailing sentiment was voiced succinctly by the reformer Henry Ward Beecher: "No man in this land suffers from poverty unless it be more than his fault—unless it be his sin" (as quoted in Monroe 2004, 451). Nor did most Americans believe that it was the government's responsibility to help the poor; rather, private charity and philanthropy was the appropriate means to assist the so-called deserving poor. Industrialization began to bring about some reconsideration of that perspective, although it would take a catastrophic economic crisis—The Great Depression—before a new view would take root (Keyssar 1986).

The second perspective sees poverty as a structural problem, specific to the ways in which societies organize their government and economy. In this view, the poor do not choose to be poor, nor is their character at issue. Rather, it is a lack of jobs and adequate housing, food, shelter, health care, and education that is the root of the problem. By the early twentieth century, many people believed that industrialization would eradicate poverty, but it actually made it worse. Neither perspective has held sway, and thus efforts to fight poverty have often been at odds.

The New Deal, President Franklin D. Roosevelt's response to the Great Depression of the 1930s, marked a significant turn in government policy for fighting poverty. The New Deal shifted primary responsibility for caring for the poor from state and local government and institutions to the federal government. The elderly, the infirmed, dependent children, and the unemployed received direct assistance from the government. During the Reagan and Bush administrations, efforts to combat poverty came principally through encouraging economic growth and private-sector philanthropy.

Poverty has been a persistent fact of life in the United States, although there is little agreement among scholars as to why. For some, the answer is in the maldistribution of wealth and income in the United States. The gap between the richest Americans and the poorest widened steadily during the twentieth century; in 2000, the wealthiest 5 percent had incomes twenty-fold greater than the poorest. Efforts to redistribute income, through taxes and government programs, have had inadequate funding and support, according to supporters of such measures. Opponents of these efforts see in the programs themselves the continuation of poverty through the expansion of the "welfare state," which, they claim, has discouraged individual initiative and created a class of citizens dependent on federal largesse. Others see a "culture of poverty," that is, poor people perpetuate their own impoverished situations, at work. Others, however, dismiss such notions, arguing that deeply embedded structural racism keeps blacks and Latinos impoverished.

What might the future hold as the baby boomers begin to retire? Politicians and policy makers have expressed concern that the boomers might bankrupt the Social Security System, given the sheer size of the cohort. Several studies, including one by the Congressional Budget Office, suggest that 70 to 80 percent of the boomers will have a "comfortable" retirement; this projection is based on the high level of education and income that boomers have earned in their lifetimes. One-fifth, however, will likely get by only with government support: Social Security, Medicare, and Medicaid. Single women are more likely to be in this group than single men or married women. In short, poverty seems unlikely to be eradicated in the boomers' lifetime. What remains constant, and exceedingly troubling, is the great disparities of wealth in the United States and the inability of the nation to close those gaps.

Bibliography

Acuña, Rodolfo. *Anything but Mexican: Chicanos in Contemporary Los Angeles.* New York: Verso, 1996.

Chafe, William H. *The Unfinished Journey: America Since World War II.* 5th ed. New York: Oxford University Press, 2003.

Frantz, Klaus. *Indian Reservations in the United States: Territory, Sovereignty, and Socioeconomic Change.* Chicago: University of Chicago Press, 1999.

Gutiérrez, David Gregory. *The Columbia History of Latinos in the United States since 1960.* New York: Columbia University Press, 2004.

Harrington, Michael. *The Other America: Poverty in The United States.* New York: MacMillan, 1962.

Katz, Michael B. *The Undeserving Poor: From the War on Poverty to the War on Welfare.* New York: Pantheon, 1989.

Katz, Michael B., ed. *The "Underclass" Debate: Views from History.* Princeton, NJ: Princeton University Press, 1993.

Keyssar, Alexander. "Poverty." In *The Reader's Companion to American History*, edited by Eric Foner and John Arthur Garraty, 858–862. Boston: Houghton Mifflin, 1991.

Keyssar, Alexander. "Unemployment." In *The Reader's Companion to American History*, edited by Eric Foner and John Arthur Garraty, 1095–1097. Boston: Houghton Mifflin, 1991.

Keyssar, Alexander. *Out of Work: The First Century of Unemployment in Massachusetts*. New York: Cambridge University Press, 1986.

Mann, Robert. *A Grand Delusion: America's Descent into Vietnam*. New York: Basic Books, 2001.

McKnight, Gerald D. *The Last Crusade: Martin Luther King, Jr., the FBI, and the Poor People's Campaign*. Boulder, CO: Westview Press, 1998.

Mink, Gwendolyn, and Alice O'Connor. *Poverty in the United States: An Encyclopedia of History, Politics, and Policy*. Santa Barbara, CA: ABC-Clio, 2004.

Monroe, James A. *Hellfire Nation: The Politics of Sin in American History*. New Haven, CT: Yale University Press, 2004.

Patterson, James T. *Restless Giant. The United States from Watergate to Bush v. Gore*. New York: Oxford University Press, 2005.

Patterson, James. *America's Struggle against Poverty 1900–1994*. Cambridge, MA: Harvard University Press, 1994.

Rodgers, Harrell R., Jr. *Poor Women, Poor Children: American Poverty in the 1990s*. 3rd ed. Armonk, NY: M.E. Sharpe, 1996.

Schultz, Jeffrey D., Andrew L. Aoki, Kerry L. Haynie, and Anne M. McCulloch. *Encyclopedia of Minorities in American Politics*. Phoenix, AZ: Oryx Press, 2000.

Unger, Irwin, and Debi Unger, eds. *The Times Were a Changin': The Sixties Reader*. New York: Three Rivers Press, 1998.

Wilson, William Julius. *When Work Disappears: The World of the New Urban Poor*. New York, Knopf, 1996.

Religion and the Baby Boomers | 7

Frank A. Salamone

n 1966, *Time* ran a cover story that asked the question, "Is God Dead?" Theologians, priests, evangelists, academics, and philosophers offered a range of views on the subject. As a philosophical matter, the question seemed very much open to debate. As a practical matter, however, there was no equivocating: according to a 1965 Harris Poll, 97 percent of Americans "believed in God." More than 120 million Americans—about 60 percent of the population—claimed a religious affiliation, and nearly half attended church services each week (*Time* April 8, 1966).

Indeed, religion remained a vital part of American society after World War II. Although in the midst of the countercultural revolution, urban riots, protests and demonstrations, and assassinations that had gripped the nation for nearly a decade, to many, it seemed that the nation had forsaken its religious beliefs for secular idols and selfish, hedonistic indulgence. In many ways, religion in the United States had been transformed and did not resemble the faiths of the baby boomers' grandparents and great-grandparents. Before World War II, religion in the United States typically was understood to mean the mainline Protestant denominations. After the war, church membership swelled, as did tithing and the establishment of new churches. A good many of these churches were located in the suburbs, further contributing to the homogeneity of suburban life and culture.

At the same time, however, there appeared challenges to the dominant narrative of American social and cultural life. The civil rights and women's liberation movements, the Cold War and anti-Communist crusade, the so-called sexual revolution, and the emergence of the counterculture all were challenges, in one way or another, to the practice of traditional, institutionalized religion. The moral voice of the civil rights movement was grounded in Protestant Christianity, yet the rightful demands of black Americans, which many mainline churches had long ignored, was unsettling. "Godless"

Communism seemed to pose both an internal and external threat to American values. The counterculture offered alternate paths in the search for spiritual comfort, such as yoga, transcendentalism, and eastern philosophies such as Hinduism and Buddhism. The free love associated with the sexual revolution was evidence for many Americans that the nation had lost its moral compass.

Appearances, however, were deceiving. As recent studies have shown, a majority of the baby boomers shared the values, including religious values, of their parents. And what would become a dominant political and social power by the 1980s and 1990s—the New Right—owed much of its growth and success to a profession of religious faith and values. What suffered in the 1960s was not religion or spiritual enlightenment but

Maharishi Mahesh Yogi, who introduced the West to transcendental meditation, gives a lecture to students at the Harvard Law School forum in Cambridge, Massachusetts, in 1968. (AP/Wide World Photos)

organized religion. One catch phrase of the 1960s was "the Establishment," and activists of every stripe were intent on challenging its authority; this included the authority of the established, mainline churches and denominations (Klatch 1999).

A Generation of Seekers

The baby boomers witnessed not only a great growth in the American population but also a shift in values—religious values in particular—within that generation. Religion changed significantly during the Baby Boom era, but it was surprisingly constant as well. Numerous scholarly debates have ensued over the ways in which the religious practices of the baby boomers differed from the practices of earlier Americans.

In a general sense, the baby boomers formed what some scholars call a "quest culture," or what Wade Clark Roof calls a "generation of seekers" (Roof 1993, 1). Many of them were dissatisfied with the values and meanings of the old culture and sought new ways of finding meaning and understanding in their world. The old spiritual authorities of Christianity or Judaism appeared to be insufficient for their means. Moreover, baby boomers seem to have drawn a clear distinction between religion and spirituality. They tended to view religion as a set of rules and practices, whereas spirituality was more of a feeling, an emotional relationship to an other, often greater, being. Roof also notes that for the baby boomers the old barriers of religion tended to blur. People were free to mix and match from a number of religions, an à la carte approach to spirituality. In the postmodern world, no one person or idea has a given monopoly on truth or religion. Things are deregulated and people can "shop" in whatever religious market they wish.

The concept of reflexivity is also an important one for the baby boomers. People look at the way in which religious and spiritual ideas fit their self-identity. Thus, Buddhist, Hindu, American Indian, African, and other views of spirituality can be brought to bear on personal needs, ideas, and values. Roof mentions that these attitudes are aided because symbols have been separated from their referents. Thus, the baby boomers are free to combine disparate symbols in unaccustomed combinations. As one boomer has written:

> Sometimes I stand in front of my little altar at home and have to shake my head in astonishment. How could a nice Jewish boy from Nebraska grow up to have an altar filled with these "graven" images? There's no golden calf on my altar, but there is a statue of the seated, meditating Buddha from India; a wooden head of the Chinese laughing Buddha; a picture of the Hindu goddess Kali; a wooden statue of the Native trickster coyote; a Thai potency amulet; and various nature fetishes. Also, on my computer is a statue of Ganesha, the Hindu elephant deity who brings good fortune.
>
> Other images and pictures get shuffled onto my altar and desk from time to time, and I admit that sometimes I get confused. For instance, Hinduism,

one of the sources of my mythological melting pot, has designated different gods and goddesses to deal with different human dilemmas. So what if I call on a deity who doesn't work on the particular problem I'm having that day? This confusion would not arise with Jehovah, who is an all-purpose God. (Nisker 2003, 1)

Certainly, something new was going on. True, something new is always going on in American religion. It is also true that something old is always continuing as well. American religious life is immensely complex and not open to simple analyses. Peter Berger states that, in meeting the challenges of the modern era, religion in America can be expressed in three ways: "by reaffirming the authority of the tradition in defiance of surrounding challenges; by secularizing the tradition; or by extracting the experiences embodied in the tradition" (Berger 1990, 22). Baby boomers, individually or in groups, have followed each of these paths of expression.

Thus, in the current spiritual scene there are sweat lodges, Promise Keepers (a evangelical Christian ministry dedicated to making men "godly influences"), and various other forms of what Berger labels Traditionalism I. There also exists Opus Dei and other forms of ultra-right-wing conservative back-to-the-basics movements. There are expressions of secular religion, such as Jesus seminar, Unitarianism, and other secularized religions. There are many fusion faiths in which pieces of various religions are put together in interesting mosaics. And, of course, there is the turning to the wisdom of the Eastern Hemisphere religions. Buddhism, Hinduism, and their variations provide answers for many baby boomers.

Importantly, the unusual, strange, and bizarre often capture the headlines, while the more traditional may not. That is true even when the less glamorous may be what is really happening. The United States, for example, still has the highest church attendance in the industrial and postindustrial world. Americans, including the baby boomers, are highly involved in religion by all usual indicators. Belief in God remains high. Religion is still very much a public thing. The fascination with new religious movements is an old strand in the American national character. Roof argues that, while American religion is typically kaleidoscopic in change, four new trends are shaping religion today: the new pluralism, the new voluntarism, the new organizational structures, and the new spirituality.

Berger uses new pluralism to refer to the increasing religious diversity of American religions. It is no longer a country of mainly Protestants, Catholics, and Jews. While other religions have been around for some time, it is only post-1960 that these other religions have really been part of America's religious landscape. Religion and culture were partners in the Eisenhower fifties. Ethnicity was not yet a means of affirming identity but religion was. Moreover, the Protestant majority has declined since mid-century, from 67 percent to 56 percent. At the same time Catholicism has grown, in part because it is a different type of Catholicism, the consequence of the Second Ecumenical Council of the Vatican, or Vatican II, which permitted mass to be sung in the vernacular, among other changes. Catholics now make up about 30 percent of the population, especially with the Hispanic population growing so quickly. The Jewish population remains at 2 to 3 percent, owing to high intermarriage and low birth rates (Roof and McKinley 1987, 15).

Growth is great among what is termed "other" faiths and "no faith" in the various polls. Since the vast influx of new immigrants beginning in the 1960s and the fascination of many of the baby boomers with Eastern religions, 8 percent of Americans say they belong to a religion other than Protestant, Catholic, or Jewish. New religions continue to spring up, or old ones find new roots in the United States. Islam is one such religion and may surpass Judaism in total U.S. membership in the early twenty-first century.

About 8 percent of Americans say they have no religious affiliation, which is eight times higher than in 1950. Add all the people with no religious affiliation to those who do not actively participate in religion and about 40 percent of Americans are cut off from organized religion. Culture and religion are not the partners they were in the 1950s. This new pluralism of the baby boomers is something different from the old pluralism of the 1950s.

A second cause of new religious change is the new voluntarism. The baby boomers have added a dimension to the individualism so dear to the American population. Choice has expanded greatly. The baby boomers have related voluntarism to what is good for the person. It is more subjective than it used to be. There is a great deal of religious selection, of cafeteria Catholics, for example. This picking is not random but rather fits an individual's moral landscape and values. People believe that they can be good Christians or Jews without attending services. A nurse named Sheila, as Robert Bellah noted in *Habits of the Heart*, declared that "I believe in God. I'm not a religious fanatic. I can't remember the last time I went to church. My faith has carried me a long way. It's Sheilaism. Just my own little voice" (Bellah 1985, 221). This attitude is widespread among baby boomers, and cuts across many sociological dimensions.

New organizational structures have emerged in American religion, not just denominational. Many special purpose groups appeal mainly to others with similar views. There are also the rather well-known religious political groups, televangelists, and other new forms of religious organization. There sometimes appears to be specialized religious groups for every illness, mental state, or way of life.

Finally, there is the new spirituality. This new spirituality takes us to the root causes or underlying forces of these new religious expressions. These forces are embodied in many overt forms: healing rituals, holistic movements, goddess worship, and various self-help programs, such as Alcoholics Anonymous. Even books on myth and fiction on religion come into this perspective. Fascination with science fiction portrayals of aliens and the paranormal have fed into this stream.

Certainly, the baby boomers have been interested in a personal spirituality. There has been an inward turning in spirituality. Religion and spirituality have been tailored to individual needs. There is a return here to the sophists who argued that man is the measure of all things. There is an individual, not institutional, permission to form one's own religion. The New Age is the logical result of the movement. Individual and divinity are fused into a single being. Spirituality, not religion, is on the rise among the baby boomers.

For baby boomers, spirituality takes on abstract concepts such as peace, unity, harmony, and inner well-being. Many best sellers deal with spiritual topics. Many books extol paths to harmony and peace. This is in keeping with the baby boomers' desire to explore faith and move forward along the journey or quest of discovery. This also is in keeping with the overall globalization of society and culture. Information on the various spiritual paths of the world and non-Western religions is at an all-time high. The Internet makes it easy to obtain information on these topics, and everyone can be an expert, at least on the surface.

Indeed, religion has taken on a self-help aspect. People seek spiritual cures in religion. If one does not work, then they go quickly to another. A feeling pervades that one should try on religions as one does shoes. If it pinches or is hard to break in, then move on. Religion has become attuned to a person's inner life, a touchy-feely sort of thing. Religion is also more than just a quest for inner meaning, a holistic experience, and a search for answers to difficult questions.

Religion as Cultural Battleground

Religion was just one of the many fronts on what became known as the "culture wars"—political conflict based primarily on opposing cultural views and values—that were waged during the Baby Boom era, battles that continue today and show little sign of ending. These conflicts typically ensued over issues such as abortion, privacy, homosexuality, marriage and the family, and the separation of church and state. These issues are sometimes referred to as "wedge" issues, because typically two clear, opposing views are held on each side of the matter. These concerns tend to be issues related to individual choice or morality and expressed in diametrically opposed terms and narratives. Abortion, for example, is a moral issue for some, whereas for others it is a right protected by the Constitution.

The origins of this particular cultural war can be found in the 1960s. The aforementioned cultural changes and social activism, an increasingly tense Cold War relationship between the United States and the Soviet Union, the threat of nuclear annihilation, and a shifting economic structure provide the context for understanding these roots.

The omnipresent threat of nuclear annihilation provided an apocalyptic context to the struggle. Many Americans equated their Christian religious beliefs and values with American values. "Atheistic" or "Godless" Communism was immoral, incompatible with American and Christian values, and thus posed a threat to the United States.

Beginning in the 1950s and continuing into the Reagan administration, an anti-Communist crusade found fertile ground in the United States. The very name of the Christian Anti-Communism Crusade (CACC), founded in 1953 and that still exists today, left no doubt about how it perceived the nature of the Communist threat.

The height of the anti-Communist crusade was in the 1950s, although it remained strong throughout the 1960s. Other issues involving religion, however, stirred great public interest. The most notable of these was the 1962 Supreme Court decision *Engel v. Vitale* prohibiting mandatory prayer and Bible reading in public schools. One woman asserted that U.S. "laws and standards" were "built on faith in God and in the church of our choice" (*Engels v. Vitale* 1962). Religion could be a powerful force for social change, as in the case of the civil rights movement, or it could be an irresistible defender of the status quo, such as the opponents of civil rights movement who couched their opposition in appeals to Christianity and the Bible. The school prayer decision became one of the rallying points for a resurgent Christian Right (as quoted in Monhollon 2002, 36).

The role that religion played in the social movements of the 1960s (other than the civil rights movement) is often played down. Religion, in particular, Christianity, played a significant role in the youth activism of the 1960s. The impersonal, alienating mass society of Cold War America led many young Americans to Christianity as a means to find fulfillment and contentment. It also provided them with a language (the teachings of Christianity) and a space (churches and ministries) from which they could try to resolve such problems as racial inequality, poverty, sexism, and, later in the decade, war (Rossinow 1998).

By the early 1970s, the religious Right found new targets to attack, most notably the feminist movement and the gay liberation movement. Many opponents of the Equal Rights Amendment (ERA), which Congress had approved in 1970 and sent to the states for ratification, for example, did so because they believed the amendment went against their religious beliefs. Some opponents of the measure argued that Christianity decreed separate roles for men and women, one that the ERA would blur, if not erase. Many opponents believed that the amendment would "legalize" homosexual relationships. One opponent, in a letter to her senator, claimed the ERA "would do away with the sacredness of womanhood, motherhood, and the home; God has never let a nation with such a demoralized society go unpunished" (as quoted in Erickson 1996, 57). Although many of those opposed to the ERA were fundamentalist Christians, not all were. The Christian Right found allies in conservatives who believed the feminist movement was threatening the moral fabric of American society. What emerged by the late 1970s was a political coalition between the Christian Right and mainstream conservatives that found a voice as the pro-family movement (Erickson 1996, 57).

Indeed, the political tenor was coming more from the right, with strong religious overtones. The sole Democrat elected president between 1968 and 1992, Jimmy Carter, openly declared in the aftermath of Watergate and the turmoil of the 1960s that he was a born-again Christian, something he shared with some 50 million other Americans in 1976. The 1970s also saw the marriage of religion and politics. Jerry Falwell, one of several evangelical ministers to broadcast their ministry on television, founded the Moral Majority. Falwell rejected what he saw as the permissiveness rampant in American society and culture, the result, he believed, of misguided Supreme Court decisions

Evangelist Jerry Falwell, founder of the Moral Majority, greets Republican presidential candidate Ronald Reagan as he arrives to address the National Religious Broadcasters in Lynchburg, Virginia, on October 3, 1980. (Bettmann/Corbis)

(*Engel v. Vitale* and *Roe v. Wade*, for example) and the 1960s counterculture. The Moral Majority attacked feminism, gay rights, abortion rights, and sexual freedom, claiming they all undermined the traditional family. Unlike previous conservative coalitions, the new conservatism coalesced around social and cultural, rather than economic, interests. The culture wars escalated in the 1980s, and baby boomers were at the center of the culture wars, as they manned the front lines on both sides of these issues.

Conclusion

The baby boomers were born in interesting times. This postwar generation was born into a prosperous but dangerous period of history. The United States never has been so rich, and most likely never will be again. Certainly, the spread of prosperity to such a large percentage of the population may never be seen again. Average workers owned homes, cars, sent their kids to college, enjoyed vacations, flew on planes, and believed that things would always get better. All that occurred under the shadow of the threat of nuclear destruction.

The Cold War dominated the thoughts of many of the baby boomers. Students participated in the infamous school drills, hiding under desks or in halls. Dirty little wars, named and unnamed, summed up in the Vietnam disaster. There were assassinations of those working for solutions. Organized religion was implicated in many of the disasters of the period.

Duane "Rick" Warren

The noted evangelical minister and author Richard Duane "Rick" Warren was born on January 28, 1954, the son of a Baptist minister and a high school librarian. Warren founded and is the senior pastor of the Saddleback Church in Lake Forest, California. His many books include the best-selling *The Purpose Driven Life*.

Warren occupies a unique place among evangelical ministers in the United States. Like many of his peers, Warren's theology is conservative, and his views on issues such as abortion and same-sex marriage are traditional.

Pastor Rick Warren, author or *The Purpose Driven Life* signs his book *The Purpose of Christmas* at Barnes & Noble bookstore in 2008 in New York. (AP/Wide World Photos)

Unlike many of his contemporaries, however, Warren has chastised other evangelicals for neglecting the environment and failing to address the causes of poverty.

After receiving his doctorate of ministry in 1979 from the Fuller Theological Seminary in Pasadena, Warren began holding services at Saddleback Church, which he founded. The church grew rapidly and eventually hosted some 10,000 worshippers each week. A permanent building for the church, which accommodated 3,500 guests, was erected in 1995. As of 2009, Saddleback is one of the largest megachurches in the United States.

As the size of his church grew, which coincided with the conservative and evangelical revival of the 1980s and 1990s, so too did Warren's influence. *Time, Newsweek,* and *U.S. News and World Report* have recognized him as a leader of significance. In 2008, during the presidential campaign, Warren's church hosted a joint appearance by presidential nominees John McCain and Barack Obama. Obama later invited Warren to give the invocation at his inauguration, which drew criticism from numerous groups on the left.

Warren appears to be a new breed of evangelicals, concerned less with divisive social issues, such as abortion and homosexuality, as with larger issues, such as poverty, global warming, and disease. Whether Warren will be able to fashion a new political coalition among Christian evangelicals, however, remains to be seen.

It is not surprising that many of the baby boomers turned to a quest for personalized religion and spirituality. The cafeteria Jews, Catholics, and Protestants still with us sprang from a legitimate quest for meaning, a meaning that could explain the inexplicable actions of leaders, political and religious. The trying out of new faiths may have had roots in fad following and curiosity, but an element of true search for inner peace and explanation always has been present. The postmodern search for meaning has its counterpart in religious quest.

The baby boomers have not been content as a group to accept pat explanations from "the Establishment." Although many of the 1960s rebels no longer man the barricades, they still are seeking a revolution, a revolution in meaning. They are attempting to find a key to put things together. Whether the truth is "out there" or "in here," the search for truth and meaning continues. Received reality and truth no longer suffice. No matter that some of the quests appear bizarre; there is glory and grandeur in the baby boomers' quest, just as there was in that of Don Quixote. The quest is where the meaning is to be found, not in stopping a chimerical arrival.

Bibliography

Bellah, Robert N., Richard Madsen, William M. Sullivan, Ann Swidler, and Steven M. Tipton. *Habits of the Heart. Individualism and Commitment in American Life*. Berkeley: University of California Press, 1985.

Berger, Peter L. *The Sacred Canopy: Elements of a Sociological Theory of Religion*. 1967. New York: Anchor Books, 1990.

Coleman, John Aloysius. "Spiritual Marketplace: Baby Boomers and the Remaking of American Religion (review)" *Spiritus: A Journal of Christian Spirituality* 1, no. 1 (Spring 2001): 109–112.

Erickson, Sonja L. "In Defense of the Family: The Fight to Rescind the ERA in Kansas, 1974–1979," Master's thesis, University of Kansas, 1996.

Herberg, Will. *Protestant-Catholic-Jew: An Essay in American Religious Sociology*. Garden City, NY: Anchor Books, 1960.

Hoge, Dean R., Benton Johnson, and Donald A. Luidens. *Vanishing Boundaries: The Religion of Mainline Protestant Baby Boomers*. Louisville, KY: Westminster/John Knox Press, 1994.

"Is God Dead?" *Time*, April 8, 1966.

Klatch, Rebecca. *A Generation Divided: The New Left, The New Right, and the 1960s*. Berkeley: University of California Press, 1999.

Melton, J. Gordon. *The Encyclopedia of American Religions*. 3rd edition. Detroit: Gale Research, 1989.

Merriman, Scott A., ed. *Religion and the Law in America: An Encyclopedia of Personal Belief and Public Policy*. Santa Barbara, CA: ABC-Clio, 2007.

Monhollon, Rusty L. *"This Is America?" The Sixties in Lawrence, Kansas*. New York: Palgrave, 2002.

Nisker, Wes. *The Big Bang, the Buddha, and the Baby Boom: The Spiritual Experiments of My Generation*. San Francisco: Harper San Francisco, 2003.

Roof, Wade Clark. *A Generation of Seekers: The Spiritual Journeys of the Baby Boom Generation*. San Francisco: Harper San Francisco, 1993.

Roof, Wade Clark. *Spiritual Marketplace: Baby Boomers and the Remaking of American Religion.* Princeton, NJ: Princeton University Press, 1999.

Roof, Wade Clark, and William McKinney. *American Mainline Religion. Its Changing Shape and Future.* New Brunswick: Rutgers University Press, 1987.

Rossinow, Douglas C. *The Politics of Authenticity: Liberalism, Christianity, and the New Left in America.* New York: Columbia University Press, 1998.

Welch, William M., and Emily Bazar. "N.J. Woman Enjoys Celebrity of Being 1st Baby Boomer." *USA Today*, December 30, 2005, 1.

Wertheimer, Jack. *A People Divided. Judaism in Contemporary America.* New York: Basic Books, 1993.

Wuthnow, Robert. *The Restructuring of American Religion. Society and Faith Since World War II.* Princeton, NJ: Princeton University Press, 1988.

The Counterculture | 8

Scott MacFarlane

Today, even the most conservative Joe can have a "bummer" day. Grown heterosexual men will hug other men. Organic foods hold down space in most every grocery store. Classic rock radio still blasts vibrant, loud music from the late 1960s and early 1970s. College students major in women's studies, environmental studies, or a variety of ethnic studies curriculums. Long hair on men is not unusual, but no more is it an indication of political persuasion. Diversity and equal opportunity are givens in the workplace and at school. Fierce debate still rages over how and when America should or should not utilize its military might. The personal computer has ushered in an information age that transformed the way we do business, communicate, educate one another, and are entertained. Industry would not dare pollute, extract resources, or develop land in the ways they did forty years ago. Within the United States and the other advanced Western societies, the counterculture of the 1960s and 1970s played a significant role in all these progressions.

To envision the breadth and magnitude of the counterculture of baby boomers that came to be at the epicenter of American social debate, it helps to imagine a permeable membrane. In the late 1960s and early 1970s, it was as though such a membrane separated the mainstream culture, then called "the Establishment," from the counterculture, often referred to as "the Movement." Strictly speaking, "the Movement" of the counterculture was a largely leaderless array of many movements—spiritual, political, lifestyle, or artistic—that challenged "the system" of "the man," also known as "the Establishment." Think of an average young man or woman working a "straight" job all week, then on the weekend dressing in paisley and bellbottoms and going to a rock festival where the new drug of choice was marijuana. Such was the permeability of this membrane separating the counterculture from the mainstream of the time. Other young people were testing the alternative side of Western culture by experimenting with

Eastern spirituality in ways that their Protestant or Catholic parents never would have considered. A young American man, between the age of eighteen and twenty-four with a low Selective Service lottery number, had to decide whether to join the military or to go "underground" and dodge the draft. Among many young people, especially by 1967 and 1968, the Vietnam War had grown increasingly unpopular.

In other words, the manner and ways in which an individual could engage the counterculture had a highly voluntary component. There were hardcore hippies and "plastic" weekend hippies. Others within the same age-group of the older baby boomers were straight, as in straitlaced. In other words, by no means were all young people in the counterculture of the late 1960s and early 1970s challenging the values, mores, materialism, and perceived hypocrisy of the mainstream, but a critical mass of youth with alternative perspectives and behaviors coalesced to fuel significant social change in ways that altered Western society from that point forward. Those at the forefront of this upsurge were highly vociferous and visible. They were no longer sharing the same ideas about freedom, liberty, and justice as the older generation or their more traditional peers.

New York Times movie critic Karen Durbin stated in a 2001 movie review that:

A female demonstrator offers a flower to military police on guard at the Pentagon in Washington, D.C., during an anti-Vietnam demonstration on October 21, 1967. (National Archives and Records Administration)

the cultural and political upheavals of the 1960s and '70s were as traumatic and transforming in their own way as the Civil War had been a century before. But it's as if we don't want to think about that time, much less risk revisiting its great and terrible vitality. (Durbin 2001, 9)

The Cold War had ushered in a frightening new age in which nuclear annihilation always loomed. The Vietnam War fueled much of the anger that divided the United States. By the late 1960s, the media had coined the terms "hawks" and "doves" to label the opposing ranks of this political divide. Most "hawks" embraced a Cold War posture that Communism had to be contained, and that to lose in Vietnam meant risking a "domino effect" whereby all the nations of Asia would fall to this godless ideology. Conversely, antiwar doves at their most theatrical extreme were typified by the individuals seen in photographs of *Life Magazine* or *The Saturday Evening Post* placing the stems of flowers in the barrels of rifles held by National Guardsmen. This was an example of the play-as-power expressiveness that gained media attention and sustained countercultural opposition to perceived military excess.

The older generation was truly baffled by this upsurge of youthful revolt and what the media called the "generation gap" between them. For example, one morning in 1969, hundreds of war protesters were camped out on the west lawn of the White House. President Richard M. Nixon, a hawkish commander-in-chief that many felt was taking too long to withdraw American forces from Vietnam, decided to visit these protesters. Awakened at dawn in sleeping bags to see the face of their reviled president staring down at them, the discussion of their differences did not turn violent, but neither did Nixon invite them inside for breakfast. In today's era of security precautions, protesters are not only not allowed so close to the White House—especially to sleep—but no American president would allow himself to be exposed to the opposition in this way.

The counterculture of the 1960s erupted in no small part because of this reaction to Vietnam, but another key ingredient played a catalyzing role as well. In the late 1950s and early 1960s, the U.S. Central Intelligence Agency (CIA) conducted a series of secretive tests on the psychological effect of lysergic acid diethylamide (LSD), the powerful hallucinogenic drug that was first synthesized in 1948 by Sandoz Laboratories in Switzerland. Called the MK-ULTRA program, the CIA was interested in the crowd-controlling impact of this substance derived from a fungus that grows on the grain of rye. Exposed to LSD during these tests were such individuals as Ken Kesey and Tom Robbins, who would become notable authors; Steve Allen, the founder of the Tonight Show; and Timothy Leary and Richard Alpert, two tenured professors from Harvard University.

Kesey, who was a part of the MK-ULTRA testing near Stanford University, admits to "liberating" a large vial of the drug from the desk of the administering psychiatrist, an amount that the author and his friends took for the first years of the 1960s. While high on peyote, Kesey had a vision of Chief Broom, the mental patient who narrates *One Flew Over the Cuckoo's Nest* (1962). In the novel, the Chief often succumbs to foggy and

Ed McClanahan

In one short work of creative nonfiction called "Another Great Moment in Sports," Ed McClanahan describes taking part in a 1968 antiwar protest on the Stanford University campus: "I know that if I have to mutter one more chorus of 'We Shall Overcome,' I'll be in danger of doing something awful that will bring down contumely and disapprobation upon the entire worldwide peace movement. Sincerity is a virtue, but these folks have OD'ed on it." McClanahan was among the lesser-known authors born in the 1920s and 1930s who contributed to our understanding and appreciation of the tumultuous counterculture of the late 1960s and 1970s. He did not enjoy the name recognition as Ken Kesey, Tom Wolfe, Joan Didion, Norman Mailer, Kurt Vonnegut, Richard Brautigan, Hunter S. Thompson, or Tom Robbins, but his literary humor was greatly appreciated by those who read him.

Born in Kentucky on October 4, 1932, McClanahan lived in California's Bay Area and taught at Stanford University during the 1960s. McClanahan was one of Kesey's band of original Merry Pranksters that gained iconic stature as proto-hippies in Tom Wolfe's breakout work of New Journalism called *The Electric Kool-Aid Acid Test* (1968). It was in the Prankster circle that he first met members of the Grateful Dead in 1965. In the March 1972 edition of *Playboy*, the author published a lengthy, award-winning article, "Grateful Dead I Have Known." The piece serves as a remarkable artifact of this era

surrealistic visions brought on by electroshock therapy as he relates this story of authoritarian excesses at the Oregon State Mental Hospital. This novel foreshadowed the intense mood of antiauthoritarianism that would manifest itself in Western society just a handful of years later. Kesey and his friends, known as the Merry Pranksters, were at the cutting-edge of shaping this new countercultural mood in 1964 when, fueled by their stash of LSD, they drove cross-country in a converted, wildly painted school bus to attend the New York World's Fair and the publisher's party for Kesey's second novel, *Sometimes a Great Notion* (1964). In 1968, author Tom Wolfe made Kesey and the Pranksters the subject of his creative nonfiction work, *The Electric Kool-Aid Acid Test*.

It has also been documented that the Beatles used the wildly painted bus of Kesey and the Pranksters as the inspiration for their 1968 movie and album, *The Magical Mystery Tour*. The influence of LSD on the Beatle's music became evident as the 1960s progressed, most notably with the album *Sgt. Pepper's Lonely Hearts Club Band*. The British band was the most influential rock group of the period, and the Beatles' experimentations in fashion, spiritual and political expression, film and visual art, and of course amplified music had a profound effect on the countercultural rebelliousness of the burgeoning youth movement.

By 1965–1966, underground chemists were making millions of hits of LSD for sale on the streets. In California, the drug was legal until October 6, 1966. The San Francisco neighborhood of Haight-Ashbury gained disproportionate notoriety as the home of "psychedelia" and, in 1967, its streets were designated as the focal point for "The Summer of Love."

for the manner in which it combined the two most notable, and seemingly contradictory, literary developments of his time: fragmented, postmodern, juxtapositional prose and the highly subjective, immersive style of the New Journalism (now called Narrative Journalism). The full version of this article was published in his collection *My Vita, If You Will*. "Grateful Dead I Have Known" ranged from an exegesis of "New Speedway Boogie," the band's statement song about the horrific stabbing death of an audience member at the 1969 Altamont Rock Festival to the misadventures of Wheat Germ, a hitchhiker and purple pill pusher whom the author brings, inadvertently, to a boisterous softball game being played near

San Francisco between members of the Jefferson Airplane and the Grateful Dead.

McClanahan excelled at creative nonfiction where he served, in grand comic fashion, as the viewpoint character, and, more often than not, the butt of his own foibles. In doing so, he explores, through comic nuance, the thorniest issues surrounding the tumultuous counterculture. By the late 1970s, the author had returned to Kentucky where he would publish two critically acclaimed works of fiction, a novel *The Natural Man* and *Congress of Wonders*, a collection of three novellas. All of these stories were set in small-town Kentucky, which was as much a focus of McClanahan's work as his countercultural subject matter.

Consequently, thousands of young people from around the nation hitchhiked to San Francisco to be a part of this low-rent, bohemian neighborhood's outrageous new "scene." The neighborhood was largely incapable of accommodating an influx of thousands of street kids. The Diggers, an anarchistic group of theatrical street performers, pilfered food from wholesalers to feed hundreds of hungry mouths. Rock groups such as the Grateful Dead, Jefferson Airplane, and the Quicksilver Messenger Service played some of their first concerts in the adjoining Golden Gate Park. By 1967, the San Francisco police, who largely had ignored the bohemian enclave in the years before, began to make wholesale busts of those taking part in the drug scene of the Haight. Likewise, the national media had descended on the neighborhood to describe the scene for a curious mainstream public. For example, *Life Magazine*, the major weekly publication of the time, did more than one cover story feature. Joan Didion, wrote an unsettling and unflattering piece for *The Saturday Evening Post* in September 1967 called "Slouching Toward Bethlehem." This cover of the *Post* said "The Hippie Cult: Who They Are, and What They Want." In other words, it was not until late 1966 and 1967 that the term "hippie" came into common usage. "Hippie" originated as a name given by older beatniks to this influx of young hipsters, or "hippies." As demonstrated with the feature in the *Post*, when the media settled on this term to label the upsurge of youthful bohemianism, the implication was largely negative. Few of those in the counterculture called themselves "hippies." More commonly, the druggies would call themselves "heads" and the longhairs were "freaks," or as Jimi Hendrix would sing, "wearing their freak flags high." Along with the

Robert Hunter

Far less of a household name than the 1960's songwriting duo of John Lennon and Paul McCartney, and less well known than Bob Dylan as a lyricist, Robert Hunter teamed with Jerry Garcia to write the bulk of the original songs by the Grateful Dead. Not only do Deadheads suggest that Hunter is among the greatest rock lyricists, Dylan asked Hunter to collaborate with him on ten of the songs on his 2009 release *Together Through Life*—which speaks highly of his talents.

Born in California on June 23, 1941, Hunter is especially noted for how well he captures a roguish American spirit. He hardly paints a sappy, romantic portrait of an America that is coming of age—whether writing that "a friend of the devil is a friend of mine," where his character is on the run and leaving behind "a wife in Chino, and one in Cherokee / the first one say she got my child, but it don't look like me" or explaining that Jack Straw from Wichita has "gotta go to Tulsa, first train we can ride / gotta settle one old score, one small point of pride." His songs exhibited a fine range, such as when he evoked the "wearin' thin" edges of

Musician Robert Hunter. (Corbis)

the rock'n'roll touring life, where the band is "truckin' off to Buffalo," and many points in between. Little did the band members know

negative portrayals, the media also romanticized and trivialized these young hippies as "flower children." Such peaceful longhairs were deemed to be part of the "flower power" movement. For these adherents of the counterculture who shared a new peace and love ethos, however, no term came to be more encapsulating than hippie. By 1969, like it or not, the members of the "Woodstock Nation" were considered by most to be "hippies."

The hippie phenomenon did not emerge overnight. The antimaterialistic, bohemian philosophy of the Beat movement of the 1950s had a profound influence on this counterculture that was flourishing by the latter part of the 1960s. Neil Cassady served as the model for Dean Moriarty, the main character in Beat author Jack Kerouac's classic picaresque novel, *On the Road* (1958). Emblematic of the segue between the Beat and hippie eras, Neil also served as the cross-country driver for Ken Kesey and the Merry Pranksters on their cross country trip in 1964. One's involvement in the counterculture or detachment from this scene was summed up by Kesey's euphemistic phrase from the bus trip: "you're either *on the bus* or that those iconic 1970 lyrics—"what a long, strange trip it's been"—would haunt their road life for a quarter century to come.

Robert Hunter possessed the sensibility of a well-read poet. For example, his song "It Must Have Been the Roses" is derived largely from William Faulkner's short story, "A Rose for Emily." While oblique literary and cultural references enrich many of Hunter's song lyrics, he did not write message music, as was common during the cultural upheavals of the late 1960s when the Grateful Dead formed. Rather, his imagistic lyrics are suggestive and highly ambiguous, allowing the listener to add his or her own narrative interpretation to the songs.

In 1960, Hunter took part in the same psychedelic drug tests as Ken Kesey, which were given at the Menlo Park, California Veteran's Hospital and funded by the CIA. Powerful psychedelics such as LSD and dimethyltryptamine (DMT) had a profound creative impact on the lyricist. On the strength of his words for "China Cat Sunflower" (I rang a silent bell, beneath a shower of pearls) and "The Eleven" (now is the time of returning /

with thought jewels polished and gleaming), he began a three-decade-long songwriting collaboration with Jerry Garcia, whom he had first met in the bluegrass scene around San Francisco in the early 1960s. His lyrics celebrate life at the edges of darkness and light, and though rarely didactic ("don't dominate the rap Jack / if you got nothing new to say"), his adages were often philosophically tantalizing ("once in a while you get shown the light / in the strangest of places if you look at it right") or ("it's just a box of rain / believe it if you need it / or leave it if you dare").

Hunter, although also a musician, seldom performed on stage with the Grateful Dead, but was the only nonplaying member of the band to be included when the group was inducted into the Rock and Roll Hall of Fame in 1994. The lyricism of Hunter's words resonated through the Grateful Dead's repertoire, and arguably, is a key component of why this band attracted a strong fan base for decades, outlasting virtually all the other bands that originated in the same psychedelic era.

off the bus." Psychedelia featured its favored drugs of marijuana, LSD, psilocybin, peyote, and mescaline. The era is typified by greatly amplified rock music, wild revelry, brightly colored clothing, and—courtesy of the pill—sex without fear of pregnancy. The counterculture of 1967 to 1972 was arguably the greatest Bacchanalian outburst (so named for the Greco-Roman god of wine and pleasure, Bacchus or Dionysus) ever witnessed in the history of humankind. Haight-Ashbury was the media focal point for this eruption. Psychedelia also flourished in New York City, London, and bohemian pockets of major cities in all the industrial Western nations. This Bacchanalian or Dionysian reaction was a direct outgrowth of Beat sensibilities.

William Everson, a Beat poet, said that "the insistence of the Beat Generation to combine jazz and poetry is quite symptomatic of the Dionysian tendency. Even the Beat novel is an open effort to sustain lyric intensity over the whole course of the work" (Everson 1981, 181). He described the opposition between the Beat/hipsters and "the man" in a way that applied, likewise, to later hippie opposition to "the system," or to "the Establishment."

This Dionysian-Apollonian model (a dichotomous model depicting light versus dark or individualism versus community) presents an archetype for the tension between the counterculture and mainstream culture. It helps explain the explosion of spiritual inquiry in the West that shattered the complacent adherence to traditional Judeo-Christianity. The Beatles, for example, went to India to learn from a guru. Among the more rank-and-file hippies, a peace and love ethos—mostly pacifist—spurred the beginnings of a movement to create an alternative, more collectivist society at the fringes of the mainstream. The communal, back-to-the-land movement at the end of the 1960s, best exemplified this phenomenon. Most of these communes failed from a combination of external and internal pressures—local authorities used zoning and health regulations to shut down the communes; freeloading or other individualistic tendencies of the communards often undermined the efforts of those making the needed sacrifices to sustain group cohesion. Certain communes still exist, and today a cohousing movement is a direct descendent of the communal movement.

In the mid-1960s, California was ironically the most politically liberal as well as the most conservative place in the country, a state that featured one of the most leftist centers of student activism in the United States at the University of California-Berkeley campus, across the bay from San Francisco, and then brought national prominence to the right-wing politics of future President Ronald Reagan, who was then governor. A growing free speech and antiwar movement was gaining momentum as the decade progressed. By 1967, many of these previously clean-cut radicals began to adopt the lifestyles, dress, and behavior of the more Dionysian hippies. Talk of revolution was in the air. The young members of the student New Left viewed this unrest in neo-Marxist terms, as the inherent stirrings of a socialist revolution, while the more Dionysian hippies thought in terms of a consciousness revolution in which the change would be more spiritual and cultural than political.

Abbie Hoffman and Jerry Rubin were affiliated with the New Left and worked creatively and disruptively to insert themselves as "spokesmen" for this burgeoning youth culture of rebellion and protest. The Students for a Democratic Society (SDS) was the most visible organization of the New Left and well in place before the Summer of Love. When the antiwar strife reached its most acrimonious at the beginning of the 1970s (before the Selective Service Draft to supply soldiers for the Vietnam War was suspended in 1972), a splinter group known as "The Weathermen," named after folk/rock singer Bob Dylan's lyric—*"you don't need a weatherman, to know which way the wind blows"*—resorted to violent means to protest the Vietnam War. The group took responsibility for many bombings, including at draft induction centers and the U.S. Capitol.

At the other end of the revolutionary spectrum were Timothy Leary and Richard Alpert, both Harvard psychology professors. In 1963, they were the first tenured academics ever fired by the university as a result of gaining considerable media notoriety extolling the psychic virtues of LSD. Leary's famous mantra of the era was to urge people to "turn on, tune in, and drop out." Alpert distanced himself from Leary's heavy proselytizing of LSD and embraced Eastern spirituality. He became a Hindu-inspired teacher and changed his name to Baba Ram Dass. In his book, *Be Here Now,* Baba Ram Dass warns psychedelic drug users that "once you get the message, hang up the phone." The more spiritually inclined tended to be non-drug-using hippies, but the hippie era was wed to psychedelia.

Interestingly, these two major thrusts of the 1960s counterculture were evident in a panel discussion in 1982 during which Abbie Hoffman and Timothy Leary (both now deceased) participated. Paul Krassner (1992), in his memoir *Confessions of a Raving, Unconfined Nut: Misadventures in the Counter-Culture,* published the exchange:

> HOFFMAN: We saw in the sixties a great imbalance of power, and the only way that you could correct the imbalance was to organize people and fight for power. Power is not a dirty word. The concept of trying to win against social injustice is not a dirty kind of concept. . . .
>
> LEARY: Abbie, you . . . have much more faith in the political system's ability to change things, and I believe with William Burroughs that it's the culture that changes—you change the way men and women relate to each other, you change the way people's consciousness can be moved by themselves, you change their music and their dress, you change the way they relate to the land and to other forms of plants and animals, and you've got yourself a revolution—to use your word, a *fuckin'* revolution—that'll make the politicians and power-mad people . . . it's gonna happen so fast they won't know it's gonna happen.
>
> HOFFMAN: . . . Tim, if you don't regard the four years you spent in prison as a political act, you took one trip too many. . . . [I]t was a political act. So to separate what is cultural from political when we are talking about American society in the fifties and sixties is an absolutely hopeless and ridiculous task. (as quoted in Krassner 1992)

Gurney Norman wrote *Divine Right's Trip,* a novel about a young hippie couple that was first published in the margins of *The Last Whole Earth Catalog,* a highly popular 1971 publication promoting appropriate technology and greater self-reliance for those partaking in the alternative reaches of the counterculture. In a 2001 television interview, the author points out how icons such as Leary and Hoffman have distorted public perception of the counterculture:

> [W]hen the media wants to treat the 1960s, the cultural revolution and the antiwar movements and so forth, it has a list—the media has a list of about 12 iconic figures who did stuff and got themselves registered by the media, in the media. They got in a database of some kind. And so when we think of the '60s, we're always shown pictures of Joan Baez and Abbie Hoffman, and others—you know, familiar people. And yet those guys don't represent the '60s counterculture and social ferment at all. They just are not representative. They only are available to an impatient media that no longer even goes out and tries to report on anything. It all has to, like, stream across the computer now. And those are the images from the '60s that are in the computer. But the '60s were not about that at all. And I could go on. . . . I think of the

1960s as when massive waves of young, earnest people set out to try to find something about themselves and to go join something. And the unknown ones . . . You see them; they're in the background of some . . . of some of the movies. But I'm kind of against icons because I think that the message is . . . stuck. It's not revealing of truth. (KET interview, 2001)

The New Left all but disappeared on the American political landscape as soon as the Selective Service Draft was suspended in 1972. The primary impetus for radicalizing America's youth—the Vietnam War—was no longer a direct threat to draft-age males. On the other hand, one of the more constructive elements of the counterculture began taking form in the environmental movement. Likewise, an underground drug culture persisted (and still does). A hippie sensibility is still readily evident at annual Rainbow Gatherings, or the Burning Man event each summer in Nevada. The Grateful Dead maintains a following of Deadheads even though Jerry Garcia, their lead guitarist and songwriter, died in 1995. The New Age movement and the explosion of organic food consumption, as well as recycling, are examples of cultural "alternatives" that owe their popularity to the 1960s counterculture.

Occurring at the same time as the voluntaristic hippie phenomenon, several liberationist movements surfaced with particular fervor at the end of the 1960s and the beginning of the 1970s. The hippie counterculture was composed of the disaffected, mostly white, children of the mainstream who, as the heirs of the Establishment, were knocking down the walls of the system from the inside. American blacks, on the other hand, were insisting on opportunities for enfranchisement. The civil rights movement had a history rooted in the struggle to abolish policies of racial segregation. Quite separate from psychedelia, and only loosely related to the growing opposition to the Vietnam War, black discontent grew increasingly violent as the 1960s progressed. The summers of the mid-1960s in the inner cities of the United States were beset by numerous ghetto riots in the mostly black neighborhoods of cities such as Los Angeles, Detroit, and Newark.

Black Muslims, such as Malcolm X, actually favored complete separation of the races through a Black Nationalism, while southern black Christian leadership, best exemplified by the Rev. Martin Luther King, favored equality of opportunity within the system. When both of these black leaders were assassinated, it fueled considerable racial resentment. More militant black leaders such as Stokely Carmichael were surfacing. In 1966, Carmichael adopted a rallying cry of "Black Power!" which spread widely. At this time, the terms "negro" or "colored," and their association with the segregationist policies of the American South came into disfavor, and, throughout American society, virtually overnight, in 1967, "black" became the acceptable way to refer to a person of African American descent.

The radical Black Panther Party, founded by Huey Newton and Bobbie Seals in Oakland, California, in October 1966, exemplified the kind of racial rage fueling a new Black Power militancy. The Black Panthers were not pacifist like most hippies, but, to achieve justice, initially espoused armed resistance to racial and class oppression. Their party platform, like that of the New Left, which was composed of mostly white, young university students, was socialist or neo-Marxist. The Black Power activists, however, were only loosely aligned with the white Left and the largely leaderless hippie phenomenon, but they all shared a countercultural disaffection directed at the mainstream, white-male-dominated establishment.

Over the course of the 1960s, the U.S. federal government enacted civil rights legislation and affirmative action programs to address issues of fair housing, discrimination, and opportunities in education. At the same time, however, federal authorities also worked covertly to infiltrate and undermine countercultural opposition to mainstream policies, often trammeling on the individual rights to free speech and dissent. Both the New Left and Black Panther organizations all but dissolved in the early 1970s at about the same time that the Selective Service Draft was eliminated.

Following on the heels of Black Power came the Red Power and Brown Power movements of Native American and Chicano activists. In 1975, the American Indian Movement (AIM), became embroiled in an armed showdown against Federal Bureau of Investigation agents in Wounded Knee, South Dakota, at the same site where a century earlier, the U.S. Army had massacred the worshippers of the Ghost Dance, a ritual that participants believed would restore their traditional Native American culture. *La Raza*, which loosely means The Race, was also prominent in the mid-1970s and exemplified Chicano activism to gain opportunities for enfranchisement. These activities and group efforts opposing the injustices of the American establishment of the 1960s and 1970s accounted for the loose amalgamation of opposition making up the many movements of the counterculture that had lost momentum by the late 1970s.

To put this period of social unrest in a global context, the American hippies, the New Left, feminists, and the Black, Brown, and Red Power movements had counterparts around the world. In 1968, the student equivalent of the New Left in France came close to toppling the capitalist government. In the Prague Spring of 1968, students and activists were fighting a different kind of establishment. As part of the Warsaw Pact following World War II, Czechoslovakia wanted more liberties from their totalitarian overlords in the Soviet Union. After the students briefly liberated the capital city, Soviet troops quickly quelled the unrest. In Vietnam, during the Tet Offensive, the tide of this protracted war took a turn against the anti-Communist Americans and their South Vietnamese allies when the strong nationalist surge of Ho Chi Minh's North Vietnamese forces and his Viet Cong allies in the south nearly toppled the South Vietnamese–held capital of Saigon. A similar wave of nationalism caused the formation of many sovereign nations in the wake of European colonialism, which peaked in 1968. Such liberationist sentiment had a profound influence on the racial unrest within the United States counterculture as well.

By 1970, social unrest extended to a burgeoning women's liberation movement whereby gender discrimination was challenged on a number of fronts, especially lifestyle and economic issues. Interestingly, women involved with the New Left were frequently strong activists within what has been called the second wave of feminism in the United States—the first wave being the suffragette movement of the early twentieth century leading, most notably, to women earning the right to vote. These women from the New Left were incensed about the treatment of women within their own movement and sought civil rights for women on a host of social fronts, including demands for equal access and treatment within the workplace. Feminism of the early 1970s also confronted sexism in the family, within romantic relationships, and interpersonally. Access to birth control methods and a woman's right to choose with regards to abortion were central to the woman's liberation movement, as were and are issues of domestic violence and sexual assault. Some lesbian feminists advocated the complete separation of women from the male-dominated society.

Feminism and environmentalism were the two major movements to surface with vigor in the 1970s. Both emerged in the wake of the 1960s counterculture, and, as such, were significant initiatives of the Baby Boom generation. The environmental movement heightened the sensitivity of the government and private sector to the impact of human activity on the world. Pollution control measures and land use practices underwent significant change as a result of growing ecological awareness and environmental concerns. This concern over the ways in which humans affect the global ecosystem continue today and came out of the countercultural opposition to establishment attitudes toward progress. The hippie counterculture, as part of the spiritual questioning of the time, was the last collective voice to widely question materialism and corporate-driven consumerism.

Reaction to the Vietnam War fueled much of the cohesion of the counterculture. Whether rooted in rock and folk music, spiritual paths, political radicalism, or back-to-the-land retreats, the cohesion and unifying idealism found in the largely leaderless counterculture of the late 1960s began to splinter in the early 1970s. In 1973, the Paris Peace Accords between the United States, the North Vietnamese, and the Vietcong seemed to promise an end to American involvement in this war. Many progressive aspects of the phenomenon, including long hair, vibrant rock and folk music, organic foods, recycling awareness, or environmental reforms, were being absorbed within the mainstream through revised government policy and business practices. An underground drug culture that mushroomed during the counterculture era persisted despite increasingly strict antidrug legislation and policies of incarceration or stiff fines. As an indicator of illicit drug consumption, in 2006, marijuana was the number-one cash crop in the State of California and number two in the State of Washington, behind only apples. Methamphetamine manufacturing and use are widely acknowledged by law enforcement officials to be epidemic, especially in rural areas.

In music, the Beatles exemplified an accessible, broadly appealing rock sound that appealed to most of the older baby boomers during the last half of the 1960s. By the early 1970s, this unifying music began to diversify into a wider spectrum of sounds with appeal to diverging audiences. This was an era in which the demographic swell of baby boomers created a large base of consumers. Many of these artists promulgated messages of separateness and rebellion that reinforced a sense of counterculture. This generational separateness of identity, a youthful idealism, and a distinct mode of communication sustained the perceived gap between the younger and older generations. The failing war effort, the psychedelics, the we-can-change-the-world idealism peaked during the period of 1967–1972. After this, the Vietnam War began to slowly wind down, and drug use patterns shifted noticeably away from strong psychedelics toward cocaine and speed. The countercultural idealism proved not to be sustainable. Even song lyrics became more banal as the 1970s progressed.

Following the folk music revival of the early and mid-1960s that spawned Bob Dylan and Joan Baez and honored lyrics filled with socially relevant messages, the end of the 1960s decade ushered in the glory days of the musician/songwriter. Folk and rock stars such as Joni Mitchell, James Taylor, Carol King, Cat Stevens, Donovan, and Loggins and Messina emerged. Conversely, the hard rock of Jimi Hendrix, Iron Butterfly, Ten Years Alter, Humble Pie, The Allman Brothers, and Santana grew progressively harder, eventually leading to the great popularity of such groups as Led Zeppelin and the heavy metal genre of rock featuring Metallica and Van Halen. Bridging the gap between the socially conscientious folk and wildly Dionysian rock were groups such as Crosby, Stills, Nash and Young and The Grateful Dead who managed a mix between the soft and the hard. Music, with its amplification and lyrical mantras, was, without rival, the ascendant communication medium of the countercultural era.

The tightest link between black and white American youth of the era stemmed, likewise, from an increasingly shared musical tradition. The euphemistically named British Invasion of such bands as the Beatles, the Rolling Stones, The Who, The Kinks, Cream, Traffic, and Pink Floyd, among others actually was composed of white English youth appropriating black American rhythm and blues and traditional blues music with its rock-and-roll backbeat. Repackaged, this sound was then delivered back to white Americans for popular consumption. Black music, most notably that of Detroit's Motown Records, also gained great crossover appeal when Marvin Gaye, Stevie Wonder, Smokie Robinson, Aretha Franklin, and Diana Ross and The Supremes became major American stars. Other black Americans such as Jimi Hendrix and Sylvester Stewart of Sly and The Family Stone arguably were hippies with their psychedelic fusion of rock, blues, and soul music. The period's music engendered greater tolerance and understanding between blacks and whites in America in the 1960s and 1970s. This influence of the era's music cannot be overemphasized.

By the time the younger baby boomers, those born between 1958 and 1964 were reaching their late teen years, the counterculture as a social force had largely desiccated. By the late 1970s, a splintering was largely complete. Those still-active hippies came to be polar opposites of the cultural spectrum from the angrier punks and skinheads who emerged. Unlike when the Beatles unified the popular music and youth culture of the late 1960s, groups such as the Sex Pistols with Sid Vicious exemplified the splintering of the music scene. At the end of the 1970s, as another example of the musical fragmentation, disco emerged as the popular craze.

Though highly successful, disco proved to be a fairly short-lived phase of popular culture. Even the more defiant subcultural entities, such as the punks, had a decidedly less potent impact on the larger culture than did the youth culture of the late 1960s and early 1970s. This is not to suggest that post-Baby Boom permutations such as Goth, with its black attire, tattoos, and piercings, are not strong statements of youthful defiance of mainstream norms, but that like many attributes of the hippies, these boldly defiant statements, over time, become appropriated by the mainstream and lose their impact as a social statement.

In the early 1980s, as a successor of the Black Power sensibility, the early expressions of hip-hop and rap began to emerge as a medium for social commentary. This musical and lyrical communication resonated within its audience. The potency of this particular voice has not diminished over the quarter century.

By 1980, the we-can-change-the-world idealism of the hippie era persisted in pockets, such as in the burgeoning environmental movement or as New Age manifestations, but it was no longer a force that threatened the status quo of mainstream America. This, however, is not to suggest that bohemianism (artistic movements outside of the mainstream) is dead. In many respects, the neo-bohemian sentiment that followed the counterculture of the baby boomers rejected this sort of idealism, or at least did not believe in its transformative potential. The darker, more jaded mood of such fringe players was again more similar to those in the Beat movement of the late 1950s than it was to the hippies with their spiritual hopefulness and collectivist idealism.

Diversity and equality of opportunity were being institutionalized rapidly through federal legislation mandating Affirmative Action, Equal Opportunity Employment, and Fair Housing. In effect, many of the struggles and disaffections of the counterculture were being addressed and absorbed by the mainstream culture. The most saleable features of the counterculture—its music, fashion, and appropriate technologies—were commoditized. This is not to suggest that issues of unfettered consumerism, unrestrained economic growth devoid of environmental sensitivity, distribution of wealth, opportunities for universal health care, choices of how and where to deploy military force, or latent racism and sexism do not persist as problems. After the mid-1970s, however, the counterculture spawned by the Baby Boom no longer existed as a potent social force, although its impact on many aspects of modern culture was profound.

Bibliography

Braunstein, Peter, and Michael William Doyle. *Imagine Nation: The American Counterculture of the 1960s and '70s.* New York: Routledge, 2002.

Dass, Ram. *Be Here Now.* Lama Foundation. San Cristobal, NM: The Foundation, 1971.

Durbin, Karen. "Together: When Love Thought It Could Defeat War." Movie Review. *New York Times*, August 19, 2001, 9.

Everson, William, "Dionysus and The Beat Generation." In *The Beats: Essays in Criticism*, edited by Lee Bartlett. Jefferson, NC: McFarland, 1981.

Kerouac, Jack. *On the Road*. New York: Viking Press, 1958.

Kesey, Ken. *One Flew Over the Cuckoo's Nest*. New York: Viking Press, 1962.

Kesey, Ken. *Sometimes a Great Notion*. New York: Viking Press, 1964.

KET interview, November 28, 2001. http://www.ket.org/livingbywords/authors/norman_interview2.htm.

Kirk, Andrew G. *Counterculture Green: The Whole Earth Catalog and American Environmentalism*. Lawrence: University Press of Kansas, 2007.

Krassner, Paul. *Confessions of a Raving, Unconfined Nut: Misadventures in the Counter-Culture*. New York: Simon and Schuster, 1992.

MacFarlane, Scott. *The Hippie Narrative: A Literary Perspective on the Counter-culture*. Jefferson, NC: McFarland, 2007.

McConnell, William S., ed. *The Counterculture Movement of the 1960s*. San Diego: Greenhaven Press, 2004.

McWilliams, John C. *The 1960s Cultural Revolution*. Westport, CT: Greenwood Press, 2000.

Miller, Timothy. *The 60s Communes: Hippies and Beyond*. Syracuse, NY: Syracuse University Press, 1999.

Miller, Timothy. *The Hippies and American Values*. Knoxville: University of Tennessee Press, 1991.

Norman, Gurney. *Divine Right's Trip: A Novel of the Counterculture*. Frankfort, KY: Gnomon, 1990.

Swingrover E. A., ed. *The Counterculture Reader*. New York: Pearson/Longman, 2004.

Whitmer, Peter O., with Bruce Van Wyngarden. *Aquarius Revisited: Seven Who Created the Sixties Counterculture that Changed America: William Burroughs, Allen Ginsberg, Ken Kesey, Timothy Leary, Norman Mailer, Tom Robbins, Hunter S. Thompson*. New York: Citadel Press, 2007.

Wolfe, Tom. *The Electric Kool-Aid Acid Test*. New York: Farrar, Straus and Giroux, 1968.

The Organization Man | 9

Matthew Johnson

Like many Organization Men, Dave Harrison's life was shaped by the Great Depression. During his childhood, his family lived on the edge of poverty and relied on each family member to survive. After enlisting in the army during World War II, he looked for the financial security that he thought large corporations provided. Harrison wrote a letter to the General Motors zone manager in New Orleans and was granted an interview. At the end of the interview, a General Motors representative asked a question that defined corporate culture in the postwar years: "Harrison, do you think?" Harrison replied, "Socially, sir" (Leinberger and Tucker 1991, 70). The bureaucratic structure of postwar corporations encouraged a rigid hierarchy that required subordination. The Organization Men of postwar America, many of whom were eager to earn salaries unavailable to their parents and just out of the hierarchical military, did not think twice about the bureaucratic structure.

Harrison justified his decision to work for General Motors in terms of financial security:

> I wanted some place to go to work that would give me security, so that my family would not have to go through what I went through. When I had the opportunity to go to General Motors, I felt that this was the place where, if I worked hard, I could stay the rest of my life. (Leinberger and Tucker 1991, 70)

Dave Harrison did stay at General Motors for the rest of his career. During his time at the company, he displayed many of the qualities that characterized Organization Men: he was loyal, prudent, averse to taking risks, and subordinate. General Motors rewarded him for exhibiting these qualities. The company soon promoted him to promotions manager for the Houston zone. His loyalty also had disadvantages. Harrison was often away from his family Monday through Friday, and the company moved him to a

Looking for financial security offered in the corporate world, organization men often put the needs of the company over their own, spending more time at the office than with family. (Getty Images)

different city three times before his daughter Joann was five. In his first twenty years with the company, General Motors transferred him nine times.

George Lamb, like many members of the Baby Boom, did not envy Organization Men. Lamb never wanted to work for a bureaucratic organization that limited individuality and expected subordination. Growing up modestly in Worcester, Massachusetts, he did not benefit from the postwar economic boom like many other baby boomers. Like Dave Harrison, he wanted the financial security that his parents could not provide for him, but he was not willing to be an Organization Man. Fresh out of Boston University Law School in 1969, he visited U.S. Steel for an interview. On a tour of the company headquarters in Pittsburg, he learned about the separate dining rooms for different management levels. Speaking of the top-level management dining room, a U.S. Steel representative told Lamb if he "worked hard he would eventually be able to eat there" (Lamb 2007). Lamb never set foot in a U.S. Steel lunchroom again. Lamb, frustrated by the hierarchical nature of the corporation, said of his experience at US Steel: "If corporate America . . . was all about where you ate lunch, I was not interested" (Lamb 2007). After briefly working for the New York state legislature, Lamb moved to Springfield, Vermont, where he joined a small firm and later started his own practice. In Springfield, Lamb found the freedom that U.S. Steel would not have been able to provide. He left work early to play golf, spent more time with his children in a day than Dave Harrison did in a week, and never moved his family. Lamb was able to "run my own show my entire career, able to come and go as I pleased. This independence has had great appeal to me. . . . I have never regretted for a moment my decision" (Lamb 2007).

The experiences of Dave Harrison and George Lamb are emblematic of the generation gap between baby boomers and their parents. Coming out the Depression, Organization Men looked for the financial security that corporations offered; and for the Organization Men who were soldiers during World War II, their experience in the highly bureaucratic and hierarchical army made for an easy transition into the corporate world. Baby boomers grew up in a different environment. The postwar economic boom allowed many young boomers to enjoy a world of mass consumption and prosperity. Even George Lamb, who had a modest childhood, did not experience anything close to Depression-era poverty. Because of the postwar economy climate, boomers did not feel the same pressure as their fathers to find jobs that provided financial stability. Just as important, by the 1970s and 1980s, when many boomers looked to start their professional careers, corporations did not offer the same stability that they offered to Organization Men. The oil crises, stagflation, and increased foreign competition forced corporations to cut costs whenever possible. Corporations quickly found that they could save money by reducing the number of managers and doing away with the bureaucratic nature of the organization. The mass firings of the 1970s and 1980s made many boomers question whether they wanted to work for a large business. Aside from the structural changes, the rise of the New Left, feminism, the counterculture, consumer activism, Vietnam, and Watergate all changed the way boomers viewed large organizations. Despite these reservations, many boomers joined Organization Men in corporate offices, but they negotiated their experience much differently. If Organization Men were loyal and put the company's interests before their own, baby boomers were individualistic and self-interested and held the corporation at arm's length.

Amanda Bennett best characterizes the Organization Man in her book *The Death of the Organization Man*: "They believed they had jobs in perpetuity. They relished the rigid corporate hierarchy. . . . They had the security that came from knowing their assigned place and the privileges and responsibilities that came from that place" (Bennett 1990, 14). The number of white-collar positions rose dramatically as corporations expanded in the postwar years. The percentage of white-collar jobs jumped

61 percent between 1947 and 1957 (Chafe 1986, 111). The growing number of large corporate enterprises in the postwar period provided for the increase in management positions. As corporations grew in size and number, the opportunity to work for small, individually owned businesses declined. In 1958, 5 million individually owned businesses dotted the American landscape outside of farming, mining, and fishing, but they provided only 15 percent of the nation's jobs (Degler 1968, 170). Large corporations began to take over the country's economy and job market after World War II.

Large bureaucratic corporations grew amid the economic devastation in Europe and parts of Asia after World War II. While parts of the world lay in ruins, the United States took over as the world's economic leader. Although businesses worried about profits in the 1950s and 1960s, in the absence of intense foreign competition, they did not look to cut every possible cost. Large corporations built a large, arguably unnecessary, bureaucracy of managers that helped sustain the prosperity of the white middle class. White men benefited most from the postwar boom. Immigration laws enacted in the 1920s, and racial, religious, and gender discrimination all reduced competition for white males. By the 1970s and 1980s, structural changes challenged America's role as the world's economic leader and white male's virtual control of the corporation (Leinberger and Tucker 1991, 127).

While Organization Men enjoyed the security and material prosperity of corporate life, a number of authors criticized the conformity that their positions produced. William Whyte's *The Organization Man* (1956) is the most famous of these critiques. Corporations promoted what Whyte (1956) called the "social ethic," a belief in belongingness as the ultimate need of the individual. Whyte argued that Organization Men lacked creativity and individuality. Other authors, such as David Riesman, joined Whyte in his criticisms of corporate culture.

Despite the criticisms of Whyte and Riesman, millions of Americans still turned to corporations for employment. The Organization Man's loyalty to corporations must be seen in the context of the Depression, postwar abundance, and Cold War anxiety. Either as a child or an adult, Organization Men experienced the harsh nature of the Depression. During the 1930s, unemployment ranged between 15 and 25 percent of all workers. In 1941, at the end of the Depression, 40 percent of American families lived below the poverty line and almost 8 million workers earned salaries below the legal minimum wage. World War II lifted the American economy out of the Depression and laid the groundwork for postwar affluence. The end of the war unleashed a huge buildup of consumer demand and left the United States as the dominant economic power in the world.

For those Organization Men who suffered through the Depression, corporate salaries in the postwar years allowed them to live a different lifestyle. Americans made up for their frugal lifestyles in the four years following the end of World War II, purchasing 21.4 million cars, 20 million refrigerators, and 11.6 million televisions each year. One million housing units were sold each year during the same period. The diverse array of new products that flashed across U.S. television screens throughout the postwar period sustained the consumption patterns of the immediate post-war period into the following decades.

Organization Men not only benefited from well-paying jobs, but also the anxiety of the Cold War gave workers a stake in national security. The Cold War was largely an ideological battle between capitalism and Communism, and by working hard for a large corporation, many men felt they played an important role in the Cold War. If Organization Men were unsure of the connection between the materials that they produced and the Cold War, then Vice President Richard Nixon reminded them in 1955. While leading Soviet Premier Nikita Khrushchev through the U.S. Exhibition in Sokolniki Park in Moscow, Nixon stopped in a model middle-class American kitchen. Stocked with a sink with hot and cold running water, a full-size refrigerator-freezer, stove and oven, automatic washer, spacious counters, and cabinets, Nixon called upon America's material comforts to prove its superiority: "Isn't it better to be talking about the relative merits of our washing machines than of the relative strength of our rockets?" (Whitfield 1996, 74).

Boomers experienced the culture of abundance and the Cold War differently than their parents. According to historian Terry Anderson, boomers' parents "transferred what they had learned fighting fascism and

Soviet Premier Nikita Khrushchev (center left) talks with U.S. Vice President Richard Nixon during their famous "Kitchen Debate" at the U.S. exhibit at Moscow's Sokolniki Park, July 24, 1959. While touring the exhibit, both men kept a running debate on the merits of their respective countries. Standing to the right is Khrushchev's deputy, Leonid Brezhnev. (AP/Wide World Photos)

tyranny [during World War II] to the new nemesis—Communism. These parents of the baby boomers saw foreign policy in black and white terms. The world was filled with good and evil forces" (Anderson 1995, 14). Anderson argues that this "mentally set the stage" for Vietnam, which boomers' parents interpreted as another World War II or Korea, "another obligation to stop aggression" (Anderson 1995, 14). Most parents had trouble understanding why their sons and daughters would question American foreign policy. Boomers had difficulty understanding why their parents viewed American foreign policy through such a narrow lens of good and evil, when American government, in boomers' eyes, was the cause of so much evil throughout the world.

Boomers also had difficulty understanding their parents concern with security and commitment to the culture of abundance. Growing up after the Depression, boomers did not view the postwar world as an escape from economic struggle. Most boomers, according to Anderson, "perceived the decade in terms of conformity and consensus, rules, and regulation" (Anderson 1995, 32). The conformist culture of "duck and cover" and crew cuts permeated their young lives. When students entered college, one student wrote, what was supposed to be "the best years of your life" turned out to be "lines, bureaucracy and crowds" (Anderson 1995, 246).

In 1962, a small group of young white college students articulated boomers' discomfort with Cold War culture. The students gathered in Port Huron, Michigan, at an American Federation of Labor-Congress of Industrial Organizations (AFL-CIO) retreat to draft a manifesto for their new organization, Students for a Democratic Society (SDS). Tom Hayden, who wrote much of *The Port Huron Statement*, grew up in Royal Oaks, a middle-class suburb of Detroit. In the suburbs, like many other boomers, he experienced the material comforts of the postwar boom, but prosperity did not overshadow the social ills that surrounded him. The opening sentence acknowledges the culture of abundance of their youth: "We are people of this generation, bred in at least modest comfort, housed now in universities, looking uncomfortably to the world we inherit" (Farber 1994, 192). Southern racism and the arms race were particular concerns for SDS, but the conformist, social ethic of the Organization Man was also concerning. *The Port Huron Statement* put forth an individualistic ethos that confronted the valued qualities of the corporation: "Men have unrealized potential for self-cultivation, self-direction, self-understanding, and creativity. . . . Work should . . . be educative, not stultifying, creative, not mechanical, self-directed, not manipulative, encouraging independence" (Leinberger and Tucker 1991, 164). Three years later, Paul Potter, president of SDS, stood in front of 15,000 like-minded boomers on Washington, D.C.'s National Mall at an antiwar protest. Potter condemned American society "that creates faceless bureaucracies and makes those the place where people spend their lives and do their work, that consistently puts material values before human values—and still persists in calling itself free and still persists in finding itself fit to police the world" (Farber 194, 139).

When the New Left began to unravel at the end of the 1960s, the counterculture offered another way for young men and women to challenge the culture of the Organization Man. Members of the counterculture cared less about buying a new car or television than breaking from the conformist culture of their parents' generation. Freedom and autonomy characterized the movement more than anything else. One hippie, critical of the mass consumer culture, wrote, "All of us started to realize that the game of life played in school and the Supermarket U. leads only to styrofoam coffins and oblivious servitude. . . . All are well trained towards indiscriminate consumption. Yet the feeling persists—there must be something greater than this" (Anderson 1995, 257). Anderson points out that if the creed of the Cold War culture and the Organization Man was the Protestant Ethic, or one that idealized hard work, "the canon of the counterculture was the Pleasure Ethic: fun" (Anderson 1995, 258). Although conservative youths outnumbered those who committed themselves to the counterculture, perhaps as many as 3 million positioned themselves within the counterculture during some period in the late 1960s and 1970s.

A smaller number of counterculture followers looked to communes to break away from mainstream culture. Communes were usually small and located in rural areas where members attempted to get away from a materialistic society. In places such as Georgeville Trading Post in Minnesota, Pandanaram in Indiana, and various farms in Southern Oregon, communards worked as a community to produce food and experimented with personal freedom. One communard wrote they were:

> Learning self-sufficiency and rediscovering old technologies that are not destructive to themselves and the land. . . . And we are doing this, as much as possible, outside the existing structures . . . Harvard, Selective Service, General Motors, Bank of America, A&P . . . CBS, DDT, USA and Vietnam. (Anderson 1995, 270)

Although a minority of those who participated in the counterculture were members of a commune, everyone who was part of the movement pledged, as one communard noted, "fond farewell to the system" (Anderson 1995, 270).

Perhaps more than the movements of the 1960s and 1970s, Watergate contributed to baby boomers' distrust of large organizations. If the ideas of the counterculture reached only a small percentage of the population, Watergate rocked the entire nation. When Nixon turned over his infamous tapes, many of the boomers who did not join the movements of the 1960s lost trust in the government. As historian Bruce Schulman argues, "Watergate added fuel to a widespread cynicism about politics. . . . It confirmed the man on the street's . . . growing distrust of America's institutions and American leaders" (Schulman 2002, 48).

In the aftermath of Watergate, President Jimmy Carter recognized that Americans did not just question the nation's political leaders but all of the country's institutions. In a 1979 speech, Carter called American's skepticism "a fundamental threat to American democracy." But more than just a threat to government:

> It is a crisis of confidence. . . . Our people are losing faith, not only in government itself but in the ability as citizens to serve as rulers and shapers of our democracy. . . .

There is a growing disrespect for government and for churches and for schools, the news media, and other institutions. This is not a message of happiness and reassurance, but it is the truth and it is a warning. (Carter 1979, para. 33, 36)

Polls supported Carter's worries. Between 1959 and 1965, Americans who expressed favorable attitudes toward corporate titans such as AT&T and General Motors increased from 69 percent to 73.5 percent. By 1977, only 36 percent of Americans expressed favorable views of America's corporate giants. Over a similar period of time, between 1962 and 1981, Americans' confidence in government declined by about 20 percent. Inflation, the oil crisis, and the Iran Hostage Crisis ensured that Carter would not change these trends.

The rise of corporate activism added to boomers' weariness of large corporations. Ralph Nader's *Unsafe at Any Speed: The Designed-In Dangers of the Automobile* (1965) shook American's confidence in the automobile industry. Nader argued that the back wheels of the 1960–1963 Chevrolet Corvair tucked under with little provocation. Nader's accusation that General Motors' executives knew about the defects, but ignored them to save money, captured the country's attention. Nader called it "one of the greatest acts of industrial irresponsibility in the present century" (Leinberger and Tucker 1991, 173). After General Motors gave Nader free publicity by trying to discredit him, sales exploded in 1966 selling 450,000 copies of his book. Nader transcended the generation gap and ideological fissures that plagued the 1960s. While millions of people ignored, even despised, the young activists of the New Left who attacked the Establishment, millions of people listened to Nader. Polls indicated that after the release of his book, Americans trusted Nader more than the government, media, and corporations (Leinberger and Tucker 1991).

Unsafe at Any Speed sparked the consumer activist movement that uncovered fraud and deception in American industries. Nader was an important part of the movement's growth. He started Public Interest Research Groups to undertake research on industrial misdeeds and to lobby Congress for new legislation that protected consumers. The findings of consumer activists had a devastating impact on members of the Baby Boom. Joann Harrison, a young member of the Baby Boom and daughter of a General Motors' Organization Man was "appalled that products were unsafe. Who would make an unsafe product? That was very eye-opening for me that people would not only make unsafe products, but also would make products that weren't any good. I was too idealistic to think that anybody would do something poorly on purpose" (Leinberger and Tucker 1991).

The environmental movement also provided evidence that damaged corporations' reputations. Rachel Carson's *Silent Spring* (1962) forced many Americans to question the advantages of technological progress in postwar America. Carson accused the chemical industry, agribusiness, and the federal government of indiscriminately using harmful chemicals. *The New Yorker* serialized the book in 1962 and, within its first year, *Silent Spring* sold 600,000 copies. CBS also aired a prime-time special titled *The Silent Spring of Rachel Carson*. By the early 1960s, the environmental consequences of big business were ubiquitous (Rothman 1998, 88–90).

Concerns about industries' negative impact on the environment did not end with the publication of Rachel Carson's book. The Santa Barbara oil spill in January 1968 brought an environmental disaster to the shores of an affluent community. The environmental consequences of industrialization had been obvious for decades in working-class communities, but the event in Santa Barbara brought environmental concerns to the mainstream. The following year, Ohio's Cuyahoga River was so polluted that it caught fire. By the late 1960s, air pollution also plagued America's biggest cities. A visible cloud over the Los Angeles skyline became one of first obvious signs of smog. Many linked air pollution to the negligence of corporations. In a famous photo, one activist held a sign that read, "Big Business Monopolizes Our Air" (Rothman 1998, 99). The sign highlights a transition in the 1960s and 1970s during which Americans took on a new ownership of the environment in face of obvious environmental changes. This new concern over the environment, especially the affects of pollution, made corporations an obvious target.

At the same time, boomers began to question the culture of abundance, and the structural factors that gave Organization Men secure, well-paying positions began to evaporate. Vietnam inflation, oil shocks, failing productivity, and the rise of global competition all slowed the American economy. Between 1973 and 1974, Organization of Petroleum Exporting Countries (OPEC) increased the price of oil 300 percent. By 1980, a barrel that cost $2.50 in 1972, cost $35. Most important, while America's productivity slowed, many of the countries devastated by World War II caught up to the United States. In 1960, the United States contributed 35 percent of the world's economic output, but by 1980, the United States contributed only 22 percent (Leinberger and Tucker 1991, 205–206).

Faced with rising foreign competition, inflation, and declining rates of production, corporations made drastic changes. Company's attempted to cut costs wherever possible, and in the process, reinterpreted the value of the bureaucracy, made up of middle managers. The Organization Men, who had once been assets to the company, became a drag on company profits. Between 1976 and 1983, the rate of corporate firing doubled. During the 1980s, more than a million managers were fired or forced to retire. During the eighteenth-month period between 1985 and 1986, nearly 300 companies including Apple, Bank of American, and Ford cut their staffs by 10 to 20 percent. Xerox cut costs by $275 million between 1980 and 1985, cutting their staff by nearly 18,000. Almost half of the jobs cut were management positions. Baby boomers stood by their fathers as corporations fired or forced them into retirement after decades of unwavering loyalty (Bennett 1990, 114).

The corporate firings had a major impact on the children of Organization Men. A large corporation forced Diane Cole's father into early retirement only two years after he relocated. Cole remembers, "I felt kind of bitter about that, how my dad was treated in that whole corporate world. I think I've always been resentful about how I think my dad was treated" (Leinberger and Tucker 1991, 214). Her father's early retirement made Cole realize how expendable Organization Men were. Carolyn Harrison's father faced a similar situation. General Motors gave her father a choice of early retirement or a transfer to Atlanta only two years before he planned to retire. It was the first time she heard her father complain about General Motors. For many children who did not consume the ideas of the counterculture, the mergers and mass firings of the 1970s led many to question the value of working for a corporation.

Importantly, the criticism came from within their homes; from their fathers who had defended the corporation throughout the postwar period. Trip Van Houston saw the changes of the 1970s and 1980s and realized that his children's experience would be much different from his. He advised his son, "You aren't going to be working in the same kind of career that I did. Make sure you build on your experience. You have to look out for yourself. Don't let yourself get locked in" (Bennett 1990, 38). Houston, like many Organization Men in the 1970s and 1980s, recognized that his children would not reap the same benefits from corporations that he had.

Some of the Organization Men who did keep their jobs during this tumultuous period did not feel that they had the same stake in the company. United Airlines pilot Bill Thomas saw the erosion of corporate loyalty in the late 1960s after United created a holding company for the airline called UAL, Inc. The holding company quickly bought hotels, resort developments, and other airlines. According to Thomas, once United became part of UAL, employees lost any concept of being part of the company: "It really belongs to some group of unknown men who own a lot of different things. . . . Who are they? I don't know. I don't know anybody who does know" (Leinberger and Tucker 1991, 212). Just as important as not knowing who the company's executives were, Thomas recalled that "when the holding company started preaching bottom line profits, that's when the pilots lost interest. There was no more hanger talk. We were all into our outside investment, our little businesses on the side. There was no more interest in the airline" (Leinberger and Tucker 1991, 212).

If baby boomers did not learn these lessons from their fathers, they soon learned it from their experience within the corporation. One of the top executives at Kodak told a manager, "no one promised us a job forever" (Bennett 1990, 253). Corporations no longer promised managers a job for the remainder of their careers. Some companies, like Kodak, tried to warn their workers not to become too attached to the company. At General Electric, according to a senior vice president, "the company wants the freedom to get rid of people when the business changes. They can't have people tied to them" (Bennett 1990, 253). General Electric prepared their employees to keep their skills and contacts up to date so they were not useless outside the company.

Members of the Baby Boom generation faced more than bureaucratic restructuring and a new corporate culture. The size of the Baby Boom exacerbated the negative effects of the economic downturn in the 1970s and 1980s. Between 1946 and 1964, 72.4 million babies were born in the United States. By 1964, 40 percent of the population was under twenty years of age. The dramatic increase in the nation's birthrate had significant effects on baby boomers' opportunities as adults. Boomers faced a level of competition that their fathers had never encountered. In 1967, when the first wave of college-educated baby boomers entered the job market, many found themselves without a job. Between 1953 and 1963, the labor force increased at a rate of about 880,000 per year. The affect of the Baby Boom on the job market is staggering. Between 1964 and 1974, the labor force increased at a rate of about 1.74 million per year (Leinberger and Tucker 1991, 120).

The recession that began in the 1970s coupled with intense job competition made baby boomers' experience in corporations much different than their fathers' experiences. If baby boomers enjoyed the economic boom as children, they suffered from its decline as adults. Between 1949 and 1973, the average income of families with two children doubled. After 1973, as baby boomers entered the job market, the average income of families with two children fell. To put the effects of stagflation into perspective, in 1986 a thirty-year-old man earned less than members of his father's generation when they first entered the job market. Facing inflation and lower salaries than their fathers, baby boomers had fewer reasons to be loyal to corporations (Leinberger and Tucker 1991, 121).

If loyalty was the most dominant characteristic of the Organization Man, self-interest may be the central quality of the baby boomers. Gone are the days when workers were expected to stay with one company for their entire working career. Baby boomers jumped from company to company, constantly in search for a new opportunity that would best serve their interests. The careers of two women illuminate this transition. When Paul Leinberger and Bruce Tucker interviewed Nancy Caton for their 1991 book *The New Individualists,* she was a foreign-exchange trader for CitiBank in San Francisco. Caton described her anxiety over working for one company for the rest of her career: "I feel I'm ready to make some sort of commitment to something and I don't really want to make it to the company, to a corporate entity to which I have no particular loyalty" (Leinberger and Tucker, 1991, 213). Laura Cory is even more emblematic of what Leinberger and Tucker call the "new individualists." Cory graduated from the University of Connecticut and then worked for a manufacturing company. Unsatisfied with her job, she went to Stanford and earned her masters of business administration and then became a certified public accountant. She immediately went to work for an accounting firm and then joined a software company. After she graduated from college, Cory changed jobs every two years. At the time of the interview, she worked for Hewlitt-Packard because of their favorable maternity policies but she explained, "once I've got children that are a couple of years old, I will probably go off to a small company again" (Leinberger and Tucker 1991, 213).

The different values of the remaining Organization Men and baby boomers often caused tension in the workplace. When one west-coast executive offered management jobs to two of the companies most prized young workers, one declined. The young employee had young children and would have to spend too much time away from his family in a

Scott Myers

Scott Myers was born in 1953 to a typical Organization Man who worked for Continental
Illinois National Bank and Trust Company. After
growing up in Park Forest, Illinois, a suburb of
Chicago, he graduated from Indiana University
in 1976 with a degree in biology and then
earned his masters of business administration
from Northwestern University. He seemed
aptly prepared for a secure management position in a large corporation, but he did not envy
the lifestyle of Organization Men. After watching his father work tirelessly for Continental,
he knew he wanted more control over his life.
The youngest of three boys, his brothers did
not supply a model path for him to follow. His
eldest brother followed in his father's footsteps, while his other sibling, Randy, worked as
a construction contractor in Boulder, Colorado.
Scott Myers wanted the respectability and financial security of his brother's position, while
also having the freedom that Randy's job provided (Leinberger and Tucker 1991, 41).

Like many boomers who went to work for
corporations, Myers quickly understood that
he would not be happy in the corporate
world. The Memorex Corporation hired him
after business school and, "I'd been there
only six months when I decided I was going
someplace else. I was in the process of leaving ever since then." But Myers stayed at the
company for ten years. Why did he stay for
so long if he was unhappy?

> The reason I stayed had nothing to do with
> loyalty. It's just whenever I got to the point
> where I actually went looking for another job,
> an opportunity would come along inside and I
> would take it. I reasoned that I would never get
> such an opportunity elsewhere because of lack
> of experience. (Leinberger and Tucker 1991, 43)

When Myers transferred from finance to
sales, he worked on a project that developed a
small in-house software company that was to

management position. The Organization Man who offered the young prospect the position was furious saying, "We made offers to the wrong persons. . . . These guys are too dumb to be managers" (Mills 1987, 169). A
typical Organization Man, loyal and willing to sacrifice for the company,
would simply ask when the company wanted him to start. The new generation of employees thought of work much differently. Many baby boomers
privileged family and quality of life over the needs of the corporation.

This tension between corporate men and baby boomers represented an
important shift in values. Organization Men searched for security in their
jobs, whereas their children wanted to feel independent and free while at
work. Baby boomers were willing to sacrifice financial security to have
more control over their work life and home life. Scott Myers, for example,
left Memorex, to develop and market a software product for computers.
Gambling on his own success, he gave up his salary and benefits to start
his own company. His brother, Randy Myers, also wanted more control
over his life. His father, an Organization Man, asked him why he would
not got to "Philadelphia or New York or Chicago or some other big city in
order to find work . . . Why Colorado? . . . There's nothing out there,
nothing happening." Myers did not want a job to dictate where he lived.
Myers responded, "for me the most important thing in life was not

be packaged and sold in the marketplace. Not long after the transfer, Burroughs bought Memorex and then merged to become Unisys. Unisys was not interested in Myers' small in-house software business and killed his division and project. Myers had been planning to leave for years, but his experience during the merger accelerated the process. The team who he had worked with on the project began talking about starting their own business and then, while still working for Memorex, began meeting on the weekends for a year and a half, defining a new product that they could sell (Leinberger and Tucker 1991, 44—45).

Before he could venture out on his own, a quote in the *New York Times* sealed his fate with Memorex. In an article published on December 7, 1986, Myers was quoted as saying that W. Michael Blumenthal, then chairman and chief corporate officer (CEO) of Unisys, did not have any loyalty to the company. After reading the article, Blumenthal wanted

him fired. Although Memorex did not fire him immediately, Myers knew it was coming and quit before the company could let him go (Leinberger and Tucker 1991, 47—50).

In the years that followed, he and his partners successfully developed a product that they sold to a large software company that made a considerable profit in 1989. With the money he made from the sale, Myers started a company with a partner that provided the type of lifestyle he wanted when he graduated from business school. His master bedroom served as his office, and he had more control over his life than ever before (Leinberger and Tucker 1991, 50—51). Myers' choice to start his own company illuminates the difference between Organization Men and baby boomers. The insecurity of a small business, without benefits and a guaranteed salary scared most Organization Men, but the freedom and control over one's life that a small business provided was idealized by many boomers.

working, but living. It makes no sense to live for your work" (Leinberger and Tucker 1991, 38).

D. Quinn Mills recognized the transition from Organization Man to individualist when he attended an alumni event at his former college. In his book, *Not Like Our Parents: How the Baby Boom Is Changing America* (1987), Mills remembers an alumni event that he attended twenty years ago where fellow colleagues were impressed by corporate positions. Corporations' size, wealth, and power carried prestige and status. By the 1980s, the status of corporations changed at alumni events, "people were most impressed when someone admitted to owning his or her own company, and working for themselves. . . . What mattered was a sense of independence, of freedom, of being one's own boss" (Mills 1987, 169).

If Organization Men were surprised by the different values that boomers brought to work, the rising numbers of women joining corporations must have been equally as shocking. Many factors contributed to the growing numbers of women in the workforce. Despite idealized images of happy housewives in American popular culture, many boomers' knew their mothers were unhappy. A 1962 Gallup poll found that only 10 percent of boomers' mothers wanted their daughters to follow in their footsteps (Rosen 2000, 43). Historian Ruth Rosen argues that boomers' aversion to their mothers' lives was the key to the postwar women's movement. By the early 1960s, young women could turn to a growing critique of gender roles expressed by writers such as Betty Friedan. In her bestseller, *The Feminine Mystique* (1963), Friedan challenged images in popular culture and described housewives who felt their lives were depressing and unfulfilling. Friedan concluded, "We can no longer ignore that voice in women that says: 'I want something more than my husband and my children and my home'" (Rosenberg 1992, 157). Women's experience in the civil rights movement and the New Left helped women realize the power of women's political organization and protest. While the civil rights movements and New Left lost much of its organizing force by the end of the 1960s, the feminist movement gained power. By the 1970s, terms such as "patriarchy" and "sexism" permeated American culture. Even though only a minority of boomers were involved in women's liberation, by the 1970s and 1980s, the idealized images of the happy housewife found important challenges in American culture and political discourse.

Structural factors contributed to the growing number of women in the workforce. Many families depended on women's wages as fewer men held jobs that paid well enough to support an entire family. By 1987, for the first time in American history, more than half of women with children under the age of one worked outside of the home. Many of these women found white-collar jobs in large corporations. Between 1972 and 1983, the number of women managers doubled to 3.5 million and the number of women in executive positions increased by 143 percent. One study, however, suggests that an increase of 143 percent is deceiving when one considers how few women filled executive positions before 1972. A 1985 study found that of 1,362 executives surveyed, only twenty-nine were women. Despite significant gains made by women during this period, the "glass ceiling" still placed limitations on their occupational mobility (Mills 1987, 189).

Joann Harrison experienced the "glass ceiling" first hand at IBM. She watched her husband, who had similar skills and training, get promoted quickly while she stayed in her starting position. Harrison described the situation:

> IBM was not overt about it but I had slower progress than a man with the same capabilities. . . . When I first joined IBM, I naively thought that if I showed them how smart I am, I'll keep moving in the ranks the way my dad did in GM. After seven years I realized that in twenty years I probably wouldn't get past third-level manager. (Leinberger and Tucker 1991, 179)

Conclusion

Structural and cultural changes contributed to the shifting views of corporate jobs among baby boomers. Increasing foreign competition, Vietnam, successive oil crises, and stagflation all helped to make boomers' experience within corporations much different from their fathers' experiences. In response to the troubled economic period, corporations cut thousands of management positions in the 1970s and 1980s. Boomers could no longer expect a corporation to provide a well-paying job for their entire career. Cultural changes also meant that many boomers did not want to work for a corporation. The rise of consumer activism, the civil rights movement, the antiwar movement, the New Left, Watergate, and the counterculture made boomers question the integrity and respectability of large organizations. Many of these movements promoted an ideal of individualism that clashed with the ideals of corporations.

Although many baby boomers criticized large organizations, as a group, they never totally rebelled against corporations in their adult lives. Like their fathers, they sat in the same offices, worked behind the same desks, and, with updated technology, performed many of the same tasks. But baby boomers negotiated corporate work much differently than the previous generation. They held the corporation at arm's length and tried not to let it control their lives. Some baby boomers were mirror images of Whyte's Organization Man, but enough baby boomers embraced a different set of values that it was obvious to Organization Men that something had changed. Baby boomers seemed to embrace Whyte's famous line: "We do need to know how to co-operate with The Organization but, more than ever, so do we need to know how to resist it" (1956, 12).

Bibliography

Anderson, Terry. *The Movement and the Sixties.* New York: Oxford University Press, 1995.

Bennett, Amanda. *The Death of the Organization Man.* New York: Morrow, 1990.

Carter, Jimmy. "Crisis of Confidence." July 15, 1979. http://www.cartercenter.org/news/editorials_speeches/crisis_of_confidence.html.

Chafe, William. *The Unfinished Journey: American Since World War II.* New York: Oxford University Press, 1986.

Degler, Carl N. *Affluence and Anxiety, 1945-Present.* Glenview, IL: Scott Foresman American History Series, 1968.

Farber, David. *The Age of Great Dreams: America in the 1960s.* New York: Hill and Wang, 1994.

Lamb, George. E-mail to author, September 12, 2007.

Leinberger, Paul, and Tucker, Bruce. *The New Individualists: The Generation after the Organization Man.* New York: Harper Collins Publishers, 1991.

Mills, D. Quinn Mills. *Not Like Our Parents: How the Baby Boom Is Changing America.* New York: William Morrow and Company, Inc., 1987.

Rosen, Ruth. *The World Split Open: How the Modern Women's Movement Changed America.* New York: Viking, 2000.

Rosenberg, Rosalind. *Divided Lives: American Women in the Twentieth Century.* New York: Hill and Wang, 1992.

Rothman, Hal. *The Greening of a Nation: Environmentalism in the United States Since 1945*. Fort Worth: Harcourt Brace College Publishers, 1998.

Schulman, Bruce J. *The Seventies: The Great Shift in American Culture, Society, and Politics*. Cambridge: De Capo Press, 2002.

Whitfield, Stephen J. *The Culture of the Cold War*. 2nd ed. Baltimore, MD: John Hopkins University Press, 1996.

Whyte, William. *The Organization Man*. New York: Simon and Schuster, 1956.

Suburbanites and Suburbia | 10

Rusty Monhollon

B ob and Mary Smith read the advertisement in the newspaper with great excitement. The developers of a new housing project outside of the city were selling single-family, three bedroom homes for less than $10,000. According to the advertisement, veterans would qualify for a low-interest loan and only a $90.00 down payment. As Bob had served in the Navy during World War II, their monthly payment for the house would be less than $70.00 per month.

Mary and Bob had lived in a cramped apartment in the city since they married, just before Bob enlisted in the Navy. They had met while they were in college; Bob had one year left to complete when he left for the Pacific, and Mary finished her degree while Bob was overseas. During the war, Mary had worked for the war department, writing articles for a government newspaper.

Their first child was born less than a year after Bob returned from the war. Using the benefits provided by the Serviceman's Readjustment Act (better known as the G.I. Bill), Bob soon completed his degree and took a middle-management position with a large company. They quickly outgrew their small apartment, as two more children were born in the next three years. Bob's salary provided more than enough income to buy a new home, so they made plans to visit the development that weekend.

As they neared the development's sales office, they grew concerned. Dozens of other young couples—several hundred people in all—were waiting in line to see the homes for sale. Their fears quickly vanished when they learned that plenty of homes were available, and, amazingly, a dozen or more were being constructed every day. The builders offered two styles of houses, both rather plain Cape Cod-style homes that sat on 7,000-square-foot lots, which seemed immense to city dwellers. Included in the sales price were new appliances. Bob and Mary signed a contract that same day, and moved in to their new home several months later. They had moved to the suburbs.

Life for the Smiths in the suburbs was different from what they had known in the city. Bob now drove to work instead of taking public transportation, of which there was very little in their new community. In fact, the Smiths purchased a second car for Mary to drive. In the city, she had walked around the corner to the grocer or took a bus downtown to shop for clothes. But now Mary spent much of her day running errands, to the grocery store or department store, or taking the children to the dentist. Bob built a two-car garage onto their home, and he later would add on two more bedrooms to the original structure. While their house was almost identical to the rest of the development when they first moved in, eventually, Bob and Mary added their style and taste to their home—just as their neighbors did with their homes—and made it distinctly theirs.

The Smiths' neighbors were much like them, as they discovered when they got to know them at backyard barbeques or school Parent-Teacher Association meetings. They were mostly young and had at least two children. All of them were white; in fact, blacks, Asians, and Mexicans were prohibited from buying homes in this development. Bob was second-generation American, the son of immigrants who arrived in the United States in 1922; so too were many of his neighbors. Almost every man in the development had been in the service during World War II, and nearly all of them were white-collar workers and commuted to work in the city. Many of the women had worked during the war but quit once they had children. Several of the women considered returning to their careers one day, but many of the men, including Bob, were adamantly opposed to their wives working. Bob felt it reflected poorly on him, suggesting he was not able to support the family on his salary. Mary Smith and the other women in the neighborhood spent their days tending to the house and children, sharing stories over coffee.

Bob advanced quickly up the corporate ladder. His new responsibilities required him to work late hours, so he often did not return home until after the children were in bed. Bob and Mary's relationship became strained from the pressures of his work and her malaise with the limitations of being wife and mother. But they remained married for more than fifty years. Their five children all attended college and all except two received degrees. One son was killed in Vietnam, and one daughter dropped out of school to join a commune. Their other children eventually married and lived near them in a new suburban development.

Bob and Mary Smith are not actual persons, nor is the housing development real. But their story, at least in its broad contours, was one that occurred repeatedly after World War II. Millions of Americans moved to the suburbs during the Baby Boom era, transforming the nation, as the historian Kenneth Jackson and others have noted, into the first suburban nation in the world.

The impact of suburbanization has been immense. The rising cultural and economic strength of the suburbs was evident soon after the boom began. "In recent years," read a 1953 article in *Fortune*,

an average of about 1,200,000 Americans moved to the suburbs every year. . . .
The middle class Suburbia, rapidly growing larger and more affluent, is
developing a way of life that seems eventually bound to become dominant in
America. It has been a major force in the phenomenal rise in the nation's
birth rate. It has centered its customs and conventions on the needs of children
and geared its buying habits to them. (as quoted in Lipsitz 1990, 46)

Between the late 1940s and the early 1960s, some 2 million new houses
were built each year, with nearly all of them detached, single-family, bal-
loon-frame homes.

Suburban culture—for better or worse—became a dominant culture in
the United States. Critics then and now have excoriated suburbia as a bastion of homogenous blandness and mind-numbing conformity. Yet by
1990, more Americans (some 120 million, or about 45 percent) resided in
the suburbs than in either cities or rural areas (Jackson 1991, 1040).

Suburbanization was an ongoing process, one that dates back to at
least the mid-nineteenth century. According to Jackson, five factors were
primarily responsible for the suburbanization of the United States: high
per capita wealth; plentiful and inexpensive land; inexpensive transportation; the predominance of balloon-framed houses; and government subsidies for housing.

As thousands of industrial jobs opened up in urban areas in the late
nineteenth and early twentieth centuries, rural migrants both from within
the United States and from abroad flooded into American cities. By 1920,
for the first time, more than half of the population of the United States
resided in urban areas. Simultaneously, a trickle of city dwellers began
moving away from the crowded and dirty inner city, which now was being
occupied by the burgeoning industrial working class, to areas on the city's
fringe that became known as the suburbs.

Suburban growth was facilitated by technological advances, especially
in transportation. In the mid-nineteenth century horse-drawn and steam-
powered streetcars had allowed wealthier residents to live beyond the city
core. By the end of the century, the rail network expanded outward,
thanks to the electrification of streetcars. These so-called streetcar suburbs
were, however, relatively small and limited primarily to the middle and
upper class.

But, beginning in the 1920s, a new form of transportation—the automobile—led to the explosion of suburban growth. The federally funded
construction of new roads and highways, in particular, the 1956 Interstate
Highway Act, pushed the suburbs beyond the reach of rail lines, making
them accessible only by automobile. In cities such as St. Louis and Kansas
City, for example, where there had been limited or no public transportation, road construction connected small outlying communities to the urban
core, creating sprawling and seemingly ill-planned metropolitan areas. New
shopping plazas, drive-in restaurants, gasoline stations, motels, and other
retail business sprung up along the so-called beltways, multilane roads that
encircled the city and allowed drivers to avoid the inner city altogether.
The consequences of suburban growth were nearly catastrophic to urban

Ron Kovic

Ron Kovic was born on July 4, 1946, the second eldest of six children. His father, a grocery clerk, and his mother, a housewife, later move the family from Wisconsin to Massapequa, New York. Kovic recalled during his childhood that he and his friends loved to watch war films and pretend they were soldiers, Marines like Sergeant Stryker, the John Wayne character in the *Sands of Iwo Jima*. As he recalled in his memoir, *Born on the Fourth of July*, he and his friends joined the Cub Scouts, marched in parades, built fallout shelters from old milk cartons, and used cardboard boxes to make rocket ships.

After graduation from high school, Kovic enlisted in the Marine Corps after hearing a rousing speech by a Marine Corps recruiter. He was motivated by the murder of President John F. Kennedy, whose inaugural speech—"Ask not what your country can do for you, ask what you can do for your country"—had stirred Kovic's red-blooded patriotism.

Kovic volunteered for a tour of duty in Vietnam and deployed in December 1965. He returned to the United States in January 1967, but he soon volunteered for a second tour in Vietnam. In January 1968, Kovic was severely wounded. A bullet struck his spinal cord, paralyzing him from the chest down. He received the Bronze Star and Purple Heart when he returned home later that year.

Kovic's injuries confined him to a wheelchair and required extensive medical care, which he received from the Veterans Administration hospital near his home. The conditions were abysmal, the medical care rote. Kovic described his room:

> The walls are almost as dirty as the floor and I cannot even see out of the window. . . . I push the call button again and again. No one comes. I am lying in my own excrement and no one comes. I begin shouting and screaming. . . . I have been screaming for almost an hour when one of the aides walks by. He sticks his head in the door, taunting me and laughing. "I'm a Vietnam veteran," I tell him. "I fought in Vietnam and I've got a right to be treated decently." "Vietnam," the aide says loudly. "Vietnam don't mean nothin' to me or any of these other people. You can take your Vietnam and shove it up your ass." (Kovic 1976, 133)

The appalling treatment and inadequate medical care he received was, to Kovic, a harsh betrayal of Vietnam veterans by their government; soon, Kovic questioned American involvement in the war itself. After the Kent State tragedy, Kovic joined Vietnam veterans against the war. He gave his first public speech against the war at Levittown High School, not far from where he had grown up.

Kovic became an impassioned critic of the war. He protested at draft centers across the country. In what he called the high point of his activism, Kovic disrupted Richard Nixon's acceptance speech at the 1972 Republican National

America, driving several cities to near bankruptcy and all into decline. Most American cities lost population. St. Louis, Detroit, and Philadelphia, for example, lost 400,000 residents between 1950 and 1980; Chicago lost more than 600,000 (Jackson 1985, 139). The decline in population meant also a decline in tax revenues for essential services.

Suburbanization also led to the class stratification of metropolitan areas, the inner city, and its surrounding suburbs. In the "walking cities" of the colonial and antebellum eras, people from all walks of life lived and worked together in a relatively compact area. With the emergence of

Antiwar activist and decorated Vietnam war hero Ron Kovic holds a sidewalk news conference in 1981 in Los Angeles to express dismay at the reception offered to freed American hostages compared with the homecoming vets received when they returned from the Vietnam War. (AP/Wide World Photos)

Convention, as it was being broadcast live. Kovic continued to speak against war and the maltreatment of veterans. In 1974, he participated in a seventeen-day hunger strike in Los Angeles, and he has protested the Gulf War and the Iraq War. In 1989, Kovic and Oliver Stone wrote a screenplay based on his life. *Born on the Fourth of July* starred Tom Cruise as Kovic, and earned Kovic the Golden Globe for best screenplay.

Ron Kovic displayed extraordinary courage in rehabilitating his life after his war injuries. His story, however, is not unique. Some 9 million Americans served during the Vietnam era, and thousands of other young men and women experienced similar horrors and despair, and demonstrated similar courage in adjusting to their lives after Vietnam.

suburbs, however, the middle and upper classes, which had the means to buy a home and to pay for transportation, could separate the workplace from their homes. Metropolitan areas became clearly delineated by class, with the poorest residents relegated to the city center, ringed by affluent suburbs.

Suburbanization accelerated after 1945. It is not a coincidence that rapid suburban growth occurred at the same time as the United States experienced its greatest period of economic growth. The economic growth of the period resulted primarily from three economic trends: (1) increased defense spending to wage the Cold War; (2) new construction, of homes, office space, and roads, among others; and (3) American's insatiable appetite for consumer goods.

Why did so many families abandon the city and flock to the suburbs after World War II? In large measure, suburban growth was the result of market forces, in particular, an acute housing shortage. There had been virtually no new construction during World War II, and demand for and cost of housing was high as the nation demobilized. With rents skyrocketing, and limited space for new construction, entrepreneurs saw the potential of building new homes on the edge of the cities. For many whites, single-family homes with manicured lawns and gardens were enticing, and a far cry from the crowded city.

Equally, if not more, important, however, was the role the federal government played in encouraging homeownership. Programs such as the Federal Housing Administration and the Veterans Administration (which was part of the G.I. Bill) guaranteed low-interest mortgages for home buyers, especially veterans. Later, Congress revised the federal tax code to permit homeowners to deduct property taxes and the interest paid on mortgages, which made homeownership even more attractive. The combination of low-interest, federally guaranteed loans and inexpensive new houses allowed millions of Americans to buy homes, most of which were built in suburban housing developments.

The role of the government in encouraging homeownership, and by extension suburban growth, can not be underestimated. Indeed, homeownership became the embodiment of the American dream, and suburbia redefined that dream by putting ownership of a single-family suburban home at its heart. By 1960, according to numerous sources, three-fifths of all American families owned their own home (Patterson 1997, 72).

Additionally, race played a significant role in suburban growth after World War II. The same federal policies that encouraged suburban growth also encouraged racial segregation in housing. Most sources agree that the postwar suburban population, for example, was about 95 percent white. African American urban migration increased after World War II, and the nation's general prosperity provided the means for many blacks to purchase homes in white neighborhoods. At the same time, many cities enacted fair housing ordinances that required public housing be made available equally to blacks. What resulted was "white flight": the white middle class packed up for the suburbs to escape growing racial tensions resulting from blacks moving into previously all-white neighborhoods. African Americans with the means to relocate were thwarted by discriminatory lending practices, racist realtors, and whites determined to keep blacks out of their neighborhood. In Cicero, Illinois, in 1951, whites broke the windows of a house recently purchased by a black family, who moved amid racial taunts and threats of violence; similar scenes played out in other communities across the nation.

The suburbs were attractive options for many Americans, especially for young, white-collar couples and returning veterans. They could afford to purchase larger homes than what they could find in the city, on larger lots and with plenty of open space. The prospect of living amid people about the same age and with similar occupations and interests was compelling. This was particularly true for stay-at-home mothers, who could turn to other women to help with child care.

Increasingly, an ideal of suburban life took root, that of the nuclear family, headed by a father who commuted to his white-collar job and a mother who cared for the home and children. Suburban life created the need for the "two-car family," one for men to drive to their jobs in the city and one for women to chauffer the children to doctor and dentist appointments, swimming pools, and baseball games, and to shop for groceries, clothing, and toys. The automobile not only helped create the suburbs but also—because there was little, if any, public transportation—became essential to sustaining the suburban lifestyle. Grocery stores, clothing stores, and other retail shops were constructed apart from residential areas, in what became known as "shopping malls" or "shopping plazas." If they chose, suburbanites could avoid the city altogether, which sounded the death knell for many downtown department stores. The emergence of the two-car family not only gave the suburbs much of its character but also was important to the nation's economic fortunes. Car ownership skyrocketed; between 1950 and 1960, automobile registrations soared from 40 to 74 million. Four out of five Americans owned a car by 1960, and 15 percent owned more than one. Car ownership was greater in the suburbs than in the cities (Patterson 1997, 316).

Suburban culture tended to reinforce rigid gender roles: men commuted to work and women stayed behind to care for the house and children. Culturally, women faced enormous pressure to stay at home and care for the house and children rather than work in the paid labor force. For many men, it was degrading if their wives worked, suggesting they were unable to support their families. At the same time, widespread assumptions about motherhood compelled many women to devote themselves wholly to their children.

As the historian Elaine Tyler May has shown, a powerful ideology of domesticity contributed greatly to the perpetuation of these gender roles. The nuclear family household, consisting of the husband and wife, and their children, became the repository for achieving the good life in America. A majority of Americans held the belief that marriage and parenthood was the surest way to happiness; many people believed childlessness was deviant. The federal government encouraged suburban growth as a way to support the ideal of the nuclear family.

Indeed, one of the best-selling books of the postwar era was Dr. Benjamin Spock's *Baby and Child Care*, which first appeared in 1946. Spock posited that the needs of the children must come before the emotional or physical needs of mothers. Paradoxically, despite the pressure on women to remain at home, the number of married women working actually increased significantly after 1945; by 1960, almost one-third of all married women were in the paid labor force (Chafe 1991, 188).

A striking feature of suburban culture was the lack of ethnicity. Studies have shown that many suburbanites were the children of immigrants, and these second-generation Americans sought to shed their ethnic heritage in

Theodore Cleaver

Theodore Cleaver was, in many ways, the consummate baby boomer. He grew up in what many would consider a stereotypical suburban community. Called "Beaver" by his family and friends, young Theodore grew up in a comfortable house replete with white picket fence in Mayfield. He lived with his older brother Wally, and his parents Ward, a white-collar professional, and June, a stay-at-home mom. Beaver attended Grant Avenue Elementary School, where he was a solid, if unexceptional, student. As a boy, Beaver enjoyed playing games with his friends Larry Mondello, Gilbert Bates, and Whitey Whitney. And, as boys were wont to do, Beaver and his friends often got into mischief. Much of his life was spent explaining the situation to his parents, and then receiving a stern lecture from his father regarding his misbehavior, accompanied by a moral lesson that would no doubt serve young Theodore well as an adult. Almost without fail, after one of his father's reprimands, his mother would comfort him with cookies and milk or his favorite meal.

Beaver Cleaver was the title character of the iconic television program *Leave It to Beaver*, which aired from 1957 to 1963. The Cleavers came to embody in popular culture the quintessential suburban family of the post-World War II era. Ward Cleaver, the stern-yet-caring, pipe-smoking and cardigan-wearing father, was a white-collar professional (although his exact job was never defined) who exemplified the ideal father. Likewise, June Cleaver epitomized the perfect wife and mother, who always wore full makeup and lovely dresses, and always had fresh-baked cookies ready when Beaver and Wally came home from school. No racial minorities lived in the fictional town of Mayfield; racial inequality, sexual discrimination, and cultural conflict were nonexistent, or at least not discussed in front of Beaver and Wally. The primary problems the Cleavers had to contend with were Beaver's frequent, if harmless, misbehavior. The idealized, middle-class suburban world that the Cleavers inhabited was idyllic, placid, and harmonious, a far cry from the reality of daily life during the Baby Boom era.

Leave It to Beaver enjoyed a long run in syndication after the series ended in 1963. In 1983, *Still the Beaver*, a made-for-television movie, premiered; it became a television series that aired for one year on the Disney Channel before being renamed *The New*

the suburbs. In the 1950s, the U.S. population was more homogeneous than before or since. In the suburbs, people of different backgrounds came together and adopted the norms of the developing national middle class. Suburbia was populated, as several scholars have noted, by a fully Americanized, fully assimilated, white middle class. "We see eye to eye on most things," remarked one resident of Levittown, "about raising kids, doing things together with your husband, living the same way; we have practically the same identical background" (as quoted in Gans 1982, 155).

As suburban life eroded ethnic distinctions, it also created a distinct culture, one that soon became dominant in the United States. In 1957, for the first time, a majority of families had incomes in the middle-class range. As more blue-collar workers participated in the middle-class culture—homeownership, financial stability, retirement security—the lines separating working class and middle class blurred. The newest consumer item,

Cast of the television series *Leave It to Beaver*, pose for a publicity portrait in this undated photo. The show, which aired from 1957 to 1963, starred, from the left, Tony Dow as Wally, Barbara Billingsley as June, Hugh Beaumont as Ward, and Jerry Mathers as Beaver. (AP/Wide World Photos)

Leave It to Beaver and airing on TBS from 1986 to 1989. In 1997, *Leave It to Beaver*, a full-length Hollywood film, was released. The show's popularity reflects, in part, the nostalgic yearnings of the baby boomers for the innocence and simplicity of youth.

television, fostered a national culture by giving Americans a shared set of experiences in two ways: (1) by watching the same television programs, and (2) by consuming the products advertised on television.

Television was instrumental in fostering this suburban, middle-class, consumer-driven culture. As numerous scholars have demonstrated, television programs in the 1950s often presented an idealized vision of family life. Programs such as *Leave it to Beaver*, *Father Knows Best*, and *Ozzie and Harriet* featured white, middle-class families living peacefully in the suburbs. Additionally, these shows popularized material comfort and the pursuit of material goods. Suburban living was portrayed as the norm for the American family. Another popular show of the era, *The Honeymooners*, depicted urban working-class families as loud and rife with conflict.

The prototype suburban community was Levittown, a housing development built after World War II on Long Island. Indeed, "Levittown" soon became synonymous with suburban life, and hundreds of similar developments spread across the nation. Levittown was the brainchild of Abraham Levitt and his sons William and Alfred. Both sons had served during World War II, William with the Seabees. William Levitt was the driving force behind the firm's growth. He understood that returning soldiers would demand housing.

Levitt and Sons' goal was to provide inexpensive housing. The company had won a government contract to construct housing for shipyard workers in Norfolk, Virginia, during the war, and it was there that the Levitts developed their construction methods. They used production methods borrowed from industry: standardized parts, vertical integration, economies of scale in materials, and specialization of labor during construction. All of Levitt's homes were built on concrete slabs to save costs. The lumber was cut to length at a lumber yard owned by Levitt and Sons. They were not builders, William Levitt once remarked, but "manufacturers."

But the Levitts did not provide merely housing; they were intent on creating a whole community. This was especially true in the second Levittown, built between Philadelphia and Trenton, New Jersey. Levitt boasted that they planned the entire development, including "every tree, color, and shrub" (Dunar 2006, 177). This emphasis on planning and community was a strong selling point. As William Levitt explained,

> The veteran needed a roof over his head, instead of giving him just a roof we gave him certain amenities. We divided it into sections and we put down schools, swimming pools, and a village green and necessity shopping centers, athletic fields, Little League diamonds. We wanted community living. (as quoted in Rybczynski 2007, 160–161)

Levitt's vision had broad appeal. One Army veteran believed Levitt "was the greatest man in the world." The veteran's wife burst into tears upon seeing their new, albeit unfinished, home in Bucks County, Pennsylvania. "Imagine it—$10 deposit, $90 at settlement and you had a house of your own! . . . We had achieved the American Dream," her husband recalled with great emotion (Blackwell 2009). Countless other couples experience similar feelings. By the early 1950s, Levitt and Sons had constructed more than 17,000 houses on Long Island. They would build some 17,000 more in Bucks County, Pennsylvania, and in Willingboro, New Jersey, some 11,000 more were erected (Bernstein 2002, 8; Gans 1982, 4; Jackson 1985, 235).

The assembly-line style of construction gave all Levitt-built houses a similar appearance. One resident recalled not being able to find his own home because it looked similar to the other homes in his neighborhood. The homogeneity of the architecture tended to reflect the homogeneity of the residents. It was this sameness, or lack of diversity, that prompted the harshest criticism of suburbia. "Everybody lives on the same side of the tracks," declared a 1954 *Saturday Evening Post* article. Suburbanites "have no slums to fret about, no families of conspicuous wealth to envy, no traditional upper crust to whet and thwart their social aspirations" (Thompson 1954, 27). The architect Lewis Mumford countered that the suburbs were "a one-class community on a great scale, too congested for effective variety and too spread out for social relationships. . . . Mechanically, it is admirably done. Socially, the design is backward" (as quoted in Levinson and Krizek 2008, 40).

Mumford was an architect who found suburbia superficial, conformist, and visually bland. Although he was perhaps the most unsympathetic critic of suburban life and culture, he was by no means the only one. In *The Crack in the Picture Window* (1957), John Keats satirically depicted suburban life as destructive of social relationships, both personal and communal. Like Mumford, Keats was critical of what he saw as the homogeneity—in architecture and ideas, especially—of suburban communities.

Others echoed this refrain. The sociologist David Riesman had even harsher criticism. In *The Lonely Crowd* (1953), Riesman likened suburban life to "a fraternity house at a small college in which like-mindedness reverberated upon itself" (as quoted in Patterson 1997, 338). Of greater significance, however, was Riesman's argument that Americans behaved according to what those around them deemed acceptable, what he called "other-directed." Some scholars later suggested that this conformity was a primary cause for the emergence of the counterculture—which was critical of the materialism of the middle class—in the 1960s. Reisman's ideas were buttressed by the work of C. Wright Mills and Willam H. Whyte, both sociologists. Mills, in *White Collar* (1951), suggested that conformity to corporate values was the price white-collar workers paid in exchange for hefty salaries. Whyte's *The Organization Man* (1956) likewise noted the stifling culture of corporate America.

Whyte also observed that suburbia was crucial to the American economy. It was, he wrote, "becoming the most important single market in the country. It is the suburbanite who starts the mass fashions—for children . . . dungarees, vodka martinis, outdoor barbecues, functional furniture, [and] picture windows. . . . All suburbs are not alike, but they are more alike than they are different" (as quoted in State Museum of Pennsylvania). As the nation's economic growth spurred the move to the suburbs, so too did the suburbs, symbiotically, fuel economic growth. This was due in large part to the Baby Boom and the emergence of youth as a consumer market.

Not all scholars believed that U.S. material abundance was beneficial. While many did not condemn capitalism per se, they did disparage the consequences of such affluence. Economist John Kenneth Gailbraith, in *The Affluent Society* (1958), argued that suburbanization, and the acquisition of material goods that it represented, undermined traditional American values.

Although the critics of suburban life were many and vocal, suburbia also had its defenders. William Levitt defended his developments by noting that the residents of Levittown were improving their housing situation. "What would you call the places our homeowners left to move out here? We give them something better and something they can pay for" (as quoted in Levinson and Krizek 2008, 40). Levitt also linked homeownership to a major concern of the postwar era: the Cold War and the threat of

Communism. "No man who owns his own house and lot can be a Communist," Levitt declared. "He has too much to do" (as cited in Jackson 1985, 231).

Other defenders challenged the sameness of suburban life. Herbert Gans, then a young sociologist, purchased a home in Levittown and found not blandness and conformity but invigorating diversity and a comfortable quality of life. "From the beginning there has been this unusual mix of liberal and conservative, Bronx born Jew and Nanticoke coal cracker," remarked one Levittown resident (as quoted in State Museum of Pennsylvania). The old middle class was not buying Levitt's houses, but the rising middle and working classes were. The houses were well built and affordable. These suburban neighborhoods provided the safe, clean, and racially segregated environments that many Americans sought. The historian James Patterson points out that:

> those who lambasted suburbia . . . tended to ignore several basic facts: the boom in building energized important sectors of the economy, providing a good deal of employment; it lessened the housing shortage that had diminished the lives of millions during the Depression and war; and it enabled people to enjoy conveniences, such as modern bathrooms and kitchens, that they had not before. (Patterson 1997, 340)

Within a few years, much of the uniformity of suburban neighborhoods began to fade as homeowners remodeled, landscaped, and transformed their homes to their own tastes. Most suburban developments lacked social services, and many had no local government. In response, residents formed voluntary associations, such as churches synagogues, bridge clubs, literary societies, recreational leagues, and Kiwanis, Lion's, and Rotary Clubs.

Yet not all suburbs were equal, and class distinctions were greater between suburbs than within them. Working-class suburbs thrived, too, typically on the edge of industrial areas. Religion also played a role in distinguishing one suburban tract from another. Jews, Catholics, and Protestants tended to socialize only with members of the same sect. Although not rigidly segregated, Catholics, Jews, and Protestants often were wary of neighbors who did not share their beliefs. Each tended to have their own clubs. Although suburbia had its critics, most Americans seemed to prefer the lifestyle it offered.

Perhaps the greatest failing of the suburbs was that they were racially segregated. Like most new suburban developments, Levittown had racially restrictive covenants limiting residents to whites. The postwar suburbs were not the first to exclude certain groups; some suburban developments not only excluded African Americans but also Jews and Catholics. Contractors, realtors, and homeowners alike contended—without any real evidence to support the contention—that black residents would drive down home prices. In 1960, in Levittown, New York, there were no black residents among the community's population of more than 80,000. William Levitt declared that:

the Negroes in America are trying to do in four hundred years what the Jews in the world have not wholly accomplished in six thousand. As a Jew, I have no room in my mind or heart for racial prejudice. But, by various means, I have come to know that if we sell one house to a Negro family, then 90 to 95 percent of our white customers will not buy into the community. (as quoted in Halberstam 1993, 141)

Levitt added that "We can solve a housing problem, or we can try to solve a racial problem. But we cannot combine the two" (as quoted in Jackson 1985, 241). The federal government reinforced this misconception by insuring loans to blacks only in specific areas. Therefore, racially segregated neighborhoods became commonplace. Levitt agreed to sell homes to blacks in 1959, after the State Court of Pennsylvania threatened to hold public hearings on housing discrimination.

This was, as many scholars have argued, a missed opportunity for the nation to address racial inequality. While racial attitudes in the North were not that much different from those in the South, suburbanization had the potential of greatly leveling the economic waters. The insatiable demand for housing, combined with federal policies that made it easy to buy a home, meant that housing developers did not need to exclude blacks to ensure the purchase of their homes. While segregated housing likely would not have been eliminated, it could have been widely reduced.

Increasingly, the suburbs came to personify the gross distinctions of wealth in the United States. Few white, middle-class Americans were aware of the extent of social injustice in the United States. Suburban living isolated many whites from the poverty of the city and parts of rural America, while popular culture—television, novels, and music—focused on enjoying the good life. This became evident in the 1980s, when the yuppie (young urban professional) emerged. Many commentators noted that many yuppies were hippies who had embraced the counterculture during the 1960s. Their conspicuous consumption in the pursuit of material accumulation to many observers seemed contradictory to the prevailing spirit of the 1960s.

The yuppies were in many ways a stereotype. Nonetheless, there did seem to be a different ethos during the late 1970s and 1980s, despite the continued, and growing, disparities in wealth. Whereas during the 1970s, the richest 5 percent earned about 10 times greater than the poorest, by 2000, that gap was 20 times greater.

Suburbia is much different today than it was sixty years ago. The first suburbs were dependent on the city they surrounded, especially for employment. Many suburbs have become large entities, however, and are no longer dependent on the urban core. The journalist Joel Garreau refers to these areas as "edge cities," which, he contends, function as cities although they look like sprawling suburban tracts. They have complex forms of government and bureaucracy that provide such services as fire and police protection, public parks, and water, and massive amounts of office space, retail space, and jobs. As a result, many suburban communities—especially those that were among the first to be developed—face social problems similar to those that have deteriorated many cities.

The suburbs—or edge cities—increasingly have provided employment in the private sector, especially in the emerging fields of computers and telecommunications, as well as the traditional fields of banking, finance, insurance, and real estate. Vast concentrations of retail shopping space, office complexes, restaurants, movie theaters, and sports arenas gave suburbanites even fewer reasons to go into the city. While many cities have revitalized their downtown in recent years, the suburbs still contrast starkly with most of urban America, particularly in how wealth is concentrated. The gentrification of many inner cities has revived those areas but also has driven up the cost of living, which, paradoxically, has displaced many poor residents.

Critics argue that we as a nation have spread out too much, what is referred to as "suburban sprawl." While many people reject that argument, several irrefutable facts can be attributed to suburban growth. Perhaps the most significant one is that the United States is wholly dependent on automobile travel, in large part because of suburbanization. With few exceptions, Americans are unable to go anywhere or do anything without driving a car to get there. Americans make hundreds of short trips each year, to buy a loaf of bread or a gallon of milk, that contribute significantly to air pollution and highway congestion, among other problems.

Suburbanization is an ongoing process, and it shows few signs of abating. Many issues with which the nation continues to struggle, such dependence on petroleum and racial segregation, derive from the construction of and movement to the suburbs. Nonetheless, the United States is, and seems destined to remain, a suburban nation.

Bibliography

Bernstein, Josh. *Willingboro, New Jersey*. Charleston, SC: Arcadia Press, 2002.

Blackwell, Jon. "1951: American Dream Houses, All in a Row." *The Trentonian*. http://www.capitalcentury.com/1951.html (accessed April 12, 2009).

Chafe, William H. *The Paradox of Change: American Women in the 20th Century*. New York: Oxford University Press, 1991.

Dunar, Andrew J. *America in the Fifties*. Syracuse, NY: Syracuse University Press, 2006.

Flink, James J. *The Automobile Age*. Cambridge, MA: Massachusetts Institute of Technology Press, 1988.

Gailbraith, John Kenneth. *The Affluent Society*. Boston: Houghton Miflin, 1958.

Gans, Herbert. *The Levittowners: Ways of Life and Politics in a New Suburban Community*. New York: Columbia University Press, 1982.

Garreau, Joel. *Edge City: Life on the New Frontier*. New York: Doubleday, 1991.

Halberstam, David. *The Fifties*. New York: Villard Books, 1993.

Jackson, Kenneth T. *Crabgrass Frontier: The Suburbanization of the United States*. New York: Oxford University Press, 1985.

Jackson, Kenneth T. "Suburbanization." In *The Reader's Companion to American History*, edited by Eric Foner and John Arthur Garraty, 1040–1043. Boston: Houghton Miflin, 1991.

Keats, John. *The Crack in the Picture Window*. Boston: Houghton Mifflin, 1957.

Levinson, David M., and Kevin J. Krizek. *Planning for Place and Plexus: Metropolitan Land Use and Transport*. New York: Routledge, 2008.

Lipsitz, George. *Time Passages: Collective Memory and American Popular Culture*. Minneapolis: University of Minnesota Press, 1990.

Mills, C. Wright. *White Collar: The American Middle Classes*. New York: Oxford University Press, 1951.

Patterson, James. *Grand Expectations. The United States, 1945–1974*. New York: Oxford University Press, 1997.

Reisman, David, with Nathan Glazer and Reuel Denney. *The Lonely Crowd: A Study of the Changing American Character*. Garden City, NY: Doubleday, 1953.

Rybczynski, Witold. *Last Harvest: How a Cornfield Became New Daleville: Real Estate Development in America from George Washington to the Builders of the Twenty-First Century and Why We Live in Houses Anyway*. New York: Simon and Schuster, 2007.

Spock, Benjamin. *Baby and Child Care*. New York: Pocket Books, 1968, 1946.

The State Museum of Pennsylvania. *Levittown, PA: Building the American Dream*. http://web1.fandm.edu/levittown/default.html.

Thompson, Craig. "Growing Pains of a Brand-New City." *Saturday Evening Post* 227, no. 6 (August 7, 1954): 26–72.

Whyte, William H. *The Organization Man*. New York: Simon and Schuster, 1956.

Primary Documents

Franklin D. Roosevelt's "Economic Bill of Rights" Speech, 1944

In his 1944 State of the Union Address, President Franklin Delano Roosevelt issued a call for an economic bill of rights. Roosevelt believed that America's future security rested on providing a solid economic foundation for all citizens. Many of Roosevelt's 'rights' were enacted in the 1950s and 1960s, particularly during the Johnson administration's Great Society.

It is our duty now to begin to lay plans and determine the strategy for the winning of a lasting peace and the establishment of an American standard of living higher than ever before known. We cannot be content, no matter how high the general standard of living may be, if some fraction of our people—whether it be one-third or one-fifth or one-tenth—is ill-fed, ill-clothed, ill-housed, and insecure.

In our day these economic truths have become self-evident. We have accepted, so to speak, a second Bill of Rights under which a new basis of security and prosperity can be established for all, regardless of station, race or creed.

Among these are:

The right to a useful and remunerative job in the industries or shops or farms or mines of this nation;

The right to earn enough to provide adequate food and clothing and recreation;

The right of every farmer to raise and sell his products at a return which will give him and his family a decent living;

The right of every business man, large and small, to trade in an atmosphere of freedom from unfair competition and domination by monopolies at home and abroad;

The right of every family to a decent home;

The right to adequate medical care and the opportunity to achieve and enjoy good health;

Table 1 Total Births and Birth Rates during and after the Baby Boom

Year	Total Number of Births	Births per 1,000 People
1940	2,559,000	19.4
1945	2,858,000	20.4
1946	3,411,000	24.1
1947	3,817,000	26.6
1948	3,637,000	24.9
1949	3,649,000	24.5
1950	3,632,000	24.1
1951	3,823,000	24.9
1952	3,913,000	25.1
1953	3,965,000	25.1
1954	4,078,000	25.3
1955	4,097,000	25.0
1956	4,218,000	25.2
1957	4,300,000	25.3
1958	4,255,000	24.5
1959	4,245,000	24.2
1960	4,258,000	23.7
1961	4,268,000	23.3
1962	4,167,000	22.4
1963	4,098,000	21.7
1964	4,027,000	21.1
Total, 1946–1964	**75,858,000**	
1965	3,760,000	19.4
1970	3,731,000	18.4
1975	3,144,000	14.6
1980	3,612,000	15.9
1985	3,761,000	15.8
1990	4,158,000	16.7
1995	3,900,000	14.6
2000	4,059,000	14.4
Total, 1965–2000	**30,125,000**	

Source: Adapted from U.S. Census Bureau, available at http://www.census.gov/statab/hist/HS-13.pdf.

The right to adequate protection from the economic fears of old age, sickness, accident and unemployment;

The right to a good education.

All of these rights spell security. And after the war is won we must be prepared to move forward, in the implementation of these rights, to new goals of human happiness and well-being.

America's own rightful place in the world depends in large part upon how fully these and similar rights have been carried into practice for our citizens. For unless there is security here at home there cannot be lasting peace in the world.

Source: Franklin D. Roosevelt, 'The Economic Bill of Rights,' January 11, 1944, in *The Public Papers and Addresses of Franklin D. Roosevelt*, ed. Samuel Rosenman (New York: Harper, 1950), 13:40–42.

Servicemen's Readjustment Act of 1944

*In 1944, President Franklin D. Roosevelt signed into law the Servicemen's Readjust-
ment Act, better know as the 'G.I. Bill.' The act provided veterans of World War II
with tuition payments and stipends for up to three years of college, and also low-
interest loans for housing, farms, and new businesses. Some 1 million veterans enrolled in college in 1946, and by 1956 more than 10 million veterans had taken
advantage of the benefits provided by the act. The G.I. Bill helped to fuel the tremendous growth of the U.S. economy in the postwar years, and accelerated the
United States' transformation into a middle-class, suburban nation.*

An Act to Provide Federal Government Aid for the Readjustment in Civilian Life of Returning World War II Veterans. . . .

    Any person who shall have served in the active military or naval serv-
ice of the United States at any time on or after September 16, 1940, and
prior to the termination of the present war and who shall have been discharged or released therefrom under conditions other than dishonorable
after active service of ninety days or more, or by reason of an injury or disability incurred in service in line of duty, . . . shall be eligible for and entitled to such course of education or training as he may elect, and at any
approved educational or training institution at which he chooses to enroll,
whether or not located in the State in which he resides, which will accept
or retain him as a student or trainee in any field or branch of knowledge
which such institution finds him qualified to undertake or pursue[.]. . . .

    The Administrator shall pay to the educational or training institution,
for each person enrolled in full time or part time course of education or
training, the customary cost of tuition, and such laboratory, library, health,
infirmary, and other similar fees as are customarily charged, and may pay
for books, supplies, equipment, and other necessary expenses, exclusive of
board, lodging, other living expenses, and travel, as are generally required
for the successful pursuit and completion of the course by other students
in the institution. . . . While enrolled in and pursuing a course under this
part, such person, upon application to the Administrator, shall be paid a
subsistence allowance of $50 per month, if without a dependent or
dependents, or $75 per month, if he has a dependent or dependents,
including regular holidays and leave not exceeding thirty days in a calen-
dar year. . . .

    . . . Any person who shall have served in the active military or naval
service of the United States at any time on or after September 16, 1940,
and prior to the termination of the present war and who shall have been
discharged or released therefrom under conditions other than dishonorable
after active service of ninety days or more, or by reason of an injury or

disability incurred in service in line of duty, shall be eligible for the benefits of this title. Any such veteran may apply within two years after separation from the military or naval forces, or two years after termination of the war, whichever is the later date, but in no event more than five years after the termination of the war, to the Administrator of Veterans' Affairs for the guaranty by the Administrator of not to exceed 50 per centum of a loan or loans for any of the purposes specified in sections 501. . . . That loans guaranteed by the Administrator shall bear interest at a rate not exceeding 4 per centum per annum and shall be payable in full in not more than twenty years. The Administrator is authorized and directed to guarantee loans to veterans subject to the provisions of this title on approved applications made to persons, firms, associations, and corporations and to governmental agencies and corporations, either State or Federal.

Source: An act to provide Federal Government aid for the readjustment in civilian life of returning World War II veterans, June 22,1944; Enrolled Acts and Resolutions of Congress, 1789–1996; General Records of the United States Government; Record Group 11; National Archives. Available at http://www.ourdocuments.gov/doc.php?flash=true&doc=76.

The Truman Doctrine, 1947

The threat of Communist insurgence after World War II soon evolved into the Cold War, which loomed ominously over the Baby Boom generation. In asking Congress for $400 million in military assistance to Greece and Turkey to fight Communism, President Harry S Truman proclaimed what would become the foundation of U.S. foreign policy during the Cold War, the containment doctrine. Truman conveniently divided the world into two factions—the free world and the Communist world— which were diametrically opposed and had little chance of peaceful coexistence. Internationally, the containment doctrine broadened American involvement in global affairs. Domestically, it contributed to the emergence of a culture that shaped the postwar era and the lives of the Baby Boom generation.

At the present moment in world history nearly every nation must choose between alternative ways of life. The choice is too often not a free one. One way of life is based upon the will of the majority, and is distinguished by free institutions, representative government, free elections, guarantees of individual liberty, freedom of speech and religion, and freedom from political oppression. The second way of life is based upon the will of a minority forcibly imposed upon the majority. It relies upon terror and oppression, a controlled press and radio, fixed elections, and the suppression of personal freedoms. I believe that it must be the policy of the United States to support free peoples who are resisting attempted subjugation by armed minorities or by outside pressures. I believe that we must assist free peoples to work out their own destinies in their own way. I believe that our help should be primarily through economic and financial aid which is essential to economic stability and orderly political processes.

Source: Address of the President to Congress, Recommending Assistance to Greece and Turkey, March 12, 1947 (Harry S. Truman Administration, Elsey Papers). Available at http://www.trumanlibrary.org/whistlestop/study_collections/doctrine/large/documents/index.php?documentdate=1947-03-12&documentid=5-9&pagenumber=1.

NSC-68, 1950

In this 1950 report prepared for President Truman, the National Security Council (NSC) called on the nation not just to contain Communism but to 'strive for victory.' To accomplish this, the NSC recommended substantial increases in defense budgets, paid for by tax increases. Perhaps as important, the NSC also recommended taking steps to maintain public support for fighting Communism, effectively putting the nation on a war footing against the Communists. Increased defense spending would be an important factor in postwar economic growth, and efforts to maintain popular support for the Cold War shaped postwar culture in significant ways.

[T]he United States now faces the contingency that within the next four or five years the Soviet Union will possess the military capability of delivering a surprise atomic attack of such weight that the United States must have substantially increased general air, ground, and sea strength, atomic capabilities, and air and civilian defenses to deter war and to provide reasonable assurance, in the event of war, that it could survive the initial blow and go on to the eventual attainment of its objectives. In return, this contingency requires the intensification of our efforts in the fields of intelligence and research and development. . . . The gravest threat to the security of the United States within the foreseeable future stems from the hostile designs and formidable power of the USSR, and from the nature of the Soviet system. . . . The risk of war with the USSR is sufficient to warrant, in common prudence, timely and adequate preparation by the United States.

. . . Attainment of these aims requires that the United States:

a. Develop a level of military readiness which can be maintained as long as necessary as a deterrent to Soviet aggression, as indispensable support to our political attitude toward the USSR, as a source of encouragement to nations resisting Soviet political aggression, and as an adequate basis for immediate military commitments and for rapid mobilization should war prove unavoidable.

b. Assure the internal security of the United States against dangers of sabotage, subversion, and espionage.

c. Maximize our economic potential, including the strengthening of our peacetime economy and the establishment of essential reserves readily available in the event of war.

d. Strengthen the orientation toward the United States of the non-Soviet nations; and help such of those nations as are able and willing to make an important contribution to U.S. security, to increase their economic and political stability and their military capability.

e. Place the maximum strain on the Soviet structure of power and particularly on the relationships between Moscow and the satellite countries.

f. Keep the U.S. public fully informed and cognizant of the threats to our national security so that it will be prepared to support the measures which we must accordingly adopt. . . .

In summary, we must, by means of a rapid and sustained build-up of the political, economic, and military strength of the free world, and by means of an affirmative program intended to wrest the initiative from the Soviet Union, confront it with convincing evidence of the determination and ability of the free world to frustrate the Kremlin design of a world dominated by its will . . . The whole success of the proposed program hangs ultimately on recognition by this Government, the American people, and all free peoples, that the cold war is in fact a real war in which the survival of the free world is at stake. Essential prerequisites to success are consultations with Congressional leaders designed to make the program the object of non-partisan legislative support, and a presentation to the public of a full explanation of the facts and implications of the present international situation. The prosecution of the program will require of us all the ingenuity, sacrifice, and unity demanded by the vital importance of the issue and the tenacity to persevere until our national objectives have been attained.

Source: A Report to the President pursuant to the President's directive of January 31, 1950 (NSC 68, April 7, 1950). Available at http://www.trumanlibrary.org/whistlestop/study_collections/korea/large/week2/nsc68_1.htm.

Internal Security Act of 1950

Amid a growing suspicion of foreigners and the rising fear of Communist subversion, Congress overrode President Truman's veto to enact the McCarran Act, as the Internal Security Act was known. Among other requirements, the law directed Communists to register with the attorney general and forbade members of totalitarian organizations from entering the country. Similar laws cropped up in many states, including Michigan. McCarthyism would reach its zenith over the next three years, and it would leave a dark cloud over American society and culture during the Baby Boom.

AN ACT

To protect the United States against certain un-American and subversive activities by requiring registration of Communist organizations, and for other purposes.

. . . As a result of evidence adduced before various committees of the Senate and House of Representatives, the Congress hereby finds that (1) There exists a world Communist movement which, in its origins, its development, and its present practice, is a world-wide revolutionary movement whose purpose it is, by treachery, deceit, infiltration into other groups (governmental and otherwise), espionage, sabotage, terrorism, and any other means deemed necessary, to establish a Communist totalitarian dictatorship in the countries throughout the world through the medium of a world-wide Communist organization. . . . The Communist movement in the United States is an organization numbering thousands of adherents, rigidly and ruthlessly disciplined. Awaiting and seeking to advance a moment when the United States may be so far extended by foreign engagements, so far divided in counsel, or so far in industrial or financial straits, that overthrow of the Government of the United States by force and violence may seem possible of achievement, it seeks converts far and wide by an extensive system of schooling and indoctrination. . . . SEC. 7. (a) Each Communist-action organization (including any organization required, by a final order of the Board, to register as a Communist-action organization) shall, within the time specified in subsection (c) of this section, register with the Attorney General, on a form prescribed by him by regulations, as a Communist-action organization. (b) Each Communist-front organization . . . shall . . . register with the Attorney General, on a form prescribed by him by regulations, as a Communist-front organization. . . . (d) Upon the registration of each Communist organization under the provisions of this title, the Attorney General shall publish in the Federal Register the fact that such organization has registered as a Communist action organization, or as a Communist-front organization, as the case may be, and the publication thereof shall constitute notice to all members of such organization that such organization has so registered.

Source: U.S. Statutes at Large, 81st Cong., 2nd sess. (1950), Ch. 1024, 987–1031.

Michigan Communist Control Law, 1952

AN ACT requiring communists and knowing members of communist front organizations to register with the Michigan state police; providing that neither the names of nominees of the communist party nor the names of communists shall appear upon the ballots in primary or general elections; providing that probable communists and knowing members of communist front organizations shall not hold non-elective positions or jobs; outlawing sabotage; and providing criminal penalties . . .

752.321 Subversive groups and elements in public and private employment and schools, finding; infiltration. [M.S.A. 28.243(11)]

Sec. 1. The legislature hereby finds and declares that there are present in the state of Michigan subversive groups and elements, particularly of the communist party and certain of its affiliated organizations, which have infiltrated into both private and public employment and into the public schools of the state. This has occurred and continues despite the existence of present statutes. The consequence of any such infiltration into the public schools is that subversive propaganda can be disseminated among children of tender years by those who teach them and to whom the children look for guidance, authority and leadership. Infiltration of these elements into the public service results in employment and retention of groups which teach and advocate that the government of the United States or of any state or of any political subdivision thereof shall be overthrown by force or violence or by any unlawful means. The legislature finds that members of such groups frequently use their office or position to advocate and teach subversive doctrines. The legislature finds that members of such groups are frequently bound by oath, agreement, pledge or understanding to follow, advocate and teach a prescribed party line or group, dogma or doctrine without regard to truth or free inquiry. The legislature finds that such dissemination of propaganda may be and frequently is sufficiently subtle to escape detection in the classroom. It is difficult, therefore, to measure the menace of such infiltration in the schools by conduct in the classroom. The legislature further finds and declares that in order to protect the children and our state institutions from such subversive influence it is essential that the laws prohibiting persons who are members of subversive groups, such as the communist party and its affiliated organizations, from obtaining or retaining employment in the public schools or state financed positions, be vigorously enforced. The legislature deplores the failure heretofore to prevent such infiltration which threatens dangerously to become a commonplace in our schools and institutions . . .

Sec. 7. The name of any communist or of any nominee of the communist party shall not be printed upon any ballot used in any primary or general election in this state or in any political subdivision thereof. . . .

Sec. 8. No person may hold any non–elective position, job or office for the state of Michigan, or any political subdivision thereof, where the remuneration of said position, job or office is paid in whole or in part by public moneys or funds of the state of Michigan, or of any political subdivision thereof, where reasonable grounds exist, on all of the evidence, from which after hearing. the employer or superior of such person can say with reasonable certainty that such person is a communist or a knowing member of a communist front organization. In cases involving a person within the classified service of the state of Michigan such hearing shall be held by the civil service commission.

Source: *Michigan Communist Control Law*, Public Act 117 (1952). Available at http://www.michigan.gov/hal/0,1607,7-160-17451_18670_18793-53650–,00.html.

Montgomery, Alabama, Code on Segregation

Although segregation existed throughout the United States, it was most blatant in the South. De facto segregation—through economic means, for example—ruled in the North; de jure segregation ruled in the South.

In 1955, the first mass protest against Jim Crow began in Montgomery, Alabama, led by twenty-six-year-old Martin Luther King, Jr. For more than a year, black citizens of Montgomery walked to and from work and to the grocer rather than ride on segregated city buses. Their challenge of the law—reprinted below—resulted in a Supreme Court ruling prohibiting segregation in public transportation.

Sec. 10. Separation of races—Required.

Every person operating a bus line the in the city shall provide equal but separate accommodations for white people and Negroes on his buses, by requiring the employees in charge thereof to assign passengers seats on the vehicles under their charge in such manner as to separate the white from the Negroes, where there are both white and Negroes on the same car. . . .

Source: Code of the City of Montgomery, Alabama (Charlottesville: Michie City Publishing Co., 1952). Alabama Department of Archives and History, Montgomery, Alabama. Available at http://www.archives.state.al.us/teacher/rights/lesson1/doc1.html.

Brown v. Board of Education, 1954

The Supreme Court's ruling in Brown v. Board of Education *overturned the doctrine of 'separate but equal,' which had given legal sanction to racial segregation in the United States for more than fifty years. Many hailed the decision as evidence that the nation was finally living up to its creed of equality; critics decried* Brown *as 'judicial activism' by a liberal court that had overstepped its constitutional bounds. The decision had significant consequences for the Baby Boom generation, and black boomers in particular. While the desegregation of the nation's schools would drag on for several decades, the decision gave hope to many young African Americans that the American promise of justice and equality would be redeemed.*

In each of the cases, minors of the Negro race, through their legal representatives, seek the aid of the courts in obtaining admission to the public schools of their community on a nonsegregated basis. In each instance, they had been denied admission to schools attended by white children under laws requiring or permitting segregation according to race. This segregation was alleged to deprive the plaintiffs of the equal protection of the laws under the Fourteenth Amendment. In each of the cases other than the Delaware case, a three-judge federal district court denied relief to the plaintiffs on the so-called "separate but equal" doctrine announced by this Court in *Plessy v. Ferguson*. . . . Under that doctrine, equality of treatment is accorded when the races are provided substantially equal facilities, even though these facilities be separate. . . . The plaintiffs contend that segregated public schools are not "equal" and cannot be made "equal," and that hence they are deprived of the equal protection of the laws. . . .

Our decision, therefore, cannot turn on merely a comparison of these tangible factors in the Negro and white schools involved in each of the cases. We must look instead to the effect of segregation itself on public education. . . .

We come then to the question presented: Does segregation of children in public schools solely on the basis of race, even though the physical facilities and other "tangible" factors may be equal, deprive the children of the minority group of equal educational opportunities? We believe that it does. . . .

To separate them from others of similar age and qualifications solely because of their race generates a feeling of inferiority as to their status in the community that may affect their hearts and minds in a way unlikely ever to be undone. . . . Whatever may have been the extent of psychological knowledge at the time of *Plessy v. Ferguson*, this finding is amply supported by modern authority. Any language in *Plessy v. Ferguson* contrary to this finding is rejected.

We conclude that, in the field of public education, the doctrine of "separate but equal" has no place. Separate educational facilities are inherently unequal. Therefore, we hold that the plaintiffs and others similarly situated for whom the actions have been brought are, by reason of the segregation complained of, deprived of the equal protection of the laws guaranteed by the Fourteenth Amendment. This disposition makes unnecessary any discussion whether such segregation also violates the Due Process Clause of the Fourteenth Amendment. . . . It is so ordered.

Source: *Oliver Brown et al. v. Board of Education of Topeka, Kansas* 347 U.S. 483 (1954). Available at http://www.ourdocuments.gov/doc.php?doc=87&page= transcript.

Executive Order 10730: Desegregration of Central High School, Little Rock, Arkansas, 1957

The first test of the Brown *decision came in 1957 in Little Rock, Arkansas. A federal court had ordered that Central High School admit African Americans. When nine African American students tried to enroll at Central they were met with resistance by whites. Governor Orval Faubus, claiming to act in the interest of preventing violence, ordered the Arkansas National Guard to the school to prevent the black students from attending. In response, President Dwight D. Eisenhower ordered federal troops to Little Rock to permit the students to enroll and to protect them as they went to classes. The dignity and courage of the black students inspired others to join the fight for racial equality. Eisenhower's action, while couched in the language of 'upholding the Constitution,' was similarly encouraging.*

WHEREAS certain persons in the state of Arkansas, individually and in unlawful assemblages, combinations, and conspiracies, have willfully obstructed the enforcement of orders of the United States District Court for the Eastern District of Arkansas with respect to matters relating to enrollment and attendance at public schools, particularly at Central High School, located in Little Rock School District, Little Rock, Arkansas; . . .

WHEREAS the command contained in that Proclamation has not been obeyed and willful obstruction of enforcement of said court orders still exists and threatens to continue:

NOW, THEREFORE, by virtue of the authority vested in me by the Constitution and Statutes of the United States, . . .

I hereby authorize and direct the Secretary of Defense to order into the active military service of the United States as he may deem appropriate to carry out the purposes of this Order, any or all of the units of the National Guard of the United States and of the Air National Guard of the United States within the State of Arkansas to serve in the active military service of the United States for an indefinite period and until relieved by appropriate orders.

SEC. 2. The Secretary of Defense is authorized and directed to take all appropriate steps to enforce any orders of the United States District Court for the Eastern District of Arkansas for the removal of obstruction of justice in the State of Arkansas with respect to matters relating to enrollment and attendance at public schools in the Little Rock School District, Little Rock, Arkansas. In carrying out the provisions of this section, the Secretary of Defense is authorized to use the units, and members thereof, ordered into the active military service of the United States pursuant to Section 1 of this Order.

SEC. 3. In furtherance of the enforcement of the aforementioned orders of the United States District Court for the Eastern District of Arkansas, the Secretary of Defense is authorized to use such of the armed forces of the United States as he may deem necessary.

SEC. 4. The Secretary of Defense is authorized to delegate to the Secretary of the Army or the Secretary of the Air Force, or both, any of the authority conferred upon him by this Order.

Source: Executive Order 10730, September 23, 1957 (Little Rock Crisis); General Records of the United States Government; Record Group 11; National Archives. Available at http://www.ourdocuments.gov/doc.php?doc=89&page=transcript.

Dr. Benjamin Spock, *The Common Sense Book of Baby and Child Care*, 1957

First published in 1946 by Dr. Benjamin Spock, The Common Sense Book of Baby and Child Care *has sold more than 50 million copies worldwide. Spock's advice influenced how the Baby Boom generation would be raised. As this excerpt from the 1957 edition illustrates, Spock cautioned against following strict feeding regimes, and encouraged parents to trust their instincts and have fun raising their children, to comfort them when they cried, and to play with them. Critics dismissed Spock's advice as 'permissive parenting.' Although his ideas went against the traditional wisdom, in many ways Spock was a traditionalist himself. Women would be the primary caregiver, he assumed, and so they should put their children's emotional and physical needs ahead of their own.*

TRUST YOURSELF. You know more than you think you do. Soon you're going to have a baby. Maybe you have him already. You're happy and excited, but if you haven't had much experience, you wonder whether you are going to know how to do a good job. Lately you have been listening more carefully to your friends and relatives when they talk about bringing up a child. You've begun to read articles by experts in the magazines and newspapers. After the baby is born, the doctor and nurses will begin to give you instructions, too. Sometimes it sounds like a very complicated business. You find out all the vitamins a baby needs and all the inoculations. One mother tells you that egg should be given early because of its iron, and another says that egg should be delayed to avoid allergy. You hear that a baby is easily spoiled by being picked up too much but also that a baby must be cuddled plenty; that fairy tales make children nervous, and that fairy tales are a wholesome outlet.

Don't take too seriously all that the neighbors say. Don't be overawed by what the experts say. Don't be afraid to trust your own common sense. Bringing up your child won't be a complicated job if you take it easy, trust your own instincts, and follow the directions that your doctor gives you. We know for a fact that the natural loving care that kindly parents give their children is a hundred times more valuable than their knowing how to pin a diaper on just right or how to make a formula expertly. Every time you pick your baby up, even if you do it a little awkwardly at first, every time you change him, bathe him, feed him, smile at him, he's getting a feeling that he belongs to you and that you belong to him. Nobody else in the world, no matter how skillful, can give that to him.

It may surprise you to hear that the more people have studied different methods of bringing up children the more they have come to the conclusion that what good mothers and fathers instinctively feel like doing for their babies is usually best, after all. Furthermore, all parents do their best job when they have a natural, easy confidence in themselves. Better to make a few mistakes from being natural than to do everything letter-perfect out of a feeling of worry.

Prenatal classes for expectant mothers and fathers are provided in many communities by the Visiting Nurse Association, the Red Cross, or the city health department. They are very helpful in discussing the questions and problems that all expectant parents have concerning pregnancy, delivery, and care of baby.

Source: Dr. Benjamin Spock, *The Common Sense Book of Baby and Child Care* (New York: Pocket Books, 1957), 1–2.

Elvis Presley and Rock-And-Roll Music

Few individuals have had as great an impact on American culture as Elvis Presley. Presley burst on the scene in the mid-1950s. He was influenced by country, gospel, rhythm and blues, and rock-and-roll music. As one record producer noted, he 'was white but sounded black.' It was his movements on stage, however, that generated reactions from opposite quarters. Presley's wild hip 'gyrations' and dancing enthralled teens and outraged parents and the older generations. He wore his hair slicked back and had long sideburns, adding a further touch of rebelliousness to his appearance. His records sold millions of copies, mostly purchased by teenagers. The excerpts below provide evidence of how little many older Americans thought of Presley, and illustrate a widening generation gap between baby boomers and their parents.

What's the matter with that insultingly stupid singer called Elvis Presslee [*sic*]? I saw him for the first time on a recent Milton Berle Show. Presslee, for my money, is straight from a burlesque house. . . . He mangles songs; his voice is flat; and his face is the epitome of pouting imbecility. I hear that the teen-agers think he's just great. IF this is true, the persons in my age group will have to relinquish their title as the "Lost Generation."

Source: Samuel P. Zadrovich, 'Who's Got the Pain?' *The Washington Post* and *Times Herald*, June 17 1956, J2. ProQuest Historical Newspapers.

The Elvis Presley craze will pass, but in the meantime teenagers are having a vicarious fling, a Greenwich Village minister said yesterday. . . . He said that Mr. Presley, "using innuendo and suggestion, by curl of lip and shake of hip, represents the revolt from the tried and true. . . . I don't think youth wants this sort of thing," adding that it is the "result of the let-down that follows every war." The teen-age set is having a vicarious fling, he explained.

Source: 'Presley Termed a Passing Fancy,' *New York Times*, December 17, 1956, 28. ProQuest Historical Newspapers.

The best description of Presley's performance on the Milton Berle show came from the chairman of the music department of Bryant High School, Harry A. Feldman, who wrote . . . "Elvis Presley, presented a demonstration which was in execrable taste, bordering on obscenity. The gyrations of this young man were such an assault to the senses as to repel even the most tolerant observer. When television entrepreneurs present such performers to millions of viewers and pronounced them great, when such deplorable taste is displayed in the presentation of primitive, shoddy and offensive material, one begins to understand the present day attitude of our youth. We in the classroom can do very little to offset the force and impact of these displays in our efforts to stem the tide toward a cultural debacle." About the only guy who ever summed up Elvis "the Pelvis" any better than that was the California policeman who, after watching him writhe around a stage, commented: "If he did that on the street we'd arrest him." . . . Where did the degeneration of popular music start? . . . The public, particularly the teen-age public, got a taste for bad music that it hasn't lost to this day. The good composers—Irving Berlin, Rodgers and Hammerstein and the like—had their songs forced off the air and with a few exceptions their songs are still off it.

Source: John Crosby, 'Could Elvis Mean End of Rock 'n' Roll Craze?' *The Washington Post* and *Times Herald*, June 18, 1956, 33. ProQuest Historical Newspapers.

Mr. Presley has no discernible singing ability. His specialty is rhythm songs which he renders is an undistinguished whine; his phrasing, if it can be called that, consists of the stereotyped variations that go with a beginner's aria in a bathtub. For the ear he is an unutterable bore, not nearly so talented as Frankie Sinatra back in the latter's rather hysterical days at the Paramount Theatre. Nor does he convey the emotional fury of a Johnnie Ray.

From watching Mr. Presley it is wholly evident that his skill lies in another direction. He is a rock-and-roll variation on one of the most standard acts in show business: the virtuoso of the hootchy-kootchy. His one specialty is an accented movement of the body that heretofore has been primarily identified with the repertoire of the blond bombshells of the burlesque runway. The gyration never had anything to do with the world of popular music and still doesn't.

Source: Jack Gould, 'Elvis Presley Rises to Fame as Vocalist Who Is Virtuoso of Hootchy-Kootchy,' *New York Times*, June 6, 1956, 67. ProQuest Historical Newspapers.

Clothing the Baby Boom, 1955

While the Baby Boom was in part a consequence of U.S. postwar economic abundance, it also contributed significantly to that growth. New products and services emerged, aimed at the growing maternity and infant markets.

When the infant becomes a gurgling reality, the happy parents, eyes already weary from reading tons of mail and ears ringing from prenatal sales talks, are sitting ducks for still another urgent barrage of commercials.

Naturally, all these cheery, well-wishing stalkers of the stork—whether they first approach the prospective parents in the early months or fly down the chimney in a dead heat with the big bird—have something to sell. Their wares and services add up to staggering figures, and it's not hard to see why. Last year, according to unofficial estimates, 4,100,000 babies—an all-time high—were born in the United States.

The maternity-clothes industry, biggest single prenatal operation, does an annual business estimated at up to $200,000,000. Layettes, cribs, baby carriages, baths, feeding accessories and toiletries, purchases of which are arranged before the baby is born, gross half a billion dollars a year. Diaper services, possibly the most vigorous competitors in the prenatal field, do an annual coast-to-coast business of $30,000,000. . . .

Then there are the friends of expectant mothers who use a diaper service themselves and either recommend the service to mothers-to-be ("and don't forget to tell them I sent you"), or actually sell their names, for a credit slip or a bonus. One Chicago diaper service has a set pay-off scale, or at least it had until recently. It offered "baby pants for two names." Hospital office employees are a good source, too. Sometimes they get nylons. . . .

Source: Murray Robinson, 'Stalking the Stork,' *Collier's*, March 4, 1955, 21–23.

The New Teenage Market, 1959

The baby boomers have been prodigious consumers their entire lives. The extent of their consumerism is evident in this 1959 article from Life *magazine.*

But to a growing number of businessmen the picture spells out the profitable fact that the American teen-agers have emerged as a big-time consumer in the U.S. economy. They are multiplying in numbers. They spend more and have more spent on them. And they have minds of their own about what they want. . . . Today teen-agers surround themselves with a fantastic array of garish and often expensive baubles and amusements. They own 10 million phonographs, over a million TV sets, 13 million cameras. . . . Counting only what is spent to satisfy their special teen-age demands, the youngsters and their parents will shell out about $10 billion this year, a billion more than the total sales of GM.

Until recently businessmen have largely ignored the teen-age market. But now they are spending millions on advertising and razzle-dazzle promotional stunts. . . . At 17 Suzie Slattery of Van Nuys, Calif., fits any businessman's dream of the ideal teen-age consumer. . . . Last year $1,500 was spent on Suzie's clothes and $550 for her entertainment. Her annual food bill comes to $900. She pays $4 every two weeks at the beauty parlor. She has her own telephone and even has her own soda fountain in the house. On summer vacation days she loves to wander with her mother through fashionable department stores, picking out frocks or furnishings for her room or silver and expensive crockery for the hope chest she has already started. As a high school graduation present, Suzie was given a holiday cruise to Hawaii and is now in the midst of a new clothes-buying spree for college. . . .

Some Fascinating Facts about a Booming Market.

FOOD: Teen-agers eat 20% more than adults. They down 3 1/2 billion quarts of milk every year, almost four times as much as is drunk by the infant population under 1. Teen-agers are a main prop of the ice cream industry, gobble 145 million gallons a year.

BEAUTY CARE: Teen-agers spent $20 million on lipstick last year, $25 million on deodorants (a fifth of total sold), $9 million on home permanents. Male teen-agers own 2 million electric razors.

ENTERTAINMENT: Teen-agers lay out more than $1.5 billion a year for entertainment. They spend about $75 million on single pop records. . . .

HOMEMAKERS: Major items like furniture and silver are moving into the teen-age market because of growing number of teen-age marriages. One third of all 18- and 19-year-old girls are already married. More than

600,000 teen-agers will be married this year. Teen-agers are now starting hope chests at 15.

CREDIT RISKS: Some 800,000 teen-agers work at full-time jobs and can buy major items on credit.

Source: 'A New $10-Billion Power: The Teen-age Market' *Life* (August 31, 1959): 78–85.

The Comic Book Code of 1954

As a distinctive youth culture emerged after World War II, juvenile delinquency became a concern for parents, educators, scholars, and politicians. The growth of this youth culture resulted from compulsory school attendance laws, new technology (television), and the sheer size of the youth population. Many people, however, identified other causes, such as films, rock-and-roll music, and comic books. One result of this debate was the Comic Book Code. The Code was written by comic book publishers following Senate hearings on the affects of comics on the young.

(1) Crimes shall never be presented in such a way as to create sympathy for the criminal, to promote distrust of the forces of law and justice, or to inspire others with a desire to imitate criminals.

(2) No comics shall explicitly present the unique details and methods of a crime.

(3) Policemen, judges, Government officials and respected institutions shall never be presented in such a way as to create disrespect for established authority.

(4) If crime is depicted it shall be as a sordid and unpleasant activity.

(5) Criminals shall not be presented so as to be rendered glamorous or to occupy a position which creates a desire for emulation.

(6) In every instance good shall triumph over evil and the criminal punished for his misdeeds.

(7) Scenes of excessive violence shall be prohibited. Scenes of brutal torture, excessive and unnecessary knife and gunplay, physical agony, gory and gruesome crime shall be eliminated.

(8) No unique or unusual methods of concealing weapons shall be shown.

(9) Instances of law-enforcement officers dying as a result of a criminal's activities should be discouraged.

(10) The crime of kidnapping shall never be portrayed in any detail, nor shall any profit accrue to the abductor or kidnaper. The criminal or the kidnaper must be punished in every case.

(11) The letters of the word "crime" on a comics-magazine cover shall never be appreciably greater in dimension than the other words contained in the title. The word "crime" shall never appear alone on a cover.

(12) Restraint in the use of the word "crime" in titles or subtitles shall be exercised.

General standards—Part B

(1) No comic magazine shall use the word horror or terror in its title.

(2) All scenes of horror, excessive bloodshed, gory or gruesome crimes, depravity, lust, sadism, masochism shall not be permitted.

(3) All lurid, unsavory, gruesome illustrations shall be eliminated.

(4) Inclusion of stories dealing with evil shall be used or shall be published only where the intent is to illustrate a moral issue and in no case shall evil be presented alluringly, nor so as to injure the sensibilities of the reader.

(5) Scenes dealing with, or instruments associated with walking dead, torture, vampires and vampirism, ghouls, cannibalism, and werewolfism are prohibited.

General standards—Part C

All elements or techniques not specifically mentioned herein, but which are contrary to the spirit and intent of the code, and are considered violations of good taste or decency, shall be prohibited.

Dialogue

(1) Profanity, obscenity, smut, vulgarity, or words or symbols which have acquired undesirable meanings are forbidden.

(2) Special precautions to avoid references to physical afflictions or deformities shall be taken.

(3) Although slang and colloquialisms are acceptable, excessive use should be discouraged and, wherever possible, good grammar shall be employed.

Religion

(1) Ridicule or attack on any religious or racial group is never permissible.

Costume

(1) Nudity in any form is prohibited, as is indecent or undue exposure.

(2) Suggestive and salacious illustration or suggestive posture is unacceptable.

(3) All characters shall be depicted in dress reasonably acceptable to society.

(4) Females shall be drawn realistically without exaggeration of any physical qualities. . . .

Marriage and sex

(1) Divorce shall not be treated humorously nor represented as desirable.

(2) Illicit sex relations are neither to be hinted at nor portrayed. Violent love scenes as well as sexual abnormalities are unacceptable.

(3) Respect for parents, the moral code, and for honorable behavior shall be fostered. A sympathetic understanding of the problems of love is not a license for morbid distortion.

(4) The treatment of live-romance stories shall emphasize the value of the home and the sanctity of marriage.

(5) Passion or romantic interest shall never be treated in such a way as to stimulate the lower and baser emotions.

(6) Seduction and rape shall never be shown or suggested.

(7) Sex perversion or any inference to same is strictly forbidden.

CODE FOR ADVERTISING MATTER

(1) Liquor and tobacco advertising is not acceptable.

(2) Advertisement of sex or sex instruction books are unacceptable.

(3) The sale of picture postcards, "pinups," "art studies," or any other reproduction of nude or seminude figures is prohibited.

(4) Advertising for the sale of knives or realistic gun facsimiles is prohibited.

(5) Advertising for the sale of fireworks is prohibited.

(6) Advertising dealing with the sale of gambling equipment or printed matter dealing with gambling shall not be accepted.

(7) Nudity with meretricious purpose and salacious postures shall not be permitted in the advertising of any product; clothed figures shall never be presented in such a way as to be offensive or contrary to good taste or morals.

(8) To the best of his ability, each publisher shall ascertain that all statements made in advertisements conform to fact and avoid misrepresentation.

(9) Advertisement of medical, health, or toiletry products of questionable nature are to be rejected. Advertisements for medical, health, or toiletry products endorsed by the American Medical Association, or the American Dental Association, shall be deemed acceptable if they conform with all other conditions of the Advertising Code.

Source: Senate Committee on the Judiciary, *Comic Books and Juvenile Delinquency*, Interim Report (Washington, DC: U.S. Government Printing Office, 1955).

The Television Code of 1952

In 1945, there were probably fewer than 10,000 television sets in the United States; by 1960 there were 46 million sets, and three-fourths of all homes had at least one set. Television's influence on the Baby Boom generation was immense. Like comic books, music lyrics, and films, however, many observers believed the medium was contributing to the low morals of youth. In 1952, television broadcasters adopted a code to regulate program content. The Senate in 1954 and 1955 held hearings to explore the possible link between television programming and the spread of juvenile delinquency. Below are excerpts from both the Senate hearings and the broadcast-ers code.

It is not enough that only those programs which are intended for viewing by children shall be suitable to the young and immature. Television is responsible for insuring that programs of all sorts which occur during the times of day when children may normally be expected to have the opportunity of viewing television shall exercise care in the following regards:

(a) In affording opportunities for cultural growth as well as for whole-some entertainment.

(b) In developing programs to foster and promote the commonly accepted moral, social, and ethical ideals characteristic of American life.

(c) In reflecting respect for parents, for honorable behavior, and for the constituted authorities of the American community.

(d) In eliminating reference to kidnapping of children or threats of kidnapping.

(e) In avoiding material which is excessively violent or would create morbid suspense, or other undesirable reactions in children.

(f) In exercising particular restraint and care in crime or mystery episodes involving children or minors. . . .

The Television Code of the National Association of Radio and Television Broadcasters, Preamble

Television is seen and heard in every type of American home. These homes include children and adults of all ages, embrace all races and all varieties of religious faith, and reach those of every educational back ground. It is the responsibility of television to bear constantly in mind that the audience is primarily a home audience, and consequently that television's relationship to the viewers is that between guest and host.

The revenues from advertising support the free, competitive American system of telecasting, and make available to the eyes and ears of the American people the finest programs of information, education, culture and entertainment. By law the television broadcaster is responsible for the programming of his station. He, however, is obligated to bring his positive responsibility for excellence and good taste in programming to bear upon all who have a hand in the production of programs, including networks, sponsors, producers of film and of live programs, advertising agencies, and talent agencies.

The American businesses which utilize television for conveying their advertising messages to the home by pictures with sound, seen free-of-charge on the home screen, are reminded that their responsibilities are not limited to the sale of goods and the creation of a favorable attitude toward the sponsor by the presentation of entertainment. They include, as well, responsibility for utilizing television to bring the best programs, regardless of kind, into American homes.

Television, and all who participate in it are jointly accountable to the American public for respect for the special needs of children, for community responsibility, for the advancement of education and culture, for the acceptability of the program materials chosen, for decency and decorum in production, and for propriety in advertising. This responsibility cannot be discharged by any given group of programs, but can be discharged only through the highest standards of respect for the American home, applied to every moment of every program presented by television.

In order that television programming may best serve the public interest, viewers should be encouraged to make their criticisms and positive suggestions known to the television broadcasters. Parents in particular should be urged to see to it that out of the richness of television fare, the best programs are brought to the attention of their children. . . .

Source: Senate Committee on the Judiciary, Subcommittee to Investigate Juvenile Delinquency, *Television and Juvenile Delinquency*, Interim Report (Washington, DC: U.S. Government Printing Office, 1955, Committee Print).

"The Constant Reiteration of Horror and Violence": A Senate Report on Television and Juvenile Delinquency

. . . During the course of its investigation, the subcommittee deemed it appropriate to explore the content of television programs that might receive attention from young people of all ages. The staff surveyed the results of studies previously made with that thought in mind. The staff conducted some surveys of its own for comparison. The results were found to be substantially in agreement. It was found that a large amount of the time during children's viewing hours is devoted to the subject matter of crime and violence. In several studies of program content, the hours from 5 to 7 P.M. on weekdays and from sign-on to 7 P.M. on Saturdays and Sundays are referred to as children's hours. However, it has been recognized that many juveniles do not limit their television viewing to those hours; and there are many who view television after 7 o'clock in the evening through the week. . . .

Concern expressed for cumulative effect of crime and horror

The cumulative effect of crime-and-horror television programs on the personality development of American children has become a source of mounting concern to parents. Several generalizations can be made concerning many of the programs shown during children's viewing hours. It was found that life is cheap; death, suffering, sadism, and brutality are subjects of callous indifference and that judges, lawyers, and law-enforcement officers are too often dishonest, incompetent, and stupid. The manner and frequency with which crime through this medium is brought before the eyes and ears of American children indicates inadequate regard for psychological and social consequences. What the subcommittee tried to determine was: Are these presentations a contributing factor in juvenile delinquency? . . .

There is reason to believe that television crime programs are potentially much more injurious to children and young people than motion pictures, radio, or comic books. Attending a movie requires money and the physical effort of leaving the home, so an average child's exposure to films in the theater tends to be limited to a few hours a week. Comic books demand strong imaginary projections. Also, they must be sought out and purchased. But television, available at a flick of a knob and combining visual and audible aspects into a "live" story, has a greater impact upon its child audience.

Source: Senate Committee on the Judiciary, Subcommittee to Investigate Juvenile Delinquency, *Television and Juvenile Delinquency*, Interim Report (Washington, DC: U.S. Government Printing Office, 1955, Committee Print).

William H. Whyte, Jr., The Organization Man, 1956

The tremendous economic growth of the Baby Boom era not only raised Americans' standard of living, but also encouraged the growth and consolidation of corporate power. Corporate culture tended toward political and social conservatism. William Whyte's The Organization Man *is the best-known critique of corporate culture. Whyte argued that corporate culture created a 'social ethic,' a belief in belonging-ness as the ultimate need of the individual. He posited that Organization Men were unimaginative, and the culture they inhabited robbed them of their individuality.*

This book is about the organization man. . . . They are the ones of our middle class who have left home, spiritually as well as physically, to take the vows of organization life, and it is they who are the mind and soul of our great self-perpetuating institutions. . . . But they are the dominant members of our society nonetheless. They have not joined together into a recognizable elite—our country does not stand still long enough for that—but it is from their ranks that are coming most of the first and second echelons of our leadership, and it is their values which will set the American temper. . . .

Whatever the differences in their organization ties, it is the common problems of collective work that dominate their attentions[.] . . . But they have no great sense of plight; between themselves and organization they believe they see an ultimate harmony and, more than most elders recognize, they are building an ideology that will vouchsafe this trust. . . .

I am going to call it a Social Ethic. With reason it could be called an organization ethic, or a bureaucratic ethic; more than anything else it rationalizes the organization's demands for fealty and gives those who offer it wholeheartedly a sense of dedication in doing so—in extremis, you might say, it converts what would seem in other times a bill of no rights into a restatement of individualism. . . .

In the Social Ethic I am describing, however, man's obligation is in the here and now; his duty is not so much to the community in a broad sense but to the actual, physical one about him, and the idea that in isolation from it-or active rebellion against it—he might eventually discharge the greater service is little considered. In practice, those who most eagerly sub-scribe to the Social Ethic worry very little over the long-range problems of society. It is not that they don't care but rather that they tend to assume that the ends of organization and morality coincide, and on such matters as social welfare they give their proxy to the organization. . . .

Thus to my thesis. I believe the emphasis of the Social Ethic is wrong for him. People do have to work with others, yes; the well-functioning team is a whole greater than the sum of its parts, yes—all this is indeed true. But is it the truth that now needs belaboring? Precisely because it is an age of organization, it is the other side of the coin that needs emphasis. We do need to know how to co-operate with The Organization but, more than ever, so do we need to know how to resist it.

Source: William H. Whyte, Jr., *The Organization Man* (Philadelphia: University of Pennsylvania Press, 2002, 1956), 3–18.

National Interstate and Defense Highways Act, 1956

The Interstate Highway Act was the largest public works project in American history. It provided nearly 90 percent of the funding for roads. As a result, the number of miles driven annually increased fourfold. The Interstate Highway Act had a pro-found impact on daily life of the Baby Boom generation by contributing to the rapid suburbanization of the postwar years.

It is hereby declared to be essential to the national interest to provide for the early completion of the "National System of Interstate Highways," as author-ized and designated in accordance with section 7 of the Federal-Aid Highway Act of 1944 (58 Stat. 838). It is the intent of the Congress that the Interstate System be completed as nearly as practicable over a thirteen-year period and that the entire System in all the States be brought to simultaneous comple-tion. Because of its primary importance to the national defense, the name of such system is hereby changed to the "National System of Interstate and Defense Highways." Such National System of Interstate and Defense High-ways is hereinafter in this Act referred to as the "Interstate System."

Source: *National Interstate and Defense Highways Act,1956*, June 29, 1956; En-rolled Acts and Resolutions of Congress, 1789–1996; General Records of the United States Government; Record Group 11; National Archives. Available at http://www.ourdocuments.gov/doc.php?doc=88&page=transcript.

National Defense Education Act, 1958

On October 4, 1957, the Soviet Union launched into outer space a small satellite called Sputnik; *Americans were stunned. In less than fifteen years, the Soviets had surpassed the United States in technological prowess, and it now had the capacity to launch rockets with nuclear payloads at the United States. Many people believed American schools had failed and, in response, Congress passed the National Defense Education Act in 1958. The act sought to strengthen graduate training and instruction at all levels in foreign languages, science, and math.*

AN ACT

To strengthen the national defense and to encourage and assist in the expansion and improvement of educational programs to meet critical national needs; and for other purposes. . . .

The Congress hereby finds and declares that the security of the Nation requires the fullest development of the mental resources and technical skills of its young men and women. The present emergency demands that additional and more adequate educational opportunities be made available. The defense of this Nation depends upon the mastery of modern techniques developed from complex scientific principles. It depends as well upon the discovery and development of new principles, new techniques, and new knowledge. We must increase our efforts to identify and educate more of the talent of our Nation. . . .

Source: *National Defense Education Act of 1958*, U.S. Statutes at Large, Public Law 85–864 (1958), 1580–1605.

John Kenneth Galbraith, The Affluent Society, 1958

Harvard economist John Kenneth Galbraith served as an advisor in both the Kennedy and Johnson administrations. In The Affluent Society *Galbraith encouraged massive investment in education, highways, and other forms of infrastructure, which he believed would be the key to the nation's continued economic stability. He was critical of the growing assumption—or conventional wisdom, as he phrased it— that simply being more productive was a sign of a robust economy. For Galbraith, mass consumerism was not an indication of a healthy economy or society.*

The final problem of the productive society is what it produces. This manifests itself in an implacable tendency to provide an opulent supply of some things and a niggardly yield of others. This disparity carries to the point where it is a cause of social discomfort and social unhealth. The line which divides our area of wealth from our area of poverty is roughly that which divides privately produced and marketed goods and services from publicly rendered services. Our wealth in the first is not only the startling contrast with the meagerness of the latter, but our wealth in privately produced goods is, to a marked degree, the cause of crisis in the supply of public services. For we have failed to see the importance, indeed the urgent need, of maintaining a balance between the two.

Source: John Kenneth Galbraith, *The Affluent Society* (Boston: Houghton Mifflin, 1958), 186.

Student Nonviolent Coordinating Committee Founding Statement, 1960

The Student Nonviolent Coordinating Committee (SNCC) emerged in the wake of the student-led 1960 lunch counter demonstrations. Young people became the critical force in pushing the civil rights movement into a new phase of nonviolent direct action. The following two documents provide a sense of the transformation that SNCC went through between 1960 and 1966, a transformation that mirrored changes taking place in the larger struggle for racial equality.

We affirm the philosophical or religious ideal of nonviolence as the foundation of our purpose, the presupposition of our belief, and the manner of our action.

Nonviolence, as it grows from the Judeo-Christian tradition, seeks a social order of justice permeated by love. Integration of human endeavor represents the crucial first step towards such a society.

Through nonviolence, courage displaces fear. Love transcends hate. Acceptance dissipates prejudice; hope ends despair. Faith reconciles doubt. Peace dominates war. Mutual regards cancel enmity. Justice for all overthrows injustice. The redemptive community supersedes immoral social systems.

By appealing to conscience and standing on the moral nature of human existence, nonviolence nurtures the atmosphere in which reconciliation and justice become actual possibilities.

Although each local group in this movement must diligently work out the clear meaning of this statement of purpose, each act or phase of our corporate effort must reflect a genuine spirit of love and good-will.

Source: Student Nonviolent Coordinating Committee founding Statement. Available at http://www.crmvet.org/docs/sncc1.htm.

John F. Kennedy's Inaugural Speech, 1961

In his 1961 inaugural speech, President John F. Kennedy issued two challenges. The first reaffirmed America's commitment to fighting Communism, the second encouraged Americans to serve their country. Both were taken up in earnest by the Baby Boom generation.

We dare not forget today that we are the heirs of that first revolution. Let the word go forth from this time and place, to friend and foe alike, that the torch has been passed to a new generation of Americans—born in this century, tempered by war, disciplined by a hard and bitter peace, proud of our ancient heritage—and unwilling to witness or permit the slow undoing of those human rights to which this nation has always been committed, and to which we are committed today at home and around the world.

Let every nation know, whether it wishes us well or ill, that we shall pay any price, bear any burden, meet any hardship, support any friend, oppose any foe to assure the survival and the success of liberty.

This much we pledge—and more. . . .

In your hands, my fellow citizens, more than mine, will rest the final success or failure of our course. Since this country was founded, each generation of Americans has been summoned to give testimony to its national loyalty. The graves of young Americans who answered the call to service surround the globe.

Now the trumpet summons us again—not as a call to bear arms, though arms we need—not as a call to battle, though embattled we are— but a call to bear the burden of a long twilight struggle, year in and year out, "rejoicing in hope, patient in tribulation"—a struggle against the common enemies of man: tyranny, poverty, disease and war itself.

Can we forge against these enemies a grand and global alliance, North and South, East and West, that can assure a more fruitful life for all mankind? Will you join in that historic effort?

In the long history of the world, only a few generations have been granted the role of defending freedom in its hour of maximum danger. I do not shrink from this responsibility—I welcome it. I do not believe that any of us would exchange places with any other people or any other generation. The energy, the faith, the devotion which we bring to this endeavor will light our country and all who serve it—and the glow from that fire can truly light the world.

And so, my fellow Americans: ask not what your country can do for you—ask what you can do for your country.

My fellow citizens of the world: ask not what America will do for you, but what together we can do for the freedom of man.

Finally, whether you are citizens of America or citizens of the world, ask of us here the same high standards of strength and sacrifice which we ask of you. With a good conscience our only sure reward, with history the final judge of our deeds, let us go forth to lead the land we love, asking His blessing and His help, but knowing that here on earth God's work must truly be our own.

Source: Inaugural Address of President John F. Kennedy (Washington, DC, January 20, 1961). Available at http://www.jfklibrary.org/Historical+Resources/ Archives/Reference+Desk/Speeches/JFK/003POF03Inaugural01201961.htm.

Executive Order 10924: Establishment of the Peace Corps, 1961

Perhaps the best example of the Baby Boom generation heeding Kennedy's rousing appeal for service to the nation was the Peace Corps. Kennedy intended the Peace Corps, which he established by executive order soon after becoming president, to be part of the global struggle against Communism. By 1966, some 15,000 volunteers had answered the call.

SEC. 2. Functions of the Peace Corps. (a) The Peace Corps shall be responsible for the training and service abroad of men and women of the United States in new programs of assistance to nations and areas of the world, and in conjunction with or in support of existing economic assistance programs of the United States and of the United Nations and other international organizations.

(b) The Secretary of State shall delegate, or cause to be delegated, to the Director of the Peace Corps such of the functions under the Mutual Security Act of 1954, as amended, vested in the President and delegated to the Secretary, or vested in the Secretary, as the Secretary shall deem necessary for the accomplishment of the purposes of the Peace Corps. . . .

Source: Executive Order 10924, Establishment and Administration of the Peace Corps in the Department of State, March 1, 1961; General Records of the United States Government; Record Group 11; National Archives. Available at http://www.ourdocuments.gov/doc.php?doc=92&page=transcript.

Executive Order 10952, 1961

Civil defense is generally associated with the 1950s. As the following document demonstrates, however, civil defense remained a concern into the 1960s.

ASSIGNING CIVIL DEFENSE RESPONSIBILITIES TO THE SECRETARY OF DEFENSE AND OTHERS

WHEREAS the possibility of enemy attack upon the United States must be taken into account in developing our continental defense program, and

WHEREAS following a thorough review and consideration of our military and nonmilitary defense activities, I have concluded that adequate protection of the civilian population requires a substantial strengthening of the Nation's civil defense capability; and

WHEREAS the rapid acceleration of civil defense activities can be accomplished most effectively and efficiently through performance by the regular departments and agencies of Government of those civil defense functions related to their established roles and capabilities; and

WHEREAS I have concluded that the undertaking of greatly accelerated civil defense activities, including the initiation of a substantial shelter program, requires new organizational arrangements:

NOW, THEREFORE, by virtue of the authority vested in me as President of the United States and Commander in Chief of the armed forces of the United States, including the authority contained in the Federal Civil Defense Act of 1950, as amended, and other authorities of law vested in me pursuant to Reorganization Plan No. 1 of 1958, it is hereby ordered as follows:

SECTION 1. *Delegation of Authority to the Secretary of Defense.* (a) Except as hereinafter otherwise provided and as is reserved to the Office of Civil and Defense Mobilization in section 2 of this order, the Secretary of Defense is delegated all functions (including as used in this order, powers, duties, and authority) contained in the Federal Civil Defense Act of 1950, as amended (hereinafter referred to as the Act), vested in me pursuant to

Reorganization Plan No. 1 of 1958 (72 Stat. 1799), subject to the direction and control of the President. Such functions to be performed by the Secretary of Defense, working as necessary or appropriate through other agencies by contractual or other agreements, as well as with State and local leaders, shall include but not be limited to the development and execution of: (i) a fallout shelter program; (ii) a chemical, biological and radiological warfare defense program; (iii) all steps necessary to warn or alert Federal military and civilian authorities, State officials and the civilian population; (iv) all functions pertaining to communications, including a warning network, reporting on monitoring, instructions to shelters and communications between authorities, (v) emergency assistance to State and local governments in a postattack period, including water, debris, fire, health, traffic police and evacuation capabilities;(vi) protection and emergency operational capability of State and local government agencies in keeping with plans for the continuity of government; and

(vii) programs for making financial contributions to the States (including personnel and administrative expenses) for civil defense purposes.

(b) In addition to the foregoing, the Secretary shall:

(i) develop plans and operate systems to undertake a nationwide postattack assessment of the nature and extent of the damage resulting from enemy attack and the surviving resources, including systems to monitor and report specific hazards resulting from the detonation or use of special weapons[.]. . . .

Source: John T. Woolley and Gerhard Peters, *The American Presidency Project* [online] (Santa Barbara, CA: University of California [hosted], Gerhard Peters [database]). Available at http://www.presidency.ucsb.edu/ws/?pid=58890.

Michael Harrington, The Other America: Poverty in the United States, 1962

Michael Harrington's 1962 best seller opened the eyes of many Americans to the depth and breadth of poverty in the United States. Harrington's descriptions of the poor were made all the more poignant amid the nation's vast aggregate wealth. The Other America put the issue of poverty squarely before Washington and the American people.

[T]ens of millions of Americans are, at this very moment, maimed in body and spirit, existing at levels beneath those necessary for human decency. If these people are not starving, they are hungry, and sometimes fat with hunger, for that is what cheap foods do. They are without adequate housing and education and medical care. . . .

The millions who are poor in the United States tend to become increasingly invisible. Here is a great mass of people, yet it takes an effort of the intellect and will even to see them. . . . The other America, the America of poverty, is hidden today in a way that it never was before. Its millions are socially invisible to the rest of us. . . . Thus, one must begin a description of the other America by understanding why we do not see it. . . .

Poverty is often off the beaten track. It always has been. The ordinary tourist never left the main highway, and today he rides interstate turnpikes. . . .

Source: Michael Harrington, *The Other America: Poverty in the United States* (New York: Macmillan, 1962), 2–3.

Betty Friedan, The Feminine Mystique, 1963

Betty Friedan was one of the founding members of the National Organization of Women (NOW). Friedan gained notoriety with the publication in 1963 of The Feminine Mystique. *Friedan identified what she called 'the problem with no name,' the cultural expectation that women should be fully content with being a wife and mother. Friedan had worked as a journalist before her marriage, but stepped down to care for her children. Friedan's critique of middle-class, suburban womanhood challenged this notion, and helped to launch the women's rights movement of the 1960s.*

The problem lay buried, unspoken, for many years in the minds of American women. It was a strange stirring, a sense of dissatisfaction, a yearning that women suffered in the middle of the twentieth century in the United States. Each suburban wife struggled with it alone. As she made the beds, shopped for groceries, matched slipcover material, ate peanut butter sandwiches with her children, chauffeured Cub Scouts and Brownies, lay beside her husband at night—she was afraid to ask even of herself the silent question—"Is this all?"

Source: Betty Friedan, *The Feminine Mystique* (New York: Norton, 1963), 15.

The Equal Pay Act of 1963

President Kennedy established the Commission on the Status of Women soon after taking office. The Commission proposed the legislation that became the Equal Pay Act, and also was instrumental in getting gender included to the kinds of discrimination prohibited by the Civil Rights Act of 1964. These acts were two tangible examples of liberal feminism making important gains for women during the Baby Boom era.

AN ACT

To prohibit discrimination on account of sex in the payment of wages by employers engaged in commerce or in the production of goods for commerce. . . .

No employer having employees subject to any provisions of this section shall discriminate, within any establishment in which such employees are employed, between employees on the basis of sex by paying wages to employees in such establishment at a rate less than the rate at which he pays wages to employees of the opposite sex in such establishment for equal work on jobs the performance of which requires equal skill, effort, and responsibility, and which are performed under similar working conditions, except where such payment is made pursuant to (i) a seniority system; (ii) a merit system; (iii) a system which measures earnings by quantity or quality of production; or (iv) a differential based on any other factor other than sex: Provided, that an employer who is paying a wage rate differential in violation of this subsection shall not, in order to comply with the provisions of this subsection, reduce the wage rate of any employee. 29 USC 206. . . .

Source: *Equal Pay Act of 1963*, Public Law 88–38 (1996). Available at http://www.eeoc.gov/policy/epa.html.

The Free Speech Movement—A Declaration of Independence, 1964

The Free Speech Movement at the University of California-Berkeley provides a good example of the intersection of student activism with other social movements, and illustrates how students used their experience in the civil rights movement to address other issues.

The Free Speech Movement at Berkeley was formed to defend the rights of free speech and political activity. Through negotiations, petitions, sit-ins, and a strike, we finally established the principle that the University may not regulate the content of speech. At the same time, the FSM has given students a new and well-deserved sense of dignity and self-respect.

Throughout this semester, however, the Regents have harassed the Berkeley campus in many ways. They are now preparing to impose new regulations that would destroy everything we fought for. In the last few months, we have become increasingly aware that it is not merely free speech and political activity to which the Regents object. They insist upon their right to govern every facet of University life—student conduct, student government, educational policy, political rights, and other areas of no proper concern to them.

The FSM, born in crisis, has never paused to organize a permanent membership nor to develop the close and continuous contacts between leaders and constituency necessary to a democratic movement. . . . Now is the time for students to join together to form a permanent, democratic membership organization to carry on the fight to free this university from outside control. The successor to the FSM shall be the Free Student Union, based upon the following declaration:

As students, we have certain rights which no agency can legitimately grant or deny; among these the right to govern our own internal affairs, to set our own standards of conduct, and jointly with the faculty to determine the form and nature of our education.

Our University exists for the extension and transmission of human knowledge. It is a community consisting of students and faculty and those who are employed to serve our needs. Final authority in this community must therefore rest with us, the students and faculty.

Yet a body external to the life of the University—the Board of Regents—claims full power to govern the University in every detail, either directly or through its agent, the administration. No rights are reserved to the University community; neither the students nor faculty deliberative bodies have any powers save at the pleasure of the Regents.

Therefore, we the students of Berkeley now establish a Union which will fight to secure our rights and to end continual outside interference.

Source: The Free Speech Movement—A Declaration of Independence (1964). Available at http://content.cdlib.org/ark:/13030/kt6g5004r8/?&query=FSM%20 DECLARATION%20OF%20INDEPENDENCE&brand=oac.

The Civil Rights Act of 1964 and the Voting Rights Act of 1965

The Civil Rights Act of 1964 and the Voting Rights Act of 1965 are perhaps the two most significant achievements of the civil rights movement. Their passage culminated a nearly 100-year struggle to ensure the rights of African Americans to vote and the equal protection of the law. The Civil Rights Act opened new opportunities for blacks, women, and other minorities in employment and education. Less than four years after the passage of the Voting Rights Act the percentage of black voters registered in the South skyrocketed: Mississippi's increased from 7 percent to 59 percent, and Alabama's jumped from 23 percent to 57 percent. Crucial to the passage of both laws was the involvement of young activists, many of which were born during the Baby Boom.

The Civil Rights Act of 1964

An Act

To enforce the constitutional right to vote, to confer jurisdiction upon the district courts of the United States to provide injunctive relief against discrimination in public accommodations, to authorize the Attorney General to institute suits to protect constitutional rights in public facilities and public education, to extend the Commission on Civil Rights, to prevent discrimination in federally assisted programs, to establish a Commission on Equal Employment Opportunity, and for other purposes. . . . [A]ll persons shall be entitled to the full and equal enjoyment of the goods, services, facilities, and privileges, advantages, and accommodations of any place of public accommodation, as defined in this section, without discrimination or segregation on the ground of race, color, religion, or national origin. . . . It shall be an unlawful employment practice for an employer—(1) to fail or refuse to hire or to discharge any individual, or otherwise to discriminate against any individual with respect to his compensation, terms, conditions, or privileges of employment, because of such individual's race, color, religion, sex, or national origin; or (2) to limit, segregate, or classify his employees in any way which would deprive or tend to deprive any individual of employment opportunities or otherwise adversely affect his status as an employee, because of such individual's race, color, religion, sex, or national origin.

Source: *Civil Rights Act of 1964*, July 2, 1964; Enrolled Acts and Resolutions of Congress, 1789-; General Records of the United States Government; Record Group 11; National Archives. Available at http://www.ourdocuments.gov/doc.php?doc=97&page=transcript.

The Voting Rights Act of 1965

. . . No voting qualification or prerequisite to voting, or standard, practice, or procedure shall be imposed or applied by any State or political subdivision to deny or abridge the right of any citizen of the United States to vote on account of race or color. . . . Whenever the Attorney General institutes a proceeding under any statute to enforce the guarantees of the fifteenth amendment in any State or political subdivision the court shall authorize the appointment of Federal examiners by the United States Civil Service Commission in accordance with section 6 to serve for such period of time and for such political subdivisions as the court shall determine is appropriate to enforce the guarantees of the fifteenth amendment[.]. . . The Congress finds that the requirement of the payment of a poll tax as a precondition to voting (i) precludes persons of limited means from voting or imposes unreasonable financial hardship upon such persons as a precondition to their exercise of the franchise, (ii) does not bear a reasonable relationship to any legitimate State interest in the conduct of elections, and (iii) in some areas has the purpose or effect of denying persons the right to vote because of race or color. Upon the basis of these findings, Congress declares that the constitutional right of citizens to vote is denied or abridged in some areas by the requirement of the payment of a poll tax as a precondition to voting.

Source: *Voting Rights Act of 1965*, August 6, 1965; Enrolled Acts and Resolutions of Congress, 1789-; General Records of the United States Government; Record Group 11; National Archives. Available at http://www.ourdocuments.gov/doc.php?doc=100&page=transcript.

The Tonkin Gulf Resolution, 1964

The Vietnam War was a defining moment for many Baby Boomers, in particular those men born between 1946 and 1954 and who accounted for the bulk of the soldiers sent to Southeast Asia. The Gulf of Tonkin Resolution gave President Lyndon Johnson great authority and wide latitude to conduct the war. By 1968, more than 500,000 soldiers were stationed in Vietnam and the country was deeply divided over the nation's continued involvement in Vietnam.

Whereas naval units of the Communist regime in Vietnam, in violation of the principles of the Charter of the United Nations and of international law, have deliberately and repeatedly attacked United Stated naval vessels lawfully present in international waters, and have thereby created a serious threat to international peace; and . . .

Whereas the United States is assisting the peoples of southeast Asia to protest their freedom and has no territorial, military or political ambitions in that area, but desires only that these people should be left in peace to work out their destinies in their own way: Now, therefore be it

Resolved by the Senate and House of Representatives of the United States of America in Congress assembled, that the Congress approves and supports the determination of the President, as Commander in Chief, to take all necessary measures to repel any armed attack against the forces of the United States and to prevent further aggression. . . .

Section 3. This resolution shall expire when the President shall determine that the peace and security of the area is reasonably assured by international conditions created by action of the United Nations or otherwise, except that it may be terminated earlier by concurrent resolution of the Congress.

Source: Tonkin Gulf Resolution; Public Law 88–408, 88th Congress, August 7, 1964; General Records of the United States Government; Record Group 11; National Archives. Available at http://www.ourdocuments.gov/doc.php?doc=98&page=transcript.

Lyndon B. Johnson, "To Fulfill these Rights," Commencement Address at Howard University, 1965

In this commencement speech at Howard University, Lyndon Johnson made his case for the Voting Rights Bill he was trying get through Congress.

In far too many ways American Negroes have been another nation; deprived of freedom, crippled by hatred, the doors of opportunity closed to hope. . . .

In our time change has come to this nation. The American Negro, acting with impressive restraint, has peacefully protested and marched, entered the courtrooms and the seats of government, demanding a justice that has long been denied. The voice of the Negro was the call to action. But it is a tribute to America that, once aroused, the courts and the Congress, the President and most of the people, have been the allies of progress. . . .

The voting rights bill will be the latest and among the most important, in a long series of victories. But this victory—as Winston Churchill said of another triumph for freedom—"is not the end. It is not even the beginning of the end. But it is, perhaps, the end of the beginning."

That beginning is freedom; and the barriers to that freedom are tumbling down. Freedom is the right to share, share fully and equally, in American society—to vote, to hold a job, to enter a public place, to go to school. It is the right to be treated in every part of our national life as a person equal in dignity and promise to all others.

But freedom is not enough. You do not wipe away the scars of centuries by saying: Now you are free to go where you want, and do as you desire, and choose the leaders you please.

You do not take a person who for years has been hobbled by chains and liberate him, bring him up to the starting line of a race and then say, "you are free to compete with all the others," and still justly believe that you have been completely fair.

Thus it is not enough just to open the gates of opportunity. All our citizens must have the ability to walk through those gates.

This is the next and the more profound stage of the battle for civil rights. We seek not just freedom but opportunity. We seek not just legal equity but human ability, not just equality as a right and a theory, but equality as a fact and equality as a result. . . .

There is no single easy answer to all of these problems.

Jobs are part of the answer. They bring the income which permits a man to provide for his family.

Decent homes in decent surroundings and a chance to learn—an equal chance to learn—are part of the answer.

Welfare and social programs better designed to hold families together are part of the answer.

Care for the sick is part of the answer.

An understanding heart by all Americans is another big part of the answer.

And to all these fronts—and a dozen more—I will dedicate the expanding efforts of the Johnson Administration.

Source: *Public Papers of the Presidents of the United States: Lyndon B. Johnson, 1965*, Volume II, entry 301, 635–640 (Washington, DC: U.S. Government Printing Office, 1966). Available at http://www.lbjlib.utexas.edu/johnson/archives.hom/speeches.hom/650604.asp.

Black Power, 1968

In this excerpt, political scientist Charles V. Hamilton explains the basic precepts of Black Power.

Black Power is concerned with organizing the rage of black people and with putting new, hard questions and demands to white America. As we do this, white America's responses will be crucial to the questions of violence and viability. Black Power must (1) deal with the obviously growing alienation of black people and their distrust of the institutions of this society; (2) work to create new values and to build a new sense of community and of belonging; and (3) work to establish legitimate new institutions that make participants, not recipients, out of a people traditionally excluded from the fundamentally racist processes of this country. There is nothing glamorous about this; it involves persistence and hard, tedious, day-to-day work.

Source: Charles V. Hamilton, 'An Advocate of Black Power Defines It,' *New York Times Magazine*, April 14, 1968, 22–23, 79–83.

Al Santoli, *Everything We Had: An Oral History of the Vietnam War*, 1981

Although readjustment to civilian life has always been difficult for veterans, it was especially difficult for Vietnam veterans because of the nature of the conflict and the course of the fighting. Santoli's recollections also suggest the generational cultural conflicts the war wrought.

We really didn't think about the future. I had no expectation of making it out of there. I don't think anybody else did, either. We didn't discuss it. We really didn't have a hell of a lot of time to sit around discussing things. I had written us off. People were too tired to cry. It was physical exhaustion—you had no energy left for anything else. You would stay awake and keep firing, drink some water, make sure your ammunition and weapon were in good shape and eat when you could, stuff some food in you just to keep fueled up so you could keep going. . . .

We did a fine job there. If it had happened in World War II, they still would be telling stories about it. But it happened in Vietnam, so nobody knows about it. They don't even tell recruits about it today. Marines don't talk about Vietnam. We lost. They never talk about losing. So it's just wiped out, all of that's off the slate, it doesn't count. It makes you a little bitter.

I still am deeply disturbed by the fact that so many people died. The young Marines that I served with thought at the time they were doing what they were supposed to be doing. Nobody had educated them in the politics of the situation. We went into the Marine Corps with the same feeling our fathers and grandfathers had gone into the service. There wasn't anybody around to tell us that we hadn't done the right thing. And then to find out later that all those people had died in vain, or that the largest percentage of the American public believed that they died in vain, is very disturbing to me. But like I say, there isn't one hell of a lot I can do about it, so I just try to roll along with it.

Source: Al Santoli, ed., *Everything We Had: An Oral History of the Vietnam War* (New York: Random House, 1981), 28–30.

Man of the Year: The Under-Twenty-Five Generation, *Time*, 1966

Although many people who were twenty-five or younger in 1966 were not Baby Boomers, this essay in Time *nonetheless suggests the ways in which youth were shaping—and would continue to shape—American life and culture.*

For the Man of the Year 1966 is a generation: the man—and woman—of 25 and under. . . .

In the closing third of the 20th century, that generation looms larger than all the exponential promises of science or technology: it will soon be the majority in charge. In the U.S., citizens of 25 and under in 1966 nearly outnumbered their elders; by 1970, there will be 100 million Americans in that age bracket. . . . Never have the young been so assertive or so articulate, so well educated or so worldly. Predictably, they are a highly independent breed, and—to adult eyes—their independence has made them highly unpredictable. This is not just a new generation, but a new kind of generation. . . .

Cushioned by unprecedented affluence and the welfare state, he has a sense of economic security unmatched in history. Granted an ever-lengthening adolescence and lifespan, he no longer feels the cold pressures of hunger and mortality that drove Mozart to compose an entire canon before death at 35; yet he, too, can be creative. Top of form . . .

The young have already staked out their own minisociety, a congruent culture that has both alarmed their elders and, stylistically at least, left an irresistible impression on them. No Western metropolis today lacks a discotheque or espresso joint, a Mod boutique or a Carnaby shop. No transistor is immune from rock 'n' roll, no highway spared the stutter of Hondas. There are few Main Streets in the world that do not echo to the clop of granny boots, and many are the grannies who now wear them. What started out as distinctively youthful sartorial revolt—drainpipe-trousered men, pants-suited or net-stockinged women, long hair on male and female alike—has been accepted by adults the world over. . . .

If they have an ideology, it is idealism; if they have one ideal, it is pragmatism. Theirs is an immediate philosophy, tailored to the immediacy of their lives. . . .

For better or for worse, the world today is committed to accelerating change: radical, wrenching, erosive of both traditions and old values. Its inheritors have grown up with rapid change, are better prepared to accommodate it than any in history, indeed embrace change as a virtue in itself. With his skeptical yet humanistic outlook, his disdain for fanaticism and his scorn for the spurious, the Man of the Year suggests that he will infuse the future with a new sense of morality, a transcendent and contemporary ethic that could infinitely enrich the "empty society." If he succeeds (and he is prepared to) the Man of the Year will be a man indeed—and have a great deal of fun in the process.

Source: 'The Inheritor,' *Time*, January 6, 1967, 18–23.

Report of the National Advisory Commission on Civil Disorder, 1968

After a series of urban riots in 1967 and 1968, President Johnson established the National Advisory Commission on Civil Disorder to investigate the causes of the violence. The commission concluded that, while there were a host of factors, white racism bore major responsibility. Johnson ignored the commission's recommendations.

What can be done to prevent it from happening again?

To respond to these questions, we have undertaken a broad range of studies and investigations. We have visited the riot cities; we have heard many witnesses; we have sought the counsel of experts across the country.

This is our basic conclusion: Our nation is moving toward two societies, one black, one white—separate and unequal.

Reaction to last summer's disorders has quickened the movement and deepened the division. Discrimination and segregation have long permeated much of American life; they now threaten the future of every American.

This deepening racial division is not inevitable. The movement apart can be reversed. Choice is still possible. Our principal task is to define that choice and to press for a national resolution. To pursue our present course will involve the continuing polarization of the American community and, ultimately, the destruction of basic democratic values.

The alternative is not blind repression or capitulation to lawlessness. It is the realization of common opportunities for all within a single society.

This alternative will require a commitment to national action—compassionate, massive and sustained, backed by the resources of the most powerful and richest nation on this earth. From every American it will require new attitudes, new understanding, and, above all, new will.

The vital needs of the nation must be met; hard choices must be made, and, if necessary, new taxes enacted.

Violence cannot build a better society. Disruption and disorder nourish repression, not justice. They strike at the freedom of every citizen. The community cannot—it will not—tolerate coercion and mob rule.

Violence and destruction must be ended—in the streets of the ghetto and in the lives of people.

Segregation and poverty have created in the racial ghetto a destructive environment totally unknown to most white Americans.

What white Americans have never fully understood—but what the Negro can never forget—is that white society is deeply implicated in the ghetto. White institutions created it, white institutions maintained it, and white society condones it.

It is time now to turn with all the purpose at our command to the major unfinished business of this nation. It is time to adopt strategies for action that will produce quick and visible progress. It is time to make good the promises of American democracy to all the citizens—urban and rural, white and black, Spanish-surname, American Indian, and every minority group.

Our recommendations embrace three basic principles:

- To mount programs on a scale equal to the dimension of the problems;
- To aim these programs for high impact in the immediate future in order to close the gap between promise and performance;

- To undertake new initiatives and experiments that can change the system of failure and frustration that now dominates the ghetto and weakens our society.

These programs will require unprecedented levels of funding and performance, but they neither probe deeper nor demand more than the problems which called them forth. There can be no higher priority for national action and no higher claim on the nation's conscience.

Source: U.S. National Advisory Commission on Civil Disorders, *Report of the National Advisory Commission on Civil Disorders* (Washington, DC: U.S. Government Printing Office, 1968).

United Farm Workers Statement, 1969

Cesar Chavez and Delores Huerta in 1962 formed the United Farm Workers (UFW) union, an effort to secure better working conditions and benefits for farm workers, many of whom were Hispanic. The UFW called a strike against grape growers in Delano, California, in 1965. It later called for a consumer boycott of all American-grown grapes. This impassioned proclamation won many people over to the cause of the UFW.

We have been farm workers for hundreds of years and strikers for four. It was four years ago that we threw down our plowshares and pruning hooks. These Biblical symbols of peace and tranquility to us represent too many lifetimes of unprotesting submission to a degrading social system that allows us no dignity, no comfort, no peace. We mean to have our peace, and to win it without violence, for it is violence we would overcome-the subtle spiritual and mental violence of oppression, the violence subhuman toil does to the human body. So we went and stood tall outside the vineyards where we had stooped for years. But the tailors of national labor legislation had left us naked. Thus exposed, our picket lines were crippled by injunctions and harassed by growers; our strike was broken by imported scabs; our overtures to our employers were ignored. Yet we knew the day must come when they would talk to us, as equals. . . .

We marched alone at the beginning, but today we count men of all creeds, nationalities, and occupations in our number. Between us and the justice we seek now stand the large and powerful grocers who, in continuing to buy table grapes, betray the boycott their own customers have built. These stores treat their patrons' demands to remove the grapes the same way the growers treat our demands for union recognition—by ignoring them. The consumers who rally behind our cause are responding as we do to such treatment—with a boycott! They pledge to withhold their patronage from stores that handle grapes during the boycott, just as we withhold our labor from the growers until our dispute is resolved.

Grapes must remain an unenjoyed luxury for all as long as the barest human needs and basic human rights are still luxuries for farm workers.

The grapes grow sweet and heavy on the vines, but they will have to wait while we reach out first for our freedom. The time is ripe for our liberation.

Source: Delores Huerta, 'Proclamation of the Delano Grape Workers for International Boycott Day,' May 10, 1969.

Corky Gonzales, "What Political Road for the Chicano Militant?" 1969

Just as the African American freedom struggle had its militant and moderate factions, so too did the movement led by Hispanics. Whereas some organizations sought economic justice, others, such as Corky Gonzales, struggled for political self-determination.

We [Mexican-Americans] have to understand that liberation comes from self-determination, and to start to use the tools of nationalism to win over our barrio brothers, to win over the brothers who are still believing that machismo means getting a gun and going to kill a Communist in Vietnam because they've been jived about the fact that they will be accepted as long as they go get themselves killed for the gringo captain; who still think that welfare is giving them something and don't understand that the one who is administering the welfare is the one that's on welfare, because, about 90 percent of the welfare goes into administration; and who still do not understand that the war on poverty is against the poor, to keep them from reacting.

Source: Rodolfo 'Corky' Gonzales, 'What Political Road for the Chicano Militant?' *The Militant* (March 30, 1970), and reprinted in *Readings on La Raza: The Twentieth Century*, ed. Matt S. Meier and Feliciano Rivera (New York: Hill and Wang, 1974), 246–47.

The Report of the President's Commission on Campus Unrest, 1970

In May of 1970, six college students—four at Kent State University and two at Jackson State University—were killed by agents of the government; the National Guard in Kent, Ohio, and the state police in Jackson, Mississippi. Violence also occurred on scores of other campuses. President Nixon established a commission to study the causes of unrest. The Scranton Commission concluded that the unrest resulted from 'a crisis of violence and a crisis of understanding,' the result of a decade of cultural and social protest and reaction.

PREFACE: TO THE AMERICAN PEOPLE

The crisis on American campuses has no parallel in the history of the nation. This crisis has roots in divisions of American society as deep as any since the Civil War. The divisions are reflected in violent acts and harsh rhetoric, and in the enmity of those Americans who see themselves as occupying opposing camps. Campus unrest reflects and increases a more profound crisis in the nation as a whole. . . .

Campus protest has been focused on three major questions: war, racial injustice, and the university itself.

The first issue is the unfulfilled promise of full justice and dignity for blacks and other minorities. Blacks, like many others of different races and ethnic origins, are demanding today that the pledges of the Declaration of Independence and the Emancipation proclamation be fulfilled now. Full social justice and dignity—an end to racism, in all its human, social and cultural forms—is a central demand of today's students, black, brown and white.

A great majority of students and a majority of their elders oppose the Indochina war. Many believe it entirely immoral. And if the war is wrong, students insist, then so are all policies and practices that support it, from the draft to military research, from ROTC to recruiting for defense industry. This opposition has led to an ever-widening wave of student protests.

A third target of student protest is the short-comings of the American university. The goals, values, administration and curriculum have been sharply criticized by many students. Students complain that their studies are irrelevant to the social problems that concern them. They want to shape their own personal and common lives, but find the university restrictive. They seek a community of companions and scholars, but find an impersonal multi-versity. And they denounce the university's relationship to the war and to discriminatory racial practices.

Behind the student protest on these issues and the crisis of violence to which they have contributed lies the more basic crisis of understanding.

Americans have never shared a single culture, a single philosophy, or a single religion. But in most periods in our history, we have shared many common values, common sympathies, and a common dedication to a system of government which protects our diversity.

We are now in grave danger of losing what is common among us through growing intolerance of opposing views on issues and of diversity itself.

A "new" culture is emerging primarily among students. Membership is often manifested by differences in dress and life style. Most of its members have high ideals and great fears. They stress the need for humanity, equality, and the sacredness of life. They fear that nuclear war will make them the last generation in history. They see their elders as entrapped by materialism and competition, and prisoners of outdated social forms. They believe their own country has lost is sense of human purpose. They see the Indochina war as an onslaught by a technological giant upon the peasant people of a small, harmless and backward nation. The war is seen as draining resources from the urgent needs of social and racial justice. They argue that we are the first nation with sufficient resources to create not only decent lives for some, but a decent society for all and that we are failing to do so. They feel they must remake America in its own image. . . .

THE NEW YOUTH CULTURE

. . . Throughout most of American history, the idealism of youth has been formed—and constrained—by the institutions of adult society. But during the 1960's, in response to an accumulation of social changes, the traditional American youth culture developed rapidly in the direction of an oppositional stance toward the institutions and ways of the adult world. . . .

An important theme of this new culture is its oppositional relationship to the larger society, as is suggested by the fact that one of its leading theorists has called it a "counter culture". If the rest of the society wears short hair, the member of this youth culture wears his hair long. If others are clean, he is dirty. If others drink alcohol and illegalize marijuana, he denounces alcohol and smokes pot. If others work in large organizations with massively complex technology, he works alone and makes sandals by hand. If others live separated, he lives in a commune. If others are for police and the judges, he is for the accused and the prisoner. By these means, he declares himself an alien in a large society with which he fundamentally is at odds.

He will also resist when the forces of the outside society seek to impose its tenets upon him. He is likely to see police as the repressive minions of the outside culture imposing its law on him and on other students by force or death, if necessary. He will likely try to urge others to join him in changing the society about him, in the conviction that he is seeking to save that society from bringing about its own destruction. He is likely to have apocalyptic visions of impending doom of the whole social structure and the world. He is likely to have lost hope that society can be brought to change through its own procedures. And if his psychological make-up is of a particular kind, he may conclude that the only outlet for his feelings is violence and terrorism. . . .

As is observed elsewhere in this report, to conclude that a student who has a beard is a student who would burn a building, or even sit-in in a building is wholly unwarranted.

But almost no college student today is unaffected by the new youth culture in some way. If he is not included, his roommate or sister or girlfriend is. If protest breaks out on his campus, he is confronted with a personal decision about his role in it. In the poetry, music, movies, and plays that students see, the themes of the new culture are recurrent. Even the student who finds older values more comfortable for himself will, nevertheless, protect and support vigorously the privilege of other students who prefer the new youth culture.

A vast majority of students are not adherents. But no significant group of students would join older generations in condemning those who are. And almost all students will condemn repressive efforts by the larger community to restrict or limit the life style, the art forms, and the non-violent political manifestations of the new youth culture.

To most Americans, the development of the new youth culture is an unpleasant and often frightening phenomenon. And there is no doubt that the emergence of this student perspective has led to confrontations, injuries, and death. It is undeniable, too, that a tiny extreme fringe of fanatical devotees of the new culture have crossed the line over into outlawry and terrorism. There is a fearful and terrible irony here as, in the name of the law, police and National Guards have killed students, and some students under the new culture's banner of love and compassion have turned to burning and bombing.

But the new youth culture itself is not a "problem" to which there is a "solution;" it is a mass social condition, a shift in basic cultural viewpoint. How long this emerging youth culture will last, and what course its future development will take, are open questions. But it does exist today, and it is the deeper cause of the emergence of the issues of race and war as objects of intense concern on the American campus.

Source: U.S. President's Commission on Campus Unrest, *The Report of the President's Commission on Campus Unrest* (New York: Arno Press, 1970), 1–5, 61–69.

"Man and Woman of the Year: The Middle Americans," Time, 1970

Richard Nixon called them the 'Silent Majority.' By the end of the 1960s, more Americans were voicing their displeasure with protests, demonstrations, challenges to authority, and violence, and demanded a return to 'law and order.'

The Supreme Court had forbidden it, but they prayed defiantly in a school in Netcong, N.J., reading the morning invocation from the Congressional Record. In the state legislatures, they introduced more than 100 Draconian bills to put down campus dissent. In West Virginia, they passed a law absolving police in advance of guilt in any riot deaths. In Minneapolis they elected a police detective to be mayor. Everywhere, they flew the colors of assertive patriotism. Their car windows were plastered with American-flag decals, their ideological totems. In the bumper-sticker dialogue of the freeways, they answered MAKE LOVE NOT WAR with HONOR AMERICA or SPIRO IS MY HERO. They sent Richard Nixon to the White House and two teams of astronauts to the moon. They were both exalted and afraid. The mysteries of space were nothing, after all, compared with the menacing confusions of their own society. . . .

Who precisely are the Middle Americans? . . . They make up the core of the group that Richard Nixon now invokes as the "forgotten Americans" or "the Great Silent Majority," though Middle Americans themselves may not be a majority of the U.S. All Americans doubtless share some Middle American beliefs, and many Middle Americans would disagree among themselves on some issues. The lower middle class, including blue-collar workers, service employees and farm workers, numbers some 40 million. Many of the nation's 20 million elderly citizens, frequently living on fixed incomes, are Middle American. So is a substantial portion of the 36 million white-collar workers. Although a hard figure is not possible, the total of Middle Americans probably approaches 100 million, or half of the U.S. population. . . . They tend toward the middle-aged and the middlebrow. They are defined as much by what they are not as by what they are. As a rule, they are not the poor or the rich. Still, many wealthy business executives are Middle Americans. H. Ross Perot, the Texas millionaire who organized a group called "United We Stand Inc." to support the President on the war, is an example. Few blacks march in the ranks of Middle America. Nor do the nation's intellectuals, its liberals, its professors, its surgeons. Many general practitioners, though, are Middle Americans. Needless to say, Middle America offers no haven to the New Left, although Middle Americans might count a number of old leftists—unionists, for example— in their numbers. They are not extremists of the right despite the fact that some of them voted for George Wallace in 1968. They are both Republicans and Democrats; many cast their ballots for Richard Nixon, but it may be that nearly as many voted for Hubert Humphrey.

Above all, Middle America is a state of mind, a morality, a construct of values and prejudices and a complex of fears. The Man and Woman of the Year represent a vast, unorganized fraternity bound together by a roughly similar way of seeing things.

Source: 'Man and Woman of the Year,' *Time,* January 5, 1970, 10–17.

Dress Code of Perryville, Arkansas, School District, 1971–1972

By the late 1960s and early 1970s, student activism had worked its way into the nation's high schools. Whereas activists born in the 1940s are often depicted as idealistic and political, boomers born later tended more toward the counterculture. Dress codes seemed archaic to most students, and their efforts to challenge them illustrate the generational divide and the larger cultural change that characterize the era, as well as the broad challenges to authority that were at the heart of student activism.

Girls: Dresses, skirts and blouses, dress slacks and blouses or pant suits may be worn. No divided skirts or dresses; no jeans or shorts may be worn. Blouses that are straight around the bottom may be worn outside the skirt or slacks. The length of the skirts or dresses will be no more than six (6) inches above or six (6) inches below the knee. Excessively tight skirts or pants will not be allowed. Girls are expected to be neatly dressed and well groomed at all times.

Girls will not come to school with hair in rollers.

Boys: Boys may wear dress or sport pants, including jeans. No frayed trousers or jeans will be allowed. Shirt tails, unless the tail is straight and hemmed, will be worn inside the pants.

Socks are required at all times. Boys will be expected to be neat and well groomed at all times. This means that their hair will be trimmed; it will not be down over the ears, in the eyes or down over the shirt collar. The face will be clean shaven—no mustaches, beards or sideburns below the ear lobes.

General: No tie-dyed clothing will be worn. Shirt or clothing having slogans, pictures, or emblems, etc. will not be worn except school approved emblems.

As amended (by memo to parents) at the beginning of the 1971–72 school year: After checking in some stores and talking with parents concerning the girls' dress, we have decided to relax the code. We will allow jeans that are made for girls to be worn providing: If the jeans open in front, a tunic or square-tailed blouse must be worn to conceal the opening. If the jeans open on the side, then an ordinary length blouse may be worn. In either case, the jeans will not be allowed if they fit too tightly.

Source: Dress Code of Perryville, Arkansas, School district, as cited in *Wallace v. Ford*, 346 F. Supp. 156 (1972).

Reference

Affirmative Action Beginning with the Kennedy administration and accelerating during the Johnson administration, the federal government established policies designed to improve the status of African Americans, women, and other economically marginalized groups. Known collectively as affirmative action, these policies sought to overcome decades of racial and gender discrimination in employment and education, among others. Although the intent of affirmative action was to "level the playing field" for women and minorities, opponents soon derided the policies as giving preferential treatment to blacks and women, and amounted to "reverse discrimination."

The Affluent Society **(1958)** Written by Harvard economist John Kenneth Galbraith, *The Affluent Society* criticized the wastefulness of Americans and the American economy. Galbraith, who later would advise both President Kennedy and President Johnson, argued that the nation's vast wealth should be directed toward building infrastructure rather than the mere consumption of consumer goods.

American Bandstand A popular television program that aired from 1952–1987. Dick Clark, who was both the show's host and producer between 1957 and 1987, introduced Top Forty songs while teenagers danced on camera; each program usually showcased at least one live performance by a popular recording artist. The show's popularity illustrates the intersection of television and consumerism, and in particular, the burgeoning teen market of postwar America. *American Bandstand* helped make rock-and-roll and pop music more accessible to the Baby Boom generation.

American Indian Movement Founded in 1968, the American Indian Movement (AIM) was a militant organization that fought for the rights of indigenous people in the United States. In 1972, AIM occupied the Bureau of Indian Affairs building in Washington, D.C. A year later, it engaged in a tense standoff with agents from the Federal Bureau of Investigation on the Pine Ridge Indian Reservation, in Wounded Knee, South Dakota.

Antiwar Movement A loose coalition of individuals and organizations opposed to American involvement in Vietnam. Pacifist and religious groups were among the first to oppose U.S. involvement, as early as 1962. By 1965, college students and faculty, and campus-based organizations became involved, and protests became more public and commonplace. Several massive demonstrations took place in 1968, 1969, and 1970. The antiwar movement began to wane after the **Kent State** shootings, but protests continued until the United States finally withdrew from Vietnam in 1974.

Area Redevelopment and Manpower-Training Acts Laws enacted in 1961 and 1962 to train workers displaced by new technology and automation.

Beat Generation The name given to a circle of poets, writers, and artists in the 1950s, and which included Allen Ginsburg, William S. Burroughs, and Jack Kerouac. The name derived from both "beatnik," a youth subculture of "hipsters" (later **"hippies"**) noted for their unconventional dress and way of life, and beatific, which implied a higher plane of consciousness and happiness. The Beats shared similar approaches to art, such as opposing social conformity, stylistic conventions, and materialism. The Beats influenced the growth of the youth **counterculture** in the 1960s.

Beatles A rock-and-roll band from Liverpool, England, composed of John Lennon, Paul McCartney, George Harrison, and Ringo Starr, that launched the so-called British invasion of rock music in 1964. Artistically and culturally, the Beatles were extremely influential. Their music evolved from simple but catchy songs about teenage romance to songs with complex musical arrangements and biting social and political commentary. Their 1967 album *Sgt. Pepper's Lonely Hearts Club Band* was the first concept album and remains one of the most influential records of the rock era.

Bellbottoms Bellbottoms were pants that had a wide flare below the knee. They were very popular among men and women in the late 1960s and early 1970s.

Birth Control Natural, mechanical, or artificial means of preventing pregnancy. Birth control became a heated topic in the 1960s amid what was called the Sexual Revolution. Controversy swirled particularly around the introduction of "the Pill," an oral contraceptive for women that was effective in preventing pregnancy. Critics assailed the Pill for contributing to the decline in morals and rising promiscuity among women, while supporters hailed it for liberating women from unwanted pregnancies.

Black Panthers In 1966, in Oakland, California, Huey Newton and Bobby Seale founded the Black Panther Party for Self-Defense. Newton and Seale intended the Panthers to protect black neighborhoods from police brutality, but it soon evolved into a revolutionary front seeking the liberation of African Americans. The Panther Party's Ten-Point Platform demanded access to education, land, and employment, the end of the draft, and reparations for past injustices, and called for blacks to arm themselves in self-defense. Official Panther chapters operated in several major cities, with perhaps several thousand members nationwide.

Black Power   An offshoot of the civil rights movement that encouraged African Americans to unite around their common heritage, and create and lead their own organizations to take control of their own communities. Black Power was a movement of active, rather than passive, resistance. It became associated primarily with young, militant activists, and frequently was misunderstood by whites. Black Power emphasized racial pride and self-determination in the struggle for political power and economic independence. Black power emphasized self-defense tactics, self-determination, political and economic power, and racial pride.

The Blackboard Jungle (**1955**)   This film features a teacher trying to reach a class of inner-city youth, but his efforts are challenged by other teachers, students, and parents. The film also featured Bill Haley and the Comet's "Rock Around the Clock," which many credit with launching the rock-and-roll era.

Brown v. Board of Education of Topeka   The 1954 Supreme Court decision that overturned the doctrine of "separate but equal" and helped spur the effort to desegregate schools and other aspects of public life in the United States.

Burning Man Project   A large, annual gathering of people held in the Black Rock Desert in northwestern Nevada. Burning Man bills itself as an "experimental community," and shares much in common with the **counterculture** of the 1960s.

Chicago '68   At the 1968 Democratic National Convention in Chicago, antiwar protestors and city police battled in the streets outside the convention hall, much of which was televised to the rest of the nation. Chicago '68 symbolized the depth of the nation's division over Vietnam and other social issues.

Chicago 7   A group brought to trial for their involvement in the protests in Chicago during the 1968 Democratic National Convention. There were originally eight defendants—Abbie Hoffman, Jerry Rubin, David Dellinger, Tom Hayden, Rennie Davis, John Froines, Lee Weiner, and Bobby Seale—but Seale's trial was separated from the others. The trial itself became something of a circus, and Hoffman especially used the occasion for street theater.

Comic Books   The most popular comic books among youth after World War II featured crime and horror stories. In the 1950s, **juvenile delinquency** became a much-discussed issue in the United States. Fred Wertham, a psychiatrist, charged in his best-selling book *The Seduction of the Innocent* (1954) that comic books—particularly those that contained crime and horror stories—were a contributing factor to juvenile delinquency and should not be sold to children under the age of sixteen. The U.S. Senate held hearings on the issue, and warned the industry to regulate itself or face regulatory legislation. The industry responded with a Code that largely self-censored the crime and horror genres.

The Common Sense Book of Baby and Child Care   First published in 1946 by Dr. Benjamin Spock, *The Common Sense Book of Baby and Child Care* has sold more than 50 million copies worldwide. Spock's advice influenced how the Baby Boom generation would be raised. Spock cautioned against following strict feeding regimes, and he encouraged parents to trust their instincts and have fun raising their children, to comfort them when they cried, and to play with them. Critics dismissed Spock's advice as "permissive parenting." Although his ideas went against the traditional wisdom, in many ways, Spock was a traditionalist himself. Women would be the primary caregiver, he assumed, and so they should put their children's emotional and physical needs ahead of their own.

Cosmopolitan   First published in the late-nineteenth century as a family magazine and then later as a literary magazine, *Cosmopolitan* transformed into a women's magazine in the 1960s under the editorial guidance of Helen Gurley Brown. Brown had penned a best-selling book titled *Sex and the Single Girl* in 1962, and she used the magazine to reach what she believed to be "liberated women." *Cosmo*, as it became known, featured provocative articles about **birth control**, premarital and extramarital sex, and female sexuality, among others. It illustrates the changing cultural norms for women in the Baby Boom era.

Council for Basic Education   Organized in 1956, the Council for Basic Education (CBE) sought to make intellectual development, rather than social development, the primary focus of education. This was in response to, in large part, a trend in American education known as **Life Adjustment**. The CBE curriculum emphasized the traditional liberal arts: English, mathematics, science, history, and foreign languages.

Counterculture   The term used to identify anything or anyone that in the 1960s seemed to challenge or reject the mainstream culture. The term was broad enough to include **hippies**, music, film, fashion, drug use, communal living, and spiritual growth and exploration, among others.

The Crack in the Picture Window (1956)   John Keats's satirical depiction of suburban life, which he portrayed as destructive of social relationships, both personal and communal.

Defense of Marriage Act   A law enacted in 1996 that allowed any state to ignore a same-sex marriage legal in another state.

The Diggers   The Diggers were a San Francisco-based improvisational theater group that embodied much of the **counterculture** of the 1960s. Anarchists at heart, the Diggers directed their street theater toward creating a noncapitalist economy in their community. This is best illustrated in what was known as Free City, where the Diggers gave away free food and people could take what they needed in Free Stores.

Doves A term used to identify opponents of American involvement in the Vietnam War, especially those in the U.S. Congress and other branches of government.

Dylan, Bob Born Robert Zimmerman, Bob Dylan was perhaps the most influential musical artist of the Baby Boom era, and one of the most influential ever. Dylan first gained notoriety as a folk artist in the same vein as Woodie Guthrie. Many of Dylan's early songs could be described as "protest" songs ("How Many Roads?", "Masters of War") that he performed with only an acoustic guitar and harmonica. By mid-decade, Dylan's interests shifted. His music was less political and featured amplified guitars and a large band. Many folk aficionados felt betrayed by Dylan's decision to "go electric," but Dylan was unmoved.

The Electric Kool-Aid Acid Test **(1968)** An account of **Ken Kesey** and the Merry Prankster's **LSD**-fueled trip across the United States in an old school bus, written by Tom Wolfe.

Elementary and Secondary Education Act (ESEA) This law, enacted by Congress in 1965, was part of President Johnson's **Great Society** and **War on Poverty**. The act greatly expanded federal funding, and policy making, for education, especially early childhood education, and sought to redress inequality in education. This meant more federal money for "educationally disadvantage" and "educationally deprived" children from poor families, in particular racial and ethnic minorities. Congress has renewed the ESEA every five years, most recently as the No Child Left Behind Act.

The Establishment A term commonly used by social activists in the 1960s to refer to the entrenched institutions and processes of power in the United States.

Fair Housing Act Congress passed the Fair Housing Act (sometimes called Open Housing Act) in April 1968, only weeks after the murder of Martin Luther King, Jr. It culminated an effort by civil rights activists, dating back at least to the turn of the twentieth century, to prohibit discriminatory practices in the buying, selling, and renting of housing.

Federal Housing Administration (FHA) The FHA was created to administer the National Housing Act of 1934. After World War II, the FHA provided loans and mortgage insurance to returning soldiers that helped fuel **suburbanization**. In 1965, the FHA became part of the newly created, Cabinet-level Department of Housing and Urban Development (HUD), and helped facilitate the expansion of home ownership.

The Feminine Mystique **(1963)** In this best-selling book, Betty Friedan revealed the "problem with no name"; the cultural and social pressures on women to be content and fulfilled with being a wife and mother.

Folk Music   Sometimes referred to as "traditional" music, folk music is usually linked with the ordinary people from the working class. Folk music enjoyed a resurgence after World War II, in part because of the spread of new media (television, radio, and recordings) but also from its close connection with the civil rights movement. Pete Seeger, Phil Ochs, Joan Baez, and (briefly) **Bob Dylan** were among the artists who used their music to speak out against social injustice.

Free Speech Movement (FSM)   A 1964 movement at the University of California-Berkeley that heralded the onset student activism. The FSM illustrates the extent to which student activism intersected with other social movements, in particular how students' experiences in the civil rights movement prompted them to address other issues. Students increasingly saw the university as an education factory, funded by government and military research, and themselves as impersonal cogs in the machine. The movement itself flared over the distribution of political literature on spots near campus, which the university previously had permitted. When a nonstudent was arrested for handing out political literature, thousands of students gathered around the police car and prevented it from moving for more than thirty hours. The movement quickly spread, instilling students on campuses all across the nation with energy and a desire to take greater control over their own lives and shape their own world.

Freedom Summer   In 1964, the **Student Nonviolent Coordinating Committee (SNCC)** organized Freedom Summer, an effort to register black voters in the South. SNCC issued a call for volunteers specifically to white college students from the North and nearly 1,000 responded. The white students witnessed the grinding poverty and violence that Southern blacks encountered daily. The murder of three civil rights workers as Freedom Summer was just beginning, including a white student, vividly illustrated to the rest of the country the extent to which whites would defend the color line in the South. The experience left a deep mark on the white student participants. Many continued the struggle in their own communities upon their return, and others used the experience to address other forms of oppression in their lives.

Generation Gap   A term that came into wide use in the 1960s to describe the vast differences between the youth culture and the older generations.

Great Society   The name Lyndon Johnson gave to his ambitious legislative program designed to eradicate poverty and provide full education and occupational opportunities for all citizens.

Greensboro Sit-in   A 1960 sit-in at a Woolworth's lunch counter in Greensboro, North Carolina, to protest racial discrimination. Led by four first-year students at North Carolina A & T University, the demonstration quickly spread to other locales in the South. The Greensboro sit-in is usually credited with launching a new phase of the civil rights movement, one of active nonviolent resistance.

Gulf of Tonkin Resolution Congressional resolution passed with only three dissenting votes (one in the House, two in the Senate) that gave President Lyndon B. Johnson near absolute power in waging the war in Vietnam.

Haight-Ashbury An area of San Francisco that became closely identified with the **counterculture** of the 1960s.

Hawks A name given to ardent supporters of the Vietnam War, especially those in the U.S. Congress and other branches of government.

High School Confidential **(1958)** A film released in 1958 that portrayed, as many others did, teenagers as immoral and adults as their salvation.

Hippies Likely derived by the **Beat's** use of "hipster," hippie became a generic term to refer to youths whose appearance, dress, behavior, and attitudes went against convention.

In Loco Parentis A Latin term meaning "in place of the parents," and which was used to define the relationship between students and institutions of higher education. The university was expected to fulfill the parental role while children were on campus. The student movement of the 1960s challenged this concept by seeking, and gaining, greater freedom over students' personal behavior.

Interstate Highway Act Passed in 1956, the Interstate Highway Act created the Interstate Highway system, the largest public works project in American history. Some 42,000 miles of limited-access, multilane roads were planned as part of the bill. The act contributed significantly to the growth of **suburbia** and helped fuel the postwar economic boom.

Juvenile Delinquency In the 1950s, a perceived increase in the incidence of misdemeanors among teens led many parents and experts to identify juvenile delinquency as an epidemic that threatened the fabric of American society. Blame was hurled at popular culture (film, music, comic books), excessive mothering (Philip Wylie's *A Generation of Vipers*), and the large number of women who worked during World War II.

Kent State On May 4, 1970, Ohio National Guard troops fired high-powered rifles into a group of students. Many of the students were gathered to protest the American invasion of Cambodia a few days earlier; many others were merely walking across campus to get to their next class. In moments, four students lay dead and several others were wounded. Kent State came to symbolize the depth of the division over the Vietnam War.

Kesey, Ken The author of several best-selling books during the 1960s, including *One Flew Over the Cuckoo's Nest*. Kesey is sometimes seen as a cultural bridge between the **Beats** and the **hippies**.

La Raza A term that refers to people who consider themselves ancestors of the indigenous people of Mexico, including those parts of the United States gained from Mexico in the War of 1846.

La Raza Unida   In the late 1960s, a group of Latino activist organizations based primarily in the southwest joined together to form *La Raza Unida* (the Unified Race). *La Raza Unida* worked to improve social and economic conditions for Hispanics through political activism.

League of United Latin American Citizens (LULAC)   Founded in 1929, LULAC claims to be the largest Hispanic organization in the United States. LULAC was a voice of moderation for Hispanics in the Baby Boom era, akin to the National Association of the Advancement of Colored People.

Levittown   Levittown was the first significant suburb of the postwar era. The Long Island, New York, development soon became synonymous with **suburbanization**, in both its positive and negative connotations.

Liberal Consensus   A broad and moderate ideological consensus that dominated American politics after World War II. Cold war liberals—Democrats and Republicans alike—rejected radicalism, were committed to defeating Communism both at home and abroad, and fervent in their faith that capitalism and the American political system would bring an end to class conflict and class inequalities.

Life Adjustment   A key curricular programs of the 1950s. The Life Adjustment curriculum emphasized preparing students for the workplace and placed less emphasis on the conventional curriculum of math, science, and reading. Courses included home economics for girls and auto mechanics for boys. Life Adjustment also stressed citizenship and the knowledge needed to be an active participant in an American democracy.

"Little Boxes"   The title of folk song written by Malvina Reynolds and popularized by the folk singer **Peter Seeger**. The lyrics were critical of the conformity of middle-class suburban life: "Little Boxes, all the same. There's a green one and a pink one; And a blue one and a yellow one; And they're all made out of ticky-tacky; And they all look just the same." *See also Suburbanization.*

Little Rock Nine   In 1957, nine African American students enrolled at Central High School in Little Rock, Arkansas. They were turned away by angry whites, who were supported by Arkansas Governor Orval Faubus. The ensuing crisis was one of the first tests of school desegregation, and ultimately necessitated in the intervention of President Dwight Eisenhower for resolution.

The Lonely Crowd (1950)   The sociologist David Reisman decried the like-mindedness and conformity of **suburbia**. He argued that suburban life forced people to behave according to what those around them deemed acceptable, which he called "other-directed."

Lysergic Acid Diethylamide (LSD)   A synthetic drug that was popular within the **counterculture** of the 1960s. Proponents of its use, most notably the Harvard psychologist **Timothy Leary**, touted the drug's therapeutic value and claimed it could raise one's consciousness and spiritual awareness. *See also MK-ULTRA.*

MAD Magazine   A publication intended for teens that was first published in 1952 by Harvey Kurtzman and William Gaines. *MAD* parodied and satirized nearly every aspect of American life and culture, from films to politics to manners. It came under fire in the 1950s during increased fears of **juvenile delinquency**, to which some critics alleged *MAD* and other publications were contributing factors.

MECha **(Movimento Estudiantil de Chicanos de Aztlan)**   A student organization formed in 1969 by Chicano students. Inspired in part by the **Black Power** movement, MECha espoused cultural pride and sought to address inequality through direct action. MECha was a radical movement that contended that the southwestern United States was seized illegally by the United States in 1848 from its legitimate owners, Mexican Hispanics. They define their struggle in national liberation terms, are active on many western university campuses, and prominent in marches against stronger immigrant border controls and immigration legislation.

Mississippi Freedom Democratic Party (MFDP)   A political party formed in 1964 by African Americans struggling for racial equality in Mississippi. The Democratic Party in Mississippi claimed that blacks had no interest in voting, but the MFDP refuted that claim by holding a mock election in which thousands of black voters turned out. The MFDP took these results to the 1964 Democratic Convention in Atlantic City, and asked to be seated as the legitimate delegation from Mississippi. Their efforts were largely rebuffed, but they brought their disenfranchisement into the public eye.

MK-ULTRA   The code name for a secret government project conducted by the Central Intelligence Agency in the 1950s and 1960s. The experiments involved giving drugs, including **Lysergic acid diethylamide (LSD)**, to unsuspecting volunteers to measure the drug's effect on brain function.

Model Cities   A program launched by the Department of Housing and Urban Development in 1966, as part of the Johnson administration's **Great Society** and **War on Poverty**. The program's intent was to provide federal funding for local projects, with the inclusion of citizen participation in planning and development. The program never achieved its goals and was ended in 1974.

Montgomery Bus Boycott   In 1955, an African American woman named Rosa Parks violated a Montgomery, Alabama, statute by refusing to give up her seat on a city bus to a white rider. Her arrest marked the beginning of the year-long Montgomery Bus Boycott. The protest, which had nearly universal support within the black community in Montgomery, culminated in a Supreme Court ruling that prohibited segregated public accommodations.

The Movement   A term generally used by participants in New Left-led social activism in the 1960s.

Mumford, Lewis   Mumford, an architect, was perhaps the most outspoken critic of the new suburban housing developments that grew rapidly after World War II.

National Organization of Women (NOW) Founded in 1966, NOW became the leading organization for advancing the cause of gender equality. NOW focused its efforts particularly on workplace equity issues, such as equal pay and opportunity.

National Education Defense Act In the aftermath of the Soviet Union's successful launch of an Earth-orbiting satellite, many people believed American schools had failed. Congress enacted the National Defense Education Act in 1958, which sought to strengthen graduate training and instruction at all levels in foreign languages, science, and math.

Office of Economic Opportunity (OEO) The OEO had responsibility for administering many of the **Great Society** programs, including Head Start, the Job Corps, and **Volunteers in Service to America (VISTA)**.

On the Road **(1957)** This 1957 novel by Jack Kerouac is usually considered one of the essential writings of the **Beat** generation.

Open University The brainchild of sociologist Paul Goodman, the Open University was an effort to create a "student-centered approach" to higher education. Scores of similar programs sprung up across the country in the late 1960s. There were no fees or tuition, and participants received a hands-on learning experience, often learning from one another. Topics ranged from philosophical issues such as just war to practical matters such as beer making.

Operation Breadbasket An extension of the Southern Christian Leadership Conference (SCLC), Operation Breadbasket sought to improve the economic conditions for African Americans, mainly in the South. In 1966, Jesse Jackson headed up Operation Breadbasket in Chicago.

The Organization Man **(1956)** William Whyte argued in this best seller that corporations created a culture, what he referred to as the "social ethic," which discouraged creativity and individuality in their white-collar workers.

The Other America **(1962)** Michael Harrington wrote *The Other America* to reveal the depth of poverty in the United States. Harrington posited that 25 percent of the population lived below the poverty line. The book caught the attention of President John F. Kennedy and helped to launch a vigorous government effort to eradicate poverty.

Peace Corps President John Kennedy established the Peace Corps in 1961, which he envisioned as part of the global struggle against Communism led by the nation's youth. By 1966, more than 15,000 volunteers had answered the call.

Playboy First published in 1953 by Hugh Hefner, *Playboy* billed itself as a men's magazine. *Playboy* featured articles on art, fashion, and politics, as well as photographs of seminude (later, fully nude) women. Critics have castigated Hefner for his objectification of women, while others have credited him with challenging the stifling social mores about sex and sexuality of the 1950s and ushering in the so-called sexual revolution of the 1960s.

Port Huron Statement Written primarily by Tom Hayden and other members of the fledgling **Students for a Democratic Society (SDS)**, the Port Huron Statement became known as the "manifesto for a generation." It condemned, among others, the debilitating consequences of modernization and the loss of genuine community among human beings.

Redlining The practice of banks to provide mortgage loans for homes in all-white neighborhoods, thus effectively shutting most African-American families out of the housing market.

Red Power In much the same way that **Black Power** became a rallying cry for black cultural pride and solidarity, Red Power espoused the same sentiment for Native Americans. The Red Power movement is usually associated with the American Indian movement.

Reserve Officers Training Corps (ROTC) A college-based program for the training of military officers. ROTC became a focal point on campus for many antiwar protesters during the 1960s.

Selective Service Act (1967) This act set eighteen to thirty-five as the age of conscription for military service. Student deferments were still allowed under the law, but expired after completing a four-year degree or reaching the age of twenty-four. Later, the act was amended to provide for a draft lottery.

Servicemen's Readjustment Act (G.I. Bill) The Servicemen's Readjustment Act, better known as the "G.I. Bill," provided veterans of World War II with tuition payments and stipends for up to three years of college, and also low-interest loans for housing, farms, and new businesses. The G.I. Bill helped to fuel the tremendous growth of the U.S. economy in the postwar years, and accelerated the United States' transformation into a middle-class, suburban nation.

Silent Spring (1962) Marine biologist Rachel Carson wrote this book as a warning against the use of chemical pesticides, particularly dichlorodiphenyltrichloroethane, or DDT. Carson is generally credited with bringing environmental concerns to a broad audience and helping to launch the environmental movement.

Sputnik The name of the satellite successfully launched into Earth orbit by the Soviet Union in 1957. The news was especially shocking to the United States, as most Americans presumed U.S. technology was far ahead of the Soviets'. As a consequence, the United States stepped up its efforts in space exploration and committed more funding to math and science education through the National Defense Education Act.

Student Nonviolent Coordinating Committee (SNCC) Formed in the wake of the lunch counter sit-ins in 1960, SNCC soon stood at the vanguard of civil rights activism in the South; it organized, for example, the 1964 **Freedom Summer**. SNCC's history in many ways mirrored that of the civil rights movement's transformation, from nonviolent direct action to the embrace of **Black Power** and separatism.

Students for a Democratic Society (SDS) Perhaps the best-known New Left organization of the 1960s.

Suburbanization The process of growth and development surrounding an urban area.

Suburbia A term for suburban life and its culture.

Summer of Love The Summer of Love was 1967, when more than 100,000 people gathered in and around San Francisco. Thousands more gathered in New York, Washington, Toronto, and cities across Europe. The event moved the **counterculture** to the forefront of public awareness.

Sunbelt The Sunbelt refers to the states along the Gulf Coast and the U.S border with Mexico. This region grew significantly during the Baby Boom, in large measure because of massive federal spending on military research and defense projects—the aerospace industry and nuclear research in particular—located in these states.

Timothy Leary A Harvard University psychologist who advocated the use of **Lysergic acid diethylamide (LSD)**. Leary's embrace of the drug, along with his oft-quote dictum "turn on, tune in, and drop out" linked him closely to the **counterculture** of the 1960s.

United Farms Workers Union A labor union formed in the mid-1960s. It emerged in the wake of strikes and boycotts of farm products led by Cesar Chavez and other workers' rights activists.

Unsafe at Any Speed: The Designed-In Dangers of the Automobile **(1965)** Ralph Nader's 1965 expose of the automobile industry helped launch the consumer activist movement. Nader accused the industry of sacrificing safety in the manufacturing of cars for cost savings and larger profits. The book shook Americans' confidence in the automobile industry. Whereas millions of Americans were apathetic or hostile to New Left social activism, many of those same people trusted Nader.

Veterans Administration (VA) Established in 1930, during the Baby Boom era the VA had responsibility for administering the G.I. Bill, in particular the medical benefits provide by the law. As such, the VA played an important role in the economic growth and development of postwar America.

VISTA (Volunteers in Service to America) The idea for VISTA originated with the Kennedy administration and was enacted as part of Lyndon Johnson's **War on Poverty**. VISTA was characterized as the domestic **Peace Corps**; volunteers worked to relieve poverty and suffering in the poorest regions of the United States.

War on Poverty In 1964, President Lyndon Johnson declared a War on Poverty" as part of his vision for the **Great Society**. A wave of new programs and offices resulted, such as the Economic Opportunity Act of 1964, the Social Security Act of 1965, Head Start, and **VISTA (Volunteers in**

Service to America). Critics assailed the legislation as social welfare and encouraging dependency, while supporters claimed such programs were necessary to overcome entrenched poverty and inequality. Rates of poverty did decline between 1964 and 1980.

White Collar: The American Middle Classes (1951)   The sociologist C. Wright Mills published this critique of middle-class, corporate America. Mills suggested that the middle class conformed to corporate values in exchange for large salaries, which left them subservient to the interests of what Mills later called the "power elite."

White Flight   Term used to describe the exodus of white homeowners to new suburban housing developments as communities began desegregating their schools. The trend hampered efforts to genuinely integrate public schools, as many communities remained segregated, not by law but by socioeconomic status.

Young Americans for Freedom (YAF)   The best-known conservative youth organization was Young Americans for Freedom (YAF), founded in 1960. YAF was critical of the course of the Cold War, the growth of the liberal welfare state, socialistic trends in American society and politics, and what they perceived as the decline of the individual and the loss of individual rights. The YAF's legacy is also significant. Many of its members were crucial to the Reagan Revolution of the 1980s and the Republican Party's capture of Congress in the 1990s.

Bibliography

The Baby Boom

Aliano, Robert J., and Anthony Mordente. *The Worst Generation: How Baby Boomers Created the Square World Order*. Philadelphia: Xlibris Corp., 2003.

Barna, George. *Baby Busters: The Disillusioned Generation*. Chicago: Northfield Publishing, 1994.

Byerly, Greg, and Richard Rubin. *The Baby Boom: A Selective Annotated Bibliography*. Lexington, MA: Lexington Books, 1985.

Delli Carpini, Michael X. *Stability and Change in American Politics: The Coming of Age of the Generation of the 1960s*. New York: New York University Press, 1986.

Douglas, Avram. *Born at the Right Time: A History of the Baby-Boom Generation*. Toronto: University of Toronto Press, 1999.

Easterlin, Richard A. "The American Baby Boom in Historical Perspective." *The American Economic Review* 51:5 (December 1961) 869–911.

Eberstadt, Mary, ed. *Why I Turned Right: Leading Baby Boom Conservatives Chronicle Their Political Journey*. New York: Threshold, 2007.

Freedman, Marc. *Prime Time: How Baby Boomers Will Revolutionize Retirement and Transform America*. New York: Public Affairs, 1999.

Gillon, Steven M. *Boomer Nation: The Largest and Richest Generation Ever and How It Changed America*. New York: Free Press, 2004.

Gross, Michael. *The More Things Change: Why the Baby Boom Won't Fade Away*. New York: Cliff Street Books, 2001.

Hamilton, Neil A. *Atlas of the Baby Boom Generation*. Detroit: Macmillan Reference USA, 2000.

Hughes, Mary Elizabeth, and Angela M. O'Rand. "The Life and Times of the Baby Boomers." In *The American People: Census 2000*. Edited by Reynolds Farley and John Haaga. New York: Russell Sage Foundation, 2005.

Jones, Landon Y. *Great Expectations: America and the Baby Boom Generation*. New York: Coward, McCann & Geoghegan, 1980.

Light, Paul Charles. *Baby Boomers*. New York: Norton, 1988.

Macunovich, Diane J. *Birth Quake: The Baby Boom and its Aftershocks.* Chicago: University of Chicago Press, 2002.

Makower, Joel. *Boom!: Talkin' about Our Generation.* Chicago: Contemporary Books, 1985.

Michaels, Joanne. *Living Contradictions: The Women of the Baby Boom Come of Age.* New York: Simon and Schuster, 1982.

Mills, Daniel Quinn. *Not Like Our Parents: How the Baby Boom Generation is Changing America.* New York: Morrow, 1987.

Novelli, William D. *50+: Igniting a Revolution to Reinvent America.* New York: St. Martin's Press, 2006.

Owram, Doug. *Born at the Right Time: A History of the Baby-Boom Generation.* Toronto: University of Toronto Press, 1996.

Phillips, Michael. *What's Really Happening: Baby Boom II Comes of Age.* Bodega, CA: Clear Glass Pub., 1984.

Pollock, Bruce. *Hipper than our Kids: A Rock and Roll Journal of the Baby Boom Generation.* New York: Schirmer Books, 1993.

Queenan, Joe. *Balsamic Dreams: A Short but Self-Important History of the Baby Boomer Generation.* New York: Henry Holt, 2001.

Roszak, Theodore. *Longevity Revolution: As Boomers Become Elders.* Berkeley, CA: Berkeley Hills Books, 2001.

Russell, Cheryl. *The Master Trend: How the Baby Boom Generation Is Remaking America.* New York: Plenum Press, 1993.

Russell, Louise B. *The Baby Boom Generation and the Economy.* Washington, DC: Brookings Institute Press, 1982.

Smead, Howard. *Don't Trust Anyone over Thirty: The First Four Decades of the Baby Boom.* Lincoln, NE: Writer's Club Press, 2000.

Stasi, Linda, and Rosemary Rogers. *Boomer Babes: A Woman's Guide to the New Middle Ages.* New York: St. Martin's Griffin, 1998.

Steinhorn, Leonard. *The Greater Generation: In Defense of the Baby Boom Legacy.* New York: Thomas Dunne Books, 2006.

Wilson, Laura B., and Sharon P. Simson. *Civic Engagement and the Baby Boomer Generation: Research, Policy, and Practice Perspectives.* London: Hawthorne Press, 2006.

Waxman, Chaim I. *Jewish Baby Boomers: A Communal Perspective.* Albany: State University of New York Press, 2001.

The Baby Boom: Memoirs and Personal Recollections

Cheever, Susan. *A Woman's Life: The Story of an Ordinary American and Her Extraordinary Generation.* New York: W. Morrow, 1994.

Hiatt, Janice Steil. *Reflections of a Baby Boomer.* Victoria, BC: Trafford, 2004.

Toth, Susan Allen *Blooming: A Small-Town Girlhood.* New York: Ballantine, 1981.

Post-World War II Overviews

Chafe, William. *The Unfinished Journey: American since World War II*. New York: Oxford University Press, 1986.

Degler, Carl N. *Affluence and Anxiety, 1945-Present*. Glenview, IL: Scott Foresman American History Series, 1968.

Halberstam, David. *The Fifties*. New York: Villard Books, 1993.

Hodgson, Godfrey. *America in Our Time: From World War II to Nixon, What Happened and Why*. New York: Vintage Books, 1976.

Jeansonne, Glen. *A Time of Paradox: America from the Cold War to the Third Millennium, 1945-Present*. Lanham, MD: Rowman and Littlefield, 2006.

Marty, Myron A. *Daily Life in the United States, 1960–1990: Decades of Discord*. Westport, CT: Greenwood, 1997.

Matusow, Allen J. *The Unraveling of America: A History of Liberalism in the 1960s*. New York: Harper and Row, 1984.

Miller, Douglas T., and Marion Nowak. *The Fifties: The Way We Really Were*. Garden City, NY: Doubleday, 1977.

Norfleet, Barbara. *When We Liked Ike: Looking for Postwar America*. New York: Norton, 2001.

Oakley, J. Ronald. *God's Country: America in the Fifties*. New York: Dembner Books, 1986.

Patterson, James T. *Grand Expectations: The United States, 1945–1974*. New York: Oxford University Press, 1997.

Patterson, James T. *Restless Giant: The United States from Watergate to Bush v. Gore*. New York: Oxford University Press, 2005.

The Sixties

Anderson, Terry H. *The Movement and the Sixties: Protest in America from Greensboro to Wounded Knee*. New York: Oxford University Press, 1995.

Berman, Ronald. *America in the Sixties: An Intellectual History*. New York: Free Press, 1968.

Bloom, Alexander, ed. *Long Time Gone: Sixties America Then and Now*. New York: Oxford University Press, 2001.

Bloom, Alexander, and Wini Breines, eds. *"Takin' It to the Streets": A Sixties Reader*. New York: Oxford University Press, 2003.

Breines, Wini. *Community and Organization in the New Left, 1962–1968*. New York: Praeger, 1982.

Burner, David. *Making Peace with the 60s*. Princeton, NJ: Princeton University Press, 1996.

Burns, Stewart. *Social Movements of the 1960s: Searching for Democracy*. Boston: Twayne, 1990.

Cavallo, Dominick. *A Fiction of the Past: The Sixties in American History.* New York: St. Martin's Press, 1999.

Chalmers, David. *And the Crooked Places Made Straight: The Struggle for Social Change in the 1960s.* 2nd ed. Baltimore: Johns Hopkins University Press, 1996.

Conlin, Joseph. *The Troubles: A Jaundiced Glance Back at the Movement of the Sixties.* New York: Watts, 1982.

Farber, David. *The Age of Great Dreams: America in the 1960s.* New York: Hill and Wang, 1994.

Farber, David. *Chicago '68.* Chicago: University of Chicago Press, 1988.

Farber, David, ed. *The Sixties: From Memory to History.* Chapel Hill: University of North Carolina Press, 1994.

Farrell, James J. *The Spirit of the Sixties: The Making of Postwar Radicalism.* New York: Routledge, 1997.

Gitlin, Todd. *The Sixties: Years of Hope, Days of Rage.* Toronto: Bantam Books, 1987.

Gottlieb, Annie. *Do You Believe In Magic? Bringing the Sixties Back Home.* New York: Simon & Schuster, 1988.

Heale, M. J. *The Sixties in America: History, Politics, and Protest.* Chicago: Fitzroy Dearborn, 2001.

Horowitz, David, and Peter Collier, *Destructive Generation: Second Thoughts about the Sixties.* New York: Summit Books, 1989.

Hurley, Jennifer A. *The 1960s.* San Diego: Greenhaven, 2000.

Isserman, Maurice, and Michael Kazin. *America Divided: The Civil War of the 1960s.* 3rd ed. New York: Oxford University Press, 2009.

Kessler, Lauren. *After All These Years: Sixties Ideals in a Different World.* New York: Thunder's Mouth Press, 1990.

Knight, Douglas M. *Street of Dreams: The Nature and Legacy of the 1960s.* Durham, NC: Duke University Press, 1989.

Lieberman, Robbie. *Prairie Power: Voices of 1960s Midwestern Student Protest.* Columbia: University of Missouri Press, 2004.

McWilliams, John C. *The 1960s Cultural Revolution.* Westport, CT: Greenwood, 2000.

Monhollon, Rusty L. *"This is America?": The Sixties in Lawrence, Kansas.* New York: Palgrave, 2002.

Morgan, Edward P. *The 60s Experience: Hard Lessons about Modern America.* Philadelphia: Temple University Press, 1991.

Morrison, Joan, and Robert K. Morrison. *From Camelot to Kent State: The Sixties Experience in the Words of Those Who Lived It.* New York: Times Books, 1987.

Olson, James S., ed. *Historical Dictionary of the 1960s.* Westport, CT: Greenwood, 1999.

O'Neill, William. *Coming Apart: An Informal History of the 1960s*. Chicago: Quadrangle Books, 1971.

Rielly, Edward J. *The 1960s*. Westport, CT: Greenwood, 2003.

Rorabaugh, W. J. *Berkeley at War: The 1960s*. New York: Oxford University Press, 1989.

Rossinow, Douglas C. *The Politics of Authenticity: Liberalism, Christianity, and the New Left in America*. New York: Columbia University Press, 1998.

Spann, Edward K. *Democracy's Children: The Young Rebels of the 1960s and the Power of Ideals*. Wilmington, DE: Scholarly Resources, 2003.

Steigerwald, David. *The Sixties and the End of Modern America*. New York: St. Martin's Press, 1995.

Unger, Irwin, and Debi Unger. *Turning Point, 1968*. New York: Scribner, 1988. Reissued as *America in the 1960s*. St. James, NY: Brandywine Press, 1993.

Violence in America

Graham, Hugh Davis, and Ted Robert Gurr, eds. *Violence in America: Historical and Comparative Perspectives*. Rev. ed. Beverly Hills, CA: Sage Publications, 1979.

The National Advisory Commission on Civil Disorders. *Report of the National Advisory Commission on Civil Disorders*. New York: Bantam Books, 1968.

African Americans, Civil Rights, and Black Power

Branch, Taylor. *Parting the Waters: America in the King Years, 1954–1963*. New York: Simon and Schuster, 1992.

Carmichael, Stokely, and Charles V. Hamilton. *Black Power: The Politics of Liberation in America*. New York: Vintage Books, 1974.

Carson, Clayborne. *In Struggle: SNCC and the Black Awakening of the 1960s*. 2nd ed. Cambridge, MA: Harvard University Press, 1990.

Early, Gerald L. *This Is Where I Came In: Black America in the 1960s*. Lincoln: University of Nebraska Press, 2003.

Eskew, Glenn T. *But for Birmingham: The Local and National Movements in the Civil Rights Struggle*. Chapel Hill: University of North Carolina Press, 1997.

Franklin, John Hope, and Alfred A. Moss, Jr. *From Slavery to Freedom: A History of African Americans*. 8th ed. Boston: McGraw-Hill, 2000.

Graham, Hugh Davis. *The Civil Rights Era: Origins and Development of a National Policy, 1960–1965*. New York: Oxford University Press, 1990.

Haines, Herbert H. *Black Radicals and the Civil Rights Mainstream, 1954–1970*. Knoxville: University of Tennessee Press, 1988.

Jamison, Andrew, and Ron Eyerman. *Seeds of the Sixties*. Berkeley: University of California Press, 1994.

Jezer, Marty. *The Dark Ages: Life in the United States, 1945–1960*. Boston: South End Press, 1982.

Jones, Charles Earl, ed. *The Black Panther Party Reconsidered*. Baltimore: Black Classic Press, 1998.

Kaiser, Charles. *1968 in America: Music, Politics, Chaos, Counterculture, and the Shaping of a Generation*. New York: Weidenfeld & Nicolson, 1988.

Kluger, Richard. *Simple Justice: The History of* Brown v. Board of Education *and Black America's Struggle for Equality*. New York: Alfred A. Knopf, 1976.

Lawson, Steven F. *Running for Freedom: Civil Rights and Black Politics Since 1941*. Philadelphia: Temple University Press, 1991.

Malcolm X, with the assistance of Alex Haley. *The Autobiography of Malcolm X*. New York: Grove Press, Inc., 1964.

Marable, Manning. *Race, Reform, and Rebellion: The Second Reconstruction in America, 1945–1982*. London: Macmillan, 1984.

McAdam, Doug. *Freedom Summer*. New York: Oxford University Press, 1988.

Morris, Aldon D. *The Origins of the Civil Rights Movement: Black Communities Organizing for Change*. New York: Free Press, 1984.

Sitkoff, Harvard. *The Black Struggle for Equality, 1954–1980*. New York: Hill and Wang, 1981.

Stoper, Emily. *The Student Nonviolent Coordinating Committee: The Growth of Radicalism in a Civil Rights Organization*. Brooklyn, NY: Carlson Publishing, 1989.

Van Deberg, William L. *New Day in Babylon: The Black Power Movement and American Culture, 1965–1975*. Chicago: University of Chicago Press, 1992.

Weisbrot, Robert. *Freedom Bound: A History of America's Civil Rights Movement*. New York: Norton, 1990.

Whalen, Charles, and Barbara Whalen, *The Long Debate: A Legislative History of the 1964 Civil Rights Act*. New York: New American Library, 1985.

Women and Feminism

Bailey, Beth. *Sex in the Heartland*. Cambridge, MA: Harvard University Press, 1999.

Blair, Karen J. *The Clubwoman as Feminist: True Womanhood Redefined, 1868–1914*. New York: Holmes & Meier Publishers, 1980.

Breines, Wini. *Young, White, and Miserable: Growing Up Female in the Fifties*. Chicago: University of Chicago Press, 2001.

Chafe, William H. *The Paradox of Change: American Women in the Twentieth Century*. New York: Oxford University Press, 1991.

Ehrenreich, Barbara, and Deirdre English. *For Her Own Good: Two Centuries of the Experts' Advice for Women*. New York: Random House, 2005.

Evans, Sara. *Personal Politics: The Roots of Women's Liberation in the Civil Rights Movement and the New Left*. New York: Vintage Books, 1980.

Freeman, Jo. *The Politics of Women's Liberation*. New York: Longman, 1975.

Friedan, Betty. *The Feminine Mystique*. New York: Bantam Doubleday, 1983.

Gere, Anne Ruggles. *Intimate Practices: Literacy and Cultural Work in U.S. Women's Clubs, 1880–1920*. Urbana: University of Illinois Press, 1997.

Gould, Bruce, and Beatrice Blackmar Gould. *American Story*. New York: Harper & Row, 1968.

Hartman, Susan M. *From Margin to Mainstream: American Women and Politics Since 1960*. New York: Alfred A. Knopf, 1989.

Harvey, Brett. *The Fifties: A Women's Oral History*. New York: HarperCollins Publishers, 1993.

Inness, Sherrie A., ed. *Kitchen Culture in America*. Philadelphia: University of Pennsylvania Press, 2001.

Kaledin, Eugenia. *American Women in the 1950s: Mothers and More*. Boston: Twayne Publishers, 1984.

Kogan, Rick. *America's Mom: The Life, Lessons, and Legacy of Ann Landers*. New York: 2003.

Meyerowitz, Joanne, ed. *Not June Cleaver: Women and Gender in Postwar America, 1945–1960*. Philadelphia: Temple University Press, 1994.

Morris, Monica. "The Public Definition of a Social Movement: Women's Liberation." *Sociology and Social Research* (1974): 526–543.

Roe, Dorothy. *The Trouble with Women Is Men*. Englewood Cliffs, NJ: Prentice-Hall, 1961.

Rosen, Ruth. *The World Split Open: How the Modern Women's Movement Changed America*. New York: Viking, 2000.

Rosenberg, Rosalind. *Divided Lives: American Women in the Twentieth Century*. New York: Hill and Wang, 1992.

Scott, Anne Firor. *Natural Allies: Women's Associations in American History*. Urbana: University of Illinois Press, 1991.

Walker, Nancy, ed. *Women's Magazines 1940–1960*. New York: Bedford, 1998.

Weiss, Jessica. *To Have and to Hold: Marriage, the Baby Boom, and Social Change*. Chicago: University of Chicago Press, 2000.

Motherhood

Chira, Susan. *A Mother's Place: Taking the Debate about Working Mothers Beyond Guilt and Blame*. New York: HarperCollins Publishers, 1998.

Bowlby, John. *Maternal Care and Mental Health*. Geneva: World Health Organization, 1951.

Feldstein, Ruth. *Motherhood in Black and White: Race and Sex in American Liberalism, 1930–1965*. Ithaca, NY: Cornell University Press, 2000.

Grant, Julia. *Raising Baby by the Book: The Education of American Mothers*. New Haven, CT: Yale University Press, 1998.

Kaledin, Eugenia. *Mothers and More: American Women in the 1950s*. Boston: Twayne Publishers, 1984.

Kaplan, E. Ann. *Motherhood and Representation: The Mother in Popular Culture and Melodrama*. London; New York: Routledge, 1992.

Ladd-Taylor, Molly, and Lauri Umansky, eds. *"Bad" Mothers: The Politics of Blame in Twentieth-Century America*. New York: New York University Press, 1998.

Layne, Linda L., ed. *Transformative Motherhood: On Giving and Getting in a Consumer Culture*. New York: New York University Press, 1999.

Taitz, Sonia. *Mothering Heights: Reclaiming Motherhood from the Experts*. New York: William Morrow, 1992.

Umansky, Lauri. *Motherhood Reconceived: Feminism and the Legacies of the Sixties*. New York: New York University Press, 1996.

Wylie, Philip. *A Generation of Vipers*. New York: Rinehart, 1955.

The Family

Child Study Association of America. *Where We Are: A Hard Look at Family And Society*. New York: Child Study Association of America, 1971.

Chudacoff, Howard. *Children at Play: An American History*. New York: New York University Press, 2007.

Coontz, Stephanie. *The Way We Never Were: American Families and the Nostalgia Trap*. New York: BasicBooks, 1992.

Coontz, Stephanie. *The Way We Really Are: Coming to Terms with America's Changing Families*. New York: Basic Books, 1997.

Cunningham, Hugh "Histories of Childhood: Review Essay." *American Historical Review* 103, no. 4 (October 1998): 1196.

Friedan, Betty. *The Feminine Mystique*. New York: Norton, 1963.

Hareven, Tamara. "Cycles, Courses and Cohorts: Reflections on Theoretical and Methodological Approaches to the Historical Study of Family Development." *Journal of Social History* 7 (Fall 1978): 97–109.

Hawes, Joseph M., and N. Ray Hiner, eds. *American Childhood: A Research Guide and Historical Handbook*. Westport, CT: Greenwood Press, 1985.

Hawes Joseph M., and Elizabeth I. Nybakken, eds. *American Families: A Research Guide and Historical Handbook* New York: Greenwood Press, 1991.

Hwang, C. Philip, Michael E. Lam, and Irving E. Sigel, eds. *Images of Childhood*. Mahwa, NJ: Lawrence Earlbaum, 1996.

Jacobson, Lisa, ed. *Children and Consumer Culture in American Society: A Historical Handbook and Guide*. New York: Praeger, 2007.

Jacobson, Lisa. *Raising Consumers: Children and the American Mass Market in the Early Twentieth Century*. New York: Columbia University Press, 2005.

Kozol, Wendy. *Life's America: Family and Nation in Postwar Photojournalism*. Philadelphia: Temple University Press, 1994.

May, Elaine Tyler. *Homeward Bound: American Families in the Cold War Era.* New York: Basic Books, 1999.

Reiss, David, and Howard A. Hoffman, eds. *The American Family, Dying or Developing.* New York: Plenum Press, 1979.

Smith, Judith E. *Visions of Belonging: Family Stories, Popular Culture, and Postwar Democracy.* New York: Columbia University Press, 2004.

South, Scott J., and Stewart E. Tolnay, eds. *The Changing American Family: Sociological and Demographic Perspectives.* Boulder, CO: Westview Press, 1992.

Spock, Benjamin. *Baby and Child Care.* 1946. New York: Pocket Books, 1968.

Weiss, Jessica. *To Have and to Hold: Marriage, the Baby Boom, and Social Change.* Chicago: University of Chicago Press, 2000.

West, Elliott. *Growing Up in Twentieth-Century America: A History and Reference Guide.* New York: Greenwood Press, 1996.

Wetzel, James R. "American Families: 75 Years of Change." *Monthly Labor Review* (March 1990): 12.

Childhood and Youth

Brunsma, David L. *The School Uniform Movement and What It Tells Us about American Education, A Symbolic Crusade.* Oxford: Oxford University Press, 2004.

Flesch, Rudolf. *Why Johnny Can't Read and What You Can Do About It.* New York: Harper, 1955.

Freire, Paulo. *Pedagogy of the Oppressed.* New York: Continuum, 1992.

Goodman, Paul. *Growing Up Absurd.* New York: Vintage, 1960.

Graebner, William. *Coming of Age in Buffalo: Youth and Authority in the Post-War Era.* Philadelphia: Temple University Press, 1990.

Hawes, Joseph M. *The Children's Rights Movement: A History of Advocacy and Protection.* Boston: Twayne, 1991.

Hine, Thomas. *The Rise and Fall of the American Teenager.* New York: Bard, 1999.

Illick, Joseph E. *American Childhoods.* Philadelphia: University of Pennsylvania Press, 2002.

Johnson, John W. *The Struggle for Student Rights:* Tinker v. Des Moines *and the 1960s.* Lawrence: University Press of Kansas, 1997.

May, Kirse Granat. *Golden State, Golden Youth· The California Image in Popular Culture, 1955–1966.* Chapel Hill: University of North Carolina Press, 2002.

Palladino, Grace. *Teenagers: An American History.* New York: Basic Books, 1996.

Wertham, Frederic. *Seduction of the Innocent.* New York: Rinehart & Co., 1954.

Students, Activism, and the University

Avorn, Jerry L. *Up Against the Ivy Wall: A History of the Columbia Crisis*. New York: Antheneum, 1970.

Cohen, Robert, and Reginald E. Zelnik, eds. *The Free Speech Movement: Reflections on Berkeley in the 1960s*. Berkeley: University of California Press, 2002.

Freeman, Jo. *At Berkeley in the Sixties: The Education of an Activist, 1961–1965*. Bloomington: Indiana University Press, 2004.

Frost, Jennifer. *"An Interracial Movement of the Poor": Community Organizing and the New Left in the 1960s*. New York: New York University Press, 2001.

Heineman, Kenneth J. *Campus Wars: The Peace Movement at American State Universities in the Vietnam Era*. New York: New York University Press, 1993.

Heineman, Kenneth J. *Put Your Bodies upon the Wheels: Student Revolt in the 1960s*. Chicago: Ivan R. Dee, 2001.

Horowitz, Helen Lefkowitz. *Campus Life: Undergraduate Cultures from the End of the Eighteenth Century to the Present*. New York: Alfred A. Knopf, 1987.

Klatch, Rebecca E. *A Generation Divided: The New Left, The New Right, and the 1960s*. Berkeley: University of California Press, 1999.

Lipset, Seymour Martin, and Sheldon S. Wolin. *The Berkley Student Revolt: Facts and Interpretations*. New York: Anchor Books, 1965.

Michener, James A. *Kent State: What Happened and Why*. New York: Random House, 1971.

Miller, James. *Democracy Is in the Streets: From Port Huron to the Siege of Chicago*. New York: Simon and Schuster, 1987.

Sale, Kirkpatrick. *SDS*. New York: Random House, 1973.

Spann, Edward K. *Democracy's Children: The Young Rebels of the 1960s and the Power of Ideals*. Wilmington, DE: Scholarly Resources, 2003.

Wallechinsky, David. *Class Reunion '65: Tales of an American Generation*. 1986. New York: Penguin Books, 1987.

Wallechinsky, David. *Midterm Report: The Class of '65: Chronicles of an American Generation*. New York: Viking, 1986.

Weaver, Gary R., and Weaver, James H., eds. *The University and Revolution*. NJ: Prentice-Hall, 1969.

Wynkoop, Mary Ann. *Dissent in the Heartland: The Sixties at Indiana University*. Bloomington: Indiana University Press, 2002.

Counterculture

Braunstein, Peter, and Michael William Doyle. *Imagine Nation: The American Counterculture of the 1960s and '70s*. New York: Routledge, 2002.

Casale, Anthony M., and Philip Lerman. *Where Have All The Flowers Gone? The Fall and Rise of the Woodstock Generation*. Kansas City: Andrews and McMeel, 1989.

Dass, Ram. *Be Here Now*. Lama Foundation, 1971.

Everson, William, "Dionysus and The Beat Generation." In *The Beats: Essays in Criticism*, edited by Lee Bartlett. Jefferson, NC: McFarland, 1981.

Kerouac, Jack. *On the Road*. New York: Viking Press, 1958.

Kesey, Ken. *One Flew Over the Cuckoo's Nest*. New York: Viking Press, 1962.

Kesey, Ken. *Sometimes a Great Notion*. New York: Viking Press, 1964.

Kirk, Andrew G. *Counterculture Green: The Whole Earth Catalog and American Environmentalism*. Lawrence: University Press of Kansas, 2007.

Krassner, Paul. *Confessions of a Raving, Unconfined Nut: Misadventures in the Counter-Culture*. New York: Simon and Schuster, 1992.

Landy, Elliot. *Woodstock Vision: The Spirit of a Generation*. New York: Continuum, 1994.

MacFarlane Scott. *The Hippie Narrative: A Literary Perspective on the Counterculture*. Jefferson, NC: McFarland, 2007.

McConnell, William S., ed. *The Counterculture Movement of the 1960s*. San Diego: Greenhaven Press, 2004.

McWilliams, John C. *The 1960s Cultural Revolution*. Westport, CT: Greenwood Press, 2000.

Miller, Timothy. *The 60s Communes: Hippies and Beyond*. Syracuse, NY: Syracuse University Press, 1999.

Miller, Timothy. *The Hippies and American Values*. Knoxville: University of Tennessee Press, 1991.

Norman, Gurney. *Divine Right's Trip: A Novel of the Counterculture*. Frankfort, KY: Gnomon, 1990.

Peck, Abe. *Uncovering the Sixties: The Life and Times of the Underground Press*. New York: Pantheon Books, 1985.

Roszak, Theodore. *The Making of a Counterculture*. Garden City, NY: Doubleday, 1969.

Rothman, Hal. *The Greening of a Nation: Environmentalism in the United States since 1945*. Fort Worth: Harcourt Brace College Publishers, 1998.

Swingrover, E. A., ed. *The Counterculture Reader*. New York: Pearson/Longman, 2004.

Whitmer, Peter O., with Bruce Van Wyngarden. *Aquarius Revisited: Seven who Created the Sixties Counterculture That Changed America: William Burroughs, Allen Ginsberg, Ken Kesey, Timothy Leary, Norman Mailer, Tom Robbins, Hunter S. Thompson*. New York: Citadel Press, 2007.

Vietnam and the Antiwar Movement

Baskir, Lawrence M., and William A. Strauss, *Chance and Circumstance: The Draft, the War, and the Vietnam Generation*. New York: Knopf, 1978.

Curry, G. David. *Sunshine Patriots: Punishment and the Vietnam Offender*. Notre Dame, IN: University of Notre Dame Press, 1985.

DeBenedetti, Charles, with Charles Chatfield. *An American Ordeal: The Antiwar Movement of the Vietnam Era*. Syracuse, NY: Syracuse University Press, 1990.

Ferber, Michael, and Staughton Lynd. *The Resistance*. Boston: Beacon Press, 1971.

Gottlieb, Sherry Gershon. *Hell No, We Won't Go!: Resisting the Draft during the Vietnam War*. New York: Viking, 1991.

Hall, James C. *Mercy, Mercy Me: African-American Culture and the American Sixties*. New York: Oxford University Press, 2001.

Halstead, Fred. *Out Now! A Participant's Account of the American Movement against the Vietnam War*. New York: Monad Press, 1978.

Kovic, Ron. *Born on the Fourth of July*. New York: Pocket Books, 1976.

Religion

Bellah, Robert N., Richard Madsen, William M. Sullivan, Ann Swidler, and Steven M. Tipton. *Habits of the Heart. Individualism and Commitment in American Life*. Berkeley: University of California Press, 1985.

Berger, Peter L. *The Sacred Canopy: Elements of a Sociological Theory of Religion*. 1967. New York: Anchor Books, 1990.

Carrol, Jackson W., Douglas W. Johnson, and Martin E. Marty. *Religion in America: 1950 to the Present*. New York: Harper & Row, 1979.

Ellwood, Robert S. *The Fifties Spiritual Marketplace: American Religion in a Decade of Conflict*. New Brunswick, NJ: Rutgers University Press, 1997.

Ellwood, Robert S. *The Sixties Spiritual Awakening: American Religion Moving From Modern to Postmodern*. New Brunswick, NJ: Rutgers University Press, 1994.

Herberg, Will. *Protestant-Catholic-Jew: An Essay in American Religious Sociology*. Garden City, NY: Anchor Books, 1960.

Hoge, Dean R., Benton Johnson, and Donald A. Luidens. *Vanishing Boundaries: The Religion of Mainline Protestant Baby Boomers*. Louisville, KY: Westminster/John Knox Press, 1994.

Marty, Martin E. *Modern American Religion: Volume 3: Under God, Indivisible, 1941–1960*. Chicago: University of Chicago Press, 1986.

Melton, J. Gordon. *The Encyclopedia of American Religions*. 3rd ed. Detroit: Gale Research, 1989.

Merriman, Scott A., ed. *Religion and the Law in America: An Encyclopedia of Personal Belief and Public Policy*. Santa Barbara, CA: ABC-Clio, 2007.

Nisker, Wes. *The Big Bang, the Buddha, and the Baby Boom: The Spiritual Experiments of My Generation*. San Francisco: Harper San Francisco, 2003.

Roof, Wade Clark. *A Generation of Seekers: The Spiritual Journeys of the Baby Boom Generation*. San Francisco: Harper San Francisco, 1993.

Roof, Wade Clark. *Spiritual Marketplace: Baby Boomers and the Remaking of American Religion*. Princeton, NJ: Princeton University Press, 1999.

Roof, Wade Clark, and William McKinney. *American Mainline Religion: Its Changing Shape and Future*. New Brunswick, NJ: Rutgers University Press, 1987.

Wertheimer, Jack. *A People Divided. Judaism in Contemporary America*. New York: Basic Books, 1993.

Wilcox, Clyde. *God's Warriors: The Christian Right in Twentieth-Century America*. Baltimore: Johns Hopkins University Press, 1992.

Wuthnow, Robert. *The Restructuring of American Religion: Society and Faith Since World War II*. Princeton, NJ: Princeton University Press, 1988.

Cold War and the Red Scare

Barson, Michael, and Steven Heller. *Red Scared! The Commie Menace in Propaganda and Popular Culture*. San Francisco: Chronicle Books, 2001.

Boyer, Paul. *By the Bomb's Early Light: American Thought and Culture at the Dawn of the Atomic Age*. New York: Pantheon, 1985.

Engelhardt, Tom. *The End of Victory Culture: Cold War America and the Disillusioning of a Generation*. New York, NY: BasicBooks, 1995.

Foster, Stuart J. *Red Alert! Educators Confront the Red Scare in American Public Schools, 1947–1954*. New York: P. Lang, 2000.

Fried, Albert. *McCarthyism: The Great American Red Scare: A Documentary History*. New York: Oxford University Press, 1997.

Fried, Richard M. *Nightmare in Red: The McCarthy Era in Perspective*. New York: Oxford University Press, 1990.

Fried, Richard M. *The Russians Are Coming! The Russians Are Coming! Pageantry and Patriotism in Cold-War America*. New York: Oxford University Press, 1998.

Goldston, Robert C. *The American Nightmare: Senator Joseph R. McCarthy and the Politics of Hate*. Indianapolis, Bobbs-Merrill, 1973.

Heale, M. J. *American Anticommunism: Combating the Enemy Within, 1830–1970*. Baltimore: Johns Hopkins Press, 1990.

Henriksen, Margot A. *Dr. Strangelove's America: Society and Culture in the Atomic Age*. Berkeley: University of California Press, 1997.

Inglis, Fred. *The Cruel Peace: Everyday Life in the Cold War*. New York: BasicBooks, 1991.

Knight, Peter, ed. *Conspiracy Nation: The Politics of Paranoia in Postwar America*. New York: New York University Press, 2002.

Kovel, Joel. *Red Hunting in the Promised Land: Anticommunism and the Making of America*. London: Cassell, 1994.

Rose, Kenneth D. *One Nation Underground: The Fallout Shelter in American Culture*. New York: New York University Press, 2001.

Rose, Lisle Abbott. *The Cold War Comes to Main Street: America in 1950.* Lawrence: University Press of Kansas, 1999.

Schrecker, Ellen. *Many Are the Crimes: McCarthyism in America.* Boston: Little, Brown, 1998.

Schrecker, Ellen. *No Ivory Tower: McCarthyism and the Universities.* New York: Oxford University Press, 1986.

Whitfield, Stephen J. *The Culture of the Cold War.* 2nd ed. Baltimore: Johns Hopkins University Press, 1996.

Winkler, Allan M. *Life under a Cloud: American Anxiety about the Atom.* New York: Oxford University Press, 1993.

Hispanic Americans

Acuña, Rodolfo F. *Anything But Mexican: Chicanos in Contemporary Los Angeles.* New York: Verso, 1996.

Acuña, Rodolfo F. *U.S. Latino Issues.* Westport, CT: Greenwood Press, 2003.

Alexander, Sandra C. *Famous Hispanic-Americans in United States History.* Greensboro, NC: Appletex Education Center, 1992.

American Journey: History in Your Hands: Hispanic-American Experience. Woodbridge, CT: Primary Source Media, CD-ROM, 1997.

Arreola, Daniel D. *Hispanic Spaces, Latino Places: Community and Cultural Diversity in Contemporary America.* Austin: University of Texas Press, 2004.

Chapman, Charles Edward. *A History of the Cuban Republic: A Study in Hispanic American Politics.* 1927. Whitefish, MT: Kessinger Press, 2005.

Chavez, Linda. *Out of the Barrio: Towards a New Politics of Assimilation.* New York: Basic Books, 1991.

De Varona, Frank, Ron Coleman, and Nick Viorst. *Latino Literacy: A Complete Guide to the Hispanic-American Culture and History.* New York: Owl Books, 1996.

Gibson, Campbell. *Historical Census Statistics on the Foreign Born Population of the United States: 1850–1990.* Washington, DC: U.S. Bureau of the Census, Population Division, 1999.

Gibson, Campbell, and Kay Jung. *The Foreign Born Population of the United States: 1850–2000.* New York: Novinka Books, 2006.

Gutiérrez, David Gregory. *The Columbia History of Latinos in the United States since 1960.* New York: Columbia University Press, 2004.

Hill, Gene. *Americans All=Americanos Todos: A Bilingual History of the Contributions of Hispanics to the Development of America.* Albequerque, NM: Añoranza Press, 1997.

Iber, Jorge, Arnold DeLeon, and Scott Zeman. *Hispanics in the American West.* Santa Barbara, CA: ABC-CLIO, 2005.

Kanellos, Nicolás, and Helvetia Martell. *Hispanic Periodicals in the United States: Origins to 1960: A Brief History and Comprehensive History.* Houston, TX: Arte-Publico, 1999.

Kanellos, Nicolás, and Cristelia Perez. *Chronology of Hispanic-American History: From Pre-Columbian Times to the Present*. New York: Gale Research, 1995.

Laezman, Rick. *100 Hispanic-Americans Who Changed American History*. Milwaukee, WI: World Almanac Library, 2005.

Navarro, Sharon Ann, and Armando Xavier Mejia, eds. *Latino Americans and Political Participation: A Reference Handbook*. Santa Barbara, CA: ABC-CLIO, 2004.

Nordquist, Joan. *Latinas in the United States; Social, Economic and Political Aspects: A Bibliography*. Santa Cruz, CA: Reference and Research Service, 1994.

Novas, Himilce. *The Hispanic 100: A Ranking of the Latino Men and Women Who Have Most Influenced American Thought and Culture*. New York: Carol Publications, 1995.

Meyer, Nicholas F. *Biographical Dictionary of Hispanic Americans*. New York: Checkmark Books, 2001.

Ochoa, George. *Atlas of Hispanic-American History*. New York: Checkmark Books, 2001.

Owsley, Beatrice Rodrquez. *The Hispanic-American Entrepreneur: An Oral History of the American Dream*. New York: Twayne Publishing, 1992.

Rosales, Francisco A. *Chicano: The History of the Mexican-American Civil Rights Movement*. Houston, TX: Arte Publico, 1997.

Stafford, Jim. *Puerto Ricans' History and Promise: Americans Who Cannot Vote*. Philadelphia: Mason Crest Publishers, 2005.

Schultz, Jeffrey D., Kerry L. Haynie, Anne M. McCulloch, and Andrew L. Aoki. *Encyclopedia of Minorities in American Politics*. Phoenix, AZ: Oryx Press, 2000.

Vargas, Zaragosa, ed. *Major Problems in Mexican American History: Documents and Essays*. Boston: Houghton-Mifflin Co., 2005.

Whately, William, Jr., ed. *Studies in Hispanic-American History*. Chapel Hill: University of North Carolina Press, 1927.

Politics and Political Culture

Andrew, John A., III. *The Other Side of the Sixties: Young Americans for Freedom and the Rise of Conservative Politics*. New Brunswick, NJ: Rutgers University Press, 1997.

Berman, William C. *America's Right Turn: From Nixon to Bush*. Baltimore: Johns Hopkins University Press, 1994.

Boaz, David, ed. *Left, Right & Babyboom: America's New Politics*. Washington, DC: Cato Institute, 1986.

Breines, Wini. *Community and Organization in the New Left, 1962–1968*. New York: Praeger, 1982.

Brennan, Mary C. *Turning Right in the Sixties: The Conservative Capture of the GOP*. Chapel Hill: University of North Carolina Press, 1995.

Carter, Dan T. *The Politics of Rage: George Wallace, the Origins of the New Conservatism, and the Transformation of American Politics*. New York: Simon and Schuster, 1995.

Erickson, Sonja L. "In Defense of the Family: The Fight to Rescind the ERA in Kansas, 1974–1979," Master's thesis, University of Kansas, 1996.

Fowler, Robert Booth. *Enduring Liberalism: American Political Thought since the 1960s*. Lawrence: University Press of Kansas, 1999.

Gosse, Van, and Richard Moser, eds. *The World the Sixties Made: Politics and Culture in Recent America*. Philadelphia: Temple University Press, 2003.

Himmelstein, Jerome L. *To the Right: The Transformation of American Conservatism*. Berkeley: University of California Press, 1990.

Isserman, Maurice. *If I Had a Hammer: The Death of the Old Left and the Birth of the New Left*. New York: Basic Books, 1987.

Karol, Wayne. *Across the Great Divide: Nixon, Clinton, and the War of the Sixties*. New York: iUniverse, 2004.

Lyons, Paul. *New Left, New Right and the Legacy of the Sixties*. Philadelphia: Temple University Press, 1996.

McGirr, Lisa. *Suburban Warriors: The Origins of the New Right*. Princeton, NJ: Princeton University Press, 2001.

Schulman, Bruce J. *The Seventies: The Great Shift in American Culture, Society, and Politics*. Cambridge: De Capo Press, 2002.

Sugrue, Thomas J. *The Origins of the Urban Crisis: Race and Inequality in Postwar Detroit*. Princeton, NJ: Princeton University Press, 1996.

The Organization Man

Bennett, Amanda. *The Death of the Organization Man*. New York: Morrow, 1990.

Leinberger, Paul, and Bruce Tucker. *The New Individualists: The Generation after the Organization Man*. New York, N.Y.: HarperCollins Publishers, 1991.

Whyte, William. *The Organization Man*. New York: Simon and Schuster, 1956.

Suburbia

Duany, Andres, Elizabeth Plater-Zyberk, and Jeff Speck. *Suburban Nation: The Rise of Sprawl and the Decline of the American Dream*. New York: North Point Press, 2000.

Baxandall, Rosalyn, and Elizabeth Ewen. *Picture Windows: How the Suburbs Happened*. New York, NY: Basic Books, 2000.

Beauregard, Robert A. *When America Became Suburban*. Minneapolis: University of Minnesota Press, 2006.

Bennett, Michael J. *When Dreams Came True: The GI Bill and the Making of Modern America*. Washington, DC: Brassey's, 1996.

Bernstein, Josh. *Willingboro, New Jersey*. Charleston, SC: Arcadia Press, 2002.

Bloom, Nicholas Dagen. *Suburban Alchemy: 1960s New Towns and the Transformation of the American Dream*. Columbus: Ohio State University Press, 2001.

Flink, James J. *The Automobile Age*. Cambridge, MA: Massachusetts Institute of Technology Press, 1988.

Gailbraith, John Kenneth. *The Affluent Society*. Boston: Houghton Mifflin, 1958.

Gans, Herbert. *The Levittowners: Ways of Life and Politics in a New Suburban Community*. New York: Columbia University Press, 1982.

Garreau, Joel. *Edge City: Life on the New Frontier*. New York: Doubleday, 1991.

Humes, Edward. *Over Here: How the G.I. Bill Transformed the American Dream*. Orlando: Harcourt, 2006.

Jackson, Kenneth T. *Crabgrass Frontier· The Suburbanization of the United States*. New York: Oxford University Press, 1985.

Jackson, Kenneth T. "Suburbanization." In *The Reader's Companion to American History*, edited by Eric Foner and John Arthur Garraty, 1040–1043. Boston: Houghton Mifflin, 1991.

Keats, John. *The Crack in the Picture Window*. Boston: Houghton Mifflin, 1957.

Kruse, Kevin M. and Thomas J. Sugrue, eds. *The New Suburban History*. Chicago: University of Chicago Press, 2006.

Levinson, David M., and Kevin J. Krizek. *Planning for Place and Plexus: Metropolitan Land Use and Transport*. New York: Routledge, 2008.

Lyons, Paul. *Class Of '66: Living in Suburban Middle America*. Philadelphia: Temple University Press, 1994.

Nicolaides, Becky M., and Andrew Wiese, eds. *The Suburb Reader*. New York: Routledge, 2006.

Teaford, Jon C. *The American Suburb: The Basics*. New York: Routledge, 2008.

Thompson, Gare. *A Suburban Community of the 1950s*. Washington, DC: National Geographic Society, 2002.

Mills, C. Wright. *White Collar: The American Middle Classes*. New York: Oxford University Press, 1951.

Reisman, David, with Nathan Glazer and Reuel Denney. *The Lonely Crowd: A Study of the Changing American Character*. Garden City, NY: Doubleday, 1953.

Rybczynski, Witold. *Last Harvest: How a Cornfield Became New Daleville: Real Estate Development in America from George Washington to the Builders of the Twenty-First Century and Why We Live in Houses Anyway.* New York: Simon and Schuster, 2007.

Whyte, William H. *The Organization Man.* New York: Simon and Shuster, 1956.

Popular Culture

Bedrock, Alan. *The "I Was a Teenage Juvenile Delinquent Rock 'n' Roll Horror Beach Party Movie" Book: A Complete Guide to the Teen Exploitation Film, 1954–1969.* New York: St. Martin's, 1986.

Berger, Michael L. *The Automobile in American History And Culture: A Reference Guide.* Westport, CT.: Greenwood Press, 2001.

Biskind, Peter. *Seeing is Believing: How Hollywood Taught Us to Stop Worrying and Love the Fifties.* New York: Pantheon, 1983.

Bodroghkozy, Aniko. *Groove Tube: Sixties Television and the Youth Rebellion.* Durham, NC: Duke University Press, 2001.

Cagin, Seth, and Philip Dray. *Hollywood Films of the Seventies: Sex, Drugs, Violence, Rock 'n' Roll and Politics.* New York: Harper & Row, 1984.

Crenshaw, Marshall. *Hollywood Rock.* New York: Agincourt, 1994.

Doherty, Thomas Patrick. *Cold War, Cool Medium: Television, McCarthyism, and American Culture.* New York: Columbia University Press, 2003.

Flink, James J. *The Car Culture.* Cambridge, MA: MIT Press, 1975.

Foster, Mark S. *Nation On Wheels: The Automobile Culture in America Since 1945.* Belmont, CA: Thomson, Wadsworth, 2003.

Gitlin, Todd. *The Whole World Is Watching.* Berkeley: University of California Press, 1980.

Hall, Mitchell K. *Crossroads: American Popular Culture and the Vietnam Generation.* Lanham, MD: Rowman and Littlefield, 2005.

Heitmann, John Alfred. *The Automobile and American Life.* Jefferson, NC: McFarland & Co., 2009.

Kieley, Genny Zak. *Green Stamps to Hot Pants: Growing Up in the 50s and 60s.* Minneapolis, MN: Nodin Press, 2008.

Lemke-Santangelo, Gretchen. *Daughters of Aquarius: Women of the Sixties Counterculture.* Lawrence: University Press of Kansas, 2009.

Lewis, Lucinda. *Roadside America: The Automobile and the American Dream.* New York: H.N. Abrams, 2000.

Lipsitz, George. *Time Passages: Collective Memory and American Popular Culture.* Minneapolis: University of Minnesota Press, 1990.

MacNeil, Alex *Total Television: The Comprehensive Guide to Programming from 1948 to the Present.* 4th ed. New York: Penguin, 1996.

Marling, Karal Ann. *As Seen On TV: The Visual Culture of Everyday Life in the 1950s*. Cambridge, MA: Harvard University Press, 1994.

Miller, James. *Flowers in the Dustbin: The Rise of Rock and Roll, 1947–1977*. New York: Simon and Schuster, 1999.

Salamone, Frank A. *Popular Culture in the Fifties*. Lanham, MD: University Press of America, 2001.

Spigel, Lynn. *Make Room for TV: Television and the Family Ideal in Postwar America*. Chicago: University of Chicago Press, 1992.

Thelen, David. *Becoming Citizens in the Age of Television*. Chicago: University of Chicago Press, 1996.

Trombetta, Jim, comp. *The Horror! The Horror! Comics the Government Saved You From*. New York: Abrams ComicArts, 2009.

Poverty and the Poor

Acuña, Rodolfo. *Anything but Mexican: Chicanos in Contemporary Los Angeles*. New York: Verso, 1996.

Chafe, William H. *The Unfinished Journey: America since World War II*. 5th ed. New York: Oxford University Press, 2003.

Frantz, Klaus. *Indian Reservations in the United States: Territory, Sovereignty, and Socioeconomic Change*. Chicago: University of Chicago Press, 1999.

Gutiérrez, David Gregory. *The Columbia History of Latinos in the United States since 1960*. New York: Columbia University Press, 2004.

Harrington, Michael. *The Other America: Poverty in The United States*. New York: Macmillan, 1962.

Katz, Michael B., ed. *The "Underclass" Debate: Views from History*. Princeton, NJ: Princeton University Press, 1993.

Katz, Michael B. *The Undeserving Poor: From the War on Poverty to the War on Welfare*. New York: Pantheon, 1989.

Keyssar, Alexander. *Out of Work: The First Century of Unemployment in Massachusetts*. New York: Cambridge University Press, 1986.

Keyssar, Alexander. "Poverty." In *The Reader's Companion to American History*, edited by Eric Foner and John Arthur Garraty, 858–862. Boston: Houghton Mifflin, 1991.

Keyssar, Alexander. "Unemployment." In *The Reader's Companion to American History*, edited by Eric Foner and John Arthur Garraty, 1095–1097. Boston: Houghton Mifflin, 1991.

Mann, Robert. *A Grand Delusion: America's Descent into Vietnam*. New York: Basic Books, 2001.

McKnight, Gerald D. *The Last Crusade: Martin Luther King, Jr., The FBI, and The Poor People's Campaign*. Boulder, CO: Westview Press, 1998.

Mink, Gwendolyn, and Alice O'Connor. *Poverty in the United States: An Encyclopedia of History, Politics, and Policy*. Santa Barbara, CA: ABC-Clio, 2004.

Patterson, James. *America's Struggle against Poverty, 1900–1994*. Cambridge, MA: Harvard University Press, 1994.

Rodgers, Harrell R., Jr. *Poor Women, Poor Children: American Poverty in the 1990s*. 3rd ed. Armonk, NY: M.E. Sharpe, 1996.

Schultz, Jeffrey D., Kerry L. Haynie, Anne M. McCulloch, and Andrew L. Aoki. *Encyclopedia of Minorities in American Politics*. Phoenix, AZ: Oryx Press, 2000.

Wilson, William Julius. *When Work Disappears: The World of the New Urban Poor*. New York, Knopf, 1996.

Index

Acosta-Colón, M., 78–79
Affluent Society, The (Gailbraith), 159
African Americans
    affirmative action, politics of, 65–66
    deindustrialization impact, 66–67
    demographics, 55–58
    freedom struggle, 58–65
    future, and, 69
    politics in 1980s and 1990s, 67–69
Albelda, R. P., 99
American Bandstand, 41
Annie Get Your Gun, 41
Attack of the Fifty Foot Woman, The, 40

Baby and Child Care (Spock), 155
baby boomers and family
    children, 12
    dual-earner model, 11
    family composition, 6
    family structure, forms of, 13
    family-strategy model, 3
    image of mother, 10
    life cycle model, 3
    nuclear families, 6
    permissive parenting, 7
    Provost, case study, 4–5
    role of families, 1–3
    women as career homemaker, 11–12
Badger Herald, 52
Bass, C., 28
Bennett, A., 135–136
black Americans *vs.* white Americans
    discrimination in housing, 57
    education, 56
    life expectancy and poverty, 58

    per capita income, 58
    urbanization, 56–57
Black Panther Party, 126
Black Power movement, 64–65
Blackboard Jungle, 40
Blob, The, 40
Bombeck, E., 23
Breines, W., 7
Bunch, C., 45
Bundy, T., 14–15
Bush, G. W., 14, 67

California Eagle, 28
Carmichael, S., 126
Carson, R., 140
Carter, J., 111, 139–140
Catholicism, 108–109
Chavez, C., 84–85
Chicago Sun-Times, 23
Christian Anti-Communism Crusade (CACC), 110
Civil Rights Act of 1964, 27–28, 60
Cleaver, T., 156–157
Clinton, H. R., 32–33
Clinton, W. J., 14
consumerism, 21–22
counterculture
    antiauthoritarianism, 120
    Black Power activism, 126–127
    Chicano activism, 127
    Dionysian Apollonian model, 124
    feminism and environmentalism, 128
    folk music revival, 129
    hippie phenomenon, 121–122
    MK-ULTRA program, 119
    play-as-power expressiveness, 119

counterculture, *continued*
    psychedelia, 120, 123
    public perception of, 125–126
    student activism, 124
    upsurge of youthful revolt, 119
    voluntary component, 118
Crack in the Picture Window, The (Keats), 159
Creature from the Black Lagoon, The, 40
Cuban American National Foundation, 83
culture, Hispanic Americans
    English proficiency, 79–80
    investment in business, 78
    purchasing power, 77
    sports, 79
    television viewers, 78–79

Defender, 27–28
Defense of Marriage Act, 14
Dionysian-Apollonian model, 124
Divine Right's Trip (Norman), 125
Donovan, M., 28

Electric Kool-Aid Acid Test, The (Kesey), 120
Elementary and Secondary Education Act
    (1951), 51
Equal Opportunity Employment Act, 96
Equal Rights Amendment (ERA), 111

Falwell, J., 111–112
Feminine Mystique, The (Friedan), 31, 44, 146
Forbidden Planet, The, 40
Free Speech Movement of 1964, 44
freedom struggle, African Americans, 58–65
    Black Power movement, 64–65
    Children's Crusade, 60
    Civil Rights Act, 60
    Greensboro sit-ins, 58–59
    Spearman, John Jr., case study, 62–63
    Student Nonviolent Coordinating Committee
        (SNCC), 59
    Voting Rights Act, 60
    Watts riot, 61
Friedan, B., 31

Gaines, W., 39–40
General Federation of Women's Club, 24, 25
G.I. Bill of Rights (1944), 19
Glaser, V., 30–31
Good Housekeeping, 26
Graham, B. N., 28–29
Great American Boycott of 2006, 87
Greensboro sit-ins, 58–59

Harrison, D., 133–134
Hayden, T., 138
Head Start, 96
High School Confidential, 40
Hispanic Americans
    activism, 83–86
    culture, 77–80
    demographics, 73–75
    future and, 86–88
    immigration, 76–77
    politics, 81–83
    roots of, 75–76
    upward mobility, 80–81
Hunter, R., 122–123

I Was a Teenage Werewolf, 40

Jackson, J., 67
Job Corps, 96
Johnson, L. B., 96, 97

Kennedy, J. F., 43, 51, 60, 96
King, Martin Luther Jr., 98
Kovic, Ron, 152–153

La Raza Unida, 86
Ladies Home Journal, 26
Lamb, G., 134–135
Lauder, E., 29–30
League for Industrial Democracy (LID), 44
League of United Latin American Citizens
    (LULAC), 83
Lederer, E., 22–23
Lee, S., 68–69
Levitt, W., 160–161
Life Adjustment curriculum, 38
Lonely Crowd, The (Riesman), 159
lysergic acid diethylamide (LSD), 49, 119,
    120, 123

Martin, M., 30
Maternal Care and Mental Health (Bowlby), 19
McCall's, 26
McClanahan, Ed, 120–121
MECha (Movimento Estudiantil de Chicanos de
    Aztlan), 86
Miami Herald, 24, 25
Mississippi Freedom Democratic Party
    (MFDP), 43
MK-ULTRA program, 119
Model Cities program, 96
Mona Lisa Smile, 31

Moral Majority, 111–112
Moseley-Braun, C., 67
Myers, S., 144–145

Nader, R., 140
National Advisory Commission on Civil
     Disorders, 63
National Association for the Advancement of
     Colored People (NAACP), 39
National Association of Colored Women's Clubs, 24
National Education Association (NEA), 39
National Hispanic Media Coalition, 78
National Institute of Latino Policy, 83
National Organization of Women (NOW), 46
Norman, N., 53

Obama, B., 67
Office of Economic Opportunity (OEO), 96–97
Omnibus, 41
On the Road (Kerouac), 122
One Flew Over the Cuckoo's Nest, 119–120
Organization Man, The (Whyte), 159
Organization Men
     bureaucracy of managers, 136
     changing values, 144–145
     corporate activism, 140
     corporate downsizing, 141–142
     culture of abundance, 137–138
     environmental consequences of
          industrialization, 140–141
     harsh nature of the Depression, 136
     job competition, 143
     personal freedom, 139
     security and material prosperity, 136
     white-collar jobs, 135–136
     women in workforce, 145–146

People en Espanol, 78
permissive parenting, 7
politics
     African Americans, 67–69
     Hispanic Americans, 81–83
     women and, 30–31
Port Huron Statement, The (Hayden), 138
Potter, P., 138
poverty and baby boom
     antipoverty programs, 96
     economic restructuring, 98–100
     of elderly people, 93
     of Hispanics and Mexican Americans, 95
     legislations, 96
     maldistribution of wealth and income, 102

Medicaid, 97
     of migrant farm workers, 94
     Office of Economic Opportunity (OEO), 96–97
     reasons for, 101
     rich and poor disparities, 92–93
     stagflation, 98
     substandard housing, 91
     in urban slums, 91
     War on Poverty, 97
Powel, C., 67
Provost, J., 4–5
psychedelia, 120, 123

religion and baby boomers
     American religious life, 108
     as cultural battleground, 110–112
     other faiths, 109
     personal spirituality, 109–110
     reflexivity, 107
     religion and spirituality, 107
     religious beliefs, 105
     voluntarism, 109
Reserve Officers Training Corps (ROTC), 46

Selective Service Act (1948), 46
Silent Spring (Carson), 140
Sometimes a Great Notion (Kesey), 120
Southern Christian Leadership Conference
     (SCLC), 43
Spanish—American War of 1898, 76
Spearman, John Jr., 62–63
Spock, B., 7–9
student activism, 42–46
     civil rights movement, 43
     free speech movement of 1964, 44
     League for Industrial Democracy (LID), 44
     political power, 43
     Student Nonviolent Coordinating Committee
          (SNCC), 43
     Volunteers in Service to America (VISTA), 44
Student Nonviolent Coordinating Committee
     (SNCC), 32, 43, 59
students and baby boom
     compulsory education, 37
     counterculture, 48–51
     culture and, 39–41
     government policy and curricular changes,
          38–39
     Great Society, The, 51–53
     student activism, 42–46
     suburbia and homogenization, 41–42
     Vietnam and, 46–48

Students for Democratic Society (SDS), 32
suburbanization
    automobile revolution, 151
    car ownership, 155
    class stratification of metropolitan areas,
        152–153
    consequences, 151–152
    economic growth, 159
    homeownership, 154
    impact of, 149–150
    lack of ethnicity, 155–156
    racial segregation in housing, 154,
        160–161
    religion, 160
    reasons for, 150
    television culture, 157–158
suburbia and homogenization, 41–42

Toth, S. A., 7
tracking, 38
Twentieth Century, The, 41

United Farms Workers Union, 83
Universal Training and Service Act,
    The, 46

Vietnam
    antiwar demonstrations, 47
    Manhattan Project, 46
    Reserve Officers Training Corps (ROTC), 46

The Universal Training and Service
    Act, 46
    Young Americans for Freedom (YAF), 47
Volunteers In Service to America (VISTA), 44
Voting Rights Act of 1965, 60

Warren, R., 113
Weathermen, The, 124
Wetzel, J. R., 6
White Collar (Mills), 159
Whole World Is Watching, The (Gitlin), 32–33
Wilder, D., 67
Williams, C. B., 30
Woman's Christian Temperance Union, 24
Woman's Home Companion, 26
women and baby boom
    advice by, 22–23
    in business, 28–30
    civil rights movement, 27–28
    consumerism and, 21–22
    as homemaker, 19–20
    magazines, 26–27
    politics and, 30–31
    women's clubs, 23–26
    women's liberation movement, 31–34
    World War II, 20–21
women's liberation movement, 31–34

Young Americans for Freedom (YAF), 47, 52
Young People's Concerts, 41